D1032423

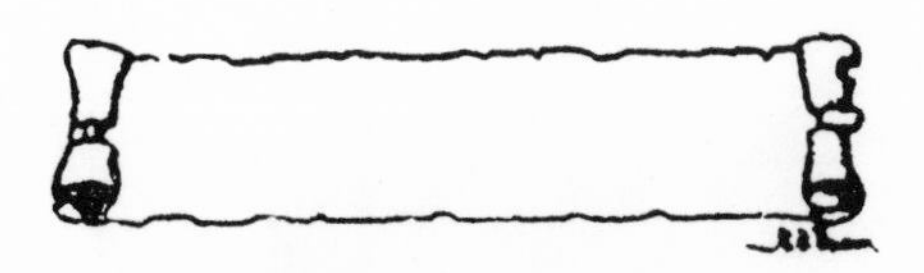

THOMAS HOPE

1769–1831

AND THE

NEO-CLASSICAL IDEA

THOMAS HOPE

1769–1831

AND THE NEO-CLASSICAL IDEA

David Watkin

JOHN MURRAY

Printed in Great Britain for
John Murray, Albemarle Street, London
by William Clowes and Sons Ltd
London and Beccles

7195 1819 9

TO MY PARENTS

Contents

Plates

The following abbreviation is used in this List
M.L. Minet Library, Lambeth

Plates

Figures in the Text

The following abbreviation is used in this List H.F. *Household Furniture and Interior Decoration executed from Designs by Thomas Hope,* 1807

Photographic Acknowledgements

Architectural Review: 24, 25
Ashmolean Museum, Oxford: 98
Birmingham Museum and Art Gallery: 15
British Museum: 30, 89, Figs. 31 and 32
Country Life, London: 20, 21, 29, 36, 37, 44, 53, 100
Fine Art Engravers, Ltd., Godalming: 38, 39, 92, 93, 94, 95, 96, 97
Fitzwilliam Museum, Cambridge: 13, 87
R. B. Fleming & Co. Ltd., London: 2, 34, 35
Cecilia Gray, London: 38
John Heesom, Cambridge: 11, 17, 18, 81, Figs. 4 and 5
Edward Leigh, Cambridge: 19, 31, 42, 46, 47, 50, Fig. 21
Metropolitan Museum of Art, New York: 41
Museum of Fine Arts, Boston: 1
National Monuments Record: 22, 23, 27, 28, 48, 51, 54, 55, 79, 91
National Portrait Gallery: 10
New Britain Museum of American Art, Connecticut: 16
Royal Institute of British Architects: 26, 29
Scottish National Buildings Record: 33, 90
Surrey County Council: 77, 78, 80
Tate Gallery, London: 14
Thorvaldsens Museum, Copenhagen: 7, 8, 9
M. D. Trace, London: 43, 56, 57, 58, 59, 60, 61, 62, 63, 64, 65, 66, 67, 68, 69, 70, 71, 72, 73, 74, 75, 76, 82, 83, 84, 85, 86
University Library, Cambridge: 4, 5, 12, 49, 88, 101, Fig. 1

Acknowledgements

It is my pleasure to thank Professor Nikolaus Pevsner, C.B.E., Ph.D., for encouraging me to undertake a study of Thomas Hope and for his assistance throughout. Special thanks are also due to Mrs. H. W. Law, Thomas Hope's great-grand-daughter, and to Mr. John Harris, Curator of Prints and Drawings at the Royal Institute of British Architects.

Some of the many others who have helped me are the Duke of Newcastle; the Duke of Wellington, K.G.; the Hon. Mary Loder; Sir John Summerson, C.B.E., D.Litt.; Professor Geoffrey Webb, F.S.A., Hon. A.R.I.B.A.; Mr. Peter Bicknell, F.R.I.B.A.; Mr. John Cornforth; Mr. Basil Cozens-Hardy, F.S.A.; Dr. R. Fortescue-Foulkes; Mr. W. T. Freelove; Mr. Mark Girouard, Ph.D.; Mr. J. L. Nevinson, F.S.A.; the late Mr. Reginald Saw and Mr. C. G. Stableforth.

I have received much help from the staff of the following institutions: American School of Classical Studies, Athens; Ashmolean Museum, Oxford; Assay Office, Birmingham; Bank of England; Baring Bros. & Co.; Bishop of Guildford's Registry; Bodleian Library, Oxford; British Museum; Messrs. Christie, Manson & Woods; Fitzwilliam Museum, Cambridge; Guildhall Library; Library of the Royal Botanic Gardens, Kew; London County Council; Metropolitan Museum of Art, New York; Minet Library, London; National Monuments Record; Public Record Office; Royal Society of Arts; Royal Institute of British Architects; St. Marylebone Central Public Library; Society of Antiquaries; Surrey County Council; University Library, Cambridge, and Victoria and Albert Museum.

I am grateful to the Right Rev. Mgr. A. N. Gilbey and also to Mr. and Mrs. Michael Jaffé for their constant generosity and encouragement; and to my friends Mr. J. P. Steadman for drawing the plans of Deepdene and the Duchess Street mansion, and Mr. Alastair Langlands for motoring me in such luxury to so many places.

Her Majesty the Queen has graciously given permission for quotation from documents in the Royal Archives, Windsor. I also wish to thank all the owners of private and public collections mentioned in the List of Plates and in the Notes for kindly allowing me to reproduce works of art and to quote from manuscripts in their possession.

The editors of the *Architectural Review*, *Apollo* and the *Burlington Magazine* have kindly given me permission to re-use material first published as articles in their journals; and Mr. Robin Middleton, Ph.D., and Mr. Alistair Rowan, Ph.D., have allowed me to quote from unpublished theses.

I am greatly indebted to the Master and Fellows of Trinity Hall, Cambridge, for giving me the opportunity to pursue these studies.

DAVID WATKIN

Preface

It is hard to suggest any parallel to the story told in this book of the eccentric offspring of a Dutch banking family who attempted to take by storm fashionable English society purely in order to influence its artistic taste. The fact that this phenomenal man had a finger in every artistic pie from architecture, painting, and sculpture to costume-design, furniture-design, and novel-writing postulates an equally varied scope for any study of him. There has thus been nothing for it but to plunge into deep and mingled waters regardless of the consequent ripples that may justifiably disturb the specialists whose areas of study are being invaded.

If the uniqueness of Thomas Hope's position as a man concerned to influence the design of all the visual arts makes the writing of a book on him such a challenge, the mystery which has for so long surrounded both him and his achievement has made him something of an enigma. Historians have darkly hinted at the decisive part he played in forming Regency taste, offering as evidence a number of oft-repeated half-truths based on secondary sources. At the same time the precise dates of his town-house and country-house, and even the appearance of the latter, have remained a mystery.[1] Moreover, his own aims and hence those of neo-classical art have been over-simplified by concentration on one aspect of them: the archaeological use of Greek forms. The disappearance of his personal papers and drawings has also helped to shroud his life and work in mystery. Less material than might have been hoped for has come to light as the result of numerous enquiries in this country and in the United States of America, where there is reason to suppose some drawings may be hidden. The many contemporary water-colours of the Deepdene, here reproduced for the first time, have, of course, been of invaluable assistance.

What has also helped in making this study is the artistic self-consciousness not only of the period as a whole but, above all, of Hope himself—as revealed, for example, in the detailed annotated bibliography with which he provided his book, *Household Furniture and Interior Decoration* (1807). In such a period the art-historian is made to feel at home. As in the Victorian age so in the neo-classical, artists were for ever saying what they were going to do, how and why they were going to do it, and how much better everyone would feel once it had been done.

This brings us to the wider question of 'the neo-classical idea', which is perhaps too ambitious a sub-title to this book. The idea of the neo-classicists, in its simplest terms, was to revive what was felt to be the failing classical tradition of the Renaissance with a pure fresh draught drawn from the original antique sources. This was to be achieved by the threefold method of excavating, publishing, and collecting.[2] That in the last phase of neo-classicism the idea became a reality in this country is due as much to the efforts of Thomas Hope as to any individual.

The eighteenth century is marked by successive attempts to move nearer to the antique world. Burlington and his circle came as close to Vitruvius as Palladio would allow, sometimes a little closer. At that moment France was still Rococo but her reaction in the 1750s was correspondingly strong. However, *le goût grec* of, for example, the furniture executed for Lalive de Jully was not yet as Greek as its description suggests.[3] The idea, in other words, was not yet a reality. Adam and the Louis XVI style went a step further but still have more of a *dix-huitième* than an antique flavour. Only by the end of the century was there assembled the vast mass of evidence from which a pure classical style could be constructed applicable to all the visual arts, fine and applied. But the available information was by now of such prodigious extent as to be barely assimilable by one man. Thus Thomas Hope was almost a *deus ex machina*. With a passionate concern for all the arts alike he had travelled for eight years in order to master the accumulated information of nearly a century. Moreover, on his return he was still rich enough to put this knowledge into practice, unimpeded by the Napoleonic Wars. The wars, unfortunately, covered exactly the period within which the final neo-classical style ought to have achieved its most prolific and mature expression. This is not to deny that they played their own part in the development of the neo-classical idea. Napoleon's romantic Imperial vision, inevitably involving military combat, made possible the discoveries of Denon and the most characteristic achievements of Percier and Fontaine, and by rendering Italy difficult of access made the traveller look more favourably on Greece. Moreover, the assembly in Paris of works of art from all over Europe not only actually realized for a few years the neo-classical vision of the universal museum but also directed afresh public attention to them, a process in which Landon's series of *Annales du Musée* (1801–17) was an important medium.

As was observed above, this is a statement of neo-classicism in its simplest terms. We have also to take into account the fact that neo-classicism was really an aspect of the growing Romantic Movement. Thus Thomas Hope's town-house contained exercises in the Egyptian, Indian, and Turkish tastes and his country-house was a study in the English Picturesque. Hope the chaste Greek evaporates in London into an incense-tainted cloud of Eastern romanticism only to reappear in the country amidst a chain of towers and terraces irregularly scattered across the steep undulations of a wooded valley. It must be our aim to discuss how far these colourful contrasts can be reconciled with the traditional picture of Thomas Hope and of neo-classicism.

I

Background and Life

> Amidst the forest of masts which covered the sea and made the port of Amsterdam into a second town ... and amidst the painted trees and marble houses of Broek, there reappear before me the servants of the great banker Hope, dressed in their gold-gallooned livery and drawn up in a row along a white marble corridor, to receive, as we went out, the gold ducat which you paid for your dinner ... [These were] The Millionaires of Amsterdam... [who] prided themselves on being frenchified, spoke only French, and lived entirely *à la Française*.[1]

This was the strange and dazzling world into which Thomas Hope was born in 1769, recalled by the Baron de Frénilly as it was in 1786, the year before Thomas left it for an eight-year tour of Europe, Asia, and Africa. He took with him, and eventually brought to England, both of the characteristics noted by de Frénilly: the concern for splendour, carefully calculated to the last penny,[2] and the belief that France was the mistress of European civilization.

The remarkable position achieved by the Hope family in the 1780s was the result of almost a century of effort. The Hopes had left Scotland in the seventeenth century to take up a commercial career in Holland, in common with a number of Scotsmen at that time. It is likely that they were even then a family of some distinction, connected to the Hopes of Craighall and Hopetoun. What is certain is that they employed commerce not merely as a means of creating sufficient wealth to enable them to live like gentlemen and to rival the aristocracy—as their English counterparts would have done—but that they made an aristocracy, as it were, of commerce in itself. In the eighteenth century they became determined to be looked up to because they were Hope and Company rather than because they enjoyed the life of the landed aristocracy. Modelling themselves, perhaps, on Italian Renaissance bankers, they created a setting at Amsterdam where works of art and lavish hospitality combined in an atmosphere of opulence and power. Two observations from the 1760s[3] give an impression of this atmosphere. Benjamin Franklin wrote: '... at Amsterdam we were Recommended to thee Hopes, who are Rank'd amounge the greatest Merchants of Europe, one of them sent us his Coach to carry us to se every thing curious in the City.'

Sir Joshua Reynolds, who painted portraits of various members of the family, said: 'I have been more particular in the account of Mr. Hope's Cabinet, not only because it is acknowledged to be the first in Amsterdam, but because I had an opportunity (by the particular attention and civility of its possessors) of seeing it oftener, and considering it more at my leisure, than any other collection.' Reynolds' observations emphasize another and most important aspect of the Hope setting: the comparative ease with which the stranger could view it. If the Hope bank was an essential part of the national life of Holland, the private dignity and wealth of the Hopes was also to be enjoyed, or at least witnessed, by the nation and its guests.

Apart from the references in journals and diaries, we are fortunate in having a visual record of the Hope world in the form of a painting by Benjamin West[4] which conveys, as clearly as any words, the nature of Thomas Hope's background (Plate 1). Here, members of the Hope family are depicted within a setting of books and papers, pictures and vases, and novel furniture. Let us look more closely into this cultured world.

On 7 March 1802 Farington records[5] that West is painting large family pictures for Mr. Hope of Cavendish Square; that they are to be half-lengths at seventy guineas each, the whole price amounting to four hundred and seventy guineas, but that Hope has offered five hundred guineas. Either Farington misunderstood the nature of the commission or a decision was taken later to replace the individual portraits by a single group; but the point to be made is that it was Henry Hope (1736–1811) who lived in Cavendish Square and there can be little doubt that it is he and not, as has long been thought, Adrian Hope who is seen seated on the left in the painting. With him are his widowed sister and her daughter, together with the latter's husband and their five children.

Henry Hope was the nephew of the Thomas Hope (1704–79) who founded Hope and Company and who was grandfather to our own Thomas Hope. Under the management of Henry Hope, our Hope's second cousin, the family business enjoyed its most successful period. Between 1785 and 1788 he built a great country house on the estate of Weglegen near Haarlem. He was a bachelor, and his heir was the eldest of his sister's three daughters, Ann (seated on the extreme right). A great favourite of her uncle's, she married at his instigation a certain John Williams (1757–1813), the son of a Cornish clergyman, who had been sent out to Hope and Company as a clerk (he is standing to the right of his wife). Williams soon became a director of the bank and on his marriage changed his name to Williams Hope. At the approach of the French armies in 1794 the Hope family moved to England. Henry Hope brought Lord Hopetoun's house in Cavendish Square—in fact the Harley Street lodge of the Duke of Chandos' proposed mansion of the 1720s[6]—and a country house at Sheen. In 1802 he made over Weglegen to John Williams Hope and commissioned from the elderly President of the Royal Academy this large portrait group. His action was possibly dictated by a desire to strengthen the precarious unity of the family. Williams Hope and his wife eventually separated, and as early as 1797 Farington had described her as 'a very proud woman, much disgusted at not being more noticed and distinguished in England than she is. In Holland she was looked up to as a vice queen would be.'[7] Samuel Rogers confirmed this judgement by observing a year later that she 'turns up her nose alike at English peeresses and English customs',[8] while her mother (seated on her right) was called a 'cross old lady' in a diary kept by a cousin of John Williams Hope. Something of the family's uneasy relationships can perhaps be sensed in the moody gazing into opposite directions of the four adults, in contrast to the affectionate grace of the children.

The setting of these characters is of equal interest. One of its more remarkable features is the large architectural model standing on a chest at the left-hand side. This handsome building is the Weglegen mansion, Het Paviljoen at Haarlem,[9] then being transferred from Henry to John Williams Hope. It contained a domed central hall flanked by two galleries for the display of the Hope picture collection. The private apartments were detached from this in a smaller two-storeyed wing. A building of the utmost elegance, it represents almost the sole instance of the introduction of the Louis XVI style into eighteenth-century Holland. How characteristic this is of the Hopes need hardly be pointed out. It seems unlikely that Williams Hope ever lived in it, and in 1806 he sold it to Louis Bonaparte, who had become King of Holland.

Worthy of comment, also, is the decoration of the urn pedestal, the chest on which the model stands, the table, and the frame of the seascape behind the family group. These are decorated in an Egyptianizing taste calculated to recall the refinement of periods remoter than the merely antique. Scholars like Thomas Hope himself and Charles Kelsall were increasingly to emphasize their conviction that Greek art was merely a more elegant re-statement of the aims and practices of Egyptian artists. Thus Kelsall designed a building (Plate 24) in which a colonnade of Egyptian columns supported one of Greek Doric columns,[10] in the same way that an Egyptian pedestal here supports a Greek vase.

The effect of the various 'properties' in West's painting is to create a vivid impression of the highly refined synthesis of cultures, the intellectual enclosure of *objets d'art* contained within the halls of a temple of the arts, that was the ideal setting for the neo-classical man of taste. The house became a museum and could, in turn, be itself displayed as a museum-piece—as Weglegen is in this picture.

The painting also establishes the extent of the precedent for Thomas Hope as collector, patron, and designer. His family gave him much to live up to. They considered that to be a Hope was a distinction of the highest order, and Thomas Hope's not always very successful attempts to become accepted in English society, and even to be elevated to the peerage, make an amusing story. It was probably not entirely a coincidence that it was Lord Hopetoun's house that Henry Hope acquired on his arrival in this country; and that Thomas Hope, in buying the Deepdene, was making his own an estate which had been described in Aubrey's *Surrey* as 'a long Hope' (one of the meanings of the word 'hope' being an enclosed valley). Leaning against the table is a portrait of, as it seems from the inscription, Adrian Hope (1709–81), one of the co-founders of the bank and promoters of the family's rise to wealth and dignity. The background of the whole family group is formed by a large Dutch canvas, the subject matter of which recalls the essential part played by shipping in the maintenance of the family's position.

Into this markedly individual family Thomas Hope was born on 30 August 1769 at Amsterdam.[11] His father, John Hope (1737–84), had entered the family business in 1762, the year in which it changed its official title to Hope and Company, and two years later married the daughter of the Burgomaster of Rotterdam, Philippina van der Hoeven (1738–1790). Thomas was their eldest son, and in 1772 and 1774 was joined by two brothers called Adrian Elias and Henry Philip respectively.

The most remarkable aspect of Thomas Hope's early life prior to his arrival in England was his extensive travelling. Even in this he was following family precedents. A Hope, doubtless his second cousin Olivier, who was a friend of Cardinal Albani, had been in Greece as early as 1760 and had later offered to accompany Winckelmann to Constantinople.[12] Thomas spent the eight years following his eighteenth birthday on what must have been the grandest of grand tours, studying architecture in Turkey, Egypt, Syria, Greece, Sicily, Spain, Portugal, France, Germany, and England. He gives us a few details in a letter of 1821: 'I resided nearly a twelve month in Constantinople; visited the arsenal and bagnio frequently; witnessed the festival of St. George; saw Rhodes, was in Egypt, in Syria, and in every other place which I have attempted to describe minutely in *Anastasius* . . . and had at one time an Albanian in my service.'[13]

It cannot be doubted that *Anastasius* is essential reading for a full appreciation of Hope's outlook and travels, quite apart from whatever literary merit it may possess in its own right. That the novel should be approached in this way was clearly envisaged by Hope. We learn from the preface that he regarded its principal function as 'adding . . . to the information, respecting the ever interesting region once adorned by the Greeks', that the plot is merely 'a fictitious superstructure', and that 'the form of biographical memoirs' was 'adopted solely with the view of affording greater facility for the introduction of minute and characteristic details'.

This immensely long and cumulative rather than coherent novel was apparently written originally in the French tongue[14] in which he had been brought up. Since the first edition of 1819 was published anonymously there was much speculation as to its author, Byron being the most popular choice. Byron, indeed, told Lady Blessington 'that he wept bitterly over many pages of it, and for two reasons—the first, that *he* had not written it, and secondly that Hope *had* . . . He added, that he would have given his two most approved poems to have been the author of *Anastasius*.'[15]

It is not unreasonable to regard the novel's picturesque extravagance as a kind of romantic wish-fulfilment, especially since that is so often what first novels tend to be. Attracted to Greece by the call of the antique, Hope was seduced by the romantic allure of Turkey in whose Empire it lay. Constantinople was the apotheosis of this ambivalence, uniting, as it does, the continents of Europe and Asia. It was the goal of the youthful dreams of Anastasius as it was those of Hope. On first catching sight of its fabled skyline, the mystery of its glistening domes made piquant by the slender minarets, Anastasius 'hardly retained power to breathe; and almost apprehended that in doing so, I might dispel the gorgeous vision, and find its whole vast fabric only a delusive dream'.[16] Like his hero Anastasius, Hope discarded his sombre native dress for the more colourful garb of the Turk (Plate 10); spent his early manhood in ceaseless travelling through Turkey to Egypt and Syria and back to Greece and Italy; and altogether abandoned the Christianity of his boyhood. Hope's own apostasy was later heightened by his dabbling in metaphysics and aesthetics, the turgid results of which he presented to the world in *An Essay on the Origin and Prospects of Man* (1831). By the time of its publication he was, ironically, dead: a circumstance which enabled his executors to suppress it entirely on account of its latitudinarian views.[17]

But it is probably unfair to press too closely the similarities between the careers of Hope and of Anastasius. The plot of Hope's novel is as extravagantly romantic as any product of the age of the Picturesque. Born at Chio as the son of a Greek Christian dragoman, Anastasius was an independent and fiery youth who ran away to sea after misbehaving with the fifteen-year-old daughter of his father's chief. Having arrived in Constantinople he put himself in the service of a Jewish pseudo-physician with whom he was incarcerated in the bagnio, the principal prison of that city. Later, on the exposure of his intrigue with a rich woman, he fled to a mosque and embraced the faith of Islam. Dressed as a Turk he travelled to Cairo and entered the service of Suleiman Bei, whose daughter he soon married. Between making a pilgrimage to Mecca and joining the Bedouin tribe of Wahhabees, the ever resourceful Anastasius found time to enter into an irregular union with the lovely Euphrosyne of Smyrna. On inheriting a fortune, he soon left the Bedouins and returned to claim his beloved son Alexis, offspring of his brief alliance with Euphrosyne. Almost everyone with whom Anastasius comes into contact dies within a matter of weeks, including his three wives, two mistresses, two illegitimate sons, his parents and his good Christian friend Anagnosti. Thus Alexis obligingly succumbs to the rigours of a fatal boat-journey from Venice to Trieste and it only remains for Anastasius himself to die. This he does at the end of the novel, aged only thirty-five.

Hope's absence from Holland between the years 1787 and 1795 was punctuated by a number of brief intervals at home.[18] He was in Amsterdam in January 1790, in April 1791, in March 1793 and in July and October 1794. From a letter written in Rome on 6 November 1793 by the Reverend Thomas Brand to the Earl of Ailesbury[19] we learn that Hope had been in Sicily in 1792 and had taken with him George Wallis, 'the English Poussin'. In December 1794 he was in Berlin, conducting business by letter with Flaxman.[20] In his *Observations* he mentions having seen the Brandenburg Gate, which had been completed in 1793. He was in Rome in 1795 with his two brothers, moving freely in English society and already beginning to purchase antiquities.[21] These dates suggest that it may have been for his protracted stay in Constantinople that he left Amsterdam in 1787. It must not be thought that Hope's most important travels were all contained within these eight years. In September 1797, for example, we hear of him in Egypt visiting the pyramids in the company of Frederick Hornemann (1772–1800), the African traveller, and a 'Major Schwartz of Göttingen'.[22]

His parents dead and Holland shattered by France, it was to England that Hope returned after the main eight-year session of his Grand Tour. On 18 January 1795 the Prince of Orange fled to England, two days later the French entered Amsterdam and proclaimed a revolutionary republic and by the 27th the Hopes, with many of their possessions, had also arrived safely in this country.[23]

From an address in Hanover Square,[24] the twenty-five-year-old heir to a large portion of the Hope fortunes attempted to launch himself in English intellectual society. Perhaps on some early unrecorded visit to England he had been elected a Fellow of the Society of Antiquaries in May 1794[25]—the year, incidentally, after Dance's and before Soane's elections. By August 1795 he was known to the Honourable Mrs. Damer and the Misses Berry,[26] close friends of Horace Walpole. Three years later his lavish hospitality was helping him to effect an entry into the smart society of Brighton. Samuel Rogers conveys the atmosphere in a letter: 'I must ride with two pretty women, and then dress for Mr. Hope's dinner and Lord Carrington's ball.'[27]

However, like other members of his family, Hope was sometimes to be made to realize that London society was a different affair from the mercantile bourgeoisie of Holland or the gay cosmopolitanism of the foreign colonies in continental capitals. Neither art nor money were sufficient in themselves to win over the hearts of Englishmen to a *nouveau-riche* foreigner. Lord Glenbervie, politician, gad-about and scholar, wrote of Thomas Hope in 1801 that he was

> Said to be the richest, but undoubtedly far from the most agreeable man in Europe . . . He is a little ill-looking man about thirty, with a sort of effeminate face and manner, and speaking a kind of language which you are in doubt whether to think merely affected or what is called broken English. He has lately given the Princess a breakfast, and has given great fêtes this and the last year to all the society of London. We do not know him and have been at none of them.[28]

The occasion which brought Hope and Lord Glenbervie together was a dinner-party given by the Princess of Wales on Tuesday, 21 July 1801, at her house at Blackheath. The other guests included Count Bernstorff and Julius Angerstein at whose elegant villa nearby, containing his famous collections, a number of the guests were accommodated for the night. However unacceptable Hope might be to Lord Glenbervie he was already moving in the world of exalted connoisseurship which always welcomed him.

In 1799 Hope acquired the grand town-mansion of the former Countess of Warwick in Duchess Street,[29] a few steps away from his second cousin in Cavendish Square. Having thus definitely established himself in this country, he felt free to travel abroad once more. By September 1799 he was in Athens and, towards the middle of the month, set off on a tour of the Morea in the company of Procopio Macri, the Levant Company's Consular Agent in Athens. By the beginning of October, however, they had returned to the Piraeus on account of the poor state of health of Macri. The consul died on 2 October whereupon Hope took the opportunity of employing the French painter Préault and a servant, who had both previously been in Macri's service.[30]

Thomas Hope's wanderlust never left him, and with the Peace of Amiens in the spring of 1802 he left England again. Samuel Rogers wrote from Paris on 4 December 1802: 'I have just heard an unexpected piece of news—Mr. Thomas Hope's death. It comes in a letter from his brother Henry, who says a merchant has written him word of it from Marseilles.'[31] The news was happily unfounded, for, by Christmas Eve 1802, Hope, as we learn from a letter which he sent to Canova on that day,[32] had been safe and sound in Naples for six weeks. He complained, however, that certain works of art which he had acquired had been confiscated in Rome by the French. In Naples as in Rome there was a colony of English visitors and residents in which Hope was, as always, both host and guest. On 16 December 1802 Lady Hester Stanhope wrote from Naples: 'Here, there are the most distinguished of our beaux: Lord Grantham, Algernon, Lord Montague, Sir Charles Douglas and Mr. Hope, Thomas Hope, I think needs no description . . . Thursday, Mr. Hope, another ball'.[33]

In March 1803 he was in Rome rescuing from oblivion the sculptor Thorvaldsen;[34] and the ending of the Peace of Amiens in May forced him to make a hasty departure from Paris.[35]

In the following year he was preoccupied with the production and effect of his pamphlet on the designs for Downing College; and with the opening of his house to the public. He had felt in 1801 that his house was still not quite ready for the discerning eyes of the artists and connoisseurs whose taste he hoped to influence. Perhaps he also felt that he himself was not yet sufficiently well known to command much attention. He was admitted to membership of the Society of Dilettanti in 1800,[36] and the following year saw his first invitation to the Annual Dinner of the Royal Academy—[37] a great step forward. Much of

1802 and 1803 he spent abroad; 1804 was to be his *annus mirabilis*. In that year he planned to launch himself, his writings, and his house in intellectual society. However, his ignorance of English ways allowed him to sail into dangerously deep and stormy waters.

The story of this near shipwreck begins on 1 February 1804.[38] On that day he sent to sixty members of the Royal Academy tickets which were to admit the bearer and three friends to the Duchess Street mansion between 18 February and 31 March. He proposed to cap this by the publication towards the end of March of his bold plea in favour of the Greek Revival, *Observations on the Plans . . . for Downing College*. But his method of inviting Academicians to view his home was hardly such as to meet with much general sympathy. At a Council Meeting of the Royal Academy on 7 February, there was criticism of what was described as the want of respect in Hope's idea of admission tickets. Members felt that they were being invited not 'to meet Company but as professional men to publish his fine place'. Moreover, when Hope's pamphlet appeared, containing an attack on Wyatt, the President of the Royal Academy, it was felt by many to be characterized by the same impertinent and dogmatic note of personal ostentation. Whatever the ultimate stimulus the pamphlet had on the Greek Revival, Robert Smirke, one of the principal exponents of that revival, observed of the pamphlet that it was 'an extraordinary piece of Egotism,—and that it might easily be answered'. He thought that 'Porden would do it well'. Even Hope's friend Samuel Rogers thought that it would be improved by having one-third of it cut out.

A more immediately unfortunate effect of the pamphlet was the decision to exclude Thomas Hope from the annual Academy Dinner to be held on Saturday, 28 April 1804. At a Council Meeting on 12 April, Sir Francis Bourgeois 'opposed Dance's proposal to invite Thomas Hope, on account of his letter to Wyatt'. West stood up for Hope at a Council Meeting on the 20th, but Bourgeois said that Wyatt felt so strongly that Hope should be excluded that 'West thought it most prudent not to press Mr. Hope's name'. On the 25th, Soane himself, who had just noticed that Hope's name was not among the guests, took up his cause in the face of continued opposition from Bourgeois.

But the decision was not reversed. To complete Hope's humiliation about two hundred copies of a satirical poem entitled *Hope's Garland* were delivered to the Royal Academy on the very day of the dinner. The following is the full text of this not very impressive piece of doggerel:

Lo! Tommy Hope, beyond conjecture,
Sits judge Supreme of Architecture,
Contracts his brows, and with a *fiat*,
Blights the fair fame of classic *Wyatt*,
And gravely proves himself alone is able
To form a Palace very like a Stable.—

Tommy to no man holds a candle;
He knows a cornice, moulding, spandle;
Despises Porticos, and Niches;
Displays a mind of mental riches;
And to support his scientific strictness,
Bids us behold his furniture and fixtures.

Tommy a Child, *Vitruvius* noted;
Transcrib'd *Pausanias*, *Euclid* quoted:
Maturer grown, sustain'd privations;
Scan'd men and Kings and distant nations;
In Flanders skated when the Sky was murky,
And bared his Limbs, and whiskers wore in *Turkey*.

Disdaining to bestride his hobby,
In closet, parlour, hall, or lobby,
In eight years hardship, toils and dangers,
'Midst *Attic* friends and *Tarter* strangers,
With depth of purse, with parts and person active,
He rov'd till roving ceased to be attractive.

Then who shall dare to doubt his knowledge
In framing plans to grace a *College*?
Or taunt him, under *Candour's* banners,
Of both ill-nature and ill-manners?
Wisdom forbid! for, to our taste's salvation,
Tommy shines forth the *Phoebus* of the *Nation*.

Fam'd for fine festivals and feeding,
Fine thoughts, fine languages, and fine breeding,
This man of men, this world's prime wonder,
Wielding his Pen as *Jove* wields thunder,
With unassuming *merit* proudly quarrels,
And adds new wreaths to all his former laurels.[39]

Smirke was present at the Academy when, between four and five o'clock, the 'garlands' arrived. Despite his lack of enthusiasm for the tone of Hope's pamphlet, he was kind enough to prevent the porter, Samuel Allen, from delivering copies of the poem to all the members.

Macmillan, publisher of the verses, and Samuel Allen were questioned closely by members of the Council at a meeting on 4 May. On the following day, it was disclosed that the verses had been sent to Henry Tresham, R.A. There was a unanimous condemnation of Tresham, and even Bourgeois, an earlier opponent of Hope, was shocked to discover that he had written the verses. On 9th May, it was decided that a resolution deploring Tresham's conduct be sent to Thomas Hope.

Thus, on 14 May, Benjamin West and Joseph Farington called at Duchess Street to convey to Thomas Hope the sympathy of the Royal Academy. The visit lasted for one hour and twenty minutes in the course of which Hope made it quite clear that he was indifferent as to the matter of Tresham's verses, but that he cared intensely about the affront of the Council in refusing to invite him to the dinner after he had been proposed by one of its members. He felt that he had some claim on the Academy through opening his house to the Academicians and their friends, and through being 'manifestly a person devoted to the Arts'. He intended never again to accept any invitation from the Academy, observing that 'others felt as he did and it had been much taken up'. West then explained that he had felt that Wyatt's word had to be obeyed because of the difficult position of the Academy at this time. These difficulties were the result of the long and tedious dispute over the powers of the Council which brought about West's resignation of the presidency in favour of Wyatt at the end of 1804. The tactful and prudent Farington suggested that it would be most high-minded of Hope to pass the matter over on the understanding that he would be invited another year, especially since the majority of the members was well disposed towards him. 'His manner was very civil,' Farington records, 'and He attended us down stairs to the door of His House, but his mind was evidently full of the subject'.

On the following day, the Marquess of Stafford, Lord Abercorn, and Payne Knight all came down firmly on Hope's side recommending that the Academy should apologise to him and extend a perpetual invitation to their annual dinners. At a Council Meeting on the 19th, attended by West, Soane, Smirke, Rossi, Bourgeois, and Farington, the latter again records that there was much discussion about Hope's business. It was beginning to harm the good name of the Academy and West observed that the 'Nobility and amateurs [were] irritated' by the rudeness of the professional artists. However, on 27 May, West read privately to the Marquess of Stafford 'the copy of the resolutions of the Council which had been read to Thomas Hope, after which, he expressed that the Academy was completely exonerated'.

So the storm in a tea-cup died down and was soon forgotten by all, except probably by Hope himself. At all events, in December 1804 West told Farington that Hope was 'following Wyatt up, having examined many of his works, and is preparing a critical examination of them'.[40] Unfortunately, this was never published.

The whole episode is significant for revealing the immense seriousness with which Hope took himself and his efforts to gain recognition in artistic circles; and the pre-eminent position occupied in such circles by the Royal Academy. His desire for acclaim seems to have been equalled only by his ignorance of how to achieve it—by his ignorance, that is, of the importance of tact in personal relationships, or even of personal relationships at all. The tickets which he sent to the Royal Academicians were, and were felt to be by their recipients, impersonal commands from a young foreigner who had spent but a few years in this country. The conceited tone of his *Observations* was no less unfortunate in its timing than was the attack which it contained on the president of the very society whose members he was seeking to impress with the style of his house.

As he said of himself, he was a man entirely 'devoted to the Arts'. Neither high-living for its own sake nor even ordinary social contacts concerned him much, nor did he see any reason why they should anyone else. His house was, in Miss Mitford's words, a 'temple of art',[41] a public museum to which access was to be gained by admission tickets, not by engraved invitation cards to dinners and parties. It was the same with his pronouncements on art and architecture. He knew himself to be right, to have travelled more, to have seen more and to have thought more than his contemporaries. In his disinterested concern for the advancement of the arts he did not regard himself as one erring human writing to another. He therefore did not consider it necessary to temper with tact or modesty either his judgements or his statement of the qualifications which he believed enabled him to make such judgements. Nor did he ever acquire an easy or pleasant social manner. In 1805 his friend Samuel Rogers said of him that he was 'a very shy reserved man and is not easily brought to live like others with the world'.[42] Malone, rather harsher, described him in 1806, the year of his marriage, as 'disagreeable, fastidious and conceited'.[43] There can be little doubt that it is to Hope that the following passage, from Rogers' *Reminiscences and Table Talk*, refers:

> A friend of mine in Portland Place has a wife who inflicts upon him every season two or three immense evening parties. At one of these parties he was standing in a very forlorn condition, leaning against the chimney-piece, when a gentleman, coming up to him, said, 'Sir, as neither of us is acquainted with any of the people here, I think we had best go home.'[44]

Maria Edgeworth describes a similarly absurd situation at a party given at Duchess Street in 1813: 'I asked Mr. Hope who someone was? "I really don't know; I don't know half the people here, nor do they know me or Mrs. Hope even by sight. Just now I was behind a lady who was making her *speech*, as she thought to Mrs. Hope, but she was addressing a stranger."'[45]

In 1804, however, the year of the Academy Dinner fiasco, Thomas Hope, as yet unmarried, was still attempting to make a name for himself. In that year he was elected to two distinguished societies: the Royal Society and the Royal Society of Arts. In the following year the Society of Dilettanti appointed him to the publication committee of their important series of books, *Select Specimens of Antient Sculpture* (1799–1807).[46] The next volume contained two plates of sculpture from Hope's collection. In March 1805 came another small indication from the same Society of the growing respect with which he was regarded. He was appointed to sit on a committee of seven, including his second cousin Henry, Benjamin West, Sir Thomas Lawrence, and Sir Henry Englefield, to consider the restoration and repair of the two great Reynolds groups which the Society owned. The committee, however, as committees so often do, merely begot further committees —one a year from 1810 to 1812—and no positive action was take until March 1817.[46]

As a relief from these activities Hope spent the autumn of 1805 at Tunbridge Wells, then beginning to give way to Brighton as a popular, provincial, social centre.[47] At the end of a gay season, Samuel Rogers wrote to his sister, on 13 October that 'tomorrow the only relic of our party will be T. Hope'.[48] A more detailed picture of the party is presented by Thomas Moore who, at Bowood in 1838, was reminiscing:

> with Miss Berry about the agreeable times we passed together at Tunbridge in 1805–6 when there were present the Dunmores, Lady Donegal, the Duchess of St. Albans, Lady Heathcote, beautiful Susan Beckford (now Duchess of Hamilton) under the care of Lady Anne Hamilton . . . Thomas Hope making assiduous love to Miss Beckford . . . Rogers and Sir Henry Englefield.[49]

Melville has suggested that William Beckford was anxious for his daughter to accept Hope's advances and looked most favourably on so wealthy a potential son-in-law; Hope, he observes, was a frequent visitor to Fonthill, as were Soane, West, and Rogers.[50] The first link between the Beckford and Hope families was that William's illegitimate brother John had been trained in a counting-house of Hope and Company.[51] Thomas Hope and William Beckford shared many characteristics. The wealth of both was derived from foreign commerce rather than from English rent-rolls and they both therefore resorted to surprise, splendour, and hospitality in an attempt to 'win friends and influence people'. By a curious irony neither, in fact, cared for society as such or for traditional country pursuits; and the tendency of both was towards the creation of a strange, inward-looking cultural world. In Beckford's case, however, this characteristic was heightened to an unparalleled degree by the ostracism inflicted upon him by society after the Powderham scandal. This isolation was at once his tragedy and the occasion of his great achievement at Fonthill.

After the daughter of the Caliph of Fonthill it was a certain Miss Dashwood who engaged Hope's attentions. Farington tells us in May 1806 that she had refused him.[43] By this time, however, he was already married. Thus the family line could be continued, the London mansion could have a mistress and Hope's acceptance in England might be completed with the assistance of the charming Irish niece of a marquess. Characteristically for the period, it was in Bath that Hope met his future wife Louisa, youngest child of William Beresford, Archbishop of Tuam, and, from 1812, 1st Baron Decies. Farington records that she did not accept his first proposal of marriage, 'but was afterwards persuaded by her friends not to refuse so splendid a prospect'.[43] Her initial reluctance was doubtless heightened by her affection for her cousin William Beresford, later Field-Marshal Viscount Beresford, whom she was to marry in the year following Hope's death.[52] With her, Beresford

> carried on a pretty lively flirtation till Mr. Hope loomed on the Bath horizon and carried off the prize. Mr. Hope came into the little Bath world with the reputation of enormous wealth, great literary ability . . . supreme artistic taste, and almost abnormal ugliness . . . Her marriage with Mr. Hope was, I believe, a happy one, though it was far from a love match.[53]

Hope clearly maintained a belief in the *mariage de convenance*, realizing that love is as much an affair of the will as of the emotions. He seems always to have been devoted to his wife and children. The marriage took place on 16 April 1806. 'On the day after the marriage the Archbishop called on Mr. Hope and handed him his wife's fortune of £3,000, which he immediately presented to her.'[43]

Whatever Hope did, he did on a grand scale. His wife played the part of a great society hostess, and the memoirs and diaries of the period are studded with references to the costly balls and parties given at the Duchess Street mansion. On the occasion of their first crowded reception, given a few weeks after their wedding, Elizabeth Spencer-Stanhope described how at 'half past eleven [in the evening] . . . we set out for Mr. T. Hope's rout, but after waiting in the street *till near one*, we found to get in was impossible!'[54]

In 1807, the year of the publication of *Household Furniture and Interior Decoration*, Thomas Hope acquired the country house and estate of the Deepdene, near Dorking in Surrey.[55] If at Duchess Street he allowed his wife to entertain the fashionable society of London, at Deepdene he seems to have held sway himself, collecting round him distinguished figures from a rarified intellectual world. Guests entertained there from 1812 to 1825 included Sir Walter Scott, Sir Humphry Davy, Sir Henry Englefield, Richard Payne Knight, Samuel Rogers, Crabbe, Washington Irving, Sismondi, and Schlegel.[56] Hope did not pursue any of the activities of the ordinary country gentleman and must have been regarded by his neighbours as a very queer fish—as indeed he doubtless was. Not for him the excitement of the chase nor the lure of rod and gun. He could derive all the thrill he needed from a bracing discussion with Davy or with Schlegel in a room full of busts and cinerary urns. And to accommodate his collections the house was always expanding in strange new directions: upwards and outwards and asymmetrically, with here a tower and there a loggia, wherever fancy demanded. By 1826 the number of bedrooms had swelled to thirty-three, although of the entertaining rooms the new library alone could boast of impressive proportions. It was to correct this balance that Henry Hope extended the house southwards after his father's death.

An early guest at the Deepdene was Miss Berry who stayed there for three days in June 1809, before those alterations had been effected which were to make the house the most remarkable in Surrey. In the day calls were paid upon the owners of neighbouring estates and in the evenings they 'looked over drawings'.[57]

Miss Berry had been present in the previous month at a ball at Duchess Street of which she wrote:

> The Princess of Wales had dined there, and stood godmother to his second son. She was holding a circle in the first drawing room when we came in. Soon afterwards all the world went to the statue gallery, where was dancing, late in beginning, as usual. Princess of Wales desired Lady Sheffield to present me to her . . . Such an over-dressed, bare-bosomed painted eye-browed figure [the Princess] one never saw![58]

Earlier in 1809 Samuel Rogers had written to Thomas Moore of a party given in Davies Street by Lady Donegall, at which were present 'the Berrys, Mrs. Damer, T. Hope, and other delectables; but I could not go, being knocked up with a cold'.[59] This was perhaps the society in which Hope found himself most at home: the Whig literary world, which included such famous blue-stocking figures as the Misses Berry and the sculptress Mrs. Damer. It was to the Berry family that Horace Walpole entrusted his books and papers on his death, and Mary Berry who edited the five-volume edition of his works published in 1798. A letter from Mrs. Damer to Mary Berry written from Park Place, London, on 1 August 1795, includes the observation: 'Lord Orford and Mr. Hope both gone this morning. I feel a sort of melancholy repose.'[26] It may be assumed from this that the youthful Hope had the privilege of meeting the aged Walpole. If Walpole, so it was rumoured, had considered marrying Mary Berry in his old age, she had attempted to form an alliance with Hope in his youth. Hope later confided to Maria Edgeworth, on her first visit to the Deepdene in April 1819, the story of Miss Berry's courtship of him.[60] After his marriage, however, Mary Berry became a close friend of Mrs. Hope. In her journal for 4 April 1810 she describes how she 'Sat a long time with Mrs. Hope; always good-humoured and unaffected. Hope and she the image of domestic comfort and good understanding.' On the following day she records that 'Lady Ellenborough called for me to go to Mrs. Hope's. An enormous assembly; the whole house open, and the Princess of Wales there.'[61]

Hope's friendship with the unfortunate half-demented Princess of Wales is less easy to understand. As early as 1801 he had given a breakfast party for her,[62] and in 1808 invited her to become godmother to his eldest son Henry.[63] It seems that he may even have gone so far as to offer her financial assistance as well as hospitality. In January 1814 Lady Charlotte Bury, Lady in Waiting to the Princess of Wales, observed in her diary—one of the principal contemporary sources for our knowledge of the strange life of the Princess—that 'H(—) has engaged to advance the Princess two thousand pounds in the course of twelve months, by instalments of five hundred each . . . She is to pay two hundred a year for the money, till the sum is paid off'[64]

In 1810 Hope acted as sponsor in society to a handsome and picturesque young man who came from Greece—a country whose cause Hope had already championed, as he was again in *Anastasius*. Lord Glenbervie, who had been so scornful of Hope in 1801, had succumbed to his magnificence by 1810. Hope, an authority on dress since the publication in 1809 of his *Costume of the Ancients*, insisted on inviting to his house this young Greek, who was described by Glenbervie as being decked out in 'the Eastern dress' so as to appear 'extremely *répandu* and *recherché*', with 'a very feminine look'. He continues to tell the story in more detail:

> I saw Mrs. Damer pay him very particular attention one night at Tom Hope's. The Persian ambassador at last took umbrage at the great success of this youth in society and went so far as to declare that he would go to no party where he was invited. One night of an assembly at Mrs. Thomas Hope's the Ambassador sent to know if this Aidé of last year was to be there, when Mr. Hope sent him word that he was invited and certainly would come if he chose, and that he could only regret it, if that should prevent his having the honour of seeing his Excellency.[65]

What must principally have absorbed Hope's attention in 1810 was the attack made on him by the French painter Antoine Dubost, who exhibited a portrait of him and his wife entitled 'Beauty and the Beast', following this up with a lengthy pamphlet of sustained abuse. As the amazing sequel to an act of patronage which misfired, this story will be told in the next chapter on Hope as 'Collector and Patron'. In 1811 Hope had the honour of sitting on a committee of three to select designs for the new Theatre Royal, Drury Lane;[66] and the following year saw the publication of his *Designs of Modern Costume*, engraved by Henry Moses.

In the early spring of 1814 he invited Lord and Lady Donegall and Samuel Rogers to stay with him. Thomas Moore wrote to Rogers on 10 April: 'The last time I heard of you, you were at Hope's with the Donegals; but I dare say, long before now, you have bid him and his magnificence farewell (*Spes et Fortuna, Valete*).'[67] In May 1814, we learn from Frances, Lady Shelley, that Prince Karl of Württemberg 'made his début' at a Duchess Street ball. 'He danced all night, and endevoured to teach about forty people a new and complicated dance . . . On being called upon to admire the house—which is certainly a fine one—he said: "C'est assez bien pour Angleterre."'[68] There is conflicting evidence as to Hope's activities later in the year. On 12 November a Miss Godfrey mentioned, in a letter written to Thomas Moore from Tunbridge Wells, that she and her friends had remained for so long at the spa that fashionable society had all departed save for 'the Fincastles, Hopes, Rogers and Lady Ellenborough'.[69] However, on the previous day Madame Reinhard described in her diary the appearance of Mrs. Hope, 'écrasée sous les poids de pierreries et des perles', at a house-warming party given in Paris by the Duchess of Kurland.[70] The case for their being in Paris rather than in Tunbridge Wells is strengthened by the historian Sismondi, who was present at 'un bal fort brillant' given in Paris by Mrs. Hope on 26 January 1815, and who dined with Mr. Hope on 14 February. Mrs. Hope continued to give balls throughout February.[71] Certainly Thomas would have been as at home in Paris as in London. Indeed he probably both spoke and wrote French more fluently and elegantly than English. So, with a Bourbon on the throne for the first time in a quarter of a century, the Hopes spent the winter-season of 1814–15 in Paris. But at the beginning of March 1815, Napoleon having made his dramatic escape from Elba, gay society in Paris came to a sudden halt and the Hopes fled to London. On 29 April Hope was present at the Annual Dinner of the Royal Academy,[72] an event which he rarely missed, once the embarrassment of 1804 had subsided.

As soon as Napoleon's fate was finally settled in the summer of 1815 and the Continent was calming down, Thomas Hope set his face once more towards Mediterranean shores. On 29 September 1815 he wrote[35] to the French archaeologist A. L. Millin to say that he was about to leave for Italy with his wife and children, though he would not be visiting Paris on the way since he had already twice been compelled to depart with haste from the capital, once in 1803 with the abrupt termination of the Peace of Amiens and again in the spring of 1815 with the return of Napoleon. The main reason for his proposed tour was, he affirmed, a wish to augment his collection, which had remained static for some time. Their journey across Europe was a lengthy one. We know that they passed through Switzerland in

1816,[73] but we do not hear of them again until September. Then Lady Caroline Capel mentioned, in a letter written from Vevay to the Dowager Countess of Uxbridge, that 'There have been some frightful robberies between this and Milan,—Lady Frances Beresford, Mr. and Mrs. Hope and Mr. (?) Leicester and his family were all stopped by bandits armed with doubled barrel guns ... they took everything from them ... and wounded one of the couriers.'[74]

Having recovered from this inconvenience they moved on to Florence where they visited the Countess of Albany, widow of Charles III. We learn of this in a letter of 5 September 1816 from Madame de Staël to the Countess:

> N'est-il pas vrai, Ma Souveraine, que vous me pardonnerez de vous envoyer encore de nouveaux sujets: M. et Mme. Hope. M. Hope est un homme très instruit, très connaisseur dans les beaux arts, et la femme est aussie jolie que gracieuse ... Vous savez que M. Hope est parent de Hope d'Amsterdam et sa femme est une Irelandaise de la plus haute naissance.[75]

One would hardly have suspected Thomas Hope of Jacobite sympathies. To move from the Princess of Wales to the Countess of Albany suggests rather a desire to become accepted in the highest quarters than a firm grasp of traditionalist principle.

By December the Hopes had reached Pisa, where their second son Charles fell ill.[76] He was rashly submitted to the charge of Lord Byron's wild travelling physician, the twenty-two-year-old John Polidori. They moved on to Rome for Christmas where Hope visited Thorvaldsen's studio and urged the sculptor to complete his statue of Jason.[77] And now poor Mrs. Hope, who in 1810 had lost a daughter,[78] was to know the grief of the death of a son. They were still in Rome in the middle of April 1817 when Hope wrote to Canova regretting that his enforced departure would prevent his visiting his studio.[79] In the same month the sad party, bereaved of the seven-year-old Charles, had reached Florence[80] on a hasty return home. In June they paused in Paris, whence Countess Granville wrote: 'Lady Jersey told me she found her way in to Mrs. Hope! I never heard of such misery, her eyes streaming with tears, unable to resist in the lightest degree her grief ... They say he was killed by seven Italian physicians. There is death in the very sound.'[81]

On the family's return to the Deepdene in the summer of 1817 Charles' ashes were buried near the edge of the park,[41] and in the following year a mauseoleum was erected over them.[82]

Between now and 1819 Hope's attention must have been engaged on the extensive alterations and additions to Deepdene. Immediately after this came the preparation of the novel *Anastasius* from notes which he had written as a young man at the end of the eighteenth century. It was the publication of this novel in 1819 which finally established for Hope an universal repute: by the year of his death it had appeared in thirteen editions in four languages.[83] He was correcting the proofs at the Deepdene in January 1819 and complaining in a letter to his publisher, John Murray, that his wife's ill-health prevented him from attending to business in town.[84] By 9 February he was in London once more, for on that day Lord Glenbervie recorded in his diary that 'Lady Charlotte and I dined at Lady Donegall's . . . [with] Mr. Thomas Hope and Mr. Ellis, son to Lord Clifden, a young man of whom Lady Donegall and Lady Charlotte had taught me to entertain a high opinion.'[85] The young George Agar-Ellis, created Baron Dover in 1831, was a man who shared Hope's tastes and enthusiasms in literature and the fine arts. Hope may have fired his interests and it was partly at Ellis' suggestion that the National Gallery was instigated in 1824. He also edited Horace Walpole's letters. Foremost among the subjects discussed that evening, Glenbervie tells us, was the reflective poem *Human Life*, by Hope's friend Samuel Rogers, which had been published that morning.

The autumn of 1819 saw the addition of a large new picture-gallery at Duchess Street.[86] In May 1820 the Austrian statesman and social figure, Philipp von Neumann, was present at a reception at Duchess Street. He referred in his diary to the new gallery and described the house as 'very fine but too crowded with ornaments'. In August of the following year Neumann attended a ball at Duchess Street, 'which was the final amusement of the season'.[87]

In the earliest 1820s the poet Thomas Moore was often present at Mrs. Hope's more informal gatherings. She was by now well-acquainted with the influential Whig family, the Hollands. In March 1823 she ornamented a distinguished party at Holland House,[88] and exactly a year later Moore describes how at Mrs. Hope's he 'got hastily through two songs, but refused any more, as there were too many people assembling. Found there the Hollands.'[89] In the autumn of 1823 the Hopes moved to Brighton for the season. The Honourable Henry Fox, later 4th Lord Holland, described in his journal how he

> grew better acquainted with Mrs. Hope, who is uncommonly pretty and very good natured with some of the drollery and none of the vulgarity of her country . . . Mr. Hope has a foolish manner and a very disagreeable voice, and says little silly nothings that make people almost disbelieve his having written Anastasius. He has a talent for drawing and has good taste. (A further acquaintance with him has made me scratch out the epithet; its place may be supplied by the word 'peculiar') but certainly nothing appears to make one think him at all equal to such a book as I believe that to be.

Fox's relationship with Mrs. Hope seems to have been of unusual intimacy. He later observed: 'Brighton got more agreeable to me lately, when I got to be a great deal acquainted with Mrs. Hope, at whose house I chiefly lived.' He dined with her on 1 January 1824 and records that: 'from Jan. 22 to Feb. 22 [I] dined almost daily with Mrs. Hope.'[90]

Certainly Thomas Hope allowed his wife every extravagance that might heighten her charm. On Christmas Day 1823 at the Brighton Pavilion she 'was dressed', according to Lady Granville, 'in solid gold, with rare birds flying in different directions out of her head'.[91] It is for precisely this dazzling rather Firbankian splendour that the Hopes became known—and where could it have found a better setting than in the Royal Pavilion?

In the summer of 1824 the Hopes were invited to stay with Lord Lansdowne at Bowood. Here they found Thomas Moore, who entertained the guests assembled at this Whig stronghold with his songs.[92] Mrs. Hope brought her *Deepdene Album* with her and invited Moore to add his own contribution to it. The poem which he provided is dated 25 August.

It may have been at about this time that Thomas and Louisa formed one of their more distinguished alliances in society—with the Duke and Duchess of Clarence, later King William IV and Queen Adelaide.

On 18 December 1824 the Duchess wrote to Mrs. Hope asking her to contribute towards a fund to assist her German fellow-countrymen who had suffered greatly from recent inundations, expressing a hope, at the same time, that Thomas had 'quite recovered from the gout'.[93] Sophy, daughter of the Duke and Duchess, came to stay at the Deepdene at the end of the month; the first visit of her parents was made in November 1826. 'Further visits followed. The Duchess brought her cousin, Princess Amelia, and on other occasions was accompanied by her mother, the Duchess of Saxe-Meiningen, and the Duchess of Gloucester.'[94]

Possibly at the suggestion of Mrs. Hope rather than Thomas, Deepdene became a centre of hospitality for those attending the Epsom Races. Philipp von Neumann conveys the atmosphere of the Edwardian country-house party when he records in his diary in May 1826 that he stayed at the Deepdene for four days for the Races.[95] He was there again exactly two years later with a big party, including Lord and Lady Gwydyr, Lord Tankerville, Lady Westmeath and Mr. and Mrs. Sidney. In December 1828 he was a guest at another house party, this time bringing with him Prince Schwarzenberg. Hope's son Henry continued to invite Epsom race-goers to stay at his house, after his father's death.[96]

If Louisa was responsible for the Epsom gatherings, Thomas had invited to the Deepdene in November 1827 a large party of 'malignants', as Whigs who had become estranged from their party were known. Samuel Rogers was present at this malignant gathering, and moved on from it to stay with Lady Holland at Brighton.[97] At the beginning of the year Thomas Moore had called at Duchess Street one February morning. He 'met there Lord Cowper. A good deal of talk about politics.'[98] The impression must not be conveyed, however, that Thomas Hope was a resolute Whig. In a letter to Louisa he says that he is 'most happy to see in the papers the issue of Sir Francis Burdett's business, for though a little of an Opposition man I am neither a Burdettite nor a Jacobin'.[99] Burdett, most rebellious of the Whig agitators, who had married the immensely wealthy daughter of Thomas Coutts, was imprisoned in the Tower of London in 1810 for his subversive activities. It was probably at this time that Hope wrote this undated letter referring to his lack of enthusiasm for violent reformers. Nor must it be supposed that Conservative society shunned the Hope entertainments. In May 1826 the Duke of Wellington's intimate friend Mrs. Arbuthnot wrote to Lady Shelley that the Duke 'said he would go to Mrs. Hope's tonight. She will be *très glorieuse* at being the first'[100] to receive him after his illness. And in February 1827 Mrs. Arbuthnot wrote in her diary that 'London is beginning to fill up and to be gay. We have just the same society as last year . . . Lady Belfast, Lady Gwydyr and Mrs. Hope are at home the Mondays, Wednesdays, and Fridays.'[101]

The Duke of Wellington had come into contact with Thomas Hope as early as 1823 through one of the latter's embarrassing attempts at becoming a peer. Mrs. Arbuthnot can tell us the sorry story:

> Wellington 'had an interview with a man who proposed to give him a gift of 10,000 pounds if he would get . . . a friend of his made a peer. The Duke was civil to the man, but told him he had made an egregious mistake in coming upon such an errand to him and sent him out of the house . . . The man, whose name is Bromley . . . had been on a similar errand to the Duke of York who had kicked him out of his house . . . The Duke had a letter from Bromley repeating the offer . . . and describing the person who wants it (the peerage) so accurately that the Duke found out who it was at once. It is Mr. Hope and what is most incredible, it seems Mr. Hope must have known of it for he took no steps to deny it when the Duke of York told him of it. The Law officers very much wished the Duke of Wellington to prosecute Bromley, but he will not do it as he does not wish to expose Mr. Hope.'[102]

It was not, perhaps, unreasonable for Mr. and Mrs. Hope to consider Thomas a suitable candidate for the peerage. He was now fifty-four, at the height of his literary and artistic prestige, was known for his dedication to the public good through his many acts of patronage and had ample wealth to be able to maintain in his private life a dignity equal to that of the suggested title; while his wife was already the the daughter and the niece of a peer and was a brilliant society hostess. However, the method adopted to attain this end could not have been more ill-conceived. The Duke of Wellington was no Lloyd George where peerages were concerned and, in attempting to bribe him, Hope revealed the extent to which he had failed to assimilate himself into the customs of English society. Nor was he content to abandon his struggle after the first rebuff. It has not before been observed that Hope reached out twice to grasp at a peerage. Louisa's cousin, early admirer and eventual husband, Lord Beresford, was a close friend of the Duke of Wellington, and she prevailed upon him to put her husband's case before the Prime Minister. She also wrote a letter to the Duke herself. Instead of the financial bribe offered earlier by her tactless husband, she now held out the more discreet, if infelicitously expressed, enticement that the talents of her eldest son, 'one of the richest commoners of the kingdom . . . may come to be useful to the support of your administration, and at a vast expense we have secured his being always in a situation to be so, as well as his younger brother as soon as his age will permit'.[103] Though the draft for this letter is undated it must have been written between January 1828 and November 1830, for the phrase 'your administration' implies that Wellington was Prime Minister at the time. Implied also is the purchase of a rotten borough, in fact East Looe.

Although Thomas did not attain the high distinction which, doubtless prompted by his wife, he desired, he was rewarded by the elevation of his eldest son Henry, 'the rich commoner', to the post of Groom of the Bedchamber to George IV in the last months of his reign. When the Hopes' friends, the Duke and Duchess of Clarence, became King and Queen, Mrs. Hope was appointed Woman of the Bedchamber to Queen Adelaide. Even this appointment did not command universal approval. In a letter to her son written on 23 July 1830, Lady Holland observed that 'Persons are surprised at Mrs. Hope being a *Woman* of the Bedchamber. The services are not dignified; & at court she cannot be admitted into the Circle, or be spoken to as her own station entitles her to otherwise. She gains the fan and gloves.'[104]

This position, of however dubious distinction, marked the climax of the family's progress in society during Hope's lifetime. For Hope himself 1830, the last full year of his life, was taken up with the preparation for the press of his curious *Essay on the Origin and Prospects of Man*.[105] At the end of this labour he was in a weak condition and fell seriously ill in January 1831. His son Adrian wrote in his diary: 'I had come to London on the 28th January on account of my father's illness. When he saw me he exclaimed, "How very, very kind". From the first I saw that there was no hope of his recovery.'[106] His friend, the

1. Benjamin West, 'The Hope Family', 1802

JOHN FLAXMAN

2. 'Hercules and Hebe', 1792

3. 'Aurora and Cephalus', *c.* 1791

novelist Miss Mitford, wrote of him in a letter: 'He had been very ill, and was getting better, but went out, in an open carriage in one of those fogs, caught cold and ... inflammation on the chest.'[107] Another novelist, Maria Edgeworth, said in a letter to her stepmother that it was scarcely possible that his death

> could strike you as much as it did me. I, who had seen him but a few days before, and who had been rallying him on his being hypochondriac ... He sent me word that if I could bear to see a poor sick man in his nightcap, I might come up.
>
> So I did, and followed Mrs. Hope through all the magnificent apartments, and then up to the attics, and through room after room till we came to his retreat, and then a feeble voice from an armchair—'Oh! my dear Miss Edgeworth, my kind friend to the last.'
>
> And I saw a figure sunk in his chair like La Harpe, in figured silk *robe de chambre* and nightcap ...

Now, as always, he spoke with great devotion of his wife and children. Miss Edgeworth 'told him laughing, that he was only ill of a plethora of happiness, that he had everything this world could give, and only wanted a little adversity. "Yes," said he, "I am happy, blessed with such a wife and such a son!"'[108]

The end came suddenly on 2 February 1831.[109] Ten days later the strange, half-foreign and ever-enigmatic connoisseur was laid to rest in the mausoleum at Deepdene,[110] which he had built for the son who died in Italy. The funeral was a simple and unpublicized affair. He had specifically requested that his body 'be deposited in the quietest manner next to that of my ever-lamented son Charles'.[111] Even here he eludes us. Though the mausoleum survives, it was sealed up for all time in 1957.[112]

His Will, made in 1818 with a Codicil added in 1824 after the birth of his fourth son Alexander, contained no surprises for those who knew him. Popular estimation had often exaggerated his fortune. In 1804 it seems to have stood at £200,000,[113] and careful investment never let it drop below this. Thus, though rich, he was not a millionaire, and the cost of everything he did or bought had to be considered in detail beforehand. Having provided in his Will for his wife, children, and servants, he made specific arrangements for the preservation of his two houses and their contents. His wife was to have the use of the Deepdene for life and it was then to pass to his eldest son, Henry. He gave: 'all my pictures, prints, drawings, statues, Greek fictile vases, engraved stones, marbles and other curiosities of that nature, and all my books, manuscripts, maps and charts . . . and my house in Duchess Street with the appurtenances and furniture—to my Executors in trust for my son Henry'. In the event of the death without heirs of his wife and children, Duchess Street and its contents were to be made over to the Trustees of the British Museum. In fact, Hope did not take sufficiently stringent measures to ensure the preservation intact of his life achievement, for his son sold the Duchess Street mansion for demolition less than twenty years after his death and had entirely remodelled the Deepdene even earlier.

The virtual disappearance of Thomas Hope's two houses, the fact that the family died out in the male line and the total dispersal of his private papers and drawings, have all contributed towards obliterating the memory of his curious achievement. The barrel has to be squeezed in order to produce even this tenuous biographical trickle. But one notices a certain duality, a certain conflict between the personality and the activities. For a man who appears by nature to have been shy and reserved,[114] if not actually aloof, haughty, and over-fastidious, he seems to have spent an uncommonly large amount of his time in giving and attending parties, routs, and balls. There can be little doubt where his real interets lay. As he observed of himself: 'From an infant, architecture was always my favourite amusement; I scarce was able to hold a pencil, when, instead of flowers, landscapes . . . of which the imitation chiefly delights . . . such children as shew a turn for . . . design I already began dealing in . . . straight lines.'[115] Nor was this a merely academic interest. If the arts had been for his immediate predecessors part of their whole princely conception of life, how much more so could they be for one who had released himself from the cares of the Bank.[116] As Hope and Company had influenced and moulded the financial life of Holland, so was Thomas Hope concerned to influence the artistic life of England. Born into a family whose members were accustomed to regard themselves as public figures, he saw clearly that he also would have to become a public figure if he were to influence taste. Hence his constantly social life. Yet his real nature seems to have been solitary and withdrawn, and such as to encourage him to build around himself a strange and private palace of art. This was the age of the transition from the private collection to the public museum—a fact which helps to account for the curious nature of the achievements of men like Beckford, like Soane, and like Hope himself. Of his own ambitions and ambivalent social position it is best to let him speak for himself in a sentence of noble ringing tones:

> I, who, though of merchant blood, am not a merchant; who though dabbling in authorship rank not among the inspired; who have only been able to bestow on a few humble artists the feeble patronage of an humble individual, have done all I could; and should I succeed in kindling for the arts a more intense and universal love, when comes the hour of death I shall think I have not lived in vain.[117]

II

Collector and Patron

> There are few names in English history which will better deserve the honours of posterity than the exalted individual, of whose gallery I am about to speak. In the very dawn of science, while yet the arts of England trembled in helpless infancy, this enlightened scholar stretched forth his fostering hand to raise the sinking child of Genius; and, not alone content with affording his own munificent support, he liberally employed his great talents and fortune in exciting a similar feeling in the minds of others. Proudly may he wear the ever-budding wreath a nation's gratitude cheerfully awards him. It is an evergreen, the gift of every voice, that must bind his brows while living, and will perpetuate his fame, shedding a fragrant odour over his memory, to the latest period of time.[1]

Thus, ecstatically, wrote Westmacott of Hope in 1824. Of all the accounts of Hope's position and influence this is probably the most enthusiastic, and it must be for us to discuss how far this praise is justified. Certainly, the whole of Hope's social and intellectual activities, outlined in the previous chapter, were for him but the background to his task of raising the standard of English taste by the threefold method of collecting the best works of art from past ages; of publicizing his own designs and productions; and of patronizing those of others. This chapter will accordingly be devoted to his patronage of living artists and to the growth of his collections.

The artist chosen by Hope as the object of his earliest recorded acts of patronage was John Flaxman (1755–1826). That Thomas Hope, at the astonishingly early age of twenty-two, should thus have singled out Flaxman from among the many and varied artists then in Rome is a strong indication of his precocious sensibility as a connoisseur. Flaxman, several years Hope's senior, was unusually enthusiastic about his commission and wrote to his parents from Rome on 3 March 1792:

> I have refused to execute any other commissions in Rome, but I have taken one to execute in England and perhaps the noblest ever brought by

> an English artist to his own country, it is the restoration of the Torso Belvidere which is believed to have been anciently a group; its restoration is to be the marriage of Hercules and Hebe, it is to be the size of the original . . . it is ordered by Mr. Thos. Hope of Amsterdam. I have bargained to make the model here and execute the marble in England.[2]

The cost was to be considerable: seven hundred guineas. Although Flaxman received a payment in Rome of £245 and another in England of £96 in July 1796,[3] the group was never executed in marble. Its vigorous strength can be appreciated in the plaster model, now bronzed, which survives at the Slade School of Fine Art (Plate 2). These forceful heroic compositions were never Flaxman's best or most characteristic achievements. By 1824 he was convinced that this proposed 'restoration' was a false notion.[4] The original idea for it, however, came not from Hope but from D'Hancarville,[5] editor of the volumes illustrating Hamilton's first collection of vases and antiquities.

Two further sculptures which Hope commissioned from Flaxman at this time were a copy in black-veined marble of the Apollo Belvedere[6] and a group of Aurora and Cephalus (Plate 3 and Fig. 13).[7] This elegant if somewhat slight composition was destined to occupy a position of singular importance at Duchess Street.

It was the fruits of Hope's next commission from Flaxman which helped elevate the sculptor to that pre-eminent position among English neo-classical artists from which he has never been deposed. This commission was for one hundred and nine illustrations to Dante, for each of which Hope was to pay Flaxman one guinea. An unpublished letter from Mrs. Flaxman to William Hayley, written from Rome on 22 July 1793, tells us something of the nature of the commission and helps to clarify the chronology of the Dante, Homer, and Aeschylus drawings:

> the set of drawings from his Divina Comedia is now compleat (both as to numbers, grace and beauty) as are the Copper Plates engraved from them but I am sorry to inform you that Mr. Hope does not mean to make them public, as he wishes to give them away himself to the chosen few, whom he may think from their taste and virtue are entitled to them, he has by a letter totally prevented Flaxman interceding for any of his friends . . . Flaxman has nearly finished another work of this kind, the Iliad and Odyssey of Homer they are larger than the Dante . . . [He] is actually

> employed in making a set of Drawings (Outlines) much larger than the former, from the Tragedies of Aeschylus, for Lady Spencer.[8]

The dichotomy between the private and the public, which existed throughout Hope's artistic life, made itself felt at the start. A few sets of the Dante plates were published for Hope by Piroli in 1793. He presented an inscribed copy of this rare edition to the Dowager Countess Spencer. A pirated French edition appeared in 1802, in 1806 Hope sold a set of Piroli's plates to Longman's for £200,[9] and thereafter numerous editions were published.

Flaxman's were the first complete set of illustrations to Dante undertaken in the eighteenth century. Although Dante was not generally appreciated until the end of the century, the Comte de Caylus, as early as 1757 remarkably enough, had recommended him as a source to modern painters adding, by way of compensation, that Virgil would inevitably play a large part.[10] It was possibly Caylus who inspired Hope and Flaxman. From the 1770's Fuseli and Reynolds had been interested in the theme, but on seeing Flaxman's Dante, Fuseli said, 'I used to think myself the best composer, but now I own Flaxman to be the greater man'.[11] Goethe and Schlegel were no less appreciative;[12] while Canova, in Rogers' words, 'who was well acquainted with his exquisite illustrations of Dante, &c., could hardly believe that a man of such genius was not an object of admiration among his countrymen'.[13]

It must be confessed, however, that in Piroli's flat rather pedestrian engravings much of the charm of Flaxman's nervous grace is lost. Nevertheless, the ethereal forms that flit across the pages are an example of the strange disembodied synthesis of Classic and Gothic that can be closely paralleled in aspects of the Dance and Soane styles. After Tischbein, Flaxman was probably the first artist completely to adopt the outline technique which became the hall-mark of late neo-classicism. The strange tense work of the Danish-German A. J. Carstens (1754–98) marks one of the highest points of the neo-classical style. His outline engravings, *Die Argonauten*, were issued in 1796 and we know that Hope possessed a copy of the rare edition published in Rome in 1799.[14]

At the time of drawing the Dante illustrations, Flaxman was probably unaware of the impact they would have. He regarded them merely as preparatory exercises for the sculpture which he hoped to execute on his return to London. On 26 October 1793 he wrote to Hayley of the Dante illustrations:

> my view does not terminate in giving a few outlines to the world; my intention is to shew how any story may be represented in a series of compositions on principles of the Antients, of which as soon as I return to England I intend to give specimens in Sculpture of different kinds, in groups of basrelieves, suited to all the purposes of Sacred and Civil Architecture.[15]

And for Hope, Flaxman executed on his return a small bust of Dante (Fig. 17), a circular bas-relief of the Birth of Bacchus[16] and a number of chimney-pieces for the Duchess Street mansion, with a bust of Thomas' brother Henry to adorn that in the dining-room (Fig. 16).[17] Hope also acquired Flaxman's original drawings for the Iliad and Odyssey.[14] These contained many examples of Greek furniture, costume, and decoration, and that Hope singled them out for mention in the bibliography to *Household Furniture* is an important fact that must not be overlooked. His enthusiasm for Flaxman was never to wane, and one of his last acts was to subscribe to the publication of a posthumous edition of Flaxman's *Acts of Mercy*.[18]

To return to Hope's early years in Rome, we can trace his first purchases of antique art made with his two younger brothers in the mid-1790s. These three rich young men, barely out of their teens, must greatly have enjoyed playing the parts of grand connoisseurs. Thomas bought from Thomas Jenkins an antique cameo depicting Caligula and a marble group of Hercules washing Diomedes' hair.[19] Henry went a step further and acquired from Pacetti a group of Bacchus and Hope from the Villa Aldobrandini and a statue of an Hermaphrodite. Adrian bought from Pacetti statues of an Apollo and and Athlete,[20] and from Pierantoni a group restored, at the enormous cost of two thousand eight hundred *scudi*, to represent Antinous offering ambrosia to Hadrian.[19] Thomas went on to acquire two further statues from Pacetti, an Esculapius from Hadrian's Villa and an Athlete,[20] and finally the two finest pieces of antique sculpture ever to adorn his collection. These were magnificent life-size Greek statues, discovered in 1797 in the mouth of the Tiber at Ostia,[21] representing, respectively, Hygeia and Athene (Plates 4 and 5). The acquisition of these was a major triumph and they were regarded throughout the nineteenth century as the work of Pheidias or his school. Most of the works purchased by his brothers also found their way into Thomas' collection.

Thomas and Henry now turned to England to take part in one of the richest sales of paintings of the age, that of the Orléans Collection. The immediate history of these paintings since their disposal by 'Philippe Egalité' in 1792, had been a complicated sequence of machinations characteristic of art-dealing in that and every age.[22] The principal sale of the Italian paintings finally took place in London between December 1798 and the end of August 1799. Sixty-six paintings still remained after this lengthy sale. They were sold in 1800. Thomas and Henry Hope seem to have approached the Sale in the careful calculating way appropriate to the sons of a banking family. Each bought about seven paintings for which each paid roughly two and a half thousand pounds, although considering the riches that were for sale, Thomas' purchases do not form a very distinguished list.[23] Perhaps of a higher quality than any of his purchases at the Orléans Sale was the Rubens 'Death of Adonis' (Plate 6), which he probably acquired at the sale at Bryan's Gallery in Pall Mall on 19 May 1798.[24] Inspired by the ending of the Tenth Book of Ovid's *Metamorphoses*, the atmosphere of doom and lamentation in this solemn canvas is heavy as thunder. Rubens seems to give us a foretaste of a sombre neo-classical world still coloured by the expansiveness of the Baroque; and it is attractive to think of the young Thomas Hope being captivated by the ponderous but heroic nudes that adorn this antique world.

Another fine work in Thomas Hope's possession was the dramatic 'Betrayal of Christ' by Guercino, acquired from the Aldobrandini Collection and now in the Fitzwilliam Museum. He also owned two paintings by Van Dyck: an 'Assumption of the Virgin', possibly that seen by Reynolds in the Hope Collection in Amsterdam,[25] and a 'Virgin and Child' now at Buckingham Palace.[26]

The French painter Antoine Dubost, however, told William Daniell in February 1808 that he thought Hope's collection so inferior to Lord Stafford's that it were better for him to sell all his 'old masters' and patronize living artists.[27] But for those who wished to collect

Renaissance and Baroque paintings, these were the golden years. Between 1795 and 1817 London was the scene of the Orléans, Calonne, Trumbull, Bryan, Fagel, Hamilton, Holdernesse, Day, Udny, Ottley, Le Brun, La Fontaine, Prince of Canino, and Prince de Talleyrand sales, as well as those of the numerous importations from all over Europe of the celebrated William Buchanan.

In 1819 Henry Hope lent to his brother the Hope Collection of Dutch and Flemish paintings which he had inherited.[28] This rich collection of nearly one hundred paintings, housed in a new gallery at Duchess Street, contained many works by artists then hardly known in England. In range and quality it rivalled the collection of the Prince Regent, who had done much to stimulate interest in Dutch and Flemish Art.

Hope's concerns, however, were more with antique and modern art and with the attempt to influence the character of the latter by promoting knowledge of the former. Thus the only major sale after the Orléans in which he was a significant purchaser was the Hamilton Sale, conducted by Christie's on 27 March 1801. Hamilton's pictures were not of high quality since they had been collected before the windfalls occasioned by Napoleon's campaigns. His vases, on the other hand, were not only of the highest possible quality but, through the frequently reprinted engravings of them published by D'Hancarville in 1766–7 and by Tischbein in 1791–5, exercised a formative influence on the late neo-classical style and particularly on the work of Flaxman. The Tischbein engravings were amongst the earliest in Europe to adopt the outline technique which Flaxman, as we have already seen, was to make his own. Flaxman had seen Hamilton's second collection in Naples, which Hope was to acquire in 1801, and wrote in a letter to Hamilton, dated 13 March 1792, 'of your superb collection of vases'.[5] There are a number of close parallels between scenes on the Hamilton vases and in Flaxman's Homer illustrations.[29]

By 1766 Sir William Hamilton (1730–1803) had acquired the collection of vases and antiquities which he was to sell to the British Museum in 1772. In 1789–90 he acquired from tombs near Naples a second collection of vases which he described, in a letter of 3 May 1796 to the Countess of Lichtenau, as 'far more beautiful and complete than the series in London', expressing at the same time his desire to deposit it at Berlin 'in the midst of men of learning and of literary academies'.[30] In 1798, fearful of Napoleon's rapacity, he shipped the vases to England in twenty-four cases. One-third was lost in a disastrous shipwreck and in 1801 Thomas Hope became the proud possessor of the surviving two-thirds for the sum of four and a half thousand guineas.[31] It was this act which immediately established him as a collector of equal importance to any in the country. He bought and sold vases, moreover, with a discerning eye and frequently enlarged his collection. Although he acquired from the Hamilton Collection just under seven hundred and fifty vases, of which half were figured, his friend A. L. Millin observed in 1806 that he now possessed over fifteen hundred vases.[32] We know that he sold one hundred and eighty in 1805,[33] but also that he acquired further vases at the Cawdor, Chinnery, Edwards, Coghill, de Paroi, Durand, Magnoncourt, and Beugnot Sales.[34]

Hope housed over five hundred vases in the three vase-rooms at Duchess Street. His son Henry sold a number of them in 1849[35] prior to moving the contents of the Duchess Street house to the Deepdene. The remaining three hundred and fifty-seven vases, sold at Christie's in 1917, were classified by E. M. W. Tillyard in his invaluable study, *The Hope Vases* (Cambridge, 1923), as comprising: one hundred and seventy-two Attic Red Figure; seventy Attic Black Figure; nine Attic Plain Black; twelve Corinthian; and the remainder various South Italian fabrics.

The importance of these vases in the development of the Hope style cannot be emphasized too strongly. They constituted an immediate and living link with Greek life with which neither antique architecture nor sculpture could begin to compete, the former because the surviving buildings represented only the public side of Greek life, the latter because of the blurring of distinctions occasioned by the constant imitation and restoration of Greek originals. Of the costumes, furniture, and fittings illustrated in Hope's *Costume of the Ancients* (1809), twenty separate items were based on works of art in his own possession, of which over half were drawn from the vase collection.

In the same year as the Hamilton Sale, Hope bought for £99. 15s. at the Bessborough Sale a huge votive foot in red porphyry, 2 ft. 11 in.

long.[36] This recalls that superb statement of the neo-classical aesthetic: Fuseli's drawing of 'The Artist moved by the magnitude of antique fragments' (*c.* 1778–9).[37]

Two years later, in 1803, came Thomas Hope's best-known act of patronage.[38] In March a disconsolate Thorvaldsen was about to return to his native Denmark after a wholly unsuccessful stay in Rome when Hope, entering his studio, professed himself delighted at a chilly but unfinished Jason (Plate 9). He expressed his delight in the most practical way by offering for the completed sculpture more than its young creator had asked. The Jason marked an important stage in Thorvaldsen's career since it was his first fully neo-classical work and, as such, showed a marked influence from Canova.[39]

Hope's patronage was not a question of vague gestures and kindly words but took the form of a legal contract as though it were still part of the affairs of Hope and Company. Thorvaldsen, however, was not to be pinned down so easily. The sculpture was still not complete by April 1806, in which month Hope's agent wrote a letter toThorvaldsen expressing Hope's desire for the finished work.[40] Eleven years passed. Thorvaldsen now observed that the Jason had been but a product of his youth and suggested that he be allowed to try another subject.[41] Hope remained unmoved: for him a contract was a contract. In April 1819 he tried force. Complaining that despite the payments he had made he had as yet received nothing in return, he handed over the whole business including contract and receipts to the bankers Torlonia and Company,[42] who were encouraged to exert the severest pressure on Thorvaldsen. Two years later it seemed that their efforts were about to be rewarded. But it was a false alarm. All that happened was that Thorvaldsen wrote an irritating letter in the course of which it was implied that time had no meaning where works of genius were concerned.[43] It was not until the spring of 1828 that Jason arrived at the Deepdene, precisely a quarter of a century after it had been commissioned. With it came a number of peace-offerings: two bas-reliefs and a bust of Hope's son Henry.[44] The bas-reliefs were iconographically complicated. 'Art and the Genius of Light' was a half-size marble copy of an original modelled in Rome in 1808 (Plate 7).[45] A crowded perhaps almost clumsy composition, it depicts Art as a seated woman with a stylus and tablet. Near her are a lyre and an owl: symbols of poetry and science. 'Cupid Received by Anacreon' was carved in 1823 as the Winter scene from Thorvaldsen's history of Cupid and Psyche.[46] It is a work of considerable elegance, closely based on antique models.

There can be no doubt that Hope comes very well out of the lengthy Jason dispute. His letter of thanks on finally receiving the statue was a model of good manners and elegance.[44] He described the statue, the reliefs, and the bust in terms of the highest praise, and their creator as the great living sculptor. If Hope's purchase of the Jason statue saved Thorvaldsen from failure, as has been held at the time and since, the episode does not shed the most attractive light on Thorvaldsen's character. He is at least revealed, for all his austere neo-classical style, as an example of the new Blake-like 'liberated' artist of the nineteenth century whose elevated conception of his art would not allow him to believe that it could be produced to order. Similarly Hope had one foot in the old world, one in the new. Despite his theories about public institutions for the encouragement of the arts in the life of the nation, his approach, as we saw with the Flaxman Dante drawings, was that of the traditional, individualist, and possessive patron.

His natural irritation at the delay over the Jason did not blind him to the merits of Thorvaldsen's art. Thus in 1817, when the dispute was going forward, he visited Thorvaldsen's studio in Rome with his wife and two sons to sit for a series of family busts.[47] Three were completed in marble: one of himself with a calm, dignified, and doubtless idealized face (Plate 8); one of his wife Louisa; and one of their son Adrian, then aged six. The bust of Henry, which Thorvaldsen sent with the Jason in 1828, had been modelled, unknown to Thomas Hope, in *c.* 1822–3. Further works by Thorvaldsen in Hope's possession were: a statue of a 'Shepherd and Dog',[34] a bronze-gilt bas-relief of 'Night',[48] a bust of Lord Wriothesley Russell,[49] and a figure of Psyche (Plate 62) given to Hope by his brother. The original was modelled in Rome in 1811 and this half-sized copy was made by Thorvaldsen for Henry Hope.[50]

In *c.* 1800 Antonio Canova (1757–1822) offered Hope a cast of his 'Perseus', which he had made for the Milanese painter Bossi and which Pius VII, refusing to allow out of Rome, placed in the Vatican

Museum.[51] Probably with good reason, Hope was unenthusiastic about casts and refused Canova's offer. Similarly, he reluctantly refused in 1805 an offer from Thomas Banks (1735–1805) of the model for his 'Achilles' (*c.* 1784).[51] This had been the work which established the popularity of this distinguished early neo-classical sculptor and for which he was made an associate member of the Royal Academy. Hope was to come into more fruitful contact with Canova a few years later. Canova's first statue of Venus was commissioned in 1805 by Queen Marie-Louise of Etruria to occupy the pedestal of the Medici Venus, recently abducted by Napoleon. A copy was made for the Prince of Canino, which soon passed into the Lansdowne Collection, and another for the King of Bavaria.[52] In 1816 or 1817 Hope had admired in Canova's studio a third copy of this Venus, uncompleted and intended for a Mr. Standish, possibly Charles Townley-Standish. Standish abandoned the contract at some point, whereupon his place was immediately taken by Hope. On 15 February 1819 Hope wrote to Canova to express his pleasure at hearing from him that instead of continuing with the Standish Venus, a new Venus, now nearly complete, had been embarked upon instead. It seems that criticism that the sight of Venus engaged in washing herself verged on the banal[53] encouraged Canova entirely to alter her pose with the result that there is almost no drapery on the Hope Venus. There were two years of delays and difficulties before Venus finally found her way to Duchess Street. Hope found her worth waiting for. On 11 March 1822 he wrote of his Venus to Canova that: 'il serait présomptueux pour moi de prétendre détailler les perfections à celui qui en est l'auteur', and that: 'je me trouve l'heureux possesseur d'un ouvrage plus précieux, plus achevé même que celui dont j'avais obtenu la promesse'. Hope writes at length in this vein, but we learn that the statue was to be placed 'au fond de ma galerie, occupant le point central d'une assez longue perspective et de quelques objets d'art intéressants . . . avec une draperie riche derrière pour faire ressortir ses blanc contours et ses reflets délicats . . . '.[52] Hope later commissioned Lorenzo Bartolini (1777–1850) to make a copy of the Venus so that he might be greeted by her at each of his houses.[54] There can be little doubt that the Hope Venus was more strictly neo-classical than the original version.[55] The greater nudity of the Hope figure, and the far more Greek severity of the line from forehead to nose, have their part to play in creating this effect.

There was no precise contemporary equivalent in painting to the glorious achievements in sculpture of Canova, Thorvaldsen, and Flaxman. Thus the products of Hope's patronage of painters were less distinguished than those of his patronage of sculptors. This, clearly, is a fault that cannot be laid at his door.

His patronage of Antoine Dubost met with results so disastrous as to be barely credible.[56] Dubost was a rising French painter whose 'Embarquement de Brutus poursuivi par les soldats d'Antinoüs' had been awarded a gold medal at the Paris *Salon* of 1799. In 1805 he arrived in England and in the following year exhibited his 'Damocles' at the Royal Academy. He had a high opinion of his work and was asking the amazing sum of fifteen hundred guineas for this canvas. In June 1807 Thomas Hope offered eight hundred guineas and the promise of one hundred persons who would subscribe towards the cost of its reproduction. He also invited Dubost to paint a portrait of his wife for four hundred guineas. Dubost accepted both offers. This began a tedious squabble, of which it will suffice to give merely an outline here.[57] Before Dubost had painted Mrs. Hope, Benjamin West was of the opinion that he was 'the first painter of the age'.[58] Having seen the completed picture he was inclined to change his opinion. Other less distinguished critics followed his lead. Nor did Hope remain silent. He asked Dubost to render less attenuated the proportions of his wife's figure as portrayed in the canvas. This Dubost was not prepared to do. He then learnt that Hope had lopped off a section of the 'Damocles' because otherwise, 'Il écraseroit . . . par son extrème hauteur ma chambre en ville.' Dubost's anger was further heightened by the fact that Hope had failed to find any subscribers to the reproduction costs of the 'Damocles' other than Sir Charles Pole, Bart., and Julius Angerstein. He was infuriated by Hope's constant advice and criticisms while he was painting his wife, but agreed to make any alterations which Hope's friends might suggest once the painting was complete if only Hope himself would refrain from commenting on its progress.[27] Under these conditions Hope refused to pay the four hundred guineas he had promised for the portrait. Dubost retaliated by producing one of the most extraordinary portraits ever painted. Against the background of the Flaxman Room at Duchess Street, it depicted Mrs. Hope being offered jewels by a monster, distinctly recognizable as her husband, out of whose mouth issued the words: 'I am sensible that I am a most horrible beast and that you can have no thoughts of me, but if you will accept of me you shall have all these riches at your disposal.'[59] This vicious painting, entitled 'Beauty and the Beast', was exhibited together with several other works by the same artist in a room in Pall Mall in the spring of 1810. A large public, including the Prince of Wales himself, willingly paid the entrance fee. On Wednesday 20 June, however, the canvas was rent asunder by the stick of the Reverend John Beresford, Mrs. Hope's brother.[60] Somewhat lacking in a sense of proportion, Dubost immediately demanded one thousand guineas in damages. Leigh Hunt now wrote an article defending Hope in the *Examiner*.[61] Dubost's own reply took the form of a sixty-page pamphlet entitled *Hunt and Hope*, published in 1810. Dubost quoted Hope as having said that although he could only afford eight hundred guineas for the 'Damocles', he agreed that it was worth fifteen hundred. He claimed that Hope had since not only cut off part of the canvas (which was true) but that he had deliberately erased the name and was telling everyone that it was the work of David! When the 'Damocles' had originally been hung next to a Benjamin West at Duchess Street, he recounted, Hope had thought that it showed up the West so unfavourably that he had asked West to touch it up. As a result West had gone out of his way at the British Institution and the Royal Academy to annoy and frustrate Dubost. Hope and West prevented his 'Venus and Diana' from being hung at the British Institution, and Hope refused to allow him to touch up his portrait of Mrs. Hope once it was hung at Somerset House.

Writers as disparate as Lord Byron[62] and Cobbett[63] referred to the dispute, the former Hope's champion, the latter Dubost's. At a dinner-party given by Joseph Farington on 2 July 1810, Dubost's 'brutal attack . . . was long a subject of conversation. Fuseli was capricious and made light of it. Lawrence opposed him.'[64] The final decision of the jury at the court-case was to award Dubost only five guineas in damages.[65]

Of commissioning portraits of himself and his family Hope was especially fond since it enabled him to combine patronage with self-perpetuation. Guy Head, who as early as the 1780's had been sent to the Hopes in Amsterdam with a letter of introduction from Reynolds,[66] had painted in Rome by December 1795 a portrait, now lost, of Thomas Hope and a brother, probably Henry.[67] There is a miniature[68] of Thomas by Henry Bone, R.A. (1755–1834); and a portrait of him in Turkish dress, painted in 1798 by Sir William Beechey (1753–1829), reminding us how far Hope was prepared to carry his admiration for civilisations which he believed less jaded than his own (Plate 10).[69] The portraits which Thomas Phillips painted in 1814 of Byron in Eastern dress are so close to Beechey's portrait of Hope as to suggest that they must have been inspired by it. In 1805 Lawrence began but never completed[70] a full-length portrait of Thomas's brother Henry in Greek dress with a red cloak and a white turban.[71] In 1826 he painted Mrs. Hope 'as an oriental Fatima, in a turban splendidly embroidered with gold and a gown of a rich glowing red. Ornamented gorgeously with jewels.'[72] Hope also commissioned Sir Martin Archer Shee (1770–1850) to paint his wife.[73] This portrait was exhibited at the Royal Academy in 1808, and in 1812 George Dawe (1781–1829), who had helped prepare the plates for *Household Furniture*, painted a further portrait of Mrs. Hope (Plate 11).[74] In this, Louisa's lithe elongated figure in a red Grecian dress descends a flight of steps and from her right arm, poised elegantly above her head, depends a trailing Grecian shawl of bright orange. This painting and indeed Louisa's posture appear to be based on a Greek vase painting (Plate 12) reproduced in Hope's *Costume of the Ancients.* An earlier portrait of Mrs. Hope by Dawe was described in 1811 as 'A faithful transcript of this fascinating woman, engaged in the most lovely of feminine employments, the nurture of her children'.[75] A painting survives by Lawrence of the short-lived son Charles as an Infant Bacchus;[76] and in 1819 James Elmes wrote of a group by Lawrence of the Hope children.[77] In May 1829 the likenesses of Mrs. Hope and two sons, Henry and Alexander, were reproduced in a more conventional way, by the art of August Edouart, the popular French silhouettist who had settled in London.[78]

With the series of busts by Thorvaldsen, artistic commemoration of the family reached its highest point. Hope also commissioned

4. 'Hygeia'

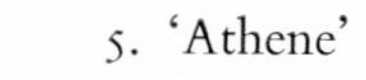

5. 'Athene'

6. Sir Peter Paul Rubens, 'The Death of Adonis'

portrait busts from William Behnes (1795–1864) of his wife and, in 1824, of their son Alexander playing with a rabbit.[79] From Lorenzo Bartolini came a bust of their eldest son Henry.[80]

We must now investigate more closely the paintings, other than family portraits, which Hope commissioned or bought directly from living artists. This was one of his most important spheres of patronage since, with surprisingly catholic tastes, he deliberately encouraged young and little-known painters and sculptors. This had far-reaching effects that were widely believed at the time to have changed the face of the art-world in England. As James Elmes observed in 1819, it was partly as a result of Hope's efforts that 'a new era is opening in sculpture'. However, he added censoriously, 'a higher degree of merit will in future be exacted for eminence in sculpture as well as historical painting, than was required when Mr. Hope began his patriotic encouragement of English art'.[81]

In May 1804 Hope commissioned from Richard Westall (1756–1836) two historical paintings at a cost of four hundred and fifty guineas.[82] One of these, 'The Expiation of Orestes at the Shrine of Delphos', must have been one of the most extreme pieces of strict neo-classicism ever executed (Plate 13). It was directly inspired by surviving works of Greek art in Hope's possession although the process of imitation is marked by a new sentimentality. The general theme was provided by a scene on one of his figured vases showing Apollo, Athene, Orestes, two human heads, and two of the Eumenides (Fig. 1). One of the latter is represented with wings, according to Millin the only known instance of this in antique art.[83] Westall was further obliged to base his figure of Athene on the Hope statue of Athene (Plate 5). This remarkable picture was exhibited at the Royal Academy in March 1805, for which occasion Hope had constrained Westall to veil Apollo's nudity—[84] a surprising lapse from classical purity on Hope's part. Westall's other grandiose mythological painting for Hope of 1805 was a painfully clumsy 'Reconciliation of Helen and Paris, after his Defeat by Menelaus' (Plate 14). Both this painting and the rather happier 'Damocles Discovering the Sword over his Head', commissioned by Hope from Westall in May 1811,[85] display much sumptuous and glistening neo-classical furniture that is markedly Hopeian in character. The 'Damocles' was a larger version of a painting by Westall (Plate 15) owned by Richard Payne Knight, then being exhibited at the Royal Academy. At an exhibition of the Water Colour Society in April 1808 Hope bought 'A View in China' by the much-travelled Westall for fifty guineas.[86] One must never be surprised by the range of neo-classical taste.

Fig. 1. 'Orestes pursued by the Eumenides'

Hope acquired as many as five paintings by Louis Gauffier (1762–1801), a follower of David, who spent the last sixteen years of his life in Rome and Florence. He was also an agreeable portraitist much in demand by the English aristocracy, and his painting of 1796 of Henry Fox, 3rd Baron Holland (1773–1840), is now in the National Portrait Gallery. Hope knew Fox and may have met Gauffier through him in Italy in the 1790s. Works by Gauffier in the Hope collection were 'Ulysses and Nausicaa', signed and dated 1798;[71] 'Hector Reproving Paris'; 'Oedipus and the Sphinx'; 'Rest on the Flight into Egypt'; and 'Vanity', dated 1791.[71] From George Dawe he acquired in 1810 a painting of 'Andromache imploring Ulysses to spare her Son';[87] and from Henry Howard (1768–1847) a scene of 'Nymphs Ravishing Hylas'. In 1809 he paid one hundred guineas for a prize canvas at the British Institution by the young William Hilton (1786–1839), 'The Burgesses of Calais before Edward III'.[77] Poor Hilton continued to his death with these grand but never very popular historical pieces.

In March 1805 Hope commissioned three canvases of Greek history from Benjamin West (1730–1820) and 'Hector Meeting Andromache' from Thomas Stothard (1755–1834).[88] One of the West paintings depicted 'Adonis contemplating Cupid, watched by Venus'; but the best known was 'Thetis bearing the Armour to Achilles' (Plate 16). It was based not exactly on a first-hand Greek source but on, perhaps, the next best thing, lines from Pope's *Iliad*: 'Th' immortal arms, the Goddess mother bears Swift to her son; her son she finds in tears, Stretch'd o'er Patroclus' corse...'[89] An engraving of this by William Bond, was dedicated to Hope 'as a small compliment for his distinguished patronage of the Fine Arts and literature of England'. Another engraving by Henry Moses is, as Irwin points out,[90] yet more strictly neo-classical than the canvas itself. The painting represents, however, a conscious return, doubtless inspired by Hope's *Costume of the Ancients*, to an archaeological accuracy which West had largely abandoned. But unfortunately for Hope, West lacked both the virtuosity and the vision of Rubens, and a comparison between his painting and the Rubens 'Death of Adonis' (Plate 6)—so similar in some respects—immediately condemns West's atmosphere of shrill emotionalism and the nasty anatomy of his strained figures.

But for the most extreme expression of the high-minded spirit of neo-classical history-painting it is to Benjamin Haydon (1786–1846) that we must turn. Moreover, when Hope first commissioned a picture from West he was already the grand-old-man of English painting, but when three years later he first bought a picture from Haydon, he was buying a picture that was Haydon's first. What he had been to Thorvaldsen he was now to become to Haydon. With the following portentous words did Haydon describe his method of approaching, at the tender age of twenty, his first canvas, a 'Rest on the Flight into Egypt': '... on 1 October 1806, setting my palette, and, taking brush in hand, I knelt down and prayed God to bless my career, to grant me energy to create a new era in art, and to rouse the people and patrons to a just estimate of the moral value of historical painting'.[91] This elevated concept of historical painting was characteristic of the moment and must have appealed to Thomas Hope; as must Haydon's further claim, in describing this picture, of having 'tried to unite nature and the antique'.[92] The completed canvas, six feet by four in size, was exhibited at the Royal Academy in 1807, and in the following year Hope honoured Haydon by purchasing it for one hundred guineas and by writing an enthusiastic account of it in the *Review of Publications of Art*, vol. II. 'The Exhibition of 1807', Haydon wrote, 'brought me before the world: my picture was considered a wonderful work for a student'.[93] Moreover, when he committed suicide in 1846 he left with his body a list of names which included Hope's, of those who had helped him to fame and 'advanced money to help me through my works'.[94]

But this was also the age of Wilkie, and if Hope never acquired a work by Wilkie himself, he did much to encourage the growth of the picturesque, sentimental, or moralizing genre-piece. 'The Music Master' by Michael Sharp, 'in the style of Metzu', won the first prize in 1808 from the Directors of the British Institution. Thomas Hope, one of the Directors, bought the painting for himself and hung it at Duchess Street where in 1819 it was warmly praised by James Elmes.[95] Hope further patronized the anecdotal revival of the early nineteenth century: in 1809 he acquired a scene of 'Officers in a Guard Room' by George Jones (1786–1869); in 1820 another painting by Sharp, 'Cup of Tea'; and in 1821 for £52. 10s. 'The Importunate Author', a scene from Molière, by G. S. Newton, R.A. In a similar vein were two water-colours by Thomas Heaphy (1775–1835), first President of the Society of British Artists. These were 'The Tired Pedlar', for which Hope paid fifty guineas at the Water Colour Society Exhibition of 1808; and a scene of village courtship entitled 'The Offer Accepted' for which, Heaphy's reputation having risen, he paid one hundred and thirty guineas at the same society's exhibition in the following year.[96] Whatever else Regency art may have been, it was not cheap.

Nor was the 'ecstatic' level of Regency art overlooked. Thus there hung at the Deepdene one of the great smoky canvases by John

Martin (1789–1854).[97] This was the 'Fall of Babylon', regarded as the finest picture at the Gallery of the British Institution in 1819 and bought there by Henry Hope for four hundred guineas.[98] Henry Hope's purchase, at the price the painter demanded, did much to raise Martin's status and the painting was again exhibited at the Egyptian Hall, Piccadilly, in 1822.[99] Martin's nearest equal, J. M. Gandy (1771–1843), was also represented with a water-colour of 'Pandemonium', based on Milton, and a 'Design for a Cenotaph'. These were at Duchess Street by 1819.[16] By the same date Hope had acquired from Robert Smirke (1781–1867) his restoration of the Temple of Athena at Sunium. The Picturesque Indian views by Thomas Daniell (1749–1840) will be referred to in a later chapter. Altogether Hope acquired five paintings by Daniell, four of them at least being specially commissioned: one in 1799, two in 1800 and a fourth in 1804. This last Hope would not allow to be shown at a public exhibition desiring rather 'that it shall be a novelty in his own house'.[100]

The presence of two paintings by Guardi of the Piazza San Marco, Venice, one with a torch-light procession, was another unusual aspect of Hope's collection. Guardi was not generally appreciated in Hope's life, though his acquaintance George Agar-Ellis, 1st Baron Dover, was his earliest champion in this country and acquired as many as fifty of his works. Hope also owned a pair of '*Fêtes Champêtres*' by Watteau and a number of Venetian views by Canaletto and Marieschi. A painting attributed with certainty to Canaletto was an exterior view of S. Salvatore, Venice,[101] but, surprisingly, was not recognized as a Canaletto at the Sale of the Hope Heirlooms in 1917. In 1808 Hope paid what was even then considered to be an exorbitant amount, five hundred guineas, for a flower-piece by James Hewlett, Hon. R.A., of Bath.[102] However, Hope was only following the example of Lord Stafford, who the year before had paid four hundred guineas for a flower-piece to which Hope's was the pair.[103] This fact, coupled with Hewlett's demand for nine hundred guineas for a similar painting, caused Hoppner to observe that 'Hewlett ought to be smothered'.[102] Hope also acquired a Stubbs and, at the British Institution in 1819 for fifty guineas, a 'View on the Boulevards' by J. J. Chalon (1778–1854).[104] Most of these were hung at the Deepdene and were probably bought as 'country-house paintings'.

Before leaving the subject of Hope's collections a few more words should be said on the sculpture. This is the best documented section because of its inclusion in Michaelis' monumental study, *Ancient Marbles in Great Britain* (1882).[105] The detailed account given by Michaelis, which does not include modern works or copies, is made up of forty-six separate items. Of these twenty had been considered worthy of plates in the Comte de Clarac's *Musée de Sculpture*, vols. III–IV, 1832–41, a work which excluded busts and reliefs. Hope possessed twenty-six sculptured figures or groups; eight heads; three busts; and a small number of torsos, cineraria, etc. After the Hygeia and the Athene,[106] the best work was probably the Apollo with Hyacinthos from Hadrian's Villa, a particular favourite of Canova's. Also from Hadrian's Villa was a finely modelled sculpture of Antinous;[107] and from Baiae came an uncommonly well-preserved Aphrodite, close in posture to the Medici Venus. These six sculptures, together with an interesting 'Dionysus and Idol', formed the cream of the collection. At the 1917 Sale, at which the whole sculpture collection together with certain Indian antiquities fetched £50,000, these seven pieces were sold for nearly £25,000.

The Egyptian sculpture, originally housed in the Egyptian Room at Duchess Street, must have been one of the most remarkable collections of its kind then in England. There were five statues of priests, two bearing the god Horus in a box before them, six canopic vases of oriental alabaster, a pair of lions, a green basalt vase, and a figure with apron and calantica considered by Michaelis to be of modern workmanship. Hope had been extremely fortunate in acquiring two of the Egyptian sculptures then being discovered in excavations of ancient Roman sites. A lion in green basalt came from Tiberius' palace on Capri, and a granite urn with bronze mounts had been found in the famous 'canope' at Hadrian's Villa.[108] This was just the approach to the Egyptian world that would have appealed to Hope. His approach was never purely archaeological. His was the subtler vision of an age of synthesis which loved to see one civilization through the eyes of another. We have to accept that to the young Thomas Hope, forming his sculpture collection in the last years of the eighteenth century, it did not greatly matter whether his Egyptian pieces were 'genuine', were Roman copies, or modern copies. It was the allusive, cumulative picture that counted. The same is true of his attitude to his classical sculpture. Thus, though we know that he had travelled in both Egypt and Greece, we have no definite knowledge of his having brought back any work of art from either country. Like his Egyptian statues, his two finest Greek ones were discovered at or near Rome. A piece which he may well have brought back from Greece—a fragment of an arm which he believed to have come from the Parthenon frieze—[109] was described derisively by Michaelis as 'anything but remarkable' and, to cap even this, carved in 'marble . . . apparently not Pentelic'![110] Hope's voice was raised at no stage in the Elgin Marbles controversy and he was not invited to sit on the Select Committee of 1816.

However, in writing a critical account of the bust of Nelson by Anne Seymour Damer (1748–1828), he stated clearly the strict neo-classical approach to modern sculpture which he had made it his aim to promote. He praised her austere bust of the hero, displaying prominently the uniform in which he had but lately won the Battle of the Nile, since 'It possesses that breadth of style which [is achieved] through carefully discarding every incidental minutiae of the feature . . . [and] exhibits, moreover, a simplicity of attitude inseparable from real dignity'.[111] This review appeared in *The Times* on 5 May 1804, and, not surprisingly, the Honourable Mrs. Damer had fifty copies of it reprinted at the Strawberry Hill private press. Though Farington considered it a 'most extravagant, and false, and ridiculous'[112] piece of writing, Hope was not deterred and acquired a bust of Isis from the same sculptress.[16] He also encouraged a number of other sculptors of similar ability to follow the principles of antique art. From John de Vaere (1755–1830), who had assisted Flaxman in the production of his group of the 'Fury of Athamas' for Lord Bristol, he acquired a copy of the Belvedere Mercury;[113] from Pisani copies of the Medici Apollino and Venus;[114] and from John Deare (1759–98) a copy of an antique Antinous. His appointment in 1805 to the publication committee of the Society of Dilettanti's *Select Specimens of Antient Sculpture* (1799–1807)[115] gave him further opportunities of influencing modern design by promoting knowledge of that of the ancients. In the same year he sat at Payne Knight's instigation on the government committee appointed to arrange the purchase by the British Museum of the first instalment of the Townley Collection. The other members of this committee were Sir Joseph Banks, Charles Greville, and Payne Knight.[116]

In the outline of Hope's life we noted his election to the artistic societies of the day as an indication of the growing respect with which he was regarded. We can now investigate these elections from the point of view of the influence which they enabled Hope to exert. The following is the amazing list of them: in 1794 the Society of Antiquaries;[117] in 1799 the Royal Institution;[118] in 1800 the Society of Dilettanti;[119] in 1804 the Royal Society [120]and the Royal Society of Arts;[121] in 1805 the British Institution[122] and select committees of the Society of Dilettanti; in 1806 the 'Committee of Taste';[123] in 1807 the Committee for the superintendence of Royal Academy Exhibition Models;[124] and finally in 1811, a slightly different appointment, the Subcommittee for the rebuilding of the Theatre Royal, Drury Lane.[125]

When in August 1801 Josiah Boydell attempted to form a body of subscribers who would become proprietors of his influential Shakespeare Gallery, founded in 1786, he received promises of financial support from Hope and Sir Francis Baring.[126] In 1805 Hope and the other subscribers to the British Institution bought the property from Boydell for £4,500 for use as their own Gallery.[122] Hope's wealth, of course, was always of the utmost assistance to him though in 1804 he told Westall that 'his fortune is not so large as supposed, but he was able to do a good deal in Art as he had not the expense of dogs and horses'.[127] Of especial importance was his invitation in 1806 to join the seven members of the newly founded government Committee for the Superintendence of Models of Public Monuments. Known as the 'Committee of Taste', this body exercised a wide control over the monuments to national heroes which had been erected in St. Paul's since 1795 as a result of the Napoleonic Wars. These monuments presented one of the greatest opportunities for bringing the 'national consciousness' within the sphere of the strictest neo-classical aesthetic. Despite the difficulties involved—not the least of which was how far modern uniforms should be represented in marble—Committee and artists combined to produce a series of monuments of a surprisingly high standard. At a meeting held on 14 June 1810 to discuss a monument to Sir John Moore,[128] Hope voted with Sir George Beaumont

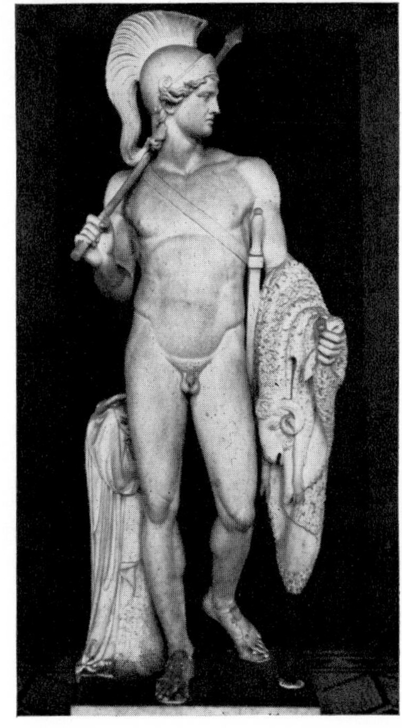

Bertel Thorvaldsen

7. 'Art and the Genius of Light', 1808

8. 'Bust of Thomas Hope', 1816–17 9. 'Jason', 1802–28

10. Sir William Beechey, 'Thomas Hope in Turkish Dress', 1798

11. George Dawe, 'The Hon. Mrs. Thomas Hope', 1812, from an engraving by Henry Dawe

12. 'Grecian Female'

13. Richard Westall, 'The Expiation of Orestes', 1804–5, from an engraving by William Bone

and Lord Carysfort in favour of Rossi as sculptor, against Sir Charles Long, the President, Payne Knight, and Henry Bankes, M.P., who voted for Bacon. The President's party won the day and the monument is generally reckoned to be one of Bacon's finest works.

As a parallel to his work for sculpture, Hope became in 1805 a founder-member and director of the British Institution. This body had as its specific aim the exhibition of paintings by young artists who were not yet ready for the Royal Academy exhibitions. The directors were expected to arouse support for the young painters by buying as many of their works as possible. Hope did not fail in this duty. A related interest of his was in the method of teaching the arts of design. As early as June 1805 he had made at a meeting of the Royal Academy what Farington described as '*too long* a prepared speech upon the necessity of Artists *drawing* . . . in which he spoke of their having models *at home* for that purpose'.[129] Two years later he published in Prince Hoare's *The Artist* a short article re-stating the problems of the instruction of design;[130] and in 1810 we hear of him busy with what he called 'the pending scheme for the redemption of the arts of engraving'.[131] Artists were to be invited to subscribe to this scheme and a committee was to be set up in the summer of 1810. But the time was hardly ripe for the setting up of government schools of design, towards which, in effect, most of these schemes tended. Haydon occupied himself much with this problem and in June 1837 sent copies of a Memorandum on the founding of a School of Design to Thomas Hope's son Henry and to Poulett Thompson.[132] At the same time the government Schools of Design were at last in the process of being set up as a result of the deliberations in 1836 of a Select Committee of the House of Commons.[133]

By his patronage of Edmund Aikin (1780–1820), George Dawe (1781–1829), and Henry Moses (*c.* 1782–1870), Hope could claim to have done much for 'the redemption of the arts of engraving'. It was Aikin and Dawe who prepared the finely detailed plates for *Household Furniture* from Hope's drawings. These engravings were among the first in the country to employ the outline technique developed by Flaxman and by Percier and Fontaine, but which, as Hope observed in 1807, 'had been woefully neglected in this country'.[134] It was Moses who brought the technique to what was, perhaps, its most sophisticated climax. In 1812 Hope commissioned from him a series of plates, introducing furniture and background settings from his Duchess Street mansion, to be published as *Designs of Modern Costume*. Two years later Moses recorded his gratitude to his patron by dedicating to him in the following words his book, *A Collection of Vases, Altars, Paterae, Tripods, candelabra, sarcophagi &c. from various museums and collections:* 'To THOMAS HOPE ESQ. whose knowledge, taste, and judgement command the esteem of all who profess and love the fine arts, this work is inscribed, in token of gratitude for various acts of kindness.' It was an enlarged version of his *Modern Costume* plates of 1812 which Moses published in 1823 as *A series of twenty-nine designs of Modern Costume drawn and engraved by Henry Moses, Esq.* (Figs. 31 and 32). The exquisite engravings for *Modern Costume* have had no greater admirer than Sacheverell Sitwell who has described them as 'superior, even, to the plates with which the works of... Percier and Fontaine are illustrated', observing that the collection 'epitomizes the age of the Regency', and finally making the extravagant claim that: 'It is probable, indeed, that these are the finest and neatest engravings that have ever made their appearance between the covers of a book.'[135]

We know the names of three of the craftsmen employed by Hope to execute the furniture for Duchess Street, some of which appeared in Moses' plates. These were Decaix,[136] a French bronzist, Bogaert, a Flemish carver still employed by Hope in 1810,[137] and the young Francis Chantrey (1781–1841).[138] Decaix and Bogaert had not been discovered without effort and Hope describes how he had personally searched 'throughout this vast metropolis teeming as it does with artists and craftsmen',[136] before he found even two of sufficient merit to execute his designs. The author of one of Hope's obituaries confirms Hope's statement of his efforts to obtain the right craftsmen, by describing how Hope had rescued both 'artists and artisans from obscurity' and recounting how he had 'heard Hope say that he had frequently traversed obscure alleys, lanes and courts to find out and employ men of skill and talent in their respective pursuits'.[139] And in his valuable study, *Patronage of British Art* (1845), John Pye refers to Hope's Essay on Design in Hoare's *The Artist* as 'an excellent paper... in which the neglect of British art is attributed to deficiency of education amongst the people', and observes that: 'At the beginning of the present century, the attention of the aristocracy was first awakened to the importance of encouraging native taste and talent in the arts, by Hope.'[140]

To appreciate to the full Hope's achievement in this field, the almost revolutionary reasons behind his patronage of obscure craftsmen must be outlined in more detail. His position was precisely that of William Morris in the 1850s. Having to furnish a house for the first time brought home to both of them how little sympathy they had for contemporary design and methods of production. The solution in each case was to have furnishings made to his own designs. Until his time, Hope observed, 'Furniture of every description, was wrought by the most mechanical processes only'; and his aim was therefore to combine the

> productions of ancient art and modern handicraft ... into a more harmonius, more consistent, and more instructive whole ... [so] that consequently almost every production of industry, rescued in some measure from the hands of the mere plodding artisan, would be enabled to give some scope to the talent of the possessor of the more liberal arts; the draughtsman, the modeller, the painter and the sculptor ... Thus ... [he] hoped to afford to that portion of the community ... [debased] by the entire substitution of machinery to manual labour ... a means of replacing the less dignified mode of subsistence ... by a nobler species of labour; one which absolutely demands the co-operation of those higher intellectual capacities which the former often allows to remain dormant ... and one in which ... the powers of mere machinery can never emulate, or supplant the mental facilities of man ... [Thus, they] might find a means first to discover the latent germs of their genius.[141]

This emphasis upon the craftsman and the necessity for drawing out his latent ability is surely something quite new, as is also the revolt against the machine. The period dominated by Messrs. Waring and Gillow and by Sheraton from, roughly, 1790 to 1810 is often regarded today as the apotheosis of English craftsmanship. Yet the introduction of machine production at this date, minimal though its effects must have been to the casual observer, was realized by Hope to be likely to have an entirely pernicious effect were it not checked or directed along different paths. Our point is confirmed by Alexander Beresford Hope in his perceptive account of his father's achievement in *The English*

Cathedral of the 19th Century (1861): 'The great fact for which Thomas Hope deserves the gratitude of posterity (a fact for which Sydney Smith was narrow enough to quiz him in the *Edinburgh*) was that he, first of Englishmen, conceived and taught the idea of art-manufacture, of allying the beauty of forms to the wants and productions of common life.'[142]

Hope's acquaintance with the engineer Matthew Boulton (1728–1809) also bears out his son's comments. Boulton, like Hope a Fellow of the Royal Society, was similarly concerned to improve the quality of everyday domestic articles. At his famous Soho Manufactory in Birmingham he insisted on a high standard of neo-classical design in the production of steel jewellery, Sheffield and silver plate, and ormolu ornaments. He had worked for a time in conjunction with Adam and much of his work found its way into the Royal collections. He interested himself especially in the problem of artistic training for craftsmen and in 1805 went so far as to send John Phillp (1780–1820)—a gifted protégé of his, apprenticed as a die-stamper and believed to be his natural son—to Hope's house in Duchess Street in order to make detailed drawings of the furniture and decoration. After this visit, Hope wrote to Boulton: 'I think myself highly honoured indeed, my dear Sir, by the great compliment you pay my taste, in thinking that the forms and ornaments I have adopted in the arrangement and finishing of my little collection of art can in any degree add to the merit of the interesting and useful productions that issue from your extensive and magnificent establishment.' Regretting that Boulton's ill-health had become so pronounced since their last meeting at Soho as altogether to prevent him from leaving Birmingham, Hope rose at the end of his letter to fine purple patch: 'You are in the predicament of a Sovereign who cannot quit his Capital: and no Capital ever diffused such beneficial influence over a whole country, as that of your creating does, in the midst of which you live.'[143]

Hope himself employed the finest craftsmen to execute his designs for household articles. As early as 1798 the great Regency goldsmith Paul Storr (1771–1844) had made for him a set of four silver-gilt baskets (Fig. 2). Also from Storr came in 1801 a silver tea-pot and circular vegetable dishes with long handles terminating in rams' heads (Fig. 3 and Plate 47), and in silver-gilt in the same year: a tea-set com-

Fig. 2. Thomas Hope, Silverware, *c.* 1800

Fig. 3. Thomas Hope, Silverware, *c.* 1800

prising tea-pot, two handled sugar-basin and cream-jug; a pair of *tazze* on lion bases; and the magnificent oviform tea-urn with a spout terminating in a panther's head and supported on an ebony stand (Fig. 2). In 1805 the firm of Rundell, Bridge, and Rundell made for him a set of four silver-gilt vases with covers.[144]

Hope's relationships with the architects William Atkinson (*c.* 1773–1839) and, over the designs for Downing College, with William Wilkins (1778–1839) will be discussed more appropriately in later chapters. In 1811 he came once more into official contact with Wilkins over the competition for the new Theatre Royal, Drury Lane. Hope had been appointed to sit on the Competition Committee of three, together with the two Whig M.P.s, Samuel Whitbread (1758–1815) of Southill and Peter Moore (1753–1828). His qualifications were the articles he had published between 1807 and 1809 on *The Structure of Our Theatres.* In these he had put forward, probably for the first time in this country, the remarkable proposal for semi-circular auditoria on antique lines. Ledoux's Theatre at Besançon (1778–84) was the first modern theatre to be designed on this principle, but it was rarely imitated save in Gilly's sketches of 1798 for a National Theatre at Berlin. England, in Hope's time, was only just adopting the horse-shoe-shaped auditorium introduced by Victor Louis (1735–1807) at the Theatre at Bordeaux in 1775–80. Hope's views naturally aroused interest, and in February 1809 Farington observed of Hope's sculptress-friend, the Honourable Mrs. Damer, that she 'looks to Thomas Hope as the man of superior taste and supports his opinion that the new Theatre at Covent Garden should be a *semi-circle* . . . that being the proper form'.[145] However, on 17 October 1811 Hope voted with Whitbread and Moore in favour of designs for Drury Lane by Benjamin Wyatt (*c.* 1775–1850) in which the auditorium was not semi-circular. In all other respects Wyatt's work was a model of chaste French elegance,[146] and for the domed Corinthian rotunda, which still survives, we have much to thank Hope and his companions. If we are to believe their report, their choice was not an easy one. Indeed they observed, perhaps at Hope's instigation, that:

> the Model and Designs exhibited by Mr. William Wilkins Junior bear full testimony to the depth of His Research amongst the great Specimens of Antiquity, and the success with which he has cultivated His natural

genius; and adapted the great examples which he has personally viewed to produce a design of great Erudition Simplicity, and Magnificence.[125]

In 1810 the architect James Elmes (1782–1862) held a meeting of architects at his house in the hope of establishing a Royal Academy of Architecture. He sent a lengthy statement of the scheme drawn up on that occasion to Thomas Hope. This was published in 1814 as *A Letter to Thomas Hope, Esq., Hereditary Governor and Director of the British Institution for promoting the Fine Arts in the United Kingdom, &c. &c. on the insufficiency of the existing establishments for promoting the Fine Arts towards that of Architecture and its Professors*; *attempting to show the cause of the decline in that branch of the Fine Arts, with some hints towards its better encouragement.* In it, he described Hope as 'one of the earliest and most liberal patrons of the British Institution . . . one of the best architectural critics of the present day, and . . . a munificent patron of the fine arts in general'. He went on, however, to contrast the recent progress of painting and sculpture, as a result of the efforts of men like Hope, with the decline in the quality of architectural design. He attributed this supposed decline to the want of patronage and of an 'academy of architecture'. It is clear, also, that he was disturbed at the architect's lack of a clearly defined professional status and function: 'You, Sir,' he wrote, 'are one of the few who can distinguish between an artist and an artisan and who would not suffer your carpenter or paper-hanger to usurp the province of your architect.'[147] As with the proposed establishment of the schools of design, the time had not quite come for architecture to take this step into the modern, professional, and public world. Elmes made a further attempt in 1819,[148] and a clear line of descent can be traced from his efforts in the second decade of the century to the establishment in 1834 of the Institute of British Architects.[149]

This chapter has shown the wide range of influence which Thomas Hope was able to exercise through his discerning patronage, and the high quality as well as the variety of the many works of art he acquired. Aged only sixty-one when he died, he had commissioned or bought works from Flaxman and Canova and as many as eleven from Thorvaldsen, a remarkable fact which, added to his having been the first to spot that sculptor's talent, more than justifies his place among the most perceptive of the neo-classical patrons and collectors of Europe.

RICHARD WESTALL

14. 'The Reconciliation of Helen and Paris, after his defeat by Menelaus', 1805

15. 'Damocles Discovering the Sword over his Head', 1811

16. Benjamin West, ‘Thetis bringing Armour to Achilles’, 1805

His Greek vases and sculpture formed one of the finest privately owned collections in the country. He had attempted to raise the standard of art-instruction by encouraging the idea of the school of design; the standard of furniture design and production by training obscure craftsmen; the standard of modern painting by liberally purchasing the works of young and unknown artists; and that of history-painting by commissioning or buying works from West, Haydon, and Westall and by publishing *Costume of the Ancients* (1809) which he described as 'A work, intended solely for the easy reference and the ready application of actual practitioners in art.' In this work, moreover, he complained, in a vision which looks forward to the decoration of the Victorian public building, that:

> corporate bodies never dream of encouraging the productions of historical works, by adorning with them their halls and meeting places ... while ministers, however lavish and profuse in other respects, continue so penurious with regard to what is most conducive to the pride and splendour of the country, as to withhold the comparatively trifling sums necessary to encourage, by adequate premiums, those performances that inspire future heroes, by nobly displaying the achievements of past worthies.[150]

And in writing this, he was but elaborating on the view which he had expressed in an article of 1807[151] that whereas sovereigns had formerly taken the initiative in matters of artistic patronage the time had now come for parliaments to replace them.

Similarly, in architecture he was looked to as a potential promoter of a scheme which resulted in what is now the Royal Institute of British Architects. He had set the youthful Wilkins on the road to success and in so doing helped bring about one of the earliest full-scale examples of the Greek Revival in English architecture. His own ideas on theatre-design were equally revolutionary. The architects J. M. Gandy and Edmund Aikin, the architectural historian John Britton, and the artist Henry Moses—who all played their part in the formation of the neo-classical outlook—all dedicated books to Thomas Hope.[152] His own architectural productions and the influence of his designs for furniture and for modern costume will be discussed in other chapters. From the point of view of position, influence, variety of patronage, and utter single-mindedness of purpose there can have been no one quite like him in this country before or since. Lord Burlington is perhaps the closest parallel, but his influence was confined mainly to the field of architecture. Moreover, Hope's achievement as 'the Apollo of Arts',[153] as Walpole had once dubbed Burlington, was given a heightened interest by coming at a moment of transition in all spheres from the private to the public. Had he lived for another ten years, which he might reasonably have expected to do, he would have seen this transition virtually effected—and that partly as a result of his own efforts. Perhaps we may be forgiven for hazarding the guess that he would not greatly have cared for this 'Servile State', this brave, new collectivist world.

III

Hope and the Greek Revival

1804 was Hope's *annus mirabilis*, as was pointed out in the first chapter. If the opening of his house to the public showed what he was capable of in practice, then the publication of his pamphlet on Downing College stated clearly his theoretical position. The story must therefore be told of how Hope came to be known as 'the Patron of Downing College'.[1]

James Wyatt had been described as architect to the college as early as 1784,[2] but it was not until the site was finally determined in 1800 that he was officially appointed architect.[3] He had prepared two designs which the Master, rather surprisingly, sent to Thomas Hope at the beginning of 1804. Hope almost immediately produced a pamphlet explaining at length how he alone in England was qualified to pronounce on architectural matters. Censuring heavily every aspect of the designs by Wyatt—then the most sought after architect in the country—he pointed out that Greek architecture, and especially Greek Doric, was the only style worthy of serious imitation and hinted coyly that Wilkins was really the man for the job. Wyatt was furious and had Hope immediately struck off the list of guests annually invited to the Royal Academy dinner. But Hope won on both counts. Soane, amongst others, championed his cause over the Dinner so that the Royal Academy sent Hope an official apology, and, of course, Wilkins, after many machinations, was eventually appointed architect to the college. As is well known, his designs (Plate 17) were, with Harrison's Chester Castle (1793–1820), the first large-scale semi-public buildings in this country that revived Greek architecture accurately. In fact, Wilkins lost his nerve over Greek Doric and only produced Greek Ionic which, to the layman, is indistinguishable from Roman Ionic.

Why, one asks, was Hope invited to air his views on this subject? Aged only thirty-four he had as yet published nothing, though he was at this moment engaged in issuing admission tickets to the Royal

Academicians for the viewing of his newly completed London home. He was also a member of the Society of Dilettanti, though not yet of the other societies to which he later became connected. We must therefore presume a personal contact between him and the Master of Downing, Francis Annesley, LL.D., F.A.S. (1734–1812). Annesley was an hereditary trustee of the British Museum and, like Hope, had early developed an enthusiasm for literature and art in which subjects he built up a considerable library.[4] He must have known what Hope's opinions would be and one presumes that these coincided with his own. He doubtless felt the need of an outside authority to lend weight to this own enthusiasm for the controversial Greek Doric.

Hope's pamphlet took the form of a letter addressed to Annesley dated 22 February 1804. Its immediate consequence was that George Byfield (*c.* 1756–1813) was invited to send in an alternative design to Wyatt's.[3] In 1805 Wilkins, Lewis Wyatt (James' nephew), and Francis Sandys voluntarily submitted designs. By 1806 the plans of Byfield and Sandys had been rejected and those by Lewis Wyatt and Wilkins submitted by the Court of Chancery to the superior judgement of George Dance, Samuel Pepys Cockerell, and James Lewis.[5] It is not surprising that Dance and Cockerell, as two of the most individual and advanced architects of the day, should have selected Wilkins' Greek designs.

It is clear from Hope's pamphlet that he had been in contact with Wilkins since the latter's return in 1804 from a three-year tour, as a Travelling Bachelor of Gonville and Caius College, of Greece, Asia Minor, and Italy. 'Mr. Wilkins has lately brought home.' Hope observed, 'and soon intends to publish, designs of a Greek temple, in the cella of which Doric columns rise on distinct bases.'[6] Wilkins' designs, as we shall see, follow closely the recommendations made in Hope's pamphlet. Still in his twenties, this was his first major commission and he may well have been glad of Hope's encouragement and assistance.

To begin at the most general level, Hope had observed: 'I could wish that instead of the degraded architecture of the Romans, the purest style of the Greeks had been exclusively adhibited.' Though referring to 'that admiration which ... none of the good living architects of the continent any longer withhold from the most chaste of orders', i.e. the Greek Doric, he said that he would be satisfied were he 'at least able to obtain that the Ionic, of a later, but still of a Grecian origin, might be preferred to a bastard order'. And it was precisely this, of course, that he was able to obtain. He also recommended that the chapel, which occupied the centre of the south range in Wyatt's as in Wilkins' designs, 'should exhibit less shallowness of projection, and less scantiness of columns', arguing that 'A portico of the height and width of this, should have presented a front of six, instead of one of four columns only.' The niches on each side should be dispensed with, since the 'merit and grace [of columns] can never be well appreciated, unless set off by the even, smooth, unadorned surface of a plain background'. In a spirit of austere functionalism, derived ultimately from Laugier, he observed: 'All pilasters I would proscribe without remission', except when used as antae. He went on to affirm that: 'I would raise the whole façade on a more elevated plinth . . . A few steps all round, would, with as much propriety as elegance, separate the inside colonnade, particularly if formed of baseless columns, from the area of the cortile.'

Wilkins adopted all of these recommendations. Thus his main porticos have six columns not four, they are raised on prominent podia or steps, pilasters and niches are never used decoratively, and columns contrast strikingly with large areas of unadorned stonework. Moreover, in looking at Wilkins' unexecuted designs for the entrance-gateway, based closely on the Greek Doric Propylaea at Athens, one recalls Hope's admiration of 'a superb town gate I saw at Berlin, imitated from the Propylaea'. In fact, Langhans' Brandenburg Gate at Berlin (1789–93) imitated the Propylaea only in general disposition, its details were basically Roman Doric.

Wilkins further followed Hope in concerning himself principally not with the internal planning and lay-out of the college, but rather with the details of its elevations. Hope had observed that 'The destination of a college admits of no great fancy in the internal distribution',[7] and turned almost at once to his discussion of the elevations. Wilkins, too, seemed prepared to accept the basic disposition of entrance-gate, hall, chapel, Master's and Professors' Lodges originally formulated by James Wyatt; although the greater detachment of block from block must be his and Hope's idea.[8] Hope's protégé was not a man of large vision. He simply happened to appear in the right place at the right time with the right knowledge of Greek architecture. Cambridge was undoubtedly the right place, and the Hope/Wilkins collaboration must now be placed in a larger setting.

Academic investigation of Greece reached a high point in a group of travelling scholars which I call the Cambridge Hellenists, and which included such men as Charles Kelsall (1782–1857), the Reverend E. D. Clarke (1769–1822), J. M. Cripps (1780–1853), the Reverend J. C. Eustace (1762?–1815), John Tweddell (1769–99), and William Wilkins (1788–1839). Of these, Wilkins was the only one trained as an architect and it was he, of course, who was responsible for introducing on a large scale revived Greek architecture. His Osberton House, Nottinghamshire (*c.* 1806; Plate 18), is the first house in England, and probably therefore in Europe, to display a temple-portico of accurate and fluted Greek Doric columns. The base for whose who wished to penetrate Greece at this time was Constantinople, where John Spencer Smythe was an admirable host at the British Embassy to his fellow-countrymen. Smythe, indeed, formed an institution known as the Ottoman Club 'in conjunction with the late Professor Sibthorp, Messrs. Hawkins, Liston, Dallaway, Wilbraham, Morrit, Stockdale, Tweddell, Cripps, Dr. E. D. Clarke, and other English gentlemen who visited Constantinople between the years 1782 and 1801'.[9] These were the years when Thomas Hope was to be found in this part of the world, and this just the society of which he would have wished to be seen as part. Indeed, we learn in a biography of John Tweddell, Fellow of Trinity College, Cambridge, that:

> Mr. Smythe's gentlemanly assiduities were not confined to Mr. Tweddell, but extended to every English traveller who had pretensions, either from learning or superior merit, to his especial favour. Mr. Hawkins, Messrs. Hope, Mr. Morritt, Dr. Clarke, Mr. Cripps, and every other of our distinguished countrymen who visited Constantinople during the period of his ministry there, experienced in like manner his uniform kindness and zealous assistance in their learned pursuits.[10]

One of the consequences of Constantinople being the gateway to Greece and of that country's being itself under Turkish sway, was that the Picturesque exoticism of Turkish life and customs impressed itself on the travelling English scholar as much as the actual Greek monuments which had ostensibly drawn him to that part of the world. As was pointed out in the first chapter, Hope took with him on his travels in 1792 the painter George Wallis and in 1799 the French artist Préault. But it must not be thought that only Grecian antiquities were recorded. The five volumes which have been preserved of the drawings made by Hope on his travels between 1787 and 1795 contain five hundred and twenty-five drawings (some in hands other than Hope's) of which the vast bulk depict life, landscape, and costume in Turkey, Asia Minor, Syria, Egypt, and Greece (Plate 19).[11] Scattered throughout the volumes are drawings of Byzantine churches, Islamic mosques, Turkish palaces, Egyptian temples, as well as views of Mycenaean and Greek sites. Thus the whole forms a composite picture of civilizations succeeding each other with none given undue emphasis or prominence. I believe it is to this that Hope refers in his Downing pamphlet when, despite having argued so emphatically for the adoption of Greek Doric, he observes of himself that:

> In bestowing (which few architects . . . can be supposed to have done) equal attention on the principle of most different and most opposite styles of architecture, I think I have learnt to entertain for none an exclusive predeliction, founded on ignorance and prejudice. Each species that has a distinct character of its own, also may display beauties of its own, provided that character be preserved . . .[12]

This last sentence Sir John Soane especially under-lined in his own annotated copy of the pamphlet. And it was precisely this Picturesque synthesis of accumulated civilizations built up around the memory of Greece and Rome which fired Hope's imagination and which, as we shall see in the next chapter, he was to put into practice so brilliantly at Duchess Street. The life and culture of the Turkish Empire was in every sense the gateway to the antique past. Thus the title-page of Hope's *Household Furniture* was framed by an elaborate border of Turkish or Islamic ornamentation. Moreover, on his return from his travels he commissioned Sir William Beechey in 1798 to paint a portrait of him in Turkish dress. If the Turkish border formed the 'entrance' to *Household Furniture*, then the Beechey portrait performed a similar function at the Duchess Street house itself, since it was hung in the staircase-hall to greet visitors on their arrival. Only when Thomas Hope's approach to his travels is seen in this light does his romantic novel *Anastasius*, written in the 1790s whilst on his travels, make complete sense as regards our picture of him as a whole. His tours were the culmination of the Grand Tours of the eighteenth century, covering a wider field and enabling more information to be accumulated than any previous tours: and the culmination of his own tours was the Duchess Street mansion.

That our comments on Hope's approach to the culture of Turkey and the Near East are not fanciful is partly justified by the existence, as has been mentioned above, of a similar approach on the part of the Cambridge Hellenists. John Tweddell, Fellow of Trinity and Hope's exact contemporary, had travelled before 1798 in Switzerland, Sweden, Germany, Poland, and Russia. The notes and drawings which he had accumulated during his travels he left in charge of Thomas Hope's friend and fellow-traveller in Greece, Procopio Macri, the Levant Company's consular agent at Athens.[13] After Tweddell's sudden death in Athens in July 1799 Lord Elgin took possession of his effects, thereby causing a chain of bitter quarrels and misunderstandings.[14] But the point of interest at the moment is that it is clear from what we know of his drawings that Tweddell's outlook must have coincided with Hope's. We know that:

> Mr. John Tweddell died possessed of extensive literary and other effects: among which were journals of Switzerland and the Crimea, in a state of finished preparation for the press; sundry MSS. having reference to antient and modern Greece; an ample collection of highly finished drawings, illustrative of Grecian antiquities, of the costumes of Russia and the Turkish empire, as well as various objects of curiosity in some of the most interesting parts of Europe.[15]

Tweddell had commissioned Préault, later employed by Hope, to record on a large scale the surviving antiquities of Greece. Referring to Préault's drawings, he observed:

> My principal collection will be uniform, of drawings about 30 inches long. I shall have *ten* large ones, of the main temples and other most interesting objects of Greece, which will be about four feet and a half, or near five feet: one of these larger ones is already finished, and a great part of the smaller size. Those of the larger dimension *are richly worth thirty guineas a piece.*

In a letter to his father written from the Island of Tenos on 18 December 1798, Tweddell reveals the full zest and enthusiasm which alone must have made endurable the remote and inconvenient travels of men like Hope:

> *My collection of Levantine Dresses* (I mean drawings of them) *is already considerable, amounting to nearly two hundred*—and will soon be greatly augmented—so that I hope one day to show the richest portfolio perhaps that was ever carried out of Greece, Asia, and Turkey. But Athens, especially, is my great object. I promise you that those who come after me shall have nothing to glean. Not only every temple, and every archway, but every stone, and every inscription, shall be copied with the most scrupulous fidelity.[16]

But death cut short Tweddell's youthful vigour. Longer lived was Sir William Gell (1777–1836), Fellow of Emmanuel College, who published in 1804 the *Geography and Antiquities of Ithaca.* It was while he was in Athens, collecting material for his next book, *Itinerary of Greece* (1810), that he met the young Sir Charles Monck, Bart.[17] Six months after the publication of Hope's Downing pamphlet, Monck set out on his honeymoon from his family seat, Belsay Castle, Northumberland. His destination was Athens and his purpose was to gather information to enable him to design a new Greek house for himself. His honeymoon was thus to be not only with his wife but with Greek architecture. The result was a son born in Athens in 1805 and called, very properly, Charles Atticus, and also the new Belsay, one of the finest Greek houses in England (Plates 20 and 21). Also in Athens was Edward Dodwell (1767–1832), of Trinity College, who had travelled in Greece in 1801 and 1805, and, with Gell as companion, in 1806.[18] He published his *Classical Tour* in 1819; made over four hundred drawings in Greece; formed a considerable collection of Greek vases, now in the Munich Glypothek; and from 1806 onwards made his permanent home in Naples and Rome, as did Gell for the last sixteen years of his life. The Reverend Edward Daniel Clarke, (1769–1822), Fellow of Jesus College, travelled as widely as Thomas Hope and Charles Kelsall: Northern Europe in 1799; Russia in 1800; Sicily, Troy, Rhodes, Cyprus, the Holy Land, and Athens in 1801; and Constantinople in 1802. From Greece he brought back to Cambridge a large statue believed to be of Ceres—in fact a caryatid from the Inner Propylaea at Eleusis—which is now in the Fitzwilliam Museum.[19] In a letter from Constantinople he speaks of possessing 'seventy-six cases of antiquities'.[18] In 1809 he published at Cambridge *Greek Marbles*, with three drawings by Flaxman of his 'Ceres' and a view of Eleusis by Sir William Gell; and between 1810 and 1823 he published six volumes entitled *Travels in . . . Europe, Asia and Africa.* Clarke knew Charles Kelsall and the latter acknowledged his assistance in the conception of a combined 'Senate-House, Public Library and Museum' proposed in his *Phantasm of an University* (1814). On Clarke's death, his memorial plaque in Jesus College Chapel was designed by Flaxman. The Reverend John Chetwode Eustace was a Roman Catholic priest who took up residence at Jesus College in 1805 to act as tutor and chaplain to Lord Petre, and whose advanced views made him extremely unpopular with the Vicar-General of the Midland District.[20] In 1807 Eustace subscribed to the publication of Wilkins' *Magna Graecia*; in 1813 he published a *Tour Through Italy* (the 3rd edition in 1815 was expanded to four volumes); and in 1814, *A Letter from Paris.* Before 1812 he had visited Dalmatia, Greece and the islands, Sicily, and Malta in company with Lord Brownlow and Robert Rushbrooke. Kelsall knew Brownlow's brother, the Reverend the Honourable Henry Cust (1780–1861), and dedicated to him the plate of the University Church in *Phantasm of an University.*

William Wilkins (1778–1839), who had been elected to a Travelling Bachelorship at Gonville and Caius College in 1801, spent the years 1801 to 1804 in Greece, Asia Minor, and Italy. He was elected a Fellow of his college in his absence and contacted Thomas Hope immediately after his return. In his *Antiquities of Magna Graecia* (1807) Wilkins acknowledged the assistance of Sir William Gell; and subscribers to the book included Thomas Hope, Gell, the Reverend John Chetwode Eustace, and Edmund Aikin. In the following year Aikin was to dedicate to Hope his own *Designs for Villas.* In a copy of *Magna Graecia*, recently presented to the library of Downing College, are pasted two designs for Greek revival buildings in the hand of Sir William Gell. The book presumably belonged to one of the circle of early nineteenth-century Cambridge Hellenists, though probably not to Gell himself since the drawings are labelled respectively in a contemporary hand, 'Sir William Gell's drawing' and 'Sir William Gell drew this forum'. The first design is for a simple building, thirteen bays by two with the central five bays pedimented and divided by six Ionic columns. In its length and austerity it is reminiscent of Wilkins' Downing designs and, as at Downing, the ground floor windows are brought down almost to ground level. The second design, for a 'forum', shows an open colonnade of eight Greek Doric columns flanked by taller two-bay wings each with three attached Ionic columns. The colonnade was to be 75 ft. 5 in. long. One can almost see Wilkins' eventual Downing designs as the fruit of a kind of collective effort by the 'advanced' dons of Cambridge with Hope's connivance. Although the main emphasis of Gell's books is topographical, he was also concerned with the application of ancient art to modern design. Amongst the plans and drawings for Belsay is one entitled 'Sir William Gell's design for the hall at Belsay'.[17] In 1828 Gell painted his own sitting-room at Rome 'in all the bright staring colours I could get, a sort of thing between Etruscan and Pompeii'.[18] Gell's strong plain colours and antique decoration recalling, perhaps, Hope's interiors at Duchess Street, were not in evidence at Belsay. Returned from Greece in 1806 with a mass of detailed drawings of Greek architecture, Sir Charles Monck began to build himself, with Gell's and possibly John Dobson's help, a grim Greek mansion void of all ornament and designed around a central columned hall or peristyle. It is a mature house and remarkable for not having a portico.[21] For most people a great portico is all that is needed swiftly to evoke an impression of Greek architecture, and architects soon found that to provide one was an easy way of achieving that end. But Monck was a man of austere integrity concerned to recapture the spirit of Greek architecture, not merely to imitate the letter. The bare chill of Belsay said concisely what admirers of Greek Art had been thinking about it since Winckelmann first pointed out its 'noble simplicity'.

Gell, as has been pointed out, helped both Monck and Wilkins. Wilkins, therefore, doubtless knew Monck's Belsay as Monck may have known Wilkins' Osberton. The closest contemporary parallel to both these houses is Wilkins' Grange Park, Hampshire (1809; Plate 22). If Osberton was just a 'portico house', the Grange was the portico house to end all such. Wilkins' patron at the Grange was the banker, Henry Drummond, who had bought the estate in 1786. It was after he returned from his travels abroad, perhaps to Greece, that Drummond began to modernize this house. There can be little doubt that he was influenced by the example of his near neighbour and fellow banker, Sir Francis Baring, who in 1803–6 had employed Dance to remodel Stratton Park, Hampshire (Plate 23). If Stratton had an unfluted tetrastyle portico, the Grange had a gigantic, fluted, hexastyle portico modelled on the Theseion itself with, on the other two sides, square columned porticos combining elements from the Choragic Monument of Thrasyllus and the Theseion.

The point to be made about Stratton, Osberton, Belsay, and the Grange is that, like the Palladian house, they are still uncompromising classic cubes. Their windows have not been turned to catch prospects nor their plans modelled to follow the irregularities of the land in accordance with the Picturesque theories of Price and Knight.[22] Rather, they are houses borne along by the earnest wind of strict neo-classicism blowing all the way from the Cambridge of Wilkins, Gell, and Kelsall.

For the moment we shall return to Cambridge in 1800: the year before Wilkins was to leave it for his all-important tour of Greece, and the year in which Charles Kelsall came up to Trinity College as a Fellow Commoner. In our discussion of Cambridge Hellenism and the part played in it by Thomas Hope, Charles Kelsall must inevitably play a lage part. In the austerity and consistency of his neo-classical outlook, he corresponds closely to the popular modern picture of Hope. Yet his interests and publications were more varied (see Appendix A), his classicism more cerebral and relentless, his social theories infinitely more *avant-garde*, than Hope's—about whose life there was more than a touch of the *ancien régime*. Born in 1782, Kelsall was the son of a prosperous member of the Council of the East India Company whose cousin had married, in Madras, Clive of India himself.[23] Charles was educated at Eton, was at Trinity from 1800–3 and then spent three years in a Wiltshire Militia regiment. He soon abandoned the army for a life of scholarship and travel. Even as an undergraduate he had visited Sicily, and the year 1807 found him in Russia with Viscount Royston. In 1808–9 he was in Sicily again, and wrote his first published book, a translation of Cicero's *Last Two*

Pleadings against Caius Verres. The most interesting aspect of this book to us at the moment is that he could not resist appending to it a *Post Script containing remarks on the State of Modern Sicily*. In this he proposes for the island a thorough process of liberal and democratic reform, which he conceived as an integral part of modern neo-classicism. In 1809 he was also in Spain with the 4th Earl of Guildford.

The year 1812 saw the publication of his first two books: the Cicero translation and a *Letter from Athens addressed to a friend in England*. If in 1819 Hope's publication of *Anastasius* was to cause Byron to weep that he had not written it himself, so Kelsall's *Letter from Athens*, published in 1812, written in Augustan rhyming couplets and calling on England to 'Pour forth thy dauntless legions, and release, The fetter'd Hellespont—ah! rescue Greece!—',[24] anticipated Byron's *Childe Harold*, published in the same year. For Kelsall everything must be liberalized, democratized, modernized—be it Sicily, the Roman Catholic Church (as we shall see later), or Greece. Ancient Greek architecture is seen as an essential part of this primitive, purifying process. So obsessed was he with the purity of Greek Doric (an extra-illustrated French edition of Winckelmann was in his library), that he even regretted the intrusion, on the Parthenon and elsewhere, of the sculptured frieze, which 'by no means harmonizes well with the simple majesty of the Grecian Doric'.[25] In a lengthy footnote to the *Letter from Athens* he praises Doric for its permanence and longevity, and is delighted to record 'the rapid progress of the present age to the attainment of true taste in architecture'.[26] As evidence of this he points to the work of Wilkins at Downing, Haileybury, and the Literary and Scientific Institute at Bath, and to Smirke's Covent Garden Theatre. To these examples he added in 1814[27] Harrison's Chester Gaol and Foulston's Assembly Rooms and Theatre at Plymouth. It is interesting to find Kelsall picking out in this self-conscious way just those buildings which the modern art historian has also isolated from the medley of late neo-classical taste. The historian must often feel his task to be remote and artificial and something inconceivable at the date about which he is writing. Kelsall, moreover, was also peculiarly aware of the international character of late neo-classicism—in which it differed from almost every other phase of Renaissance architecture. Thus he mentions in the same breath as Wilkins and Smirke, Quarenghi's Horse Guards Riding Stables (1800–4) and de Thomon's Theatre and Exchange, all at St. Petersburg, and de Thomon's Theatre at Odessa. He also praises 'some buildings' at Berlin, the Exchange at Trieste and, above all, Paris where 'grecian architecture triumphs ... a better school for young architects, than either Rome or Venice'.[26]

What was probably Kelsall's greatest achievement was published in 1814 under the title *Phantasm of an University*.

> You, Oxonia, and you, Cantabrigia, are the two national establishments of science and art. On you the eyes of a great part of the nation are invariably fixed. Take at last measures to keep pace with the improvements made in the present age, in all the departments of science and art. I deny that universal science is centred in mathematics, in the classics, in the composition of Greek and Latin odes, in theology, in occasional declamations. I want great statesmen, orators, ambassadours, lawyers, physicians, surgeons, painters, sculptors, architects, agriculturalists.[28]

Thus Britannia addresses her universities in the *Phantasm*, and Kelsall takes up her theme proposing the drastic reform, both academically and architecturally, of Oxford and Cambridge. The sweeping changes outlined are astonishingly advanced for so early a date, the demand for reform becoming pronounced only in the 1830s. Kelsall's views, however, are much more the outcome of the earnest intellectual neo-classicism of *c.* 1800 than of the preoccupation with political reform of twenty or thirty years later. His ideal university was to be composed of six colleges devoted respectively to the study of Civil Polity and Languages; Fine Arts; Agriculture and Manufactures; Natural Philosophy; Moral Philosophy; and Mathematics. Like Kelsall, Thomas Jefferson was obsessed by the notion of reconciling liberty and equality and imagined that a system of universal education would be of assistance in this process. Kelsall's scheme affords the closest parallel to Jefferson's design of *c.* 1817 for the University of Virginia.[29] It also anticipated the foundation of London University; and only in modern times has his own University of Cambridge fully adopted his recommendations concerning the variety of subjects to be taught. An extended period of world-travel would follow the university course. This enormous cultural Phantasm, this 'Nurse of Universal

Fig. 4. Charles Kelsall, Detail of Design for College of Fine Arts, 1814

Science',[30] as Kelsall calls it, is in many respects directly inspired by the abstract wishful-thinking of French Grand Prix projects from the 1780s onwards for public libraries, academies, and museums in an austere megalomaniac style. Each college was to consist of a large rectangle of detached buildings forming a courtyard larger than Lincoln's Inn Fields. In the centre of four of these courts was a much smaller court following more closely the traditional college plan, though with a campanile in the centre. The six colleges were to be grouped so as to form a rectangle leaving a large open space in the centre to contain the university church and a tripartite building that was a combination of senate-house, public library, and museum. The plan and elevations may owe something to the chaste Greek repetition of Wilkins' detached blocks at Downing College, but more to the vast geometrical patterns of French projects. J.-P. Gisor's Plan for a Museum of 1779[31] is a particularly close parallel. French in taste are the end bays of the curious College of Fine Arts with their enormous caryatids, inset panels of sculptural relief, and so on (Fig. 4). Indeed the Observatory (Fig. 5), to stand in the middle of the Botanical Gardens, is directly based on a 'House for a Cosmopolitan' designed by A. T. L. Vaudoyer in Rome for Debrac in 1785. It was reproduced in C. P. Landon's *Annales du Musée* in 1805, where Kelsall doubtless saw both it and Debracq's remark, characteristic of the contemporary shift of emphasis from the local to the universal, that he wanted 'regarder la terre entière comme son domaine, et, enfin, qu'il était COSMOPOLITE'.[32]

An extraordinary feature of the College of Mathematics (Plate 24) was superimposed tiers of attached columns, the lower seemingly Greek Doric but with neither bases nor capitals, the upper ordinary baseless Greek Doric. Kelsall, however, describes the lower as 'a specimen from the Egyptian Thebes', so that the point of the juxtaposition lies in its 'forming as it were a link between the architecture of Egypt and of Greece, and exhibiting at one view, the root and the flower of the Doric order'.[33] Here are the beginnings of that spirit which culminated in the emphasis of 'Great Exhibition art' upon the narrative and the instructive. At the same time the close combination of Egyptian and Greek models is a feature of both Duchess Street and Deepdene. The archaeological interest of the day coupled with the neo-classical search for a style that was pure and primitive, un-

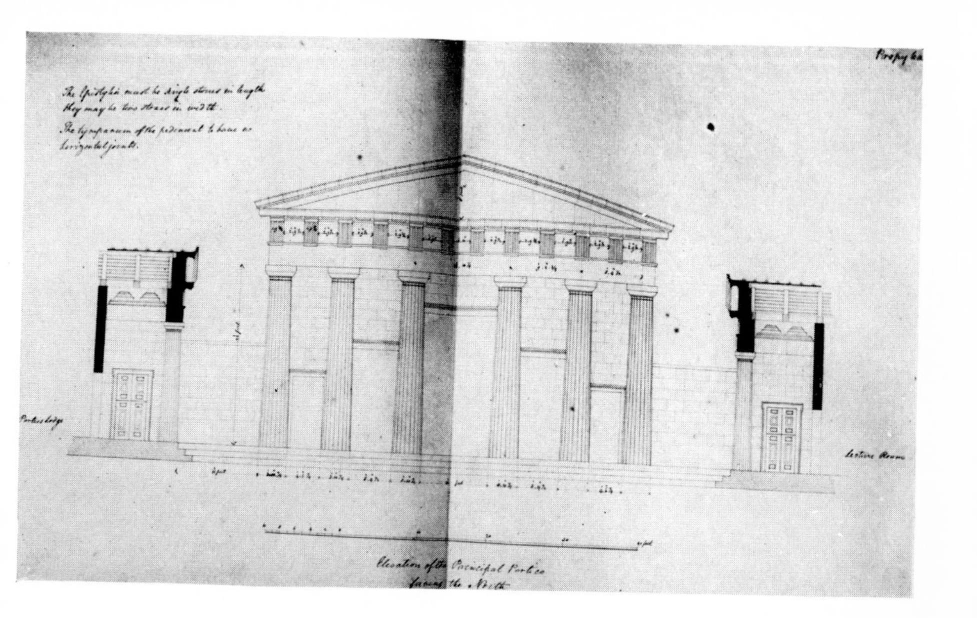

WILLIAM WILKINS
17. Design for Propylæa at Downing College, *c.* 1804
18. Osberton House, *c.* 1806

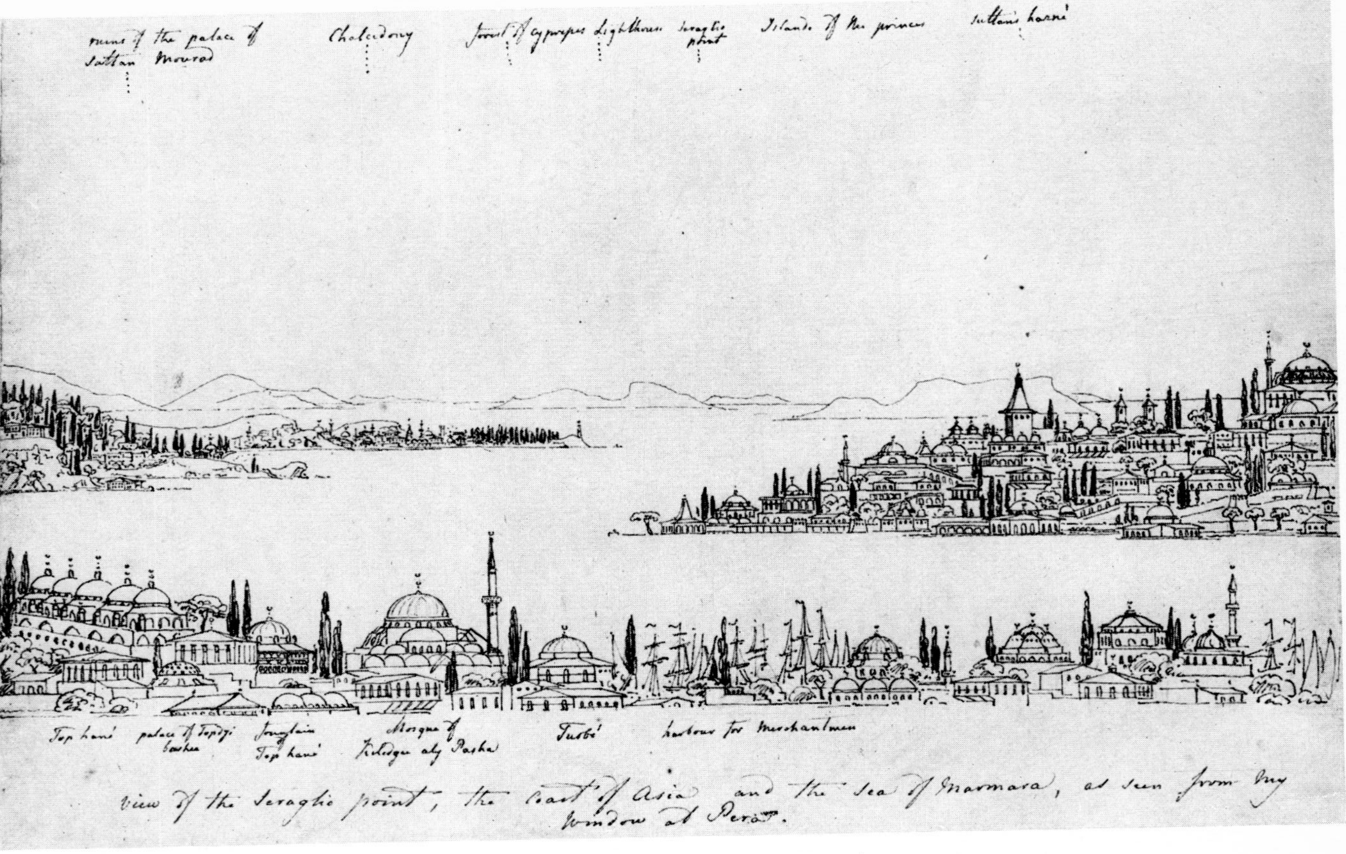

19. THOMAS HOPE, View of Constantinople, *c.* 1798

corrupted by the taint of civilized decadence, encouraged the revival of Egyptian design. If Roman architecture was, as Hope observed, 'only that of the Greeks when on the decline, divested of its primitive consistency and breadth and chastity',[34] was it not possible that Egyptian architecture contained an elemental dignity more powerful, even, than that of the Greeks?

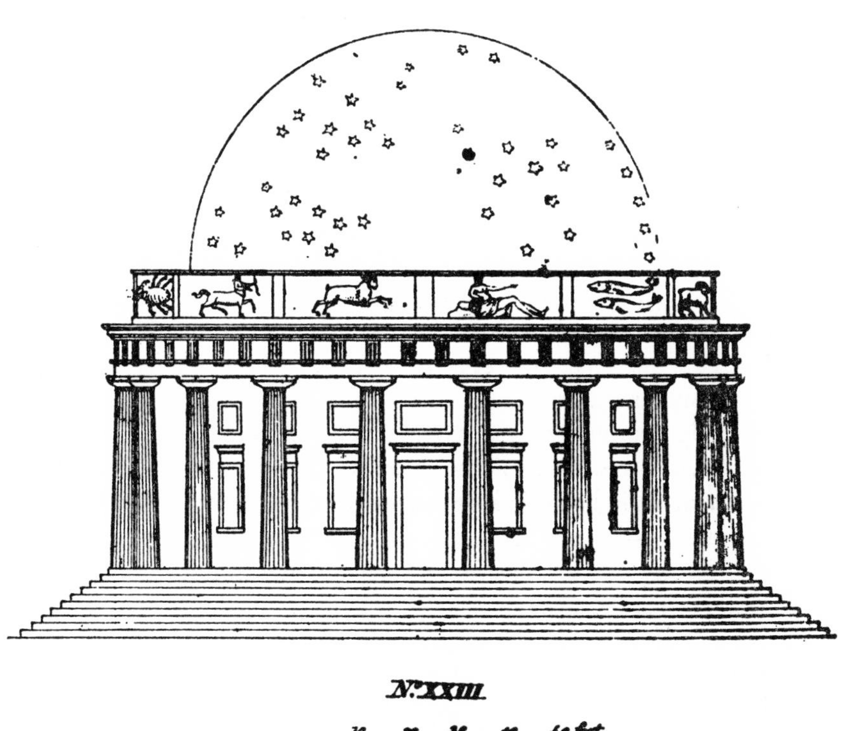

Fig. 5. Charles Kelsall, Design for an Observatory, 1814

Few Englishmen at that date can have acquired the first-hand knowledge that Kelsall was able to in 1807 of the major monuments of Russian neo-classicism erected under Catherine II and Alexander I. In describing his university buildings, he observes that his first intention was to have great ranges of one-storeyed buildings with Greek Doric colonnades, but that he afterwards considered that many of these would present 'a barrack-like appearance'. The bleakness, however, was not to be lightened by any arches or too many pediments, for it was pediments, he believed, which 'deface the Winter Palace at St. Petersburg'[35] (1754–62), designed by the Rococo architect Count Bartolommeo Rastrelli. More to his taste was the remarkable Tauride Palace (1783–88) at St. Petersburg. This was the work of Starov (1743–1808), who had studied at Paris under de Wailly in the 1760s and had brought to Russia what was newest in France, just as Cameron was to bring the English style. What also engaged Kelsall's attention were the Theatre and Exchange at St. Petersburg by Thomas de Thomon (1754–1813). The former was derived from de Wailly's Odéon in Paris, and the columns of the latter, 'though unfluted, were based upon those of the Temple of Poseidon at Paestum, and are one of the earliest examples, on such a scale, of the revival of this early, almost archaic Doric order'.[36] Kelsall also praises the work of 'my friend the Chevalier de Guarenghi, Architect to the Emperor'.[37] Giacomo Quarenghi (1744–1817) came to Russia in 1780 from Italy and was the introducer of yet another style, an austere Palladianism.

If the four large courts at the corners of Kelsall's university campus were partly inspired by the vast grandeur of Russian and French neo-classicism, the smaller traditionally planned courts which these enclosed were entirely English in conception. In fact they were in the Norman style—'Saxon' to Kelsall (Plate 25). Inaccurate though his nomenclature may have been, the architectural details are far from hazy and romantic. They represent the fruits of what was amongst the first scholarly surveys of English Norman architecture. It is hard to point to any neo-Norman designs of such extent and completeness earlier than these. Adam's Culzean (1777–90), Nash's Killy Moon (1803), Smirke's Eastnor (begun 1812), and the work at Belvoir after 1816, all adhere, in varying degrees, to a Picturesque, round-arched, castellated tradition. The first signs of a more academic approach are Lugar's Tulliechewan Castle, Dumbartonshire (1808),[38] and Henry Hakewill's Old Wolverton church, Buckinghamshire (1810–15), with Hopper's Gosford Castle, County Armagh (1819), and Penrhyn Castle, Caernarvonshire (1827–47), as the mature climax. On the whole, neo-Norman architecture was not common before the 1840s.

Kelsall observes that these designs are 'composed of what I consider the best parts of the few genuine Saxon specimens remaining in

England' and will, he hopes, 'prove that this style of architecture, though destitute of the symmetry which characterizes the Grecian and pure Roman buildings, becomes nevertheless agreeable if rightly understood and applied'.[39]

The vast majority of the University buildings, in the classical style, presented 'almost all the specimens of orders to be seen in the ruins of Greece and Italy'.[40] Thus, what is to be emphasized is that the very buildings become themselves edifying and instructive, become a complete museum of styles. The great classical courts are like display-cases each enclosing a precious gem in the rarer styles of Norman and Gothic. Kelsall's boast that almost all the surviving orders of Greek and Roman architecture were employed in his designs seems to be hardly an exaggeration. The scholarship is monumental and as a work of synthesis the designs are an exact parallel to Hope's decorative synthesis in *Household Furniture*. Kelsall, indeed, like Hope, employed a number of artists to execute engravings for publication of his own designs. And of his three artists the most famous, Henry Moses (1782–1870), had been employed by Hope just two years before in the preparation of the plates for his *Designs of Modern Costume* (1812).

It is a characteristic and significant fact that almost the only periodical in which the *Phantasm* was reviewed was French, the *Magasin Encyclopédique*, edited by Hope's archaeologist friend, A. L. Millin. The reviewer was unenthusiastic about the architectural plans but saw that the scheme's chief importance lay in its social and philosophical implications: 'mais ce sont les idées morales et politiques d'un système d'instruction, qui embrasse toutes les branches des connoissances et la destination de l'homme en société, qu'il faudroit apprécier car se sont elles qui font le mérite d'un aussi important ouvrage.'[41]

With the publication of the *Phantasm* achieved, Kelsall was off on his travels once more. In 1814 he was in France, in 1816 in Italy and Austria, in 1817 in Zurich and Brussels. In Brussels he wrote and published there in 1818, *Constance and Eugenie, or an Evening on Mount Vernon the seat of General Washington. A Political dialogue discussing the Constitution of the United States.* In the following year he further championed the cause of what he believed to be political liberty by a translation of *The Funeral Oration of the Doge Loredano at Venice*, to which he appended *Some Remarks on the Venetian scheme of Civil Polity*.

In 1819 he walked from Rome to Arpino to visit the remains of Cicero's villa, where he was horrified to find no memorial to him. Thus his book *Classical Excursion from Rome to Arpino*, published in 1820, suggests how a remedy might be provided. Like many of his works, the book is made the occasion of a number of philosophical and social digressions. In these his ambiguous relationship with the Roman Catholic Church first emerges, to be more fully exploited in his *Horae Viaticae* (1836). Here, as in all subjects, it is a primitive purity for which he searches. Architecturally, he finds the Pantheon superior to St. Peter's and, philosophically, the Mahommedanism he saw in Constantinople superior to Catholicism. Nevertheless, he outlined a scheme for 'purifying' St. Peter's, in which the Bernini colonnade was to be retained but St. Peter's itself to be remodelled with rows of giant Greek Doric columns.

There could be no more telling example of the advanced neo-classical reaction against anything that savoured of mere elegant artificiality than Kelsall's observation, in the course of his classical meanderings, that he would 'prefer to see the temple of the Erectheus, surrounded as it is by monuments of Turkish barbarism, than in the sprucest lawn, laid out by the Reptons and the Browns'.[42] That remark, eminently characteristic of the second phase of the Picturesque, was made in 1819. In the same year Thomas Hope was still remodelling the Deepdene. In April Maria Edgeworth visited the house and wrote of it in her diary that it was 'like some of the views in Athenian Stuart of Turkish buildings, grotesque and confused among trees in no one particular taste'.[43] The significance of Hope's Turkish enthusiasms has already been outlined.

His elaborate Cicero monument in the Amalthaea at Arpino, which he describes in detail at the end of the book, was intended to provide 'something full as satisfactory as cross-keys and tiaras':[44] that is, he believed that intellectual culture had to be elevated to a degree of importance that would enable it to compete with, if not to take over from, the Church. The monument was to take the form of a rotunda, based on the Pantheon, with a statue of Cicero centrally placed under the *œil-de-bœuf* in the roof. The rotunda was to be surrounded by an Ionic colonnade, imitated from the Temple of Bacchus at Teos. It was to be flanked by top-lit wings containing fourteen frescoes, divided by fasces, depicting significant events in the life of the orator. The artists for these were to be selected by 'a committee of three of the first antiquaries or connoisseurs in Rome'.[45] Between groups of frescoes were be painted *trompe l'œil* statues in recesses of Poetry, Eloquence, Law, and Philosophy. This whole narrative and literary monument to classical genius was to be set in a romantic and Picturesque landscaped garden suggestive of a Belanger-like decay. Here there would be mournful poplars twined about with vines, a ruined tree-grown archway half submerged in water, seats, *cippi*, and statues including a seated figure of Cicero's mother at the head of the 'island'. Elsewhere, a footbridge over the river Fibrenus took the form of the top half of a large archway flanked by Doric columns.

This whole conception was a development of the theme, essential to the 'intellectualism' of neo-classicism, of the Monument to Genius or Virtue.[46] This recurs again and again from Stowe and Aaron Hill's 'moral rock-garden' to von Klenze's great Walhalla at Regensburg of 1830–42. Kelsall's idea is close to Napoleon's creation, after 1796, of the Virgil Monument in the park at Mantua with its Elysian fields filled with a hundred statues of ancient and modern figures of different nationalities. Kelsall attempted to create this atmosphere in the home he made for himself from 1841 onwards at Hythe, nine miles from Southampton. This was known as the Villa Amalthaea, a direct echo of his Ciceronian Amalthaea at Arpino. Behind the sea-wall was a row of nine stone busts on pedestals of Homer, Pythagoras, Dryden, Milton, Newton, and so on, and in the garden was a lead copy of the 'Dancing Faun' from Pompeii.

Nor was this the only monument he planned. He intended at one time to leave £1,000 to Christ's College, Cambridge, to pay for a Milton Memorial to be erected in the Fellows' Garden. This was to take the form of a small temple in the Delian Doric order, for which three architectural drawings are preserved at Morden College. In 1823 he published a little pamphlet entitled *The First Sitting of the Committee on the Proposed Monument to Shakespeare*, an amusing parody (though presumably springing from a serious desire to see such a monument), of the deliberations of a committee composed of authors and eccentrics from different centuries.

One of Kelsall's most unusual productions was his book *Horae Viaticae* (1836), which contained diaries of his tour from St. Petersburg to Vienna in 1807 and of his travels in Scandinavia in 1835. But what engages our attention more than these is the extraordinary and unexpected novelette which he appended to this work. Perhaps the only literary parallel to this strange story, in which Kelsall invents his own Pope, Urbano Nono, is Baron Corvo's *Hadrian VII* (1904). But of more significance than this are the changes in the Church effected by 'the *radical Pope*', as Kelsall calls him. He convenes a Council 'to simplify and purify the sacred pivot of Christianity'[4] in hopeful preparation for the reception back into its fold of the separated brethren. The changes include the introduction of vernacular languages and of a more democratic method of papal election, the simplification of vestments and ritual and the reorganization of the Curia. Changes in the administration of the Papal States involve the abandonment of all hereditary aristocratic titles and the replanning of the city of Rome along modern neo-classical lines with Greek Doric market places and so on. The Pope himself 'conceives such a mortal hatred against the old trumpery at the altars, that he orders a great mass of the wooden and silver candlesticks to be burned. He has been known to ask for a ladder, and to tear away with his own hands the silk curtains fringed with gew-gaws.'[48] Kelsall anticipates 'the demolition of the vile turrets put up at the Pantheon by Urban VIII'.[49]

There can be no doubt that Kelsall saw himself in the character of Urbano Nono, just as Corvo was to in Hadrian VII. Pope Urban shares Kelsall's outlooks and sympathies even to the extent of having played in his youth the violin and of possessing violins made by the best-known masters.

If Kelsall's *Phantasm* anticipated the University of London and the reform of the ancient universities, so did his vision of a 'purifying' Council of the Roman Catholic Church anticipate the Second Vatican Council—though by one and a half centuries. The astounding originality of Kelsall's observations cannot be over-emphasized. There is, almost without a doubt, absolutely no parallel before the opening years of the twentieth century to Kelsall's demands for simplification, purification, and abandonment of all that is implied by the word 'triumphalism' (used today by many Catholics in a pejorative sense).

It is not merely this that is extraordinary, but that he anticipates also the reasons adduced for the introduction of these reforms. His criticisms, in other words, are by no means just those of a traditional Protestant shocked by Roman post-Tridentine splendour. Listen to his Pope using language indistinguishable from that of John XXIII or Paul VI, but surely unprecedented before: 'But I trust, my dear Cardinal, that a new era is opening for Catholicism, that those nations, *separated, in a great degree, through our own fault*, from the unity of doctrine, and worship, will return to within the pale of the one and original religion.'[50] Kelsall further developed a strange ecumenicism of his own in the triple crosses which he erected on the roof of the Villa Amalthaea and which still survive there. A Latin inscription on a stone let into the wall explains that the lower cross signifies Old Catholicism, the middle Protestantism, and the upper cross the 'Reformation of Both'.

Sedlmayr in *Verlust der Mitte* (1951) and Kaufmann in *Von Ledoux bis Le Corbusier* (1933) have both implied, though from widely differing standpoints, that advanced neo-classicism was the breeding-ground for the democratic, collectivist ideals of modern society and architecture. On the whole, however, the modern art historian—except when he discusses modern architecture and abandons all objectivity—is reluctant to be considered a prophet, a herald of change. But if one wished to support the thesis of Sedlmayr and Kaufmann—and there is much to be said for their position—then surely one could point to no more convincing evidence than Kelsall. Soaked in neo-classical art, architecture, and theory, not even, really, very interested in the Picturesque, he did not hesitate to take his every view-point to its logical extreme, and in doing so became the modern man, as none other of his generation dared.

See, for example, his little pamphlet, *Remarks Touching on Geography especially that of the British Isles* (1822). This looks simple enough at first sight yet it contains, like so many of his works, revolutionary proposals. He sets out in detail a system for dividing Great Britain and Ireland into Departments, partly inspired by Napoleonic precedent. It was a logical rationalized attempt to take account—like the 'five-year plans' of modern times—of 'the drift of population and commerce, etc', to do away with duplication of the names of towns and rivers, to promote 'the purification of geography . . . [and] the gradual melioration of the representative system', to turn new populous cities into capitals in place of some of the older towns whose peak had been reached in the Middle Ages, and to ensure that 'the cobwebbed and antiquated scaffolding of counties, ridings, wapentakes, lathes, and hundreds, which adds such useless perplexity to our laws, falls to the ground'.[51] Kelsall would have rejoiced at the recent destruction of the Isle of Ely and the Soke of Peterborough, and regretted that Rutland should have escaped the improver's hand. In his horror of all that is individual, eccentric, anomalous, inherited, and in his desire for everything to be 'brought into line', systematized, and, ultimately, made cosmopolitan, he anticipates the dominant trends of modern thought.

Despite his wealth and talent Kelsall seems to have moved hardly at all in the social and intellectual circles in which Thomas Hope was so often to be found. Thus the journalists and diarists of the period are silent about him, though notes of births and deaths in the family are to be found in the *Gentleman's Magazine*. He was a scholarly recluse much out of England on his foreign travels. His books, moreover, were mostly published privately at his own expense, some of them abroad and many—for some inexplicable reason—under varying pseudonyms. They were not, therefore, much reviewed or discussed in contemporary periodicals. His impact has been virtually nil and despite his fifteen publications he does not even appear in the *Dictionary of National Biography*. I know of only one contemporary reference to him that reveals anything of his personality, but that so perceptive and straightforward that it makes up for much. The entry in Benjamin Robert Haydon's diary for 1 April 1828, reads: 'Worked at Ariadne. My employer, C. Kelsall the traveller called and liked it. He is a singular, nervous, intelligent good hearted imaginative creature, excellent in taste and classical and refined in information. I like him much.'[52] I do not suppose that we shall get any picture more sensitive and accurate than this of this strangely forgotten neo-classical genius.

Kelsall has bulked large in this chapter since he represents what happened when strict neo-classicism—a movement in the forefront of which Hope was placed temporarily by his Downing pamphlet—

Country Life

Country Life

Sir Charles Monck, Bart., Belsay Castle, 1806–17
20. Entrance Front 21. Hall

22. William Wilkins, Grange Park, 1809
23. George Dance the Younger, Stratton Park, 1803–6

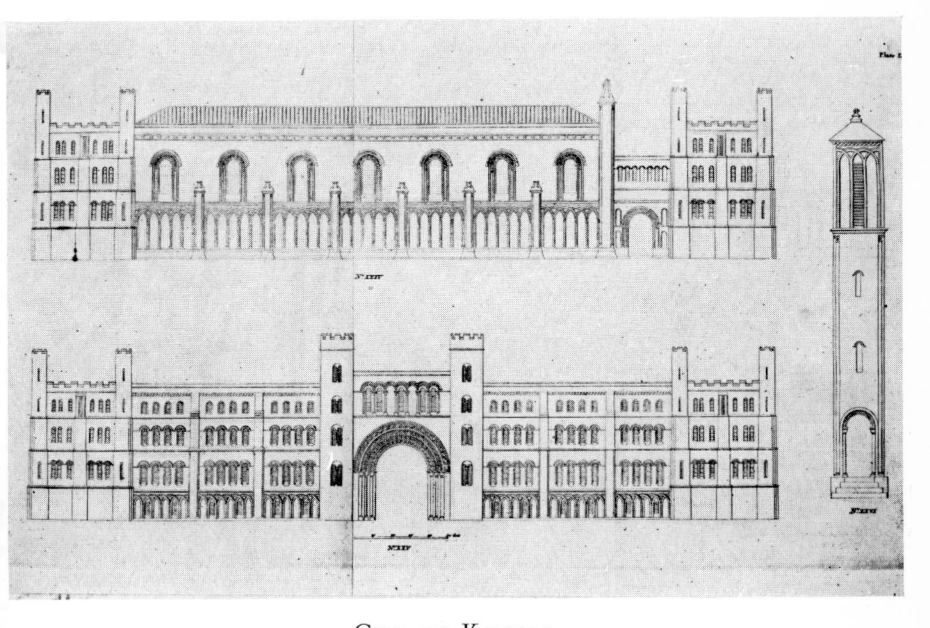

CHARLES KELSALL
24. Design for College of Mathematics, 1814
25. Design for College of Natural Philosophy, 1814

26. AUGUSTIN PAJOU, Cook Monument, Méréville, *c.* 1786

JOSEPH GANDY

27. Doric House, Bath, *c.* 1803–18

28. Storrs Hall, 1808, from a watercolour by J. C. Buckler

29. William Hardy, Portico, Letheringsett Hall, *c.* 1808–9 *Country Life*

30. James Paine the Younger
Design for Stables at Ugbrooke Park, *c.* 1779
31. S. Nelson, Temple at The Mote, 1800

32. Robert Mitchell, Design for a Greek House, 1801
33. James Playfair the Elder, Cairness House, 1792–7

was concentrated on to the exclusion of all else. It has been outlined in some detail since it was a way in which neo-classicism generally and Hope in particular, might have developed but did not. In our own time, architects like Behrens and Gropius have claimed to have made this development themselves. This is not the place to discuss the validity of that claim and instead we shall return to the 1800s to follow the alternative route of neo-classicism.

This alternative is already present in Hope's crucial pamphlet of 1804 and a further two quotations from it should reveal what I have in mind. Thus, for all his adulation of the strict austerity of the Greek Doric, Hope cannot help criticizing the standard books of engravings of Greek buildings because in '... the least unfaithful, the least inaccurate even, such as Stuart's Athens, Revett's Ionia, no adequate idea can be obtained of that variety of effect produced by particular site, by perspective, a change of aspect, and a change of light;'[53] and Sir John Soane, in the margin of his own copy of Hope's pamphlet, wrote of this phrase that it was 'worthy of the most serious consideration'. Thus, in order to recapture some of the lively richness lacking in the pages of Stuart and Revett, Hope recommended that the porticos at Downing be made as deep as possible so as to give 'to the entire facade more motion, more picturesqueness, and more dignity'.[54] What these quotations show, then, is that in the very document which is supposed to have established Hope, in Summerson's phrase, as 'a doctrinaire Neo-classicist',[55] the signs are already apparent of a dissatisfaction with the cold flat reproduction of Greek details from Stuart and Revett onwards, beyond which Wilkins' architecture, ironically, rarely went. We have already hinted at the way in which Hope bypassed this difficulty at his London house and will also show, later, how at the Deepdene he embraced wholeheartedly, as Wilkins never did, the English theories of the Picturesque. There are a number of stages in the development of Hope's approach to modern Greek architecture. The doubts and criticisms raised in his Downing pamphlet were emphasized in an article, *On Grecian and Gothic Architecture*, published in 1808. Here, it was precisely for its freely adaptable character that he praised Greek architecture. Observing how it was more adaptable 'to the peculiar exigiencies of every object', he referred to the 'nicety with which its richness may be proportioned to the peculiar character of every work'. Having established this point, he proceeded to argue that:

> nothing less than a total misapprehension of these principles could so often make modern architects apply the vigorous symmetry of the ancient temple . . . to the private habitation [of a modern Englishman, . . . or] give the box of a London citizen that exact correspondence of external forms, to which the villa of a Roman emperor, even of Hadrian himself, did not aspire.[56]

Later on in his life, this demand for picturesque freedom brought him round to a grudging admiration for Roman architecture. Thus, in his two-volumed *Historical Essay on Architecture*, published posthumously in 1835, he pointed out that there was far more local variety of style in Greek architecture than was generally recognized, but actually censured the dark timidity of the Greek interior, observing how enormously it lost through the lack of the 'curve and swell'[57] introduced by the Romans.

The Picturesque is, of course, a subject in itself and will be treated separately in a later chapter. To conclude this chapter, let us turn to a problem which is raised in my mind by an attitude that is prevalent throughout Hope's Downing pamphlet. The attitude is apparent in chance phrases such as: 'that admiration which . . . none of the good living architects of the continent any longer withhold from the most chaste of orders': Greek Doric. Why should Hope have supposed that continental architects were more enthusiastic than English about the revival of Greek Doric? Nothing, as I shall show (see Appendix B) could have been further from the truth. Was it that this alien Dutchman, attempting to impress his superior merits on English society, fell back upon undue adulation of continental architects as a sort of unconscious self-justification or self-defence? It is unlikely that Hope had in mind countries other than Germany and France. We know that Hope was in Germany in 1794, but by this time probably no building had been erected there with Greek Doric details. In Berlin the Police Riding School of 1792[58] had a number of stunted unfluted Doric columns, but hardly on a scale to solicit much attention or admiration. Two Municipal Theatres in the latest 90s—at Danzig by the city-architect Held, and at Glogau—were adorned with full-scale unfluted Greek Doric columns; and then in *c.* 1800 Heinrich Gentz's Old Mint at Berlin and David Gilly's Vieweg House at Brunswick were two fine and austere neo-classical compositions introducing fluted Greek Doric columns, though on a small scale, probably for the first time in Germany. It is not to be presumed that Hope had seen the numerous unexecuted sketches by Friedrich Gilly of the 1790s in most of which Greek Doric columns played an essential role. Thus, on the whole, it is hard to imagine that it was to Germany that he was referring. German neo-classical architecture reached a high point only later under Gilly's pupil Schinkel, who was only twenty-three at the time of the publication of Hope's pamphlet.

Turning to France, a different picture presents itself though, again, hardly one which justifies Hope's suggestion that pure Greek Doric was a norm on the Continent. Ledoux was obviously the pioneer, but the number of his executed buildings that incorporated pure Greek Doric details was slight: the Hôtel Montmorency, Paris (1772), the Besançon Theatre of three years later and the Barrière de Monceau in Paris of *c.* 1784. There were two Greek Doric garden buildings: one by Belanger at the Folie de Ste. James, Neuilly (1777),[59] another by Augustin Pajou at the Parc de Méréville (*c.* 1786; Plate 26).[60] And in Paris there were a further two or three such buildings: Antoine's Hôpital de la Charité (1778–81)[61] and Bruneau's Maison Chenot of 1790 in the rue de Provence.[62] Hope knew Paris well and was doubtless acquainted with a number of these Parisian examples, but I think it unlikely either that he knew many more instances than these or, indeed, that there were many more instances in 1804.

There can be no doubt that England, so scorned by Hope, was by 1804 in advance of every other country in Europe, so far as the use of the Greek Doric style was concerned.[63] By 1804 versions of fluted Greek Doric columns had been employed on at least twenty-five occasions in this country, and probably on many more that are not yet dated or recorded. Moreover, by a curious irony, four of these instances are due to Wyatt himself: the arch-villain of Hope's pamphlet! Wyatt had introduced colonnades that were variants of Greek Doric, i.e. though the shafts were fluted and baseless, the caps and necking bands were Roman Doric, at Castle Coole, County Fermanagh (1788–98), and at Stoke Park, Buckinghamshire, in *c.* 1800. He used similar columns in the 90s at Gresford Lodge, Cheshire, and Ottershaw Park, Surrey, both on lodges or entrance gateways. The most convincing of the pre-1804 examples and the closest to the unexecuted Grand Prix projects (which Hope may have had in mind) is Thomas Harrison's magnificent Chester Castle apparently designed as early as 1788 and erected in 1793–1820. It was Harrison's suggestion to Lord Elgin in 1799 that he should acquire casts and drawings of Greek works of art which resulted in the eventual acquisition of the Elgin Marbles. With that, of course, we are back in the world of the travelling Hellenists. The house which Harrison built for Lord Elgin in the late 1790s at Broomhall, near Dunfermline, Fifeshire, was not, however, markedly Greek in its details. A bulky neo-classical house of eleven bays by three, it was later altered by Porden and Gandy-Deering.

A reason for Hope's unfavourable comparison of England to the Continent may, perhaps, be found in the invention in France of the unfluted Greek Doric order. To appreciate the significance of this invention, the nomenclature of the Greek Doric and Tuscan orders must be reviewed and revised.[64] In the Renaissance there was an almost wilful misunderstanding of what Vitruvius had indicated as constituting the Tuscan order. Inigo Jones at Covent Garden was one of the few architects to realize that it involved simple tetrastyle temples of wooden construction, or seeming to be so, with widely spaced columns, plain friezes and broadly projecting eaves. However, in the Renaissance anything came to be called Tuscan that displayed unfluted columns and plain friezes. Often it was only the absence of metopes and triglyphs that distinguished this 'Tuscan' order from Roman Doric and, with the feeble yet rigid standardization of the orders insisted on by Renaissance theorists, the great variety amongst Roman Doric originals was forgotten. However, with Greek Doric there was no such ambiguity of title partly because it had not been employed for so long and thus never adapted. It clearly had fluted columns with neither astragals nor bases, and with metope and triglyph friezes. In France in the 1770s and in England a decade later, as the chronologies show, advanced architects introduced a quite new order that combined elements from both Greek Doric and Tuscan but which can properly be classified as neither. This new order always had unfluted columns, like the Tuscan order, but with neither astragals nor bases, like the Greek Doric. Sometimes there were metopes and triglyphs in the frieze, which, as much as anything, must rule out the possibility of this order being known as plain Tuscan. The difficulty of pinning it down to a known style was expressed as early as 1787 by Thiéry, who wrote of the cloister of Brongniart's Capuchin Convent of 1781 that, 'formé de colonnes toscanes, sans base, [il] retrace en petit les anciens monuments de Poestum'.[65] There is no serious ancient Greek precedent for this order—unless it be the unfinished columns of the temple at Segesta—and I suggest that it should be known as unfluted Greek Doric or, perhaps more indicatively, as 'Primitivist'. It was used repeatedly in France from 1772 onwards (my chronology represents only a selection of the known instances). A little-known building by Brongniart, the thatched cottage which he erected *c.* 1780 for M. Montesquiou in the Parc de Maupertuis near Coulommiers,[66] shows exactly the primitivism of the moment. With its unfluted Greek Doric colums, it is the missing link between Laugier's and Chamber's illustrations in the 1750s of the 'primitive hut' and Soane's use of primitivism at Hammells Park and Betchworth. Indeed, Soane's Hammells dairy of 1783 is probably the first appearance of this order in England, and is very close to Brongniart's cottage at Maupertuis. It was Soane, particularly, who used this French order in England, and of the fifteen examples in the chronology seven are attributed to him.

On the whole it was the Greek Doric which England, unlike France or Germany, made her own in these years. Yet within that category there is far more variety than might appear at first sight. Though less stylistically original than the 'Primitivist' order, the Greek Doric represented something more uncompromising and daring, something less easily confused with Tuscan. But even in England there was sometimes a reluctance to make these columns fully Greek Doric. Perhaps this is partly the reason for Revett's adoption of the almost entirely unfluted columns of the Delian order at Standlynch (*c.* 1766) and Ayot St. Lawrence (1778). Thomas Johnson's Warwick Gaol (1779–82) we know was to have been fluted, but somehow the carvers never got to work. The ambiguity of feeling towards Greek Doric is revealed in the development of J. M. Gandy's Doric House, Sion Hill, Bath (Plate 27). According to Ison, in the first plans for this house and gallery for the painter Thomas Barker, the street façade consisted of a tall windowless storey raised on a plinth. It was divided into five bays by fluted Greek Doric columns and boasted a sculptured frieze.[67] However, the house as built in *c.* 1818 differed in a number of ways from the first project. One of the most significant changes was that the columns lost their flutes, and the house, as a result, has a quieter more French air. But that the effect is still intended to be Greek Doric, despite the absence of triglyphs and metopes in the frieze, is borne out not only by the details of the capitals and necking of the columns, but by the name 'Doric House' which has stuck to it. Another change in design is one which must make the house almost an archaeological joke: this is that it seems fair to read its *exterior* as a version of the two-storeyed *interior* of a Greek temple. The relative proportion to each other of the two storeys of columns must make this reading almost certain. If so, Gandy has not dared to develop the strange idea to the full and has wrongly inserted a modillion cornice between the two storeys. The archaeological vein of this little composition, and its surprising transposition of internal features to an exterior, make it an exact and rare contemporary parallel to what Thomas Hope was doing with furniture design: Hope was ridiculed for bringing the shield of a Roman soldier indoors and using it as a firescreen, as Gandy might be ridiculed for his game at Doric House. But both, surely, constitute an essential artistic parallel to the religious 'development of doctrine' and are no more indefensible than, say, the decoration with little temple pediments and columns of interior door-cases.

There is more to say concerning the liberties taken by architects with Greek forms, for the Greek Revival from Stuart and Revett to Hope's furniture was a living organic thing, not a dead reproduction. Whiffen observes of Revett's Ayot St. Lawrence church that 'The detail of the exterior is of course impeccably Greek.'[68] But this is far from the case. Just as the side wings are, as has been recognized, Palladian in form though Greek in implication, and were originally intended to have been capped by towers, so the portico itself is a synthesis of Greek and later classical motifs. Triglyphs and metopes are disposed in the frieze in a completely un-Greek way, leaving 'demi-metopes' at the ends; and the two central columns are further apart from each other than from the end columns.[69] The same un-Greek handling of a triglyph and metope frieze occurs at Dance's portico at Stratton Park, the columns of which are also unfluted—though the whole is always supposed to be pure Greek; and again at James Green's house, Buckland Filleigh, Devon (*c.* 1809–10), inside which fluted Greek Doric columns are used with elegance and confidence.[70]

Another half-way stage in the acceptance of pure Greek is represented by the use of stopped flutes on Greek Doric columns, for which there is no ancient Greek precedent. Latrobe employed them at Hammerwood, Sussex, in 1793; then Soane at Tyringham, Buckinghamshire, in 1795, and at Bentley Priory, Middlesex, three years later. His Princes Street vestibule at the Bank of England was planned with them in 1804 but lost them in execution. The device was used by Gandy in 1808 for the columns of his colonnade at Storrs Hall, Westmoreland (Plate 28).[71] A year later the scholarly Soane at Moggerhanger, Bedfordshire, actually used columns with partially stopped flutes. He probably took this idea from the so-called 'portico of Philip, King of Macedon' on Delos, illustrated in 1794 in the third volume of Stuart and Revett's *Antiquities of Athens*.[72] Exactly similar columns appear in *c.* 1808–9 on the remarkable portico of Letheringsett Hall, Norfolk, designed by its owner William Hardy (Plate 29).[73]

Other little games that architects played with Greek columns were their use on plain square blocks, as at Wyatville's Woolley Park, Berkshire (1799),[74] and Green's *porte-cochère* at Buckland Filleigh; and less common, the combination of Greek and Roman Doric which Wyatt used at Castle Coole and Stoke Park, and Wyatville at Woolley Park. These, incidentally, were also the sort of hybrid columns with which Payne Knight had adorned the chimney-piece of his drawing-room at Downton Castle as early as the 1770s.

This glance at the variety of early Greek Revival work shows that, so far as is known, when Hope used pure Greek Doric columns in his gallery at Duchess Street in 1800, he was the first to employ them in any English interior.[75]

Though a number of varieties of Greek Doric had been employed quite extensively on exteriors, it must not be thought that the habit was spread equally throughout the country by Hope's time. A glance at the chronology suggests that large parts of the country were left untouched before 1810 by the new fashion. The un-Greek counties include Cornwall, Dorset, Essex, Suffolk, Huntingdonshire, Rutland, Leicestershire, Oxfordshire, Lincolnshire, Derbyshire, Durham, and Cumberland. For the most part they are counties at the extremities of the country or remote from London influences. In the Greek areas, London, of course, dominates with its seven examples and then Hertfordshire with five. Next come Sussex, Hampshire, and Cheshire with four examples each; Middlesex, Buckinghamshire, Northumberland, and Warwickshire with three. All the remaining counties have but one or two examples each. Northumberland and Cheshire, though counties far from London, happened to have strong local architects. Who were the patrons commissioning this advanced and rare work? The largest proportion came no longer from the Whig aristocracy who had patronized and created the Vanbrughian, Palladian, and Adam phases, but from a group—eighteen of them—that one may describe as ordinary commoners. The next largest group consists of public buildings, churches, etc., of which there are sixteen. Then come the country gentry and the old aristocracy, each with eight. Finally a comparatively new and important class, the bankers, for whom five of these buildings were erected. And what of the architects themselves? Of the twenty-two in our chronology all but six were London men. The widely scattered locals are James Green of Exeter, Thomas Harrison of Chester, Thomas Johnson of Warwick, John Kent of Southampton, and David Stephenson and William Stokoe, both of Newcastle. Of the sixteen London-based architects, Soane appears eleven times, James Wyatt seven, and Gandy and Wilkins four times each; Stuart, Revett, and Bonomi all have two examples each. It should be pointed out that the architects of five of these Greek works are unknown, and that four were designed by amateurs for themselves.

What is surprising is not that there were so many Greek Doric exteriors at this time in England, but that there were so few. As early as 1762, the first volume of Stuart and Revett's *Antiquities of Athens* had presented, in a way to facilitate imitation, detailed drawings of the Gateway to the Agora, Greek Doric in style though Roman in date—

just such a combination as would have appealed, one would have thought, to those not absolutely in Sir William Chambers' camp of regarding the Greek Doric as a style fit only for the Hottentot and the Baboon.[76] The remarkable but unexecuted designs of *c.* 1779 for stables at Ugbrooke, Devon (Plate 30), by James Paine (1745–1829) are an interesting experiment—but why were there so few imitations of the Agora Gateway? We have alluded earlier to the portico of Letheringsett Hall as an example of the Greek Doric erected immediately prior to 1810. The following quotation from an unpublished description of the house, apparently written on 12 June 1809 by a friend of its owner and designer, helps to show how revolutionary the style was regarded at even that date: 'A complete Grecian colonnade is so seldom applied to common purposes of architecture . . . that the attempting was at first a constant theme of conversation and criticism, and of course those were loudest in their censures who were the least informed, and whose own observations were confined to what was passing at home.'[77] In 1788 the second volume of Stuart and Revett gave drawings of the Parthenon itself and of the Choragic Monument of Thrasyllus. Why, again, did England have to wait for twenty years until Wilkins at Grange Park produced a grand building that united monumentally pure Greek Doric and the Thrasyllan order? There is, in fact, an interesting intermediary stage between Stuart and Revett in 1788 and Wilkins in 1809—though whether the effect of this is to emphasize or minimize the time-gap is hard to say. This intermediary stage is a design for a Greek Revival house (Plate 32) published in 1801 by Robert Mitchell, a Scottish architect of some distinction, whose interiors are normally close to the Cameron/Holland offshoot of the Adam style. The Greek design is one of three illustrations to *An Essay to elucidate the Grecian, Roman and Gothic architecture*, which is appended to his folio-volume, published in English and French, of *Plans and Views in Perspective with Descriptions of Buildings erected in England and Scotland* (1801). The Greek Doric house is probably the most convincing and successful of the three illustrations and its extreme similarity to Grange Park can hardly be considered a coincidence.[78] Thus Hope's protégé, by baldly imitating at Grange Park the work of another man, takes us back to the beginning of this chapter where we saw him blindly following the recommendations of

Thomas Hope. Hope, I think, was not very happy in his choice of architects: Wilkins and Atkinson. The next chapter will show how successfully he was able to put his theories into practice at Duchess Street without the aid of either of these architects.

IV

The Duchess Street Mansion

On his arrival in this country Thomas Hope lost no time in establishing himself in a distinguished setting. His first address, as a young man of twenty-six, was 2, Hanover Square. His second cousin, Henry Hope, took up residence at the former Hopetoun House off Cavendish Square, where he soon became noted both for his lavish hospitality and his patronage of art.[1] The Hope Collections, which the family brought from Holland in 1795, were deposited at 2, Hanover Square,[2] in which house Thomas was probably joined by John Williams Hope, a Director of the bank and heir to Henry Hope. But Thomas was anxious to acquire a larger house of his own, and four years later purchased from the Dowager Lady Warwick her enormous mansion in Duchess Street, off Portland Place. She was the sister of Sir William Hamilton, whose vases Hope was soon to acquire.

Her house, properly known as 1, Mansfield Street, was built as part of the Portland Place development by Robert Adam for his old friend Major-General Robert Clerk.[3] Although the original building lease was granted to Clerk, the first tenants were Lady Warwick, from 1771 to 1774, and Sir Thomas Wynn, Bart., later Lord Newborough, from 1774 to 1780. After the death in 1773 of her first husband, the Earl of Warwick, the Dowager Lady Warwick married General Clerk, her landlord, and together they lived in the house from 1780 until his death in 1797. Lady Warwick then let the house for a year, until its purchase by Hope in 1799.[4]

We know that Thomas Hope possessed a set of drawings for this house which referred to its having been begun in 1768 for Lady Warwick at her own expense.[5] Plans, elevations, sections, and designs for its interior decoration survive among the Adam drawings at Sir John Soane's Museum.[6] The first drawing, for the South elevation, is in a different style of draughtsmanship from the others and is dated 1779. The second drawing, for the South front of the courtyard, is labelled 'First design for General Clark's house', implying that it had been superseded. It must, however, be observed that the rate-books show that the house was complete by 1771; the date 1779 on the first drawing may well be inaccurate, since the Adam drawings were almost certainly labelled and dated by William Adam many years after their execution;[7] and the designs can be related to descriptions of the house under Hope's ownership. There can thus be little doubt that the Soane Museum designs represent substantially the house which Hope bought. However, apart from the difference in technique of the first design, some of the others also display inconsistencies. Thus the ground-floor plan (Plate 34) shows a curved North front with an eight-columned *porte-cochère* following its line, which are both absent from the elevation shown in Plate 35.

The house was bounded on the East by Adam's Chandos House and its stables, which still survive today, on the south by Queen Anne Street, on the West by Mansfield Street and on the North by Duchess Street. Access was gained through a forecourt in Duchess Street, and at the back there was a long narrow garden looking on to Queen Anne Street. There was thus something of the air of the Parisian *hôtel* about the plan and disposition of the house which must have appealed to Hope. Clerk had spent much time in Paris in the 1760s, where he 'acquired a place in French society',[8] a fact which may help to account for the Gallic plan. The South or back elevation looking on to the garden was nine bays by three, with the central three bays divided by four attached Ionic columns without a pediment. The designs show decorative panels between the windows of the first and second floors and balconies to all the first-floor windows. It seems that these ornamental devices were not executed.[9] The long West front along Mansfield Street was largely devoid of windows or decoration. In the entrance-wall in Duchess Street there were two gateways leading into the courtyard. On either side of the courtyard were short three-storeyed wings containing coach-house, kitchens, and servants' quarters.

Inside the house itself, the ground-floor was entirely given over to the servants, except for the staircase hall and a circular entrance-hall, twenty-four feet in diameter, which was in the centre of the house at the front. To the right lay the staircase-hall, divided into two portions by a columned screen. From the first portion, which was semi-circular, one saw through the screen the staircase, rising in one arm, returning in two. The principal reception rooms, including even the dining room, were all *en suite* on the first-floor. Above, on the second-floor, there were three private entertaining-rooms, three bedrooms and servants' quarters.

The designs for ceilings, chimney-pieces and shutter-panels are all of an unobtrusive elegance. It seems that Adam relied for effect in this house on size and plainness rather than on elaborate polychrome decoration. A novel feature was that all the rooms, both in the house and in the courtyard wings, had ceilings in the form of segmental vaults (Plate 35), constructed with tiles or flat bricks.[10] Equally novel was the absence of basement or attics, the pitch of the roofs being too shallow to allow for the introduction of rooms. The small proportion of bedrooms to reception-rooms emphasizes the difference in the rôles played in English society by the town house and the country house. To gain space for the reception-rooms, since the offices were on the ground-floor, the staircase was relegated to the extreme end of the building, a position unusual for a house of that size. Thus Adam could keep all the principal rooms on one floor and arrange them in a free yet logical manner.

So in 1799 to a wealthy, thirty-year-old bachelor, in the throes of forming a great collection, this house seemed an ideal home. It was a grand house, a slightly French house, with few bedrooms but many reception-rooms, and capable of further expansion into the courtyard wings; its interiors, though elegant, were not of so elaborate an ornamentation as could not easily be transformed to display a more correct taste.

There can be no doubt that Hope began his alterations and improvements as soon as possible after his purchase of the house in 1799. In that year the rates rose from £350 to £500 per annum, and in 1800 in the July–August number of the *Magasin Encyclopédique*, edited by Hope's friend A. L. Millin, it was observed that in London:

> On s'entretient beaucoup de la superbe galerie de tableaux, de vases, de statues, de pierres gravées, etc. de l'ingénieux HOPE . . . Elle n'est pas encore achevée; mais on travaille assidûment à l'arrangement des vastes salles qui doivent former cette galerie. M. Hope avoit recueilli ces trésors

en Italie, en Allemagne, en France, etc. Il n'y aura rien en Angleterre qui puisse être comparé à cette collection.[11]

It is reasonable to assume that the house was largely complete in 1801, and on 23 July in that year Lord Glenbervie wrote of Hope in his diary: 'He is a great traveller and collector at any expense of *vertu* of all sorts, pictures, marbles, Hetruscan (*sic*) vases, fossils, etc., etc., etc., and he has furnished his magnificent house (late General Clarke's and Lady Warwick's) in Mansfield Street with a profusion of those things as well as the most costly furniture.'[12] It was certainly complete by the end of 1803,[13] for on 1 February 1804 Hope sent out admission tickets to members of the Royal Academy.

In suggesting the disposition of rooms in the remodelled house (Fig. 6), we may begin with the assumption that as far as possible he left intact both the structure of the house and the function of many of its principal apartments. There are a number of reasons for this assumption. To start at the most mundane level, there was the question of cost. Hope always had a banker's eye where money was concerned. Though he was lavish there was no waste, and if he could re-use chimney-flues and door-openings, then we can be sure he would. Moreover, the modern habit of gutting a building leaving only the façades, and then entirely remodelling the interior hardly presented itself as a serious possibility in the 1790s. Another reason is that we know that at the Deepdene Hope was to leave more or less intact the old house and the function of a number of its rooms, transforming its appearance by judicious decoration not by wholesale structural alteration. His reasons for this procedure at both his houses were not merely those of convenience and economy but, almost certainly, part of a desire to be seen as belonging to England's traditional, influential, and fashionable society. Both his houses had been built towards the end of the eighteenth century by distinguished English gentlemen. He wanted to be accepted as part of that tradition and therefore preserved the whole paraphernalia of ante-rooms, drawing-rooms and boudoirs in a way that contrasts strikingly with Soane who, a complete eccentric from first to last, abandoned immediately the trappings of the *salon*.

What we know about the arrangement of the show-rooms at Duchess Street is this: Britton and Pugin tell us that they were all on

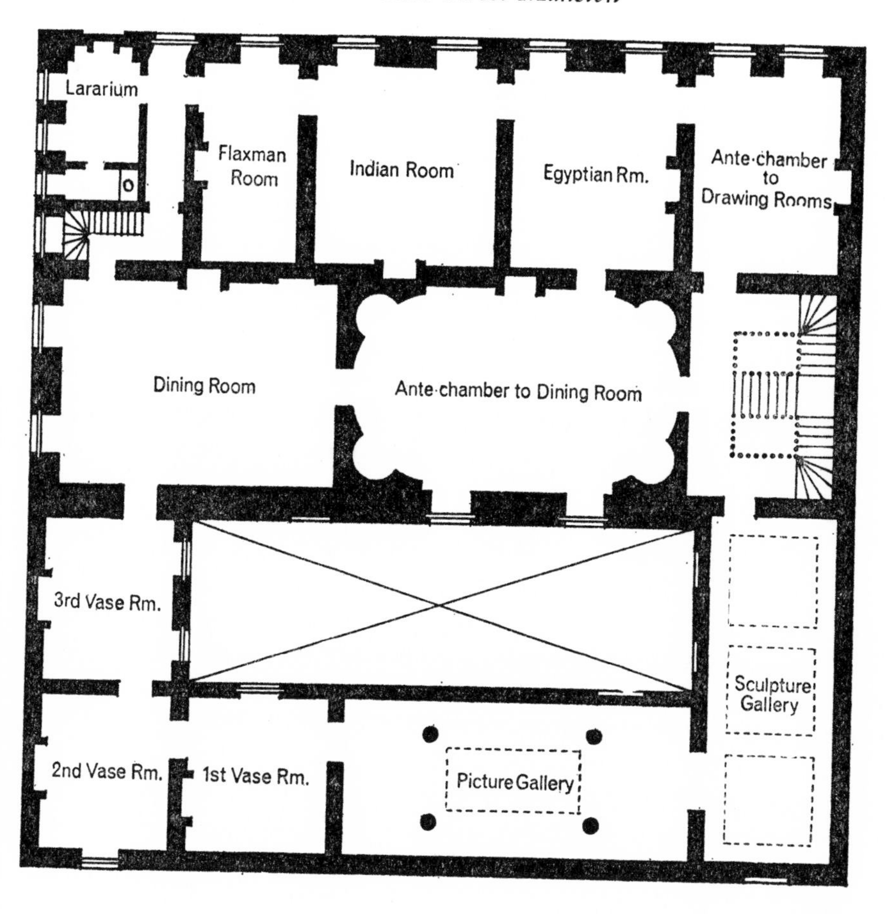

Fig. 6. Suggested 1st floor plan of the Hope Mansion in Duchess Street, London, *c.* 1800

the first-floor, that the sculpture-gallery was on the West side of the courtyard, the picture-gallery on the North and the vase-rooms on the East.[9] The expected arrangement of the three vase-rooms in a sequence on the east side cannot have occurred for the following reasons.

Firstly, the first vase-room which Hope shows in *Household Furniture* has a flat ceiling, and we know that all the rooms in the wings were segmentally vaulted; and secondly, the arrangement of doors and windows in the second vase-room does not correspond to what would have been possible—for example, the chimney-piece and door would have been on the courtyard side. A glance at the suggested plan shows how the evidence of Hope's plates can be made to fit what we know of the house from Adam's plans and from Britton and Pugin's account. With the sequence of the other rooms, it is more difficult to be certain, for Hope seems to give up strict geographical sequence in the arrangement of his plates.

It is clear from the Adam drawings that the main drawing-rooms were the two in the middle of the south front. From the position of chimney-piece and doors, it seems certain that Hope's Indian Room was the eastermost of these two and that adjacent to it on the west was the Egyptian room. The Flaxman or Star Room is revealed in Hope's plate as being rectangular and seems to fit perfectly in size and in the position of the chimney-piece with the original first-floor bedroom. The Lararium seems to have been smaller still. As there was no room so small and mysterious on the first-floor it follows that Hope must have formed it himself. Since no one actually lived or slept on the first-floor, the old writing-closet and powdering-room must have been unnecessary. The complicated arrangement of niches in front of the chimney-piece in the writing-closet probably gave the idea for the strange Lararium chimney-piece. It only needed to remove the thin wall between writing-closet and powdering-room to create a tucked-away and intimate chamber, 9 ft. 6 in. wide by 14 ft. 6 in. long, which would do perfectly for the Lararium. The dining-room Hope doubtless retained for its original function since it was conveniently placed by the back-stairs for service from the kitchens underneath it.

This suggested arrangement of Hope's rooms makes some sense of the order of plates in *Household Furniture*. Having ordered them clockwise and geographically for the first five rooms, he was unlikely to abandon all order for the remaining five. The pattern for the second five is that he began with the principal drawing-room, the Indian or Blue Room, from there glanced backwards into the adjacent Flaxman Room, then moved clockwise from the Indian to the Egyptian

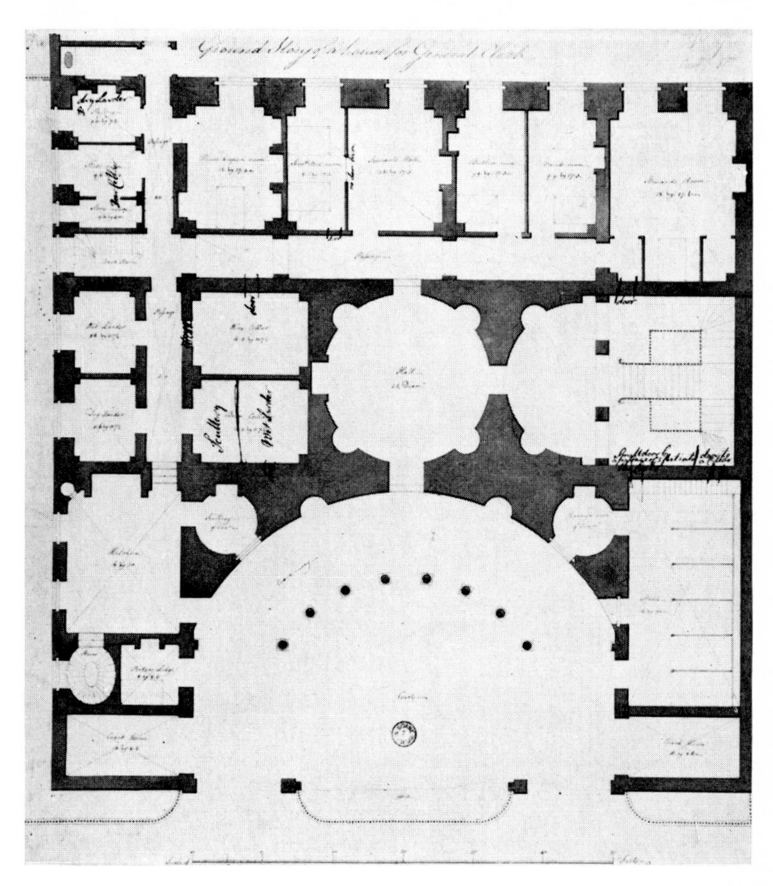

Robert Adam, No. 1, Mansfield Street, 1768–71?
34. Ground-floor plan 35. Elevation to Courtyard

Country Life

Country Life

11, Montagu Terrace, London

36. Back Drawing Room 37. Front Drawing Room

38. Thomas Hope, Egyptian Clock, *c.* 1800

THOMAS HOPE

39. Egyptian Couch, *c.* 1800 40. Egyptian Chair, *c.* 1800

Room and so on through the 'Room for entertaining company before dinner' (which he does not show) into the dining-room and from there, still clockwise, into the nearly adjacent Lararium.

Finally, there is the question of the Flemish Picture Gallery which was added in 1819. We know that the dimensions of this were about 50 ft. by 20 ft. and that it was lit by a raised clerestorey. It must almost certainly have been added in the garden at the rear of the house, probably at the extreme east end where it would least obscure the south-facing windows of the main first-floor apartments. On a visit to the house in February 1827, Prince Pückler-Muskau observed that: 'On a sort of terrace on part of the house are hanging-gardens; and though the shrubs have only three feet of earth, they grow very luxuriantly.'[14] This charming feature was doubtless related to the roof of the new Picture Gallery and was probably added at Mrs. Hope's request as compensation for the depletion of her flower-gardens occasioned by its erection.

The first recorded commission for work at Duchess Street is that of August 1799 for a painting by Thomas Daniell as a companion to one by Pannini. These were hung in the Indian Room where they formed essential almost architectural decorations, and it is to be assumed that by 1799 the rooms were already taking shape in Hope's mind if not in the actual house. With work under way, Hope thought it appropriate to make a visit to Greece, the ultimate source of his enthusiasms. He spent the autumn and winter of 1799–1800 abroad and, intellectually refreshed, threw himself on his return in 1800 into the remodelling process at Duchess Street. Commissions are now recorded until the end of 1801. On 1 July 1800 he paid Flaxman £157. 10s. for a marble chimney-piece and the cost of its erection in the house, and in the same month Thomas Daniell was painting two more pictures for the Indian Room. On 9 November Hope made a further payment to Flaxman, of £200, for another marble chimney-piece, and on 28 December of the following year paid him five guineas for a model of a chimaera. The house now virtually complete, Thomas Hope left the country for a year and was travelling abroad from May 1802 until the following May. In October 1803 he paid Flaxman £84 for a marble bust of his brother, Henry Philip, which adorned the chimney-piece in the dining-room. This was accompanied by a payment of

£1. 9s. 9d. to Flaxman's men for cleaning and mending statues—[15] a finishing touch to make all things new for the discerning eyes of the Academicians and for the general public.

From the beginning, the first-floor apartments were to be opened, museum-like, to the public. Neither Hope nor his wife ever lived in them, but had their own suites of smaller rooms upstairs.[16] He compiled an explanatory catalogue[17] of his collections and galleries, a copy of which was doubtless left in the house for the use of visitors. In 1809 the painter Martin Archer Shee in a footnote to his unusual and lengthy poem *Elements of Art*—a fascinating statement of the neo-classical approach to patronage and the arts—observed that in times when continental wars prevented Englishmen from seeing the art of those countries, it was Thomas Hope who

> . . . took the lead in offering to the public this desirable indulgence. The facility with which admission was obtained to view his magnificent establishment and the assembly of interesting objects which it contains, may be said to have given the first impulse to that liberality which has so materially contributed to our gratification and instruction.[18]

Tickets were issued to those desirous of inspecting the mansion. The normal method of obtaining a ticket was by 'An application signed by some persons of known character and taste', or by 'The personal introduction of any friend of the family', but to persons of greater distinction, such as the Royal Academicians, Hope himself sent out unsolicited tickets of invitation. 'Visitors are admitted on the Monday during the season of the nobility being in town',[19] explained Westmacott in 1824, although from the references in contemporary memoirs to visits paid to the house, it would appear to have been opened rather more frequently. From Soane, Dance, and the Princess of Wales downwards, that whole social and artistic world of the English Regency, immortalized in Daniel Maclise's brilliant *Portrait Gallery*, moved at one time or another through the halls and galleries of Duchess Street. The house acquired something of the *réclame* that Strawberry Hill[118] had earlier, and in issuing admission tickets and compiling a catalogue of his collections, Hope was following Walpole's precedent closely.

The house was demolished in 1851[20] and no record of it, photographic or otherwise, was made at that time. It is possible, however, to piece together a very clear picture of its appearance from Hope's own thorough record of it in the text and illustrations to *Household Furniture*; from the accounts of it in Westmacott's *British Galleries* and Britton and Pugin's *London*; and from the surviving furniture. The authority of *Household Furniture* is unimpeachable. Hope himself insisted[21] that all its plates represented pieces actually made, and we know from the furniture and fittings in existence today that the plates are of an almost incredible accuracy.

The visitor would begin his tour in the staircase-hall, a room dominated by Beechey's portrait of Thomas Hope in Turkish dress, painted in 1798 (Plate 10).[22] Thus, his first introduction to the house was through the remote exoticism of a culture other than his own, just as the title-page of *Household Furniture* was framed by an elaborate Turkish border. Hope comments upon the significance of this border in the notes to his book and this may be an appropriate moment to discuss this characteristic example of his cultural outlook. The 'congelations and stalactites' of this Turkish decorative border were, he believed, derived from the 'Grecian architects of the lower empire' and were 'remarkable for the play, or rather the flicker, of light and shade'. With them, were decorated 'most of the Greek churches and Mohammedan mosques', they were a consistent feature of Saracenic monuments in Arabia, Egypt, Persia, India, and Spain, and in England appeared in the form of the 'zig-zags ... and chevrons ... improperly ... denominated Saxon'.[23] Thus does Hope justify his Turkish excursions as historically meaningful and, by virtue of the picturesque flicker of light and shade, visually arresting.

So, musing on the interwoven strands of which his culture was formed, the ideal visitor would pass into the Sculpture Gallery (Fig. 7), a long room with a coffered ceiling lit by three raised lanterns. Hope, ever anxious to combine refinement of expression with echoes of the primitive source, describes how this coffering 'imitates a light timber covering'.[24] This simple setting contained some of the less remarkable sculpture, for Hope had no intention of giving away everything at the start. Thus the statues which lined this narrow room seemed to point the way to the rest of the house and to show, for there were many modern copies, how the antique world is seen with modern eyes. There were copies of the Belvedere Apollo and the Belvedere Mercury by Flaxman and de Vaere respectively, and of the Medici Apollino and the Medici Venus, both by Pisani. A pair of antique urns were displayed, as well as a pair of Piranesian candelabra.

Fig. 7. Thomas Hope, Sculpture Gallery, Duchess Street, *c.* 1800

From the Sculpture Gallery was approached the Picture Gallery (Figs. 8 and 31), a top-lit, two-storeyed room in the wing which Hope had added to enclose the courtyard on the fourth side. This was probably the room which most closely approximates to the accepted notion of Hope the Greek, inspirer of the academic austerity of Downing College. A precise anthology of classical quotations, it included columns, supporting the large sky-light, that were imitated from the Temple of the Winds; a trabeated roof from the Theseion; four Doric columns from the Propylaea; and the columns, entablature, and pediment of an organ from the Erectheion. What engages the attention is

Fig. 8. Thomas Hope, Picture Gallery, Duchess Street, *c.* 1800

not merely the presence of the Greek details—though they were rare enough in 1800—but the form which the room took: that of a temple. Thus, with the organ at the far end it deliberately assumes, as Hope observed, 'the appearance of a sanctuary'.[25] Designed as a small Ionic temple, the organ was decorated with much iconographical care. Hope described how, 'The car of the god of music, of Apollo, glides over the center of the pediment. The tripods, sacred to this deity, surmount the angles. Laurel wreaths and other emblems, belonging to the sons of Latona, appear embroidered on the drapery, which, in the form of an ancient peplum or veil, descends over the pipes . . . '[25] The whole room can be seen as an attempt to create not merely a museum, but something yet purer than that—the Greek *μουσεῖον* or sanctuary dedicated to the Muses. The effect is to make a religion of the arts. In an article published in the same year as *Household Furniture*, Hope described how 'the first musaea, or repositories of the Muses, (as they were most appropriately denominated) . . . [were] nurseries of . . . modern art'.[26] So his own *μουσεῖον* was a sanctuary for the arts of music, painting, and sculpture as well as for decorative design and architecture. The paintings, hidden behind long curtains in Hope's view, though revealed in Westmacott's, were originally of the popular Italian seventeenth century schools, some of which Hope had acquired at the Orléans Sale in 1798. After *c.* 1805 he added the great canvases of Greek mythology which he was commissioning from artists like West, Dawe, and Westall. His Canova Venus was eventually housed here, together with a considerable number of busts and bronze vases.

This room must have been the first as well as one of the most uncompromising attempts to impose the forms of a Greek temple upon an English interior. Wilkins followed Hope's example at the Grange in 1809, though here it was an exterior to which the uncompromising Greek forms were applied. In his *Historical Essay on Architecture* (1835), Hope was to censure the application of the templar style to domestic architecture in words which followed closely what he had written as early as 1808.[27] How far does this objection conflict with his own practice at Duchess Street? The answer can be found partly in his definition of good furniture and, by implication, of architecture: that it should have beauty, character and appropriate meaning. The public architecture of the Greek temple was justified at Duchess Street because the house was always something more than a private residence and was also a temple or sanctuary of the arts. Thus, what was wholly 'characteristic' and 'appropriate' at Duchess Street was indefensible at the Hampshire seat of a country gentleman. The nature of this conflict must play an important part in any discussion of Hope's influence. He may have been responsible in part for the revival of archaeological forms in furniture and architecture, but it seems that this brought him little pleasure. The mere application to modern design of antique and pre-antique features was a worthless process if it was not informed by a whole social and cultural outlook. The furniture at Duchess Street, everywhere symbolic of the purpose and meaning of the room which it adorned, would be meaningless where

Fig. 9. Thomas Hope, 1st Vase Room, Duchess Street, *c.* 1800

it would not be vulgar if reproduced at random elsewhere. But this it undoubtedly was, and while it is almost to be expected that the high-minded artistic innovator will be distressed at the work of his admirers—Ruskin's horror at the mass-produced Venetian Gothic of the London suburbs being well known—it can be maintained that Hope's case was a special one. To imitate forms which had been worked out against the dual background of Duchess Street and to transfer them to a wholly private and domestic setting was to distort, if not entirely to miss the point.

From the Picture Gallery one made one's way back to the body of the house through a sequence of three vase-rooms. These contained over five hundred vases, the bulk of them deriving from the second Hamilton Collection, from which Hope had acquired about seven hundred and fifty vases in 1801. Probably echoing Hope's catalogue or

Fig. 10. Thomas Hope, 2nd Vase Room, Duchess Street, *c.* 1800

at least, his sentiments, Westmacott described the Hope vases as,

> . . . the most interesting and unique collection in the world. Independent of their great variety, and varied elegance of form, they are doubly valuable as specimens of ancient history and costume, every object presenting some new and highly-instructive design, tending to correct and refine the taste, and direct the student to the purest style of Greek art.[28]

What is also striking about these rooms is the pains that Hope took, as throughout the house, to ensure a meaningful and appropriate

Fig. 11. Thomas Hope, 3rd Vase Room, Duchess Street, *c.* 1800

connection between the object displayed and its setting. The vases had been found in tombs near Naples and, in the first room (Fig. 9), were therefore displayed in columbaria. In this recreation of the original setting of the vases, symbolic furniture also had its part to play. Open cupboards in the first room, which contained Hope's fictile

Fig. 12. Thomas Hope, Indian Room, Duchess Street, *c.* 1800

vases, were divided by terms adorned with the head of the Indian or bearded Bacchus, since the scenes depicted on the vases 'relate chiefly to Bacchanalian rites . . . connected with the representations of mystic death and regeneration'.[29] In the second room (Fig. 10) cupboards were decorated with the Dionysiac staff entwined with the ivy-leaves of Bacchus. Two pairs of consoles in the form of panthers in this room and, in the third room (Fig. 11), a table supported by three bronze chimaerae, and benches with similar terminations, were directly inspired by the furniture discovered at Pompeii. Hope considered that these, together with 'bronze candelabra and a few other utensils, of a quiet hue and a sepulchral cast, [were] analogous to the chief contents'[30] of these rooms.

Far from sepulchral was the note struck by the Indian or Blue Room, the principal of the drawing-rooms (Fig. 12). Decorated in the 'Saracenic or Moorish' taste, its exotic colours and even aromas must be described by Hope himself. The segmental vaulted ceiling, copied from those in Turkish palaces, was a

> . . . canopy of trellice-work, or reeds, tied together with ribbons. The border and compartments display foliage, flowers, peacock's feathers, and other ornaments of a rich hue, and of a delicate texture, which, from the lightness of their weight, seem peculiarly adapted for this lofty and suspended situation . . . As the colours of this room, in compliance with the oriental taste, are everywhere very vivid, and very strongly contrasted, due attention has been paid to their gradual lightening, as the eye rose from the skirting to the cornice. The tint of the sofa is deep crimson; that of the walls sky blue; and that of the ceiling pale yellow, intermixed with azure and with sea-green. Ornaments of gold, in various shades, relieve and harmonize these colours. Round the room are incense urns, cassolettes, flower baskets and other vehicles of natural and artificial perfumes.[30]

Westmacott observes, more simply, that 'The decorations of this apartment are in the most costly style of Oriental splendour; the curtains, ottomans, &c., are all of rich damask silk',[31] and that the carpets are Persian. The room corresponds exactly to one belonging to a Greek in Constantinople, described in *Anastasius* as: 'furnished in all the splendour of eastern magnificence. Persian carpets covered the floors, Genoa velvet clothed the walls, the gilt trellis work overcast the lofty ceilings. Clouds of rich perfumes rose on all sides, from silver censers.'[32] This room, then was a precise statement of Hope's unique romantic vision, his blending of the Greek and near Eastern cultures.

Despite the fanciful colouring of such rooms, the chill outline engravings which Hope employed to facilitate accurate imitation of the objects depicted have given birth to the idea that the actual interiors were as chill as their delineations. Hope was himself aware of the possibilities of misrepresentation, but though he believed that 'a mere lineal engraving' was not always the best solution, in the case of this book the 'strong contrast of the light and shaded parts . . . the harmonious blending, or the gay opposition of the various colours', could have been conveyed only by 'enhancing its price to such a degree as must have defeated its principal purpose'.[21]

In this room were hung three large Indian views especially commissioned from Thomas Daniell (1749–1840). A 'Mosque in Hindustan' was painted in August 1799 for one hundred and thirty guineas, to hang as a pair to a view by Pannini of the 'Campo Vaccino' or Forum in Rome. Two upright paintings by Daniell of 'Temples on the Ganges at Benares' and of the 'Taj Mahal' followed in July 1800. The Daniells and the Pannini were identically framed within heavy borders of fasces and were exactly balanced in size both as regards each other and the wall spaces. The union of painting, sculpture, and architecture, which John Britton so much admired at the Soane Museum,[33] was also a real concern for Hope. He knew that it was that union which had characterized the great achievements of the past, and was determined to recreate it again—even at the risk of outraging the sensibilities of the 'pure artists', as is shown in his cutting down of Dubost's canvas 'Damocles' in order to accommodate it to the proportions of the Duchess Street rooms. The classical Pannini view was doubtless intended to harmonise with the classical and rather sculptural furniture in which the winged lion played a more than prominent part. The fire-screens, quaintly formed by shields supported on javelins (Fig. 27) were acquired by Edward Knoblock (Plate 36); and a pair of the bizarre pendant wall-lights, or a contemporary variant of them, found its way into the collection of Sir Albert Richardson.[34] In carved, ebonized, and gilt wood with Graeco-Egyptian decorations, these lights may now be seen at the Royal Pavilion, Brighton.[35] (For a list of surviving objects designed by Hope, see Appendix E.)

No less remarkable was the adjacent Flaxman or Star Room (Fig. 13). The *raison d'être* of this apartment was to provide a setting both meaningful and magnificent for the sculptural group of Aurora visiting Cephalus on Mount Ida, which Hope had commissioned from Flaxman in Rome in the early 1790s. The subject of this sculpture dictated the iconography of the whole room which was, as Hope observes, 'rendered . . . analogous to these personages, and to the face of nature, at the moment when ... the goddess of the morn, is supposed to announce approaching day'.[36] In an attempt to heighten this sensation, azure, black, and orange satin curtains were draped over looking-glasses edged with black velvet on three sides of the room.

Hope's description of the symbolic intentions of all these culminates

Fig. 13. Thomas Hope, Flaxman Room, Duchess Street, *c.* 1800

in a romantic purple patch, in which he shows how the combined tints of draperies, ceiling, and accessories suggest: '. . . the fiery hue which fringes the clouds just before sunrise . . . [while] in a ceiling of cooler sky blue are sown, amidst a few unextinguished luminaries of the night, the roses which the harbinger of day . . . spreads on every side around her.'[36] The curtains were parted mysteriously in three places to reveal the Flaxman group and its reflections in the large looking-glasses placed opposite to each other on the side walls. In Hope's depiction of the room, the eye is pleasingly confounded by this device into supposing for a moment that the room contains not one but three pieces of sculpture.

The iconographical treatment of this room was of an astonishing degree of consistency and intricacy. The pedestal on which the Flaxman sculpture stood was adorned with torches, garlands, and wreaths emblematic of Cephalus and his mistress. These were disposed around a diadem of stars bisected by the fatal dart which Aurora gave her lover. On either side appeared the sinister head of Jupiter, Serapis, or Pluto, figurative of death. Opposite the chimney-piece stood a large table, which still survives, of which the front legs were composed of pairs of the Horae, the four goddesses of the seasons. In the frieze above their heads were four medallions representative of the deities of night and sleep. On the table stood an extraordinary Egyptian clock (Plate 38), which recently appeared in a London sale-room and has since been acquired by the Brighton Pavilion.[37] It consists of an elegant black basalt figure of the horned Isis—introduced into the room because she was symbolic of the moon—standing between two hieroglyphic blocks of finely-worked ormolu. The frames of these blocks and the plinth are of a warm red marble. The actual clock is held before her by the goddess, pressed close to her stomach. This object, of a type more familiar from the period of the Great Exhibition, affords another example of the way in which, in his concern to bring domestic articles within the sphere of narrative art, Hope prefigured the work of his Victorian descendants.

The chimney-piece of the Flaxman Room was of black marble ornamented with a band of nine stars made of gilt bronze. A pair of owls, their presence justified by their nocturnal associations, supported the shelf.

Round the top of the room was a broad frieze on which were depicted the heads of Aurora and of Cephalus, and the animals, instruments, and emblems of the chase, favourite pursuit of Cephalus. 'Round the bottom of the room', observes Hope, 'still reign the emblems of night.'[36] The nature of this last symbolical gesture, presumably hidden by the curtains in Hope's view, remains a mystery. What also cannot be conveyed by Hope's engraving is the sense of dramatic wonder conveyed by this veiled tent-like room, suggestive in its tints of 'rosy-fingered dawn' (a phrase quoted by Hope) still overshadowed by the inky blackness of chimney-piece and table, the whole flashing and glinting as rays of light caught the gilt stars and decorations and were in turn reflected by the ubiquitous mirrors. What is equally to be stressed is that all this was conceived as a setting for a sculpture by Flaxman, commonly regarded as the most chaste of English neo-classical sculptors. What emerges, then, is the supreme importance of the setting to an appreciation of Regency works of art; and the difficulty, if not impossibility, of divorcing the Picturesque from the neo-classical.

But the room has not yet yielded all its secrets. On either side of the Flaxman sculpture stood a heavy table, close variants of which survive at the Brighton Pavilion,[38] on which were displayed elaborate glass cases. These contained, respectively, a marble arm supposedly from one of the Lapithae on the Parthenon metopes, and a stalactite from the grotto at Antiparos. Each of these was disposed 'upon a velvet cushion, with all the care of a costly jewel'.[39] Thomas Hope is sometimes regarded today merely as the champion of the austerest form of the Greek Revival. The rich eclecticism of Duchess Street should be sufficient to reveal the inadequacy of that picture, but that he should give precisely the same honour and emphasis to a stalactite as to a fragment by Pheidias creates the demand for some quite other reappraisal. To say that he saw them both in the same light may be an over-simplification, but he saw that they both combined rarity with remoteness or primitiveness. Each had classical associations, but it remained for him to create a refined and evocative setting in which art and nature could say their piece together. In this remarkable neo-classical attempt to suggest that the spirit of antique art is coincidental with that of eternal nature Hope was giving an idiosyncratic visual expression of the views of the painter William Hodges (1744–97). In his *Travels in India* (1793), Hodges discussed at length the architectural effect of the cave having been man's first home. He described the 'incrustations of snow-white spar or stalactite, which either form undulated hangings on their sides, or icicles dripping from their roofs in the shape of columns, pillars, &c.', and went on to point out that

Fig. 14. Thomas Hope, Egyptian Room, Duchess Street, *c.* 1800

'These are the peculiar glories and features of the grotto of Antiparos.'[40]

Following Hope's sequence of plates we leave the Flaxman Room and, crossing the Indian Room, enter the 'Egyptian or Black Room' (Fig. 14)[41] Here, the walls were adorned with a large frieze of figures from Egyptian papyrus rolls, the lunettes at two ends of the room being painted with feigned drapery, the martial associations of which made it popular in French Empire interiors. The segmental ceiling was painted in a criss-cross pattern to resemble quilting, and double doors—two sets on three sides of the room—were decorated in a rather similar way. The visitor must have felt as though he were shut inside a cushioned basket. 'The prevailing colours', wrote Westmacott echoing Hope's language, 'both of the furniture and ornaments are that pale yellow and bluish green which hold so conspicuous a rank among Egyptian pigments skilfully relieved by the occasional introduction of masses of black and gold.'[41] The accuracy of these descriptions of the colours of the sumptuous and uncompromising furniture is borne out by the curious wall-lights, now owned by the Duke of Wellington,[42] and by one of the two great couches and two of the four arm-chairs which survive today at Buscot Park, Berkshire, in all their bright archaic splendour as one of the prime monuments to Hope's imaginative genius (Plates 39 and 40). Their authoritative note is due partly to the characteristically opulent and permanent nature of their materials, partly to the historical accuracy of their decoration.[43] Thus the winged sun-god Ra appears in bronze on the rails of the arm-chairs, and the cow, symbol of the goddess Hathor, on their backs. The arm supports are formed by exquisitely detailed seated figures of Egyptian priests which are echoed in miniature by the canopic vases, also in bronze, which surmount the backs of the chairs. On the mahogany couch, panels are decorated with bronze mounts depicting the jackal-headed god Anubis facing the hawk-headed Horus; gilt brass scorpions appear on the sides; and the sacred beetle or scarab in bronze on the feet. The terminal blocks are surmounted by pairs of *couchant* lions finely carved in bronze. The rail, in black paint, is decorated with a frieze of gilt rosettes and the brackets beneath more than hint at Greek decorative forms. Some of the sources for Hope's Egyptian details will be outlined in the last chapter.

The materials in the room were exotic and monumental: granite and serpentine, porphyry and basalt. On a table opposite the windows stood a basalt cup flanked by two short obelisks containing idols and supporting canopic vases. Beneath the table crouched a lion also made from basalt. An identical table with similar ornaments stood opposite the chimney-piece. The chimney-piece itself was a striking feature carved in black marble in imitation of the façade of a sepulchral chamber hewn from the rock on the coast of Southern Turkey, near the site of the city of Antiphellos. Hope observed that it 'represents a screen of rude and massy timberwork in which may be discerned the upright posts, transverse beams, rafters, wedges, bolts.' He intended the composition to convey a sense of primitive monumentality and permanence, describing how the original works ' . . . amaze the intellect, through the immensity of their size, and the indestructibility of their nature.' He thus particularly censured the 'Modern imitations . . . of lath and of plaster, of callico and of paper, [which] offer no one attribute of solidity or grandeur . . . and can only excite ridicule and contempt.'[44] In so doing he anticipated Soane's sharp censure, in a lecture given after 1809, of 'the paltry attempt to imitate the character and form of . . . [Egyptian] works in small and confined spaces'.[45] If Hope's work could not entirely escape Soane's criticism, it certainly escaped his own. One imagines that even today the surviving pieces would long resist unpremeditated attempts at destruction.

By a pleasing conceit the picture over the chimney-piece depicted the 'Rest on the Flight into Egypt', by Louis Gauffier (1762–1801). On the wall opposite hung a curious composition by Gauffier painted in 1791.[46] Entitled 'Vanity', it depicted two Roman women in a courtyard of unfluted Greek Doric or Primitivist columns. A painting by Sablet of 'Ruins with Figures' hung between the windows and opposite was a painting possibly intended to depict the 'Finding of Moses', in which pyramid and temple played a more than usually dominant role. As in the Indian Room several apparently heterogeneous paintings were identically and unusually framed. Here they were given arresting star-studded borders and played an essential part in the whole decorative scheme. Since the arrangement and furnishing of these rooms was obviously so selfconscious and carefully deliberated a process, the mingling of cultures represented by these pictures must have been part of a definite plan. The spirit of an early and primitive culture, and that of classical Rome were interpreted, combined, and displayed by the daring hand of modern neo-classicism.

Some of the smaller Egyptian figures in this room, including the one in the centre of the chimney-piece, still survive in the collection of

Fig. 15. Thomas Hope, Sideboard in the Dining Room, Duchess Street, *c.* 1800

the present Duke of Wellington, but the prize exhibit was doubtless the Egyptian Mummy which lay in a glass case near the centre of the room. The case rested on a large block with sloping sides and open at the centre like a gateway. Two seated priests wearing animal masks guarded the entrance to this gateway, and over it hovered a winged Isis, emblematic of the immortality of the soul. Within this shrine stood, on the floor, an antique cinerary urn of Egyptian or oriental alabaster. Not, on the whole what one would expect to find in a gentleman's London drawing-room! But, of course, it is not so very far removed from the eerie tomb-like effect of Soane's Sculpture Museum at Lincoln's Inn Fields. It must be pointed out, however, that this part of Soane's house was not formed until 1808 and the magnificent sarcophagus for the Mummy of Seti I which was housed in the Sepulchral Chamber, was not acquired by Soane until as late as 1824.[47] At Lincoln's Inn Fields, moreover, there was no Mrs. Hope constantly throwing open the rooms and galleries to London society for her grand routs and balls. Were the cinerary urns and Mummies, one wonders, removed for these gay occasions? Probably not. The Regency man of taste could take these things in his stride.

The dining-room seems to have been altogether a more chaste and sober apartment (Fig. 15). Even here Hope's insistence on appropriate or symbolic decoration had resulted in a highly eccentric chimney-piece (Fig. 16). The centre-piece of this was the bust, carved by Flaxman in 1803, of Hope's brother Henry Philip. In accordance with Greek practice the pose of the bust, at Hope's request,[48] was severely frontal and not angled in the manner of Roman and later sculptors. Hope must be regarded as a pioneer in this aspect of the strict neo-classical aesthetic, so characteristic of the busts by Thorvaldsen. Henry Philip seems to have been known by the second of his Christian names since his bust is inscribed *φιλιππος*. The unusually large pair of antique horses' heads on either side of the chimney-piece, projecting far into the room from canted terms, were not the anomalies in a dining-room that they at first sight appeared. They were in fact justified because Philip in Greek means 'horse-lover'! In the same room the simple sideboard was appropriately adorned with the emblems of Bacchus and Ceres, and the cellaret beneath it with amphorae and figures 'allusive to the liquid element'.

Fig. 16. Thomas Hope, Chimney-piece in the Dining Room, Duchess Street, *c.* 1800

Perhaps the last room which the visitor entered and which Hope shows us in his plates was the most astonishing of all, certainly it was the one for which least precedent existed. This was the 'Lararium', a small 'Closet or Boudoir fitted up for the reception of a few Egyptian, Hindoo, and Chinese idols, and curiosities' (Fig. 17).[49] In this strange

Fig. 17. Thomas Hope, Lararium, Duchess Street, *c.* 1800

room pillars supported a ceiling of bamboo arches from which depended tasselled tent-like drapery. Equally arresting was the chimney-piece, the lower part of which, like that in the Egyptian Room, imitated Epyptian temple architecture, the stepped superstructure serving as a display stand for the idols and curiosities. The whole was set against a background of looking-glass creating that effect of ambiguous surprise familiar to us from the Soane Museum and from an elaborate chimney-piece designed by Percier and Fontaine for a Prince in Poland.[50]

Not only were the Eastern cultures represented but also the classical and the Christian. The whole stepped pyramid of the chimney-piece was surmounted by an early seventeenth-century Italian bronze of the famous Marcus Aurelius statue in Rome, while over the shelf was a wooden relief depicting Bacchus and Ariadne beneath a grape-vine. Balancing each other, somewhat surprisingly, were small busts of Dante and Napoleon in a semi-circular niche, the former by Flaxman; and there was also—not shown in Hope's view—a large ivory crucifix upon which the body of Christ was nearly two feet long.[51]

There could surely be no more cogent example than this amazing 'Lararium' of the kind of romantic historicism which, we suggest, characterized Thomas Hope and the late neo-classical movement. Within a light natural grotto of bamboo the different religions of the world are united together in terms of their romantic and artistic appeal. The new man investigates and displays the achievements of the past, but at one remove from them. His outlook is detached and relativist. Hope's 'Lararium', in which Hindu idol rubs noses with Christian crucifix, is little different in spirit from André Malraux's '*Musée Imaginaire*' and the belief which inspired it in the supremacy of art over life and, in Malraux's words, that modern man has inherited a world-culture in default of a religion.[52] A solid sofa from this room, originally with a figured frieze along the back (Fig. 27), survived, bereft of its frieze, in the collection of Edward Knoblock (Plate 37).

This completes the tour of those rooms which had been shown to visitors since the beginning of 1804. No major change seems to have been effected for fifteen years until in the autumn of 1819 Thomas

Hope added a gallery (Plate 41) in order to house the Hope Collection of about one hundred Dutch and Flemish paintings inherited by his brother Henry Philip. The accounts of Westmacott and of Britton and Pugin make it clear that Thomas Hope was the architect of this addition, William Atkinson—then supervising alterations at the Deepdene—the executant. Westmacott gives the dimensions of the gallery as 48 ft. by 22 ft., Britton and Pugin as 42 ft. by 19 ft. by 25 ft.[53] A continuous clerestory of round-headed lights, supported on shallow coving, was only slightly shorter in length and breadth than the whole room. The flat ceiling above this was coffered and adorned with gilt paterae. At one end, the panels of two mahogany doors were inlaid with classical figures and decorations finely engraved in brass—a device which appears again at the Deepdene. Round the end of the room opposite to these doors was a light-blue ottoman, and around the remaining walls were disposed beneath the pictures tables and bronze casts of classical sculptures. Down the centre of the room was an invention by Hope consisting of a mahogany screen displaying on each side ten paintings which could be swung on hinges for the greater ease of the connoisseur. Above these and on either side of them were a dozen ormolu lamp-brackets; and below were shelves or compartments designed to contain large folios of engravings and books on the fine arts. Along the top of this art-historian's paradise were ranged bronze figures and classical vases. The whole conception was in keeping with that new self-conscious attitude to the art of the past which prepared the way for the birth of art-history.

Hope's knowledge of and interest in such technical details connected with the display and study of works of art is one of the most consistent features of the house. It was, indeed, his own one-man achievement and since he felt that he could rely on no antecedent common tradition he became acquainted, Morris-like, with the technique of production in a way which in the immediate past few other connoisseurs could have done. In describing a writing-table he observed how 'the insulated ornaments ... are in bronze ... left simply to exhibit its own green patina',[54] are cast so as to be simply reproduced, do not weather or soil and can be removed to adorn new pieces of furniture or can perhaps be gilded, sometimes a necessary precaution in our damp climate. He realized that the superb con-

41. Thomas Hope and William Atkinson, Flemish Picture Gallery, Duchess Street, 1819, from a drawing by R. W. Billings

42. Picturesque view of Blenheim, 1825
43. THOMAS HOPE and WILLIAM ATKINSON, Deepdene, 1818–23

struction and the durability of his furniture set it in a class apart from much contemporary work, and complained that 'In England much more attention is generally paid to the perishable implements of the stable than to the lasting decoration of the house'. Whereas most modern furniture was constructed of materials as flimsy as its decorations were trivial and was, therefore, for ever being discarded and replaced, productions like his own 'may be preserved in families, from generation to generation, as a valuable portion of the patrimonial estate'.[55] This passionate desire to create something fixed and enduring for all time must be seen as an essential part of the full neo-classical aesthetic. While there doubtless exists a tendency, aggravated by the rise of popular education, for every age to regard itself as having reached a point from which advancement in material comfort would be as impossible as regression would be insupportable, the neo-classical approach, being one first and foremost of accumulation and synthesis, was especially prone to a belief that further development would be undesirable if not inconceivable.

Further technical details which Hope cited in favour of his furniture were that the metal and ebony inlay, which adorned the typical chair, were not only suited to mahogany, 'so much in use in this country', but also enlivened the appearance of the article without recourse to the raised ornaments which both get rubbed and collect dust and dirt. In Paris, of course, this technique was 'carried to a great degree of elegance and perfection',[56] so that the metal ornament and its ground of stained wood were stamped and cut out together.

To sum up the total effect of this remarkable house, let us quote a few words from Thomas Hope himself:

> In forming my collection and in fitting up my house, my object has neither been an idle parade of virtu, nor an ostentatious display of finery. I have observed with regret, that most persons employed in our manufactures or in furnishing our habitations, are rarely initiated even in the simplest rudiments of design, whence it has happened that immense expense has been employed in producing furniture without character, beauty or appropriate meaning.[17]

The triple requirement of 'character, beauty, and appropriate meaning' was emphasized by Hope a second time at the end of

Household Furniture, and we have shown the symbolical system which it engendered at Duchess Street. It is the creation of this whole evocative and narrative framework which distinguishes Hope so sharply from the collectors of earlier periods. He tends towards a kind of historical relativism that comes very close to that of the modern museum in which individual rooms are completely furnished in the different styles of the past. It must, at the same time, be remembered that he believed that the refining hand of neo-classicism could weld these styles into a new unity as well as make its own unique contribution. His furniture well exemplifies this, reiterating and amplifying as it does hints given by the works of art to which it was placed in immediate contiguity. The architect and designer Richard Brown, whose furniture designs are closely modelled on Hope's, actually recommended that the different rooms of the house be laid out in the styles of different centuries.[57] Thus, a walk through the 'period rooms' at the Victoria and Albert Museum—one of which contains furniture from the Duchess Street mansion—gives one a curious sensation of the neo-classical aesthetic, hardly intended by those who laid them out.

V

Hope and the Picturesque

There are three starting points for this chapter: firstly, a comparison between an early nineteenth-century Picturesque view of Blenheim (Plate 42)[1] and a view of the Deepdene (Plate 43); secondly, Thomas Hope's praise of Wyatt's Pantheon and his reference to its closeness to Hagia Sophia; and thirdly, his essay, *On the Art of Gardening*.

What the two views have in common is that they show architecture disposed in, almost scattered over, the landscape. The massing and irregular disposition, the jumping skyline, the rich and uneven play of light and shade, architecture as an incident in a dramatic landscape to which it is, ultimately, subordinate: that is what we see and that is what the Picturesque aesthetic was concerned to create. The eighteenth century came increasingly to believe that Vanbrugh had achieved this—even if it meant, as in this engraving, distorting his work to prove the point—and so gradually attempted to recreate it. Since no one dared to handle classical architecture asymmetrically, this process took a long time—in fact over a century. By 1823, however, the Deepdene had been remodelled by Thomas Hope as the apotheosis of the Picturesque in which architecture has taken on all the characteristics of landscape and, indeed, is barely discernible in the midst of it. Even the laundry-maid is subjected to the Picturesque discipline so that we can see her struggling up-hill through the dense undergrowth in order to deck with her damp sheets some suitably Picturesque eminence. The Picturesque aesthetic was invented in 1709 by Vanbrugh. For well over a century and, perhaps, for much longer, the theories which he outlined in his Memorandum of 11 June 1709 on the preservation of Woodstock Manor dominated much English artistic practice and theory. Thus the extraordinary attempt was made to make both nature and architecture look like what neither is: a picture.

The Memorandum is remarkable not so much because Vanbrugh wishes to preserve the building but because of the reasons he adduces for doing so. He argues for the preservation of buildings of distant times, because '... they move more lively and pleasing Reflections (than History without their aid can do) on the Persons who have inhabited them; on the remarkable things which have been transacted in them, or the extraordinary occasions of erecting them.'

Here the case is formulated for the first time for buildings that are evocative, associational, and which recall periods more remote and perhaps more colourful than our own. Vanbrugh continues:

> There is still more to be said on other considerations. That part of the Park which is seen from the North Front of the new building has little variety of objects Nor does the country beyond it afford any of value. It therefore stands in need of all the helps that can be given... Buildings and Plantations. These rightly dispos'd will indeed supply all the wants of Nature in that place. And the most agreeable disposition is to mix them: in which this old Manour gives so happy an occasion for; that were the enclosure filled with Trees (principally fine Yews and Hollys) promiscuously set to grow up in a wild thicket, so that all the buildings left might appear in two risings amongst 'em, it would make one of the most agreeable objects that the best of Landskip painters can invent.[2]

What is revolutionary here is this conscious savouring of the effects of the natural landscape and of its inter-relations with architecture, as early as 1709, when Louis XIV is still on his throne and is to be for another six years. We witness at the same time the birth of that idea that nature must be fulfilled, must be made more like herself than she really is, and that not by imposing on her a formal human discipline but by bringing out her latent characteristics. Thus a 'promiscuous' mingling of trees and irregular buildings set in a natural landscape, 'rightly dispos'd will indeed supply all the wants of Nature in that place'. This, with the romantic attitude to the past and the consequent emphasis upon the narrative, associational, and evocative characteristics of buildings, forms a deliberately Picturesque whole—Picturesque because the justification as well as the model for this heightening of the charms of the natural landscape are the idyllic pastoral scenes by 'the best of Landskip painters', that is the Bolognese eclectics and their French disciples.

Vanbrugh's Memorandum has been dwelt on because the theoreticians at the end of the century, Price, Knight, and even Hope himself, who are supposed to have invented Picturesque theory, produced hardly a single idea that the Memorandum does not contain in embryo. In answering the inevitable question of why Vanbrugh should have developed these revolutionary ideas so early, one begins at the most practical level. This is that his refurbishing of Woodstock Manor for his own occupation and without the Duchess of Marlborough's knowledge needed, when news of it was brought to her ears, a sudden and complete justification. Vanbrugh was thus forced to create the Picturesque theory on the spur of the moment as an excuse for his actions. Had the Duchess been a less forceful character, Vanbrugh's feeling for the Picturesque would doubtless have remained implicit rather than explicit. One ought also to take into account the circumstances in which Blenheim was built. It was from the start a monument of display to be built from almost unlimited resources. It was different, therefore, from Versailles to which it has been compared, for though Versailles was certainly a monument of display it also fulfilled a precise political and governmental function and provided lodgings for the numerous courtiers who were themselves a part of that system. But Blenheim had no such justification. Its sole *raisons d'être* were national pride, splendour, and aesthetic pleasure. The spirit is perfectly conveyed by the way in which numerous models of ornaments for the roof were hoisted up to the roof by workmen, while Duchess and architect stood back to select for execution those they found most aesthetically pleasing.[3] Thus the circumstances of Blenheim's erection encouraged just those tendencies towards the creation of pure aesthetics in which Vanbrugh had already begun to indulge at Castle Howard. What I point to here is his decisive abandonment of the traditional English grouping of the lord of the manor's house with the parish church and village houses. The old home of Henderskelfe Castle and the entire village and church were swept away to make way for the grand new mansion house.[4] Perhaps Vanbrugh was the first to do this. At any rate it became a norm in eighteenth-century England and its significance lies in the consequent creation of an independent cultured world divorced from the life of the manor or the church. To generalize, we may say that, in eighteenth-century terms, it is a concept essentially Whig and not Tory; and it is the Whigs for whom Vanbrugh worked and who at this moment begin to dominate the political and cultural life of the country from their vast bleak mansions, from Woburn, Holkham, and the rest, set proudly alone in the midst of parks miles from anywhere or anything. At Castle Howard, Vanbrugh and Hawksmoor created a whole world of drama and grandeur covering several square miles. If Versailles was linked on one side to its geometrical gardens, on the other to the geometrically planned town of Versailles, itself linked to Paris, Castle Howard was an heroic and magnificent inward-looking universe of its own, shut off from the outside world by an extraordinary chain of almost mediaeval fortifications, walls, and bastions. We feel that such ramparts must enclose the solitary Gothic dream of Beckford at Fonthill; and indeed this creation of an autonomous and private artistic domain is a recurrent feature of the Picturesque, governing the achievements of Thomas Johnes at Hafod as much as Thomas Hope at Deepdene.

What Vanbrugh had attempted in the way of outbuildings and fortifications at Castle Howard he repeated in miniature from 1717 onwards at his own house, Vanbrugh Castle on Maze Hill at Greenwich. There is a sense, indeed, in which this house is more Picturesque, grouped more freely with its landscape, than its offsprings Strawberry Hill and Downton Castle; only the Deepdene fulfilling all its promises. William Stukeley's view of 1721[5] shows how the house, with its subsidiary fortifications and gateways, formerly ran freely over the hill, interrupted by bursts of trees, as the Woodstock Memorandum had recommended. Vanbrugh had bought a considerable amount of land here which he crossed with winding paths and adorned with eccentric houses and gateways. Like the Claremont Belvedere, shaded romantically on its lofty hillock by Surrey pine and fern, Vanbrugh Castle looks essentially the creation of a later age than Vanbrugh's. This impression is heightened by its being built of a harsh, yellow-grey, London stock-brick that has neither weathered nor mellowed, so that the whole seems to have strayed from the abutments to some Early Victorian railway embankment.

This characteristic grand austerity first appeared in the hall at Blenheim. The hall at Castle Howard had been modern Roman—that is Baroque—whereas that at Blenheim was ancient Roman, a significant shift. The bold plain arcading of the Blenheim hall recalls some great Roman aqueduct, straddling a flat plain and seems to mark the beginning of that obsession with the austere heroic scale of Roman public buildings which the engravings of Piranesi so much encouraged and which was so fundamental to the development of Picturesque neo-classicism. This preoccupation of Vanbrugh's flowered in such creations of his imagination as the tall arched chimneys of Kings Weston (1711–14). These may well derive from Perrault's dramatic engraving of 1684 of a demolished Roman temple at Bordeaux, and, indeed, in the arcuated massiveness and the octagonal towers of his Paris Observatory (1667) Perrault had himself attempted to recapture something of this Roman romanticism.[6] Thus the text to a contemporary engraving of it by Perelle observes that: '... outre la Magnificence de sa Structure, on y voit une solidité qui la fait prendre de loin pour une Citadelle.'

How much that fortress-like spirit must have appealed to Vanbrugh, and how close to the Observatory is his own Seaton Delaval in plan and even elevation. But the plan of Seaton Delaval, as also of Vanbrugh's own houses at Esher and Greenwich is, at the same time, English and Jacobean in inspiration. For Vanbrugh's heroic mediaevalizing spirit had been anticipated in a chain of buildings which led from Wollaton to Hardwick and Lulworth and reached a climax in John Smythson's Bolsover Castle, Derbyshire (1612–16).[7]

It was exactly at the moment of Bolsover that Inigo Jones began his attempt to impose upon English architecture the cold forms of Italian Palladianism. But his attempt was not altogether popular or successful and there can be little doubt that Vanbrugh looked back beyond his smooth classicism to an heroic past of which Bolsover had been the latest evocation. And when Burlington re-echoed Jones' plea there were, again, those who found this unsatisfying, who felt that architecture ought really to be something altogether more grand and romantic than this. Vanbrugh stands between these two Palladian revivals, looking back to something more picturesque and heroic than even continental Baroque; and after Vanbrugh it was to be to Vanbrugh himself that men looked back. The key moments are these: Walpole on the Sublime at Castle Howard in 1772;[8] the Adam brothers' Preface of 1773;[9] Reynolds in his Discourse of 1786;[10] Price[11] in 1798; Knight in 1805;[12] and finally Soane in 1815, who, echoing Price, observed that: 'The young architect, by studying the Picturesque effects of his works will learn to avoid the dull monotony of minor Artists and be led to think for himself and acquire a taste for his own.'[13]

Dunglass, in Haddingtonshire (Plate 44), built for Sir James Hall, Bart., in 1807–13 by Richard Crichton, was a deliberate realization of Price's neo-Vanbrughian Picturesque recommendations.[14] Here, indeed, Hall went so far as to invite a landscape-painter, Alexander Nasmyth, to select a suitably Picturesque site for the house and to suggest its general disposition before ever the opinion of the architect had been sought. This was the inevitable and ultimate consequence of Vanbrugh's recommendation that architecture be governed by the same rules that governed 'the best of Landskip painters'.

Another aspect of the sympathy for Vanbrugh and the Picturesque is the desire to break down 'the dull monotony',[13] the four-square solidity of the Palladian apartment. Thus in the rooms of Adam and Wyatt, Dance and Soane, spatial relationships were blurred and veiled by means of concealed or top lighting and intricate vaulting arrangements. The 'swelling and sinking',[9] to use Adam's suggestive phrase, of his constant curves and apses occupy a pivotal place in this development. Thus even Byzantine architecture appealed to him and he made a fine drawing of the interior of San Vitale at Ravenna, making it appear almost Adamish in its decorative detailing.[15] This church's replacement, as Pevsner observes, of 'a clear spatial distinction by a floating and welling of space from the centre into the surrounding outer layer',[16] struck a particular chord in Adam's heart. He also owned a drawing of Hagia Sophia at Constantinople. Nor is it a coincidence that the interior of Wyatt's Oxford Street Pantheon of 1770 was based not, as its title suggests, on the Roman Pantheon but on Hagia Sophia. Thus Wyatt, too, at the start of his career evinced dissatisfaction with the Roman/Palladian idea of even a domed space. This brings us back to Thomas Hope and to the second of the three reference-points which were indicated at the beginning of this chapter. The Pantheon was the only building by Wyatt which Hope was prepared to praise and in so doing he was the first to point out that Hagia Sophia was its model. In criticizing Wyatt's Downing designs in 1804, he observed that:

> The portico is that, not of the Roman Pantheon, but of the Pantheon in Oxford-Street; and however much credit I am willing to give the archi-

tect of that temple of pleasure for the inside thereof, though borrowed from the very different kind of temple consecrated by Emperor Justinian to Divine Wisdom, yet I must doubt that a man of taste would ever quote its outside portico among the fine architectonic productions of our time.[17]

The Picturesque and exotic impact made by the Pantheon is also revealed in the rather more imprecise reflections on it of Horace Walpole. In April 1771 he observed: 'It amazed me myself. Imagine Balbec in all its glory!', and in a letter of a year later he enlarged on his reactions:

> There has been a Masquerade at the Pantheon, which was so glorious a vision that I thought I was in the old Pantheon, or in the Temple of Delphi or Ephesus, amidst a crowd of various nations, and that formerly *Panthoides Euphorbus eram*, and did but recollect what I had seen. All the friezes and niches were edged with alternate lamps of green and purple glass, that shed a most heathen light, and the dome was illuminated by a heaven of oiled paper well painted with gods and goddesses.[18]

This romantic widening to a point beyond the merely Roman of the range of references of the Classical Revival, so as to include Byzantine spatial effects and an atmosphere of Delphic mystery and drama, is obviously central to our period. A parallel are the Picturesque extravaganzas, the romantic compositions of semi-ruinous classical buildings,[19] which were the obsessive product of Adam's spare time. It is hard to resist the thought that these Piranesian visions are what he would really have chosen to execute had his clients allowed him. Indeed in 1786 he illustrated two projects for ruinous bridges 'in imitation of the Aquaducts of the Ancients',[20] designed to adorn the parks at Bowood and Sion. Beyond this there is a point to be made so obvious that it is normally overlooked, namely that the views of his interiors in his *Works in Architecture* do not illustrate them as they really are, but as if they were the Picturesque compositions in light and shade that he spent his spare time in devising. To see Adam in this light makes clearer his position in the Picturesque movement than if we seek, as is sometimes done, a Picturesque handling of external forms at Compton Verney or at Osterley. Moreover, his fantastic drawings surely place him in a line of development from Piranesi to

Gandy. All three used the fanciful, highly imaginative and Picturesque, creative architectural drawing as a method of escape from the strait-jacket of classicism. All three were obsessed by decay in one form or another.

For Soane, too, Vanbrugh was, as he put it, 'the Shakespeare of architects',[21] and where Vanbrugh had landscaped his exteriors Soane was to landscape his interiors. And indeed the liberation movement, the concern for Picturesque spatial ingenuity from Wyatt's Pantheon to the Soane Museum, is normally an affair of interiors only, which is why the Deepdene stands out the more remarkably. Dance's marvellously lit and vaulted rooms at Cranbury Park, Hampshire, of the 1790s are the missing link between Adam and Soane. Soane's work is, of course, the climax and apotheosis of the Picturesque interior. As early as 1792 in his diagram for the Bank Stock Office he had discarded the Adamesque trappings which had still adorned his spatial experiments in the drawing-room at Wimpole, and had landscaped an interior letting the wind, as it were, blow through it and form its undulations so that we almost feel we are walking through woodland opened out by Capability Brown. Later in life he created a more complex and intricate spatial ingenuity as in the suspended canopy-vault of the Privy Council Chamber in Whitehall (1823–4). Soane may have taken the idea for such a suspended vault with side windows rising above it from the ingenious vaulting and lighting arrangements in the side aisles of Henry VII's chapel at Westminster Abbey. Where the aisle fan-vaults meet the outer walls of the aisles they are suspended three-dimensionally in the air, touching the walls only at the shafts dividing the bays, so that the undulating windows reach up above them and free of them, throwing their umbrella-like form into dramatic silhouette. Again, the point to be made is that which we learn from Hope's observations on the Pantheon: how *recherché* the neo-classical architect became in his attempts to enliven the classical discipline with a new Picturesque vigour. Indeed it was realized in Soane's own day that a close parallel could be drawn between his own work and that of the landscape architect. Thus in 1827 John Britton, at a time when he was engaged in recording the external Picturesque effects of the Deepdene, pointed out how admirable a description of the Soane Museum interiors were Pope's lines of advice to Lord Burlington on the art of gardening: 'Let not each beauty ev'rywhere be spy'd When half the skill is decently to hide. He gains all points who pleasingly confounds Surprizes, varies and conceals the Bounds.'[22]

Once in the world of landscape-gardening we are at the heart of the Picturesque. Thomas Hope's position in and contribution to the development of this must now be discussed, using as a basis our third reference-point, his essay *On the Art of Gardening*, published in 1808[23] and again in 1819 as a preface to Mrs. Hofland's lavish publication on the Duke of Marlborough's house and gardens at Whiteknights. A superficial glance at this essay would suggest that Hope had diverged decisively from the Picturesque. Thus the essay opens with the following condemnation of current practice and theory: 'It has been much the fashion of late years, in this country, to commend no features in that product of human industry, a Garden, which should not appear as if still remaining the mere spontaneous work of unassisted Nature.' He complains how, 'Surfeited at last with symmetry carried to excess, we have suddenly leaped to the other extreme', so that: 'From the threshold of the still ever symmetric mansion one is launched in the most abrupt manner into a scene wholly composed of the most unsymmetric and desultory forms of mere Nature, totally out of character with those of that mansion.'[24] This was the central problem in the phase of the Picturesque inaugurated by Price and Knight. It was the result not merely of a dissatisfaction with the method of landscaping employed by Capability Brown, but with the dichotomy between the regular Palladian villa and the irregular landscaped park. Pevsner argues, from an interpretation of the multiform meanings given in the eighteenth century to the word 'nature', that for the men who originally laid out these houses and gardens there was no such dichotomy.[25] While this is doubtless true, it is equally true that by 1800 a dichotomy was felt to exist and that the method of resolving it, of making a unity of building and setting, was either to architecturalize the landscape or to landscape the architecture. Thus, in an implied criticism of the obsession of Price and Knight with 'rough' ivy-clad architecture, Hope observes that since some of us have been '. . . unable to make the grounds harmonize with the mansion, we attempt to harmonize the mansion with the grounds, by converting that mansion itself into a den or quarry.' He especially censures

> . . . the total exclusion of all the variety, the relief, the sharpness, which, straight, or spherical, or angular, or other determinate lines and forms might have given to unsymmetric and serpentining forms and surfaces . . . [since] Nature herself . . . superadds those features of regular symmetry of colours and shapes, which . . . form a more striking contrast with the more desultory modifications of her huger masses.

And so, in a passage almost Ruskinian in the acuity and perception of its organic descriptions, Hope observes that if we 'Examine the radii of the snow-spangle, the facettes of the chrystal, the petals of the flower, the capsules of the seed, the wings, the antennae, the rings, the stigmata of the insect and the butterfly . . . we shall find . . . [there] reigns the nicest symmetry of outline and correspondence of parts.' So we see how Hope the chaste Greek was driven by the Picturesque to make a detailed first-hand observation of Nature in her most minute and fundamental aspects. Yet, as is characteristic of the moment, the scientific symmetry which he perceived in the organic world was used by him only to justify a further heightening of Picturesque romanticism. Hence a purple patch in which he praises the effects of

> . . . the suspended gardens within Genoa, and of the splendid villas about Rome . . . those striking oppositions of the rarest marbles to the richest verdure; those mixtures of statues, and vases, and balustrades, with cypresses, and pinasters, and bays; those distant hills seen through the converging lines of lengthened colonnades; those ranges of aloes and cactuses growing out of vases of granite and of porphyry scarce more symmetric by art than these plants are by nature.

If the first or Capability Brown phase of the Picturesque had been initiated by Vanbrugh's drawing of attention to Italian landscape paintings, and the second was the move of Price and Knight away from Brown's artificial smoothness, the third phase was the result of a more empirical observation of the gardens which the Italians themselves had formed within their so much admired landscapes. In this third phase Hope appears as something of a pioneer. He goes on to indicate the new unity between house and setting which might be created by the new wave of Italianism:

> ... the cluster of highly adorned and sheltered apartments that form the mansion ... shoot out, as it were, into ... ramifications of arcades, porticoes, terraces, parterres, treillages, avenues, and other such still splendid embellishments of art, calculated by their architectural and measured forms, at once to offer a striking and varied contrast with, and a dignified and comfortable transition to, the more undulating and rural features of the more extended, more distant, and more exposed boundaries.

The justification for regarding this development as part of the Picturesque movement is that Hope is anxious to show how it can be reconciled with the precise aesthetic demands made by Price and Knight: '... if we wish for variety, for contrast, and for brokenness of levels, we can only seek it in arcades and in terraces, in steps, balustrades, regular slopes, parapets ... we cannot', he adds sternly, 'find space for the rock and the precipice'.[26]

In order to place Hope's views historically some account must be given of the varying tendencies within the development of the Picturesque movement. The landscape-garden, though first appearing in a complex rather Rococo form, was the child of that new, liberal, and rational world of the early eighteenth century which was determined to harmonize its activities with what was being revealed by Newton and others as the eternal order of the universe. Thus the well-known epitaph on Newton by Pope captures perfectly the spirit of the moment: 'Nature and Nature's laws lay hid in Night: God said, *Let Newton be*!, and All was *Light*.'[27] For the garden to partake of this light and clarity, then, all that was necessary was for it to imitate Nature and Nature's laws. Whether this implied an imitation of Nature as she is, or in the tamed idealized form first captured in the gardens of the ancients was an ambiguity never to be resolved. It was, of course, an ambiguity that had existed among the ancients themselves. This had been revealed in an important publication of 1728 dedicated to Burlington, called *The Villas of the Ancients Illustrated*, by Robert Castell.[28] Castell showed that Pliny's garden contained not only portions laid out formally in strict regularity, but also an *Imitatio Ruris* with hills, rocks, and cascades in an agreeable disorder like the confusion of many landscape scenes, and a *Pratulum*, a compromise between the two which imitated Nature in her simplest most charming aspects, at once preserving her irregularity and disposing the parts with the greatest art. Now it was exactly this compromise, this balance, which was the precarious achievement of the mid-eighteenth century as typified by Capability Brown. The slightest shift in emphasis would clearly be sufficient to tilt the scales in favour of the regular garden. And the growing concern of the century for something more fundamental, more primitive—the Greek Doric, the savage Norse Sagas of the poet Gray—the embarrassment at the sweet artificiality of the moment, which even Adam felt about his own work, so producing his roughly romantic compositions—led to a weighting of the scales away from the smooth *Pratulum* in favour of the wilder *Imitatio Ruris*. The appearance of the fully formulated Picturesque aesthetic in the 1790s is the formal justification for this swing to a wilder irregularity. The Picturesque theoreticians, Gilpin, Price, Knight, Repton, and Hope, were all united in their antipathy to the placid artificiality of the Capability Brown park. To that manner they would prefer almost anything, even the old-fashioned formal garden. And it is especially significant that they should do so, for the formal garden is one of the two extremes that the *Pratulum* will tend to fade off into once the balanced compromise is upset. Thus, surprisingly, Price, Knight, and Repton are all mildly enthusiastic about the old English terraced garden. Their reasons are in part negative, that is to say that they perversely forced themselves into a position of admiring anything which Capability Brown thought objectionable. Uvedale Price's own position, always confused with that of the painter, as regards the Italianate architectural garden may be appreciated in this quotation from his Essay *On Decorations near the House*:

> I know very little of the history of the old Italian gardens, and of their dates; but it is probable that several of them, which may have served as models for those of later times, were made during the most flourishing period of painting—and as some of the greatest painters were likewise architects, and were employed by their patrons in making designs for the *houses* of their villas, it is not improbable that they might have been consulted about the *gardens*.[29]

In the following years Price and Knight saw the path that taste was likely to take and in 1805 Knight spoke enthusiastically of 'the hanging terraces of the Italian gardens', observing of them that 'Such decorations are, indeed, now rather old fashioned; but another revolution in taste, which is probably at no great distance, will make them new again.'[30]

Two years later these tentative Italianate enthusiasms were formulated by Thomas Hope for the first time into a whole-hearted and coherent recommendation of the Italian architectural garden. His Picturesque evocation of distant hills framed by cypress and balustrade was to become in the popular imagination the background for romance of all kinds, from his own day to at least the 1930s. Passages in Repton's *Fragments on the Theory and Practice of Landscape Gardening* of 1816 suggest that he was becoming ever more inclined to accept the formal garden, but he died two years later without ever having created one, even on a small scale.

Perhaps at about the time of writing his essay *On the Art of Gardening* Hope made the designs for a villa which are reproduced in Plates 46 and 47.[31] These clearly show *one* of the two Picturesque solutions to the eighteenth-century dichotomy, but not the other. They show, that is, the landscaping of architecture but not yet the architecturalization of the landscape. Observe how with their low spreading roofs juxtaposed against a taller pivotal tower, the loosely grouped limbs of the villa precisely echo the forms of the trees which are so intimately linked with them. Attached to the designs are notes, also in Hope's hand, which draw attention to what he believes to be their especial merits. First and foremost comes the essentially Picturesque notion of the importance of growth and change: 'It is to be observed', Hope's account opens, 'that No additions can spoil the regularity of this plan'. The other observations are all of a practical not an aesthetic nature. Thus Hope points out how

> . . . the doors of the drawing room are so situated as not to occasion any draught . . . there is a staircase placed between the eating room, and the servants hall, in order to prevent the noise in the latter being heard . . . The kitchen is at the further end of the house in order to prevent any smell, yet near enough for dinner to come up hot . . . The ladies chamber communicates separately with the passage and entrance so that she may either go out, or have access to any room separately, without being obliged to pass thro' any other. Her closets are perfectly retired and

secluded from both noise and sight and can be overlooked from no room whatever . . . All the rooms are on the same floor, except the servants bedrooms, which being over the offices, and having a staircase entirely to themselves form a distinct quarter, entirely unconnected with the rest.

This immense concern for the practical conveniences of the day-to-day running of a small house is one of the most noticeable contributions to architecture of the Picturesque aesthetic and its preoccupation with the *genius loci*. It is interesting to see how even Hope, the grand connoisseur dwelling in marble halls and whose own kitchens he had probably never so much as entered, was impelled by his Picturesque enthusiasms to make convenient arrangements for the placing of the coal-hole, the lighting of the scullery. Yet despite these mundane preoccupations one cannot but feel that Picturesque and impractical aesthetics govern the design as a whole. Thus though the square tower at the back is the essential visual pivot to the whole composition, it is impossible to place its foundation walls when we look at the ground-floor plan. At another level, the whole Villa seems designed for a climate at once more clement and less variable than the English. Assuming that the drawing-room window faces south, then it is the only one in the whole house to do so; even if it faces west, the only south-facing window is that of the second bedroom. And this drawing-room window looks, in Hope's view, for all the world like a screen of open columns. The plan, of course, suggests that it is not but from the purely aesthetic point of view it would obviously be preferable if the climate allowed it to be. Again, the circular room no. 17, envisaged by Hope as a 'Boudoir, library, or bath', would be in the latter case calculated to produce a chill in the hardiest individual, it being connected with the bedrooms only by a draughty open veranda. Having made these small criticisms, the significance of the designs remains: they represent an attempt to achieve Picturesque irregularity in terms of the classical tradition, whereas the overwhelming majority of such attempts fell back on the Gothic style as a ready-made answer, as an easy way out.

Precisely this attitude towards Gothic is criticized by Payne Knight in *An Analytical Inquiry into the Principles of Taste* (1805), which Hope had probably read by the time of making these designs, certainly by the time of his essay, *On the Art of Gardening*. Knight observed:

Country Life

44. Richard Crichton, Dunglass, 1807–13

45. Henry Goodridge, Lansdowne Tower, 1825

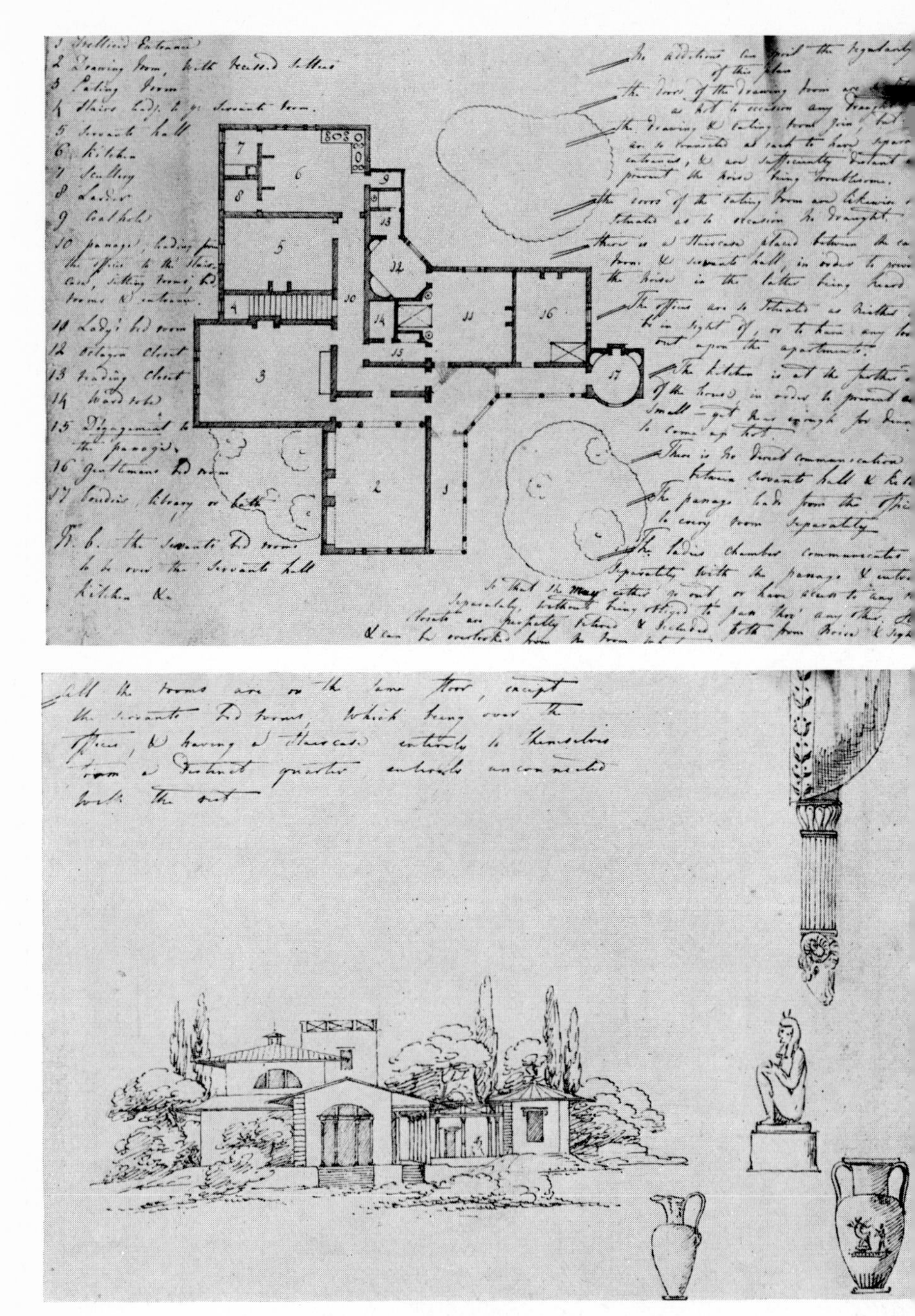

THOMAS HOPE, Design for a Villa

46. Plan 47. Elevation

'Some few attempts have lately been made to adopt the exterior forms of country-houses to the various characters of the surrounding scenery, by spreading them out into irregular masses: but ... our ideas of irregularity in buildings of this kind, have been habitually associated with those of the barbarous structures of the middle ages ...' Although at his own house, Downton Castle, he had used castellated architecture in order to create irregularity, he justified Downton by claiming that it possessed 'the advantage of being capable of receiving alterations and additions in almost every direction, without injury to its genuine and original character.'

It hardly needs to be pointed out how close to this is Hope's own observation about his villa design, that 'no additions can spoil the regularity of this plan'. But Knight also went on to outline a new phase of the Picturesque which Hope was not to take up until his designs for the Deepdene. Knight continues:

> It has already been observed that the architecture of the Gothic castles ... is of Grecian or Roman origin, but if it were not, there could be no impropriety in employing the elegancies of Grecian taste and science, either in the external forms and proportions, or interior decorations of houses built in that style: for, surely, there can be no blamable inconsistency in uniting the different improvements of different ages and countries in the same object ...

Finally, he comes down decisively in favour of a belief that:

> The best style of architecture for irregular and picturesque houses, which can now be adopted, is that mixed style, which characterizes the buildings of Claude and the Poussins: for as it is taken from models, which were built piecemeal during many successive ages; and by several different nations, it is distinguished by no particular manner of execution, or class of ornaments; but admits of all promiscuously, from a plain wall or buttress, of the roughest masonry, to the most highly wrought Corinthian capital.[32]

If Cronkhill, to which we shall return later, and the Deepdene are the buildings which put into practice most fully Knight's proposals, an intermediary stage, forming a close parallel to Hope's villa designs, is represented by J. M. Gandy's two volumes published in 1805, of *Designs for Cottages, Cottage Farms and other Rural Buildings* and *The Rural Architect*. The surprisingly free and irregular little buildings that Gandy shows are in a less sophisticatedly Pompeiian, a more consciously vernacular manner than Hope's, but nevertheless constitute a close parallel to Hope's. In the preface to this volume Gandy speaks of '... a question submitted to the Public, whether Architectural Designs, in general should be uniform, that is, having corresponding fronts on each side of a centre, or whether they should be composed of parts dissimilar, though harmonious'. Gandy himself obviously came down firmly on the side of buildings 'composed of parts dissimilar, though harmonious', a phrase which aptly summarizes the artistic method employed by Hope in his villa designs. It is not surprising, then, that Gandy dedicated to Hope this first volume of his designs, published in January 1805. Hope, he observed in the dedication, is 'a Name which will ensure respect wherever the Arts are known'. It seems reasonable to assume that Gandy had seen such drawings by Hope as those we have been discussing and that they had together debated the possibilities of this new style.

One of the few buildings actually erected in this free vernacular manner was Cronkhill in Shropshire by Nash. Built in about 1802 for Lord Berwick's agent at nearby Attingham Park, a house whose interiors Nash was remodelling in a subdued Empire style, the original design in the Soane Museum shows unexecuted outbuildings and windows in a style extremely close to Gandy's 1805 designs and to Hope's villa plan. There is even at one point a small spire. Exactly this feature, borrowed from romantic Italian landscape-paintings, reappears at the dairy and kitchen wing of the Deepdene. The source for Cronkhill, and probably also for Nash's Sandridge Park, Devon (1805), was undoubtedly sketches in Claude's *Liber Veritatis*. These were certainly used as a source by Uvedale Price and are referred to by him as often as the actual paintings themselves. Indeed, he describes[33] a picturesque bridge over a ravine, no. 67 in the *Liber Veritatis*, which may have inspired a high bridge erected by Thomas Hope at the Deepdene. We know that Knight possessed as many as 273 drawings by Claude which he left to the British Museum in 1824.

A later but related development is the work of Henry Edmund Goodridge (*c.* 1800–63). I refer especially to his Lansdowne Tower of 1825 (Plate 45) and a house of three years later on Bathwick Hill, not previously attributed to him, called Montebello (Plates 48 and 49). Lansdowne Tower was built for Beckford whose Fonthill Abbey had been in every sense a landmark in the Picturesque movement, and not least because of its cross-shaped plan. Such a plan, apart from creating variety, depth, and richness is particularly susceptible to growth and additions. Its influence is seen in designs like that of Hope's for an irregular villa and even, perhaps, in Barry's eminently Picturesque new Palace at Westminster. However, Hope seems to have sown doubts about Fonthill in Beckford's mind, by observing in 1804: 'I have often regretted that in the new building at Fonthill, where had the Grecian orders been employed, a mansion might have arisen, unrivalled in the most distant parts of the island, a style had on the contrary been adopted, which subjected every one of its details to disadvantageous comparisons with the cathedral at Salisbury.'[34]

We are fortunate in possessing, in the unpublished typescript of the Farington Diary, an account of Beckford's immediate reaction to Hope's criticisms of the as yet uncompleted Fonthill. On 29 March 1804, the month in which the Downing pamphlet appeared, Beckford gave dinner in London to Benjamin West. Afterwards, Beckford read the pamphlet for the first time and, as Farington reported, 'He said Tom Hope was right in his remarks. He said He felt the force of what he observed of the Abbey at Fonthill.'[35] Hope had probably visited Fonthill, and in 1805 was 'making assiduous love' to Beckford's younger daughter. There are reasons for supposing that Beckford was anxious for his daughter to accept Hope's advances, looking most favourably on this wealthy connoisseur as a prospective son-in-law. However, in 1810 his younger daughter married the Marquess of Douglas and Clydesdale, heir to the Duke of Hamilton, a far greater catch than Thomas Hope since it landed a peerage, as much desired for their respective families by Beckford as by Hope. And the references to Hope in 1807 and 1822 in Beckford's letters to Franchi only suggest a further gloating over possessions lacked by Hope.[36] However, when commissioning for himself a new towered residence in 1825, he repented of his Picturesque extravagance in the Gothic taste at Fonthill and jumped, instead, on to the neo-classical band wagon. In the sophisticated and imaginative classical composition of the Lansdowne Tower,[37] described by Brockmann surprisingly as a 'rather dull design',[38] Goodridge showed Beckford how he could follow Hope's advice about 'employing the Grecian orders' to create 'a mansion . . . unrivalled in the most distant parts of the island', and yet still be Picturesque. To emphasize the point, Beckford laid out, between it and his house in Lansdowne Crescent, a chain of gardens forming Picturesque vistas with waving pampas-grass and pools, a grotto and 'the finest ride upon turf in Europe'.[39]

Goodridge went on to develop this theme further at Bath. To the man of truly Picturesque sensibility, Bath was thought by the 1800s to be no more Picturesque than Capability Brown. In the course of a discussion on the Picturesque value of the skyline, Price observed that:

> . . . the summits of mere houses in towns, may be very material in the general view; as when a town happens to be placed on the side of a hill, where the ascent is steep, and the ground irregular—for, as in such cases the houses rise above each other with sudden changes in their level and direction, their tops are more distinctly seen, and from a greater variety of different points. In situations of that kind, were an architect with a painter's eye, to have the planning of the whole, he would have an opportunity of producing the richest effects, by combining his art with that of painting—by varying the characters of the buildings, and particularly of their summits, according to the place which they were to occupy . . . As I recollect my admirations of the circumstances I have just mentioned at Tivoli, so I remember my disappointment the first time I approached Bath . . . how little the buildings are made to yield to the ground, and how few trees are mixed with them . . .[40]

In the 1820s the steep upper slopes of Bathwick Hill, commanding a magnificent vista southwards towards Combe Down and Prior Park, were as yet undeveloped. The young Goodridge, quite possibly inspired by the Price passage just quoted, saw and took this opportunity of bringing the true Picturesque to Bath. Thus in 1828 he began to build for himself on a choice site half way up the hill an asymmetrical, classical or Italianate villa which he called, very properly, Montebello. Terraced houses had been built much lower down the hill—the kind criticized by Uvedale Price—but this was the first large detached villa in Bathwick. It is obviously within the tradition of Cronkhill and the Hope villa design, but one's fears that, like much Picturesque building, it will just be a tawdry affair of stucco are not justified. Goodridge had the advantage of fine Bath stone and, like his Northumberland contemporary John Dobson, was a master in the subtle handling of bands of razor-sharp masonry. This is particularly in evidence at the octagonal tower at the south end of the house, which is of a sophisticated originality that just escapes being Italianate. Like details of the Lansdowne Tower, it is probably inspired by the Tower of the Winds. The tent-like conservatory at the other end of the house has a distinct Regency feel, but the campanile rising above and behind it is, on the other hand, a foretaste of the heavy Italianism of the immediate future. Goodridge's purpose in erecting this villa was partly to house his growing collection of Italian paintings, a number of which he acquired from his patron Beckford.[41] The new Italianism proved popular and, under Goodridge's influence, Bathwick Hill came to be to Bath what Fiesole was to Florence. Montebello was thus joined by villas known as Casa Bianca, La Casetta, and Fiesole. Goodridge's Casa Bianca, set at the summit of a steep slope next door to Montebello, has already made the transition to the solid Italianism of the Early Victorian villa, with its first-floor loggia framed by an opening of pilaster-strips in the form of a Venetian window and its inevitable tower. Opposite Montebello there rose in *c.* 1832 another rambling Italianate villa called Oakwood built, again as a picture-gallery, by Benjamin Barker.[42] The grounds of this villa slope irregularly down to Smallcombe Valley. The Italophile Walter Savage Landor, whose life was divided between villas in Fiesole and Bath, described Bath as England's Florence;[43] and a slightly later atmosphere is caught in a romantic evocation of 1864 which recounts how 'at the end of Henrietta Street, a precipitous wooded hill arises, thickly dotted with villas, and at night illuminated by stars of gas-light, that twinkle through so many casements'.[44] Thus Goodridge's Picturesque experiment at Bath shows how, encouraged by a dramatic 'Italian' landscape, it merged imperceptibly into an Italianate Revival. We have already observed this shift in the Picturesque theoreticians and the next chapter will show it in some detail at the Deepdene.

So far we have discussed only examples of the Picturesque landscaping of architecture. The time has come to show an example of that being combined with the architecturalization of the landscape. A perfect instance of this is provided by the Grange, Hampshire, discussed in the chapter on the Greek Revival. What concerns us about it at the moment is the heroic attempt made after the Napoleonic Wars to bring this uncompromising block-like house into line with the latest theories of the Picturesque.[45] Designed by an architect who in 1804 had been a protégé of Thomas Hope it was already out of date on its completion in 1809, since by 1808 Hope had moved on to a position of attacking those 'modern archiects [who] apply the vigorous symmetry of the ancient temple . . . to the private habitation'[46] of a modern Englishman.

Now exactly these sentiments were echoed in a description of the Grange written in 1826, in which the question was raised: ' . . . how far those cumbrous proportions and that Doric severity, which according to Vitruvius were reserved to honor the major deities, are applicable to the purposes of villa architecture'.

The anonymous author, probably J. C. Loudon, censures Wilkins' transformation of a seventeenth-century country-house into a Greek temple, on the grounds, principally, that ' . . . convenience . . . [has] suffered considerably in the adaption of the templar style, and by heightening the ground floor . . . without acquiring those noble proportions of which this operation has totally deprived the upper floor'.[47]

Again, Hope was to condemn those who, 'by building houses in the shape of temples have contrived for themselves most inappropriate and uncomfortable dwellings'.[48] The happy solution at the Grange was to call in C. R. Cockerell to add a lower 'L'-shaped wing at the south-west end of the Wilkins house and then to link the whole yet more firmly to the setting by means of a conservatory and architectural gardens (Plates 50 and 51). Cockerell's elegant Ionic design for the dining-room, with a chimney piece by Flaxman,[49] is on paper watermarked 1821 and survives at the R.I.B.A. Library. This would have been the first room to be added, since it adjoined the old house. Then, at right angles to it, were added 'the ladies' apartments',[50] which opened into the lavish conservatory. We know that this was erected in the autumn of 1824 and that the gardens were added in 1825–6.[51] The effect of these extensions was to throw out an embracing arm, as it were, to force the house to lie down with the landscape. In doing so, much that we regard as characteristically Victorian was anticipated. Thus the conservatory, 70 ft. long by 40 ft. wide and 21 ft. high, had been manufactured entirely from iron and glass by Messrs. Jones and Clark in Birmingham, and then, transported to Hampshire, workmen had reassembled it, Crystal Palace-like, on the spot. It was believed at the time, probably correctly, that it was 'not surpassed by anything of the kind in the United Kingdom'.[50] Moreover, the designs for the large formally Italianate gardens, before the west and east fronts, are probably the earliest in the country. The whole house, then, affords a perfect example of the way in which Picturesque planners felt obliged to impart to the house something of the irregularity of the natural setting, and to the setting something of the formality of the house. As was remarked of the Grange in the *Gardener's Magazine* in 1826: 'The ornamental scenery, immediately surrounding the garden, fronting the house, partakes of the symmetry of its architecture; [though] it is not entirely finished . . .'[51]

With the development of the Italian garden went, as we began to see at Goodridge's Montebello, an Italianate architecture. Since the round arch was felt to be more plastic and Picturesque than the straight column, this style combined features from the Early Christian, Byzantine, Romanesque, and Italian architectures into an amalgam best summed up as the *Rundbogenstil.* Though Thomas Hope never designed in this manner, he made an important contribution to the literature of the subject by his detailed studies of Early Christian, Italian Romanesque and Gothic of which plates from his own drawings formed, rather surprisingly, the bulk of the illustrations to his *Historical Essay on Architecture.* It cannot be doubted that the plates in this standard two-volumed work, published posthumously in 1835, formed an essential source-book for many an early Early Victorian architect. As early as 1792 Samuel Pepys Cockerell had remodelled the old Norman church at Tickencote in Rutland in a Norman style.[52] He provided the open-topped south tower and inscribed the exteriors with a precise calligraphic decoration whose sharp abstract clarity is somehow almost savage and coarse. A version of this style achieved a menacing and compelling expression in two buildings designed by Fontaine. The Chapelle Expiatoire was erected for Louis XVIII in the

Rue d'Anjou, Paris, in 1815–26 to house the remains of Louis XVI and Marie-Antoinette in an attempt to expiate the crime of regicide. Though the austere interior of the chapel could have been executed for Napoleon, the cloisters are in the macabre part Romanesque, part Gothic, part Classical manner of these strange years of transition.[53] It appears again, with none of its novelty lost, in the Chapelle-Saint-Ferdinand erected by the same architect in the Avenue Pershing at Neuilly. The Duke of Orléans had been killed in a carriage accident near the spot, and the chapel was raised in 1843 to his memory. The interior is a parallel to that of the Chapelle Expiatoire, whereas the outside, and especially the porch,[54] is adorned in a wild yet mechanical manner that refuses to be Italianate, Romanesque, or Classical.

At this point we must return to Goodridge. Exactly five years after the Chapelle-Saint-Ferdinand he added an impressive entrance-range (Plate 52) to the gardens surrounding the Tower at Lansdowne which he had built for Beckford. This is a fine composition of high originality, grouping picturesquely with the Tower itself. Its imaginative and sharply-cut detailing is at once part of the contemporary Romanesque revival and yet looks back to Soane. Thus the frequent half-cylindrical acroteria echo the dumpy 'swiss-roll' forms which adorn oddly the Soane family tomb of 1816 in St. Pancras Gardens. The strange and harsh eclecticism at Lansdowne, however, is softened by the Picturesque, by the winding path that leads to the unexpected vista framed by the piquant fronds of the monkey-puzzle.

Perhaps the most amazing expression of this savagely detailed almost mystically intense Romanesquoid manner are Thomas Hopper's interiors of the 1830s and 40s at Penrhyn Castle, Caernarvonshire. The flight of fancy is furthest in the design of the staircase (Plate 53), where the truncated umbrella-pendentives, evocative of Dance, and especially the adjacent lunettes are encrusted with a seething yet metallic decoration almost Indian in its remote profusion. With that, of course, we are some way from the world of Hope, but he can nevertheless be seen as occupying, theoretically, a position in the *Rundbogenstil* movement which captured men's imaginations between the two successive waves of Italianism: the 'Claudeian' and the 'Renaissance'. His studies of Early Christian, Byzantine, and Italian

HENRY GOODRIDGE, Montebello, *c.* 1828–30
48. View from the road 49. Garden front

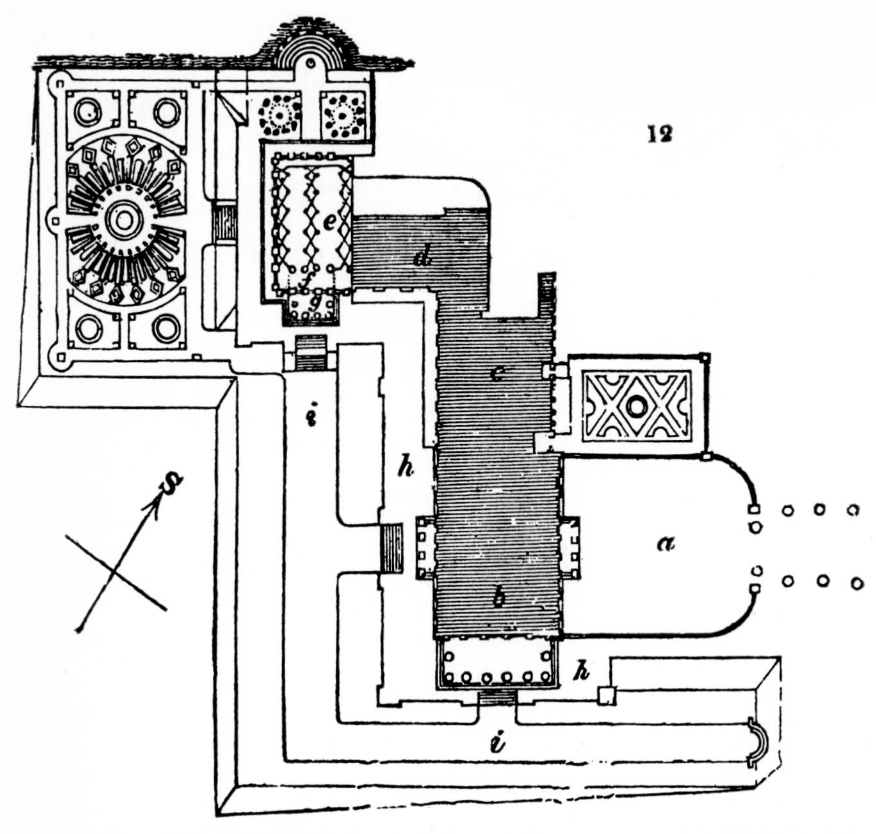

WILLIAM WILKINS and C. R. COCKERELL, Grange Park,
1809 and 1821–6

50. Plan 51. View

52. HENRY GOODRIDGE, Detail of Entrance Gateway, Lansdowne Cemetery, 1848

Country Life

53. THOMAS HOPPER, Staircase, Penrhyn Castle, *c.* 1827–47

54. George Dance the Younger, Vestibule, Laxton Hall, 1811

Romanesque architecture were amongst the first to appear in this country, and were much used by Ruskin himself.[55]

The last part of this chapter will be devoted to an aspect of the Picturesque so far kept out of the discussion because of its more intangible nature. I refer to a kind of theological justification of the aesthetic doctrine worked out by Vanbrugh and his successors. It is a tenuous philosophical system developed by Shaftesbury and Rousseau, playing with ambiguous terms like 'reason' and 'nature' and weaving its way throughout Picturesque Romanticism. An early but very complete and little-known development of this theme, showing precisely how it was related to the idea of landscape-gardening, is a detailed proposal of 1734 by Aaron Hill for a 'moral garden'. The philosophical idea behind this garden runs something like this: nature is pure, purity is moral, morality is free, freedom is independence. There is some justification for seeing the landscape garden as linked to the English eighteenth-century idea of political liberty. The open-air monument to morality, to men of genius and to the classical virtues, which was such a feature of the park at Stowe, is taken up in the great abstract structures—dedicated to the Cult of Moral Values, or the New Ethics—in the parks of Ledoux's *Ville Idéale de Chaux*, published in 1804. It also finds a curious expression in the moral festivals devised in the 1790s by David for the leaders of the French Revolution. At the same time that a moral significance was being attached to the landscaped park and its monuments, so was a religious significance to the rôle of art and the collector. That this theory is not far-fetched is justified by the existence of Beckford at Fonthill Abbey, who specifically saw himself as the abbot of a monastery dedicated no longer to God but to culture. Germany particularly develops this theme, so that for Goethe and others the artist comes to be regarded as a priest or prophet. Goethe spoke of the artist as 'the anointed of God'.[56] The place where the works of artists are united together, that is the Museum, becomes, as it was at Fonthill, a church. Thus Schinkel, designing in 1823 his famous Altes Museum at Berlin, wrote of it how it was to 'exalt' the visitor, 'to be the sanctuary in which the most precious was stored'.[56] It is at this point that Thomas Hope the collector reappears to make his own contribution. In 1821 was published the first and only volume of *The Magazine of the Fine Arts and Monthly Review of Painting, Sculpture,*

Architecture and Engraving. The introductory article states precisely the aesthetic position reached at this moment: 'True taste, we argue, is conducive to virtue; and the Fine Arts produce the food by which this taste is nourished.'[57] Now the first plate in this magazine depicts Hope's Picture Gallery at Duchess Street, enthusiastically referred to later in the text, and the second shows the Gallery of the British Institution, of which society Hope was a founder member. Hope had himself observed of his Picture Gallery that, with the organ at the far end, it assumed 'the appearance of a sanctuary,' and had also described his Lararium as a 'tabernacle'. To find out where the belief that 'true taste is conducive to virtue' was shortly to lead, one has only to read Pugin. So often seen as the first characteristic thinker of the nineteenth century, he is surely equally to be regarded as a complete product of eighteenth-century artistic philosophy.

The long preceding paragraph has outlined the developments which made possible the tenets of 1821. We can now justify this general view by isolating a few aspects of it in more detail. An especially significant scheme is that for a 'moral garden' (Fig. 18) proposed in 1734 by Aaron Hill, the dramatist and dilettante of Pope's circle. He first mentions his project in a letter to Lady Walpole, dated 30 May 1734. He describes how he is laying out his garden in Petty France, Westminster, as a model for a larger scheme which he hopes to execute in the country. The Moral Garden was to be laid out in a large expanse of woodland with, in the centre, an artificial hill. The hill was to be surrounded first by cornfields and meadows containing a thatched cottage, then by a series of walks and canals probably arranged in a terraced fashion, and finally by a walled cloister walk. The point of thus sealing off the hill from the surrounding woodland was that although arrival at the Temple of Happiness which surmounted the hill was the goal of admission to the garden, it was to be achieved by following only one path. Thus four large grotto-passages and eight smaller winding gravel walks—each with a different theme, like Ambition, Power, Intellect, and so on—all appeared to lead directly to the Temple of Happiness, but in fact only one of them did so. The passages and walks were all to be approached from the circumference of the woodland, where their presence was indicated by appropriate statues of virtues and vices. Windows in the grottoes

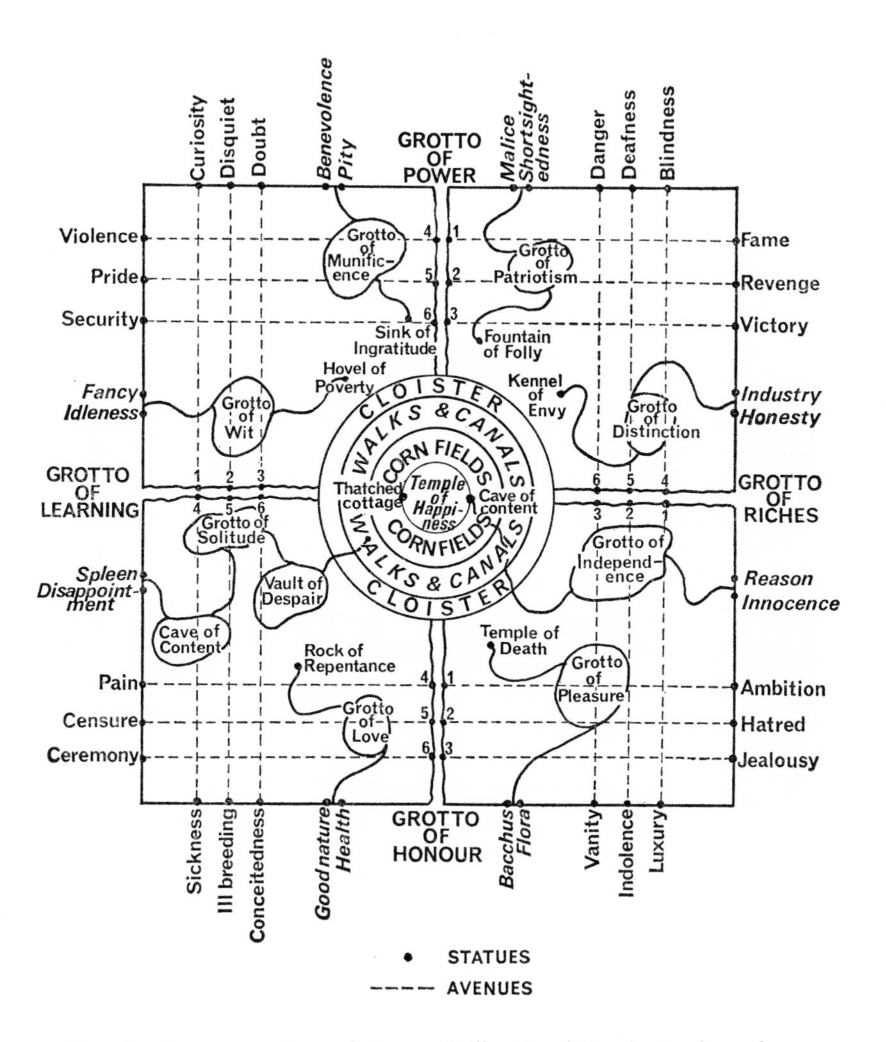

Fig. 18. Reconstruction of Aaron Hill's Moral Rock Garden of 1734

commanded views down avenues which were also terminated by appropriate statues. All the grottoes eventually opened into the cloister-walk; and the winding paths, passing through appropriately named caves, fields, and temples, ended up at various symbolic points: all, that is, save one which conducted the fortunate visitor to the Cave of Content from which alone access might be had to the Temple of Happiness. Everywhere there was to be narrative and symbolic decoration. Thus, in the Grotto of Power were to be: 'represented, in *shell-work*, of all sizes and colours, the forms of military weapons, antient and modern; as also the ruins of old castles and towers.—And from caves up and down within the rocks, hang chrystals of salt-petre—the foundation of that friend of power, gunpowder.'

Similarly, the Grotto of Riches was to be: 'composed, chiefly, of glass-house clinkers, illuminated by pieces of transparent crystal and coloured glass jewels, representing rubies, emeralds, &c.', and enlivened by the appearance of little narrative scenes: 'one rock represents *Potosi*, in *Peru*, where *Indians* (in little figures) are busy, at the several tasks, of breaking, raising and smelting the silver ore'. The Rock of Repentance rises in the midst of a wilderness of briar, thistle, and furze and is 'covered over with moss, out of which water drops, weeping and melancholy'; and the Temple of Death is 'in an area, surrounded by yew-trees and filled with tombs'.

Finally, the visitor, so many times disappointed, sets out on a path flanked by statutes of Reason and Innocence which conducts him through the woodland: 'to the grot of INDEPENDENCE; into which having entered, you pass down a straight, short, hollow way, and rise, on a sudden, among corn fields, within the center, in view of the house of Content, and in the path to the Temple of Happiness'.[58]

So that is it. It is the strange combination of Reason, Innocence, and, above all, Independence that is to lead man to the promised land. Nothing could show more clearly the contemporary concern to unite reason and nature and moral philosophy in the new medium of the landscape-garden or, at any rate, in its first tentative expression as the 'wiggly wildernesses,'[59] in Pevsner's phrase, of Bridgeman, Pope, and Hill. There can be little doubt that Hill's grotto-passages were directly inspired by the one which Pope had created as early as 1719 under a road, in order to connect his house with the garden opposite.

Also in this garden there was an artificial hill with a spiral pathway round it.[25] Despite the thoughts that Aaron Hill's Moral Garden may recall of Bunyan or even Dante, and despite the fact that it was produced in a nominally Christian age and culture, Hill's whole comprehensive scheme of life and morals is worked out with no acknowledgement to the Christian values. We hear nothing of Faith or Hope or Charity. What we do hear of is the supreme and essential nature of Independence. By contrast, religion, and especially Roman Catholicism, is seen more and more as essentially a Picturesque and romantic affair of the emotions. And if art rather than religion is the supreme end of man, the new priest will be he who acts as a patron of the arts or who, at any rate, collects and displays existing works of art. No clearer evidence of a tendency towards such an outlook could be afforded than by the existence of Beckford at Fonthill. Fonthill was an abbey, but an abbey devoted no longer to the worship of God but of the arts. Beckford was its abbot and he envisaged that after his death pilgrims would come to venerate his shrine, but not as that of a man of piety, but as a great patron of the arts. The diarist Farington gives us confirmation of this when he records of Fonthill in 1798 that: 'The abbey to be endowed, and cathedral service to be performed in the most splendid manner that the Protestant religion will admit. A gallery leading from the top of the church to be decorated with paintings, the works of English artists. Beckford's own tomb to be placed at the end of this gallery, as having been an encourager of art.'[60]

But for a realization of some of the Rousseauesque theories of Aaron Hill it is to France that we must turn. Hill had perhaps borrowed the idea of geographically plotting the emotions on a map from the *Littérature Précieuse* of seventeenth-century France, from the little charts drawn up by Mademoiselle de Scudérie. Perhaps this approach is especially French. What I point to at the end of the eighteenth century in France is the whole visual technique of narrative symbol which played such an enormous part in popularizing the Revolution in France. In the preface to his *Symbol and Satire in the French Revolution*, E. F. Henderson, asks: 'In what period of the world's history do we meet with so many fables and personifications, symbols, satires and emblems? The dawn of French liberty is like the dawn of the world's religion.'[61]

The high point of this movement was doubtless the symbolical festivals devised by J.-L. David, which united all the arts into a captivating, narrative, propagandist, and almost religious whole.[62] The Festival of Unity and Indivisibility began at dawn on 10 August 1793 in the form of a procession, attended by over 200,000 people, starting on the site of the Bastille and stopping at a number of halts or stages, rather like the Stations of the Cross. From the Fountain of Regeneration, for example, spurted forth water which all present were obliged to drink, and of course from a single cup. Another of the stations was designed in the form of a temple stylistically close, ironically, to the detested pre-Revolutionary *barrières* by Ledoux. Another of David's festivals, the Festival of the Supreme Being, staged in 1794, is closely related to schemes like that of Aaron Hill. The final stage at this Festival was the Mountain erected over the Altar to the Fatherland. In front of this half-natural, half-artificial setting, dotted with grottoes and swathed with incense, Robespierre himself burnt away with a torch a number of statues representing atheism, discord, ambition, and so on, at last setting light to some wood which revealed, triumphant beneath, the statue of Wisdom. This is obviously an exact parallel to Hill's system of paths, grottoes, and statues in which various virtues, vices, and moral attitudes were accepted or rejected until only one was left.

The references we have made to Rousseau ought to be followed up by a glance at the neo-classical feeling for the picturesqueness of the primitive. One aspect of this has been discussed in the chapter on Greek Doric. If, as we have seen, Thomas Hope was a pioneer in the internal application of the Greek Doric order at Duchess Street, that house was also remarkable for its Egyptian and Indian or Turkish rooms. A discussion of these Revivals, which form an obvious part of the picturesqueness of the primitive, has been reserved for a chapter on 'The Hope Style: Sources, Parallels and Influences', and the present chapter will be concluded by an investigation of some of the work of Dufour, a man whose art is Picturesque at every possible level.

The panoramic wallpapers produced by Joseph Dufour and others in early nineteenth-century France might be regarded as a substitute for the picturesque landscaped parks which it was hardly possible to create during the Napoleonic Wars. It has not before been recorded that two sets of Dufour's papers—the 'Voyages du Capitaine Cook', and the 'Paysage Indien'—were brought to this country, to Laxton Hall in Northamptonshire.[63] We know, on the other hand, of at least two hundred sets in North America.[64] Americans and Frenchmen had, after all, shed blood together in a common cause against the English, the cause of 'Liberty'; and it is well known how much the men of the Revolution in France were encouraged by the success of the revolting colonies. The discoveries by Captain Cook and others of the gay primitive communities of New Zealand and the South Sea Islands lent support to the concept of the 'noble savage' and doubtless enabled the liberated colonists to identify themselves sentimentally with the savages, to regard themselves as being similarly free and untrammelled, and at the beginning not the end of civilization. An English parallel is formed by the Norse sagas of the poet Gray.

The primitive and exotic discoveries of Cook were early translated into the current Picturesque idiom. Thus in 1776 William Hodges, who had acted as draughtsman on Cook's second voyage, exhibited at the Royal Academy, 'A view taken in the Bay of Otaheite Peha'. This romantic landscape in the Wilson tradition is now at the National Maritime Museum. It was Hodges' book, *Select Views in India* (1786), which Reynolds was to recommend architects to use as a source for imitations of 'the Barbarick Splendour of . . . Asiatick buildings'.[65]

As would be expected, the landscaped park is the medium for the next stage of the Cook enthusiasm. After Cook's death in 1779, monuments were erected to him in parks in England and France. At Stowe, a Cook monument took the form of a pedestal ornamented with a medallion and surmounted by a globe.[66] This seems to have inspired another globed monument to Cook erected in the grounds of The Vache, near Chalfont St. Giles, Buckinghamshire, by Sir Hugh Palliser.[67] This was probably the Commodore Palliser referred to in an earlier example of exotic primitivism, a painting by John Russell exhibited at the Royal Academy in 1769 and entitled, 'Portraits of Micoc and her son Tootac, Esquimeaux Indians, brought over by Commodore Palliser'. In France, a Cook monument in the park at Méréville formed the centre-piece of a little island planted with exotic trees and intended to recall one of Cook's own islands (Plate 26).[68] This probably dates from a year or so after the Stowe monument, since

Jean-Joseph de Laborde, the banker who caused it to be erected, did not acquire the property of Méréville, near Etampes, until 1784. Designed by Augustin Pajou, the temple was an early example of the revival of Greek Doric, an order whose primitive associations were suited to its function here. Square, with a column at each corner and an entablature surmounted by a squat, heavy attic, the temple contained a funerary stele and an urn. It is perhaps worth mentioning a description by Horace Walpole of Lord Holland's artificial ruins near the sea-shore at Kingsgate, Kent, in which he observed that 'a view of them might be passed for a prospect in some half-civilized island discovered by Captain Cook'.[69] As a parallel to Méréville, a conscious attempt to create a 'half-civilized island' was made early in the nineteenth century in the gardens at Mareham Manor, Lincolnshire. Here, Henry Roberts, who had travelled with Sir Joseph Banks on Cook's second voyage, adorned his grounds with huts in imitation of those he had seen at Tierra del Fuego and New Holland.[70] If Commodore Palliser had brought to England a pair of Esquimeau Indians, Captain Furneaux took it upon himself in 1774[71] to introduce into this country a native of Tahiti called Omai, of whom Reynolds himself painted a full-length portrait. The introduction into the sophisticated neo-classical world of piquant figures from primitive societies such as Esquimeaux and Tahitians, was taken a step further by Hope who not only introduced such a character—the young Greek Aidé, decked out 'in the Eastern dress . . . with a very feminine look'—but had actually decorated rooms in his house, based on those in Turkish palaces, that would serve as appropriate settings for such persons. As a result of Omai's visit, there was presented at Covent Garden in 1785 'Omai: or a Trip round the World,' for which magnificent sets were designed by Philip de Loutherbourg.[72] Reynolds, present at the first night, is recorded as having 'expressed the utmost satisfaction at all the landscape scenes'.[73] In Paris three years later a similar dramatic entertainment was presented, entitled 'La Mort du Capitaine Cook';[74] and between 1789 and 1797 Johann Zoffany painted Cook's death,[75] basing the figure of Cook on the Ludovisi Gladiator and that of his murderer on the Townley Discobolus in such a way as to present both Englishman and savage as noble, classical heroes.

55. JOSEPH DUFOUR, 'Dance of the Otahïti Girls before King O-Too', 1806

56. THOMAS HOPE and WILLIAM ATKINSON, Temple, Deepdene, 1818–23

THOMAS HOPE and WILLIAM ATKINSON, Deepdene, 1818–23

57. North Lodge 58. Entrance Front

The association, therefore, at Méréville, of Greek Doric with this romantic primitivism was, as we have suggested, no coincidence. It was a logical extension of the parallel which many travellers had drawn between the forms, manners, and costumes of the natives of Tahiti and those of ancient Greece. This romantic idealizing vein makes an early appearance in the writings of Louis de Bougainville, who had visited Tahiti in 1768, a year before Cook. 'I never saw men better made', he wrote, 'and whose limbs were more proportionate: in order to paint a Hercules or a Mars, one could nowhere find such beautiful models.' He described how a Tahitian girl appeared to him 'as Venus . . . herself to the Phrygian shepherd, having . . . the celestial form of that goddess', and observed of that island as a whole that 'one would think himself in the Elysian fields'.[76] These sentiments are echoed in Banks' *Journal . . . in H.M.S. Endeavour*, and carried to a yet more fanciful extreme in his MS. entitled *Thoughts on the manners of Otaheite* (1773).[77] The case of George Forster, who had travelled on Cook's second voyage, brings us a little closer to the Greek Doric at Méréville, since he was an enthusiastic and early disciple of Winckelmann. He actually used Winckelmann's phrase 'noble simplicity', to describe the appearance of the Tahitians.[78]

Having presented something of the philosophical and artistic background, we can now turn again to Dufour. In 1806 he exhibited a wallpaper, twenty sections long, designed for him by J. C. Charvet and entitled 'Voyages du Capitaine Cook'. It was a great success and at least four sets were exported to North America. Dufour moved from Macon to Paris in 1807 where he began to print further exotic wallpapers such as 'Les Français en Egypte', of which twelve sets went to America, a 'Paysage Turc' and, in 1815, a 'Paysage Indien'.[79] The French demand for Indian scenes corresponds to the popularity in this country of the pictures of the Daniells, and Dufour's picturesque views of landscapes and temples might be based on their work.

The 'Voyages du Capitaine Cook' and the 'Paysage Indien' form unexpected adornments to two bedrooms at Laxton Hall, Northamptonshire, a gaunt neo-classical house built in 1805–11 for George Freke Evans by Humphry Repton and his son John Adey Repton. One is tempted, though there is no evidence, to ascribe the introduction of these papers to George Dance, who, in 1812, provided the house with a great bleak hall in a spirit more French than English (Plate 54). The wallpapers, which are not complete, are cut up into sections and applied rather arbitrarily to the walls in odd strips and panels. But Dufour always envisaged considerable variety in the grouping, combination, and method of display of his papers. The colours are strong, rich, and dark and the scenes of native-dances, tiger-hunts, and so on are imaginative, well-detailed, and full of incident. Fanciful though they may appear, the ceremonies and dances, including many of the actual characters shown, are nearly all based on scenes recorded as having taken place on Cook's travels. (Plate 55 shows the 'Dance of the Otahïti Girls before King O-Too'). It will be observed how, in accordance with Forster's views, many of the dancers are depicted with clothes and hair-styles reminiscent of those of the ancient Greeks. The larger of the rooms contains scenes from the 'Paysage Indien' and with its bold decorative panels of Indian views and buildings is very similar to the Indian room at Duchess Street, adorned with the Indian paintings of Thomas Daniell.

Although such decorative ensembles were comparatively rare in England, something of the sort seems to have existed in the early 1820s at Clewer Lodge, Windsor. Here J. Ramsbottom had his sitting-room adorned with figures in 'Turkish, Dalmatian, and Hindoo costumes, spiritedly painted', the dining-room walls being 'painted with marine and other views'.[80] In the Villa Vittoria at Pesaro the Princess Caroline, godmother to Thomas Hope's eldest son, created in 1818–19 her own parallel to her husband's yet more exotic extravagances at Brighton. A whole suite of rooms in her villa was adorned with Turkish and Levantine figures and landscapes, while other apartments were fitted out in the Chinese taste.[81]

It should be pointed out that even the representation of Indian life and landscape was sometimes endowed with a moral significance. Irwin refers to a play by W. Richardson called *The Indian*, presented in 1790 at the Theatre Royal, Richmond, in which the Indian appears as a symbol of liberty in contrast to the tyranny of Europe'.[82] Such an approach, however, was rarely given so explicit an expression. There was certainly this high seriousness, this intellectual self-consciousness about Dufour's Cook wallpaper. As evidence for this one can point to a booklet which he wrote about this wallpaper and published in

An XIII (1804–5) at Macon, under the title of *Sauvages de la Mer Pacifique*. This document is of especial interest since it confirms the observations which we have made concerning the significance and implications of the artistic enthusiasm for the primitive. I refer to Dufour's hope, expressed in the course of his pamphlet, that his wallpaper will assist 'in creating by means of new comparisons, a community of taste and enjoyment between those who live in a state of civilization and those who are at the outset of the use of their native intelligence'.[83] We must not forget that this approach was heightened at the time by a relativist belief that savages, like those on Tahiti, had reached a similar point of development to the ancient Greeks, so far as life and manners were concerned. This belief is given perfect expression by Payne Knight at exactly the moment of the Dufour pamphlet. Probably referring to Tahitians,[84] he observed in 1805 that 'the attitudes and gestures of savages . . . are extremely dignified and graceful'. He went on to describe how 'In the fine age of the arts of Greece, civilization had just arrived at that state, in which the manners of men are polished, but yet natural.'[85]

The apt summary, in the quotation from Dufour's pamphlet, of the artistic scene of the 1800s may be taken as a convenient ending to this chapter. As the eighteenth century wore on, the term 'Exotic' came often to be synonymous with 'Picturesque';[86] and as we began this chapter by showing the sources for Hope's use of the Picturesque at the Deepdene, it may be appropriate to end it with Dufour's justification for his use of Picturesque Exoticism in the interiors at Duchess Street. For here, we cannot doubt that daring stylistic juxtapositions created precisely Dufour's 'new comparisons', his new 'community of taste and enjoyment'.

VI

The Deepdene and the Development of the Picturesque

In May 1807, the year after his marriage and of the publication of *Household Furniture*, Thomas Hope acquired the country house and estate of the Deepdene, near Dorking in Surrey. In doing so, he followed fairly closely his practice at Duchess Street of acquiring a well-established late eighteenth-century house of some quality. As his town house had been built by Adam for persons well known in London society, so had his country house been a residence until 1791 of the Dukes of Norfolk. His acquisition of ready-made houses was not prompted solely by convenience. Hope never was. These houses made it clear that he wanted to enter society at that traditional level, and would only then begin his alterations, transformations, and the imposition of his own taste.

Beyond all this, however, there was another aspect of the Deepdene that must have appealed to Hope. It was at this moment that he was beginning to concern himself with the Picturesque theories of Price and Knight, and there can be no doubt that the steep hills and rolling woods of central Surrey are still, and must have been much more so when in a condition of relatively wild remoteness as in the 1800s, amongst the most 'Picturesque' parts of the country, in the precise sense in which the word was used in 1800. That is to say, they are like an 'excited' version of a Capability Brown park on the very grandest scale. Thus, Leith Hill is the highest point in south-east England; and a topographer recently described how from Newlands Corner one sees 'range after range of hills composing themselves as elegantly and harmoniously as a Claude landscape'.[1] But what is of equal significance is that these dramatic undulating vistas seem already to have had their own effect on the gardens of a number of Surrey houses. Italianate influence was felt strongly in the second half of the seventeenth century at Chilworth Manor and Albury Park, both near

Guildford, and at Wotton House and the Deepdene, both near Dorking.

It seems to have been in the 1640s and earliest 50s[2] that the diarist John Evelyn, with the architectural assistance of his cousin Captain George Evelyn, made a deliberate attempt to create in the grounds of Wotton House the kind of steeply terraced garden that was so often the accompaniment to the Italian villa. The upper part of the hill was artificial and in the lower part Evelyn contrived a Roman Doric temple,[3] rather crudely detailed perhaps, but then who else could boast of a Doric garden-temple at all in 1649? Not five miles away at Deepdene, the Honourable Charles Howard in about the same years was remodelling his own gardens in a yet more dramatic Italianate manner. Howard had the advantage, which Evelyn had not, of possessing on his estate a naturally 'U'-shaped hill which lent itself to terraced treatment. In August 1655 Evelyn records in his diary that he '. . . went to *Darking* to see Mr. Chas. Howard's Ampitheater Garden, or Solitarie recesse, being 15 Ackers, invironed by an hill: he shew'd us divers rare plants . . . Caves, an Elaboratory'.[4] A passage from Camden's *Britannia* gives a more detailed description of this unusual garden:

> The situation . . . is somewhat surprising, by reason of the risings and uniform acclivities about it, which naturally resemble a Roman amphitheatre . . . Now it is most ingeniously cast and improved into gardens, vineyards, and other plantations, with frequent grots here and there, beneath the terraces leading to the top, from whence one has a fair prospect of that part of Surrey and Sussex.[5]

The account of the Deepdene from Aubrey's *Antiquities of Surrey* uses to describe it the word 'hope', one of the meanings of which is 'a long valley'. I imagine that Thomas Hope knew of this and that it must have appealed to him. Aubrey writes:

> A long Hope, i.e. according to Virgil, *deductus vallis*, is contrived in the most pleasant and delightful solitude for House, Gardens, Orchards, Boscages, &c., that I have ever seen in England; it deserves a poem, and was a subject worthy of Mr. Cowley's muse. Mr. Howard hath cast this Hope into the form of a Theatre, on the side whereof he hath made several narrow walks, like the seats of a theatre . . which are bordered

> with thyme, and some cherry trees, myrtles etc. Here were a great many orange trees and syringas . . . The pit as I may call it, is stored full of rare plants and choice flowers. In the hill, on the left hand, being sandy ground, is a cave digged thirtysix paces long, four broad and five yards high; and at about two-thirds of the hill . . . he hath dug another subterranean walk or passage, to be pierced through the hill, through which you have the vista, over all the south part of Surrey and Sussex, to the sea. The south side of this hill is converted to a vine-yard, of many acres of ground . . . On the West of this garden is a little Building, which is divided into a Laboratory and a neat Oratory, by Mr. Howard . . . The house was not made for grandeur, but retirement; a noble hermitage, neat, elegant and suitable to the modesty and solitude of the proprietor.[6]

The subterranean passage through the hill, which was soon blocked by falling sand,was an idea taken up in the same years by the Earl of Arundel at Albury Park near Guildford. The garden was again laid out in terraces to designs by John and Captain George Evelyn and in 1676 a cavern in imitation of a Roman Bath was excavated beneath the principal terrace. Evelyn records in September 1670 that he went '. . . to *Alburie* to see how that Garden proceeded, which I found exactly don according to the Designe and plot I had made, with the *Crypta* through the mountains in the park, which is 30 pearches in length, such a *Pausilippe* is no where in England besides: the Canals were now digging, and Vineyards planted.'[7] This passage shows that even the subterranean passage was deliberately Italianate in inspiration, being an echo of the Grotta di Posilippo near Naples.

The last in this list of Italian gardens in Surrey is the walled garden at Chilworth Manor, just a mile or so from Albury, which is laid out in terraces up the side of a hill.

The atmosphere of the Deepdene as the picturesquely Italianate and classical retreat of the sensitive scholar and man of ideas was clearly ideally suited to Thomas Hope. Created at that moment in the seventeenth century when the English nobleman, and especially the house of Howard, conceived a passion for collecting coins and antiquities in imitation of his Italian Renaissance predecessors, it was especially fitting that the estate should have been brought to its finest and fullest neo-classical expression by the hand of Hope. There can be little doubt that the amphitheatrical and terraced lay-out of the gardens which greeted Hope on his arrival in 1807, did much to influence his encouragement of 'the suspended gardens within Genoa and the splendid villas about Rome' in his essay on *The Art of Gardening*, published in the year after his acquisition of the Deepdene. The movement towards an acceptance of the formal Italian garden by the late Picturesque theoreticians, amongst whom Hope's essay justifies him a place, is one of the more surprising features of this period.[8] The history of the Deepdene in the seventeenth century helps to explain it.

The house (Fig. 19) which Thomas Hope bought had been built by the 10th Duke of Norfolk between the years 1777 and 1786.[9] It was a compact mansion of thirteen bays and two and a half storeys, with a large canted bay in the centre of the north-west front, the whole very much in the manner of an architect like Sir Robert Taylor at, for example, Asgill House, Richmond, of 1757–8. There were six entertaining-rooms, three of which could boast statuary marble chimney-pieces, and nine principal bedrooms. The library, dining-room, and billiard-room were, surprisingly, ornamented with stained glass, some of which Hope seems to have retained. He also retained intact, despite all his alterations and additions, the structure and the room-divisions of this house.

With the house went over one hundred acres of arable and pasture land and a twelve-roomed farm-house. The Sale Catalogue described the 'Pleasure ground or park ... [with] luxurious forest trees ... walks, rural retirements, grottoes, cavern, terrace, the Pleasure Garden with alcoves, grottoes, a Canal of Water, two hot-houses and the Kitchen Garden and melon-ground.'

All this was sold by auction to Thomas Hope in one lot at noon on Tuesday, 26 May 1807, at Garraway's Coffee House, Exchange Alley, Cornhill. Thus, for the sum of £9,030,[10] Thomas Hope became an English country gentleman.

It was not from the Duke of Norfolk that Hope purchased the estate but from Sir Charles Burrell, Bart., whose father William Burrell, antiquarian and topographer, had acquired it from the dissolute 11th Duke in 1791. Sir Charles Burrell moved to Sussex where in 1809 Nash created for him the marvellously Picturesque and castellated Knepp Castle, near West Grinstead. The only permanent adornment left by the Burrells seems to have been the verses eulogistic of

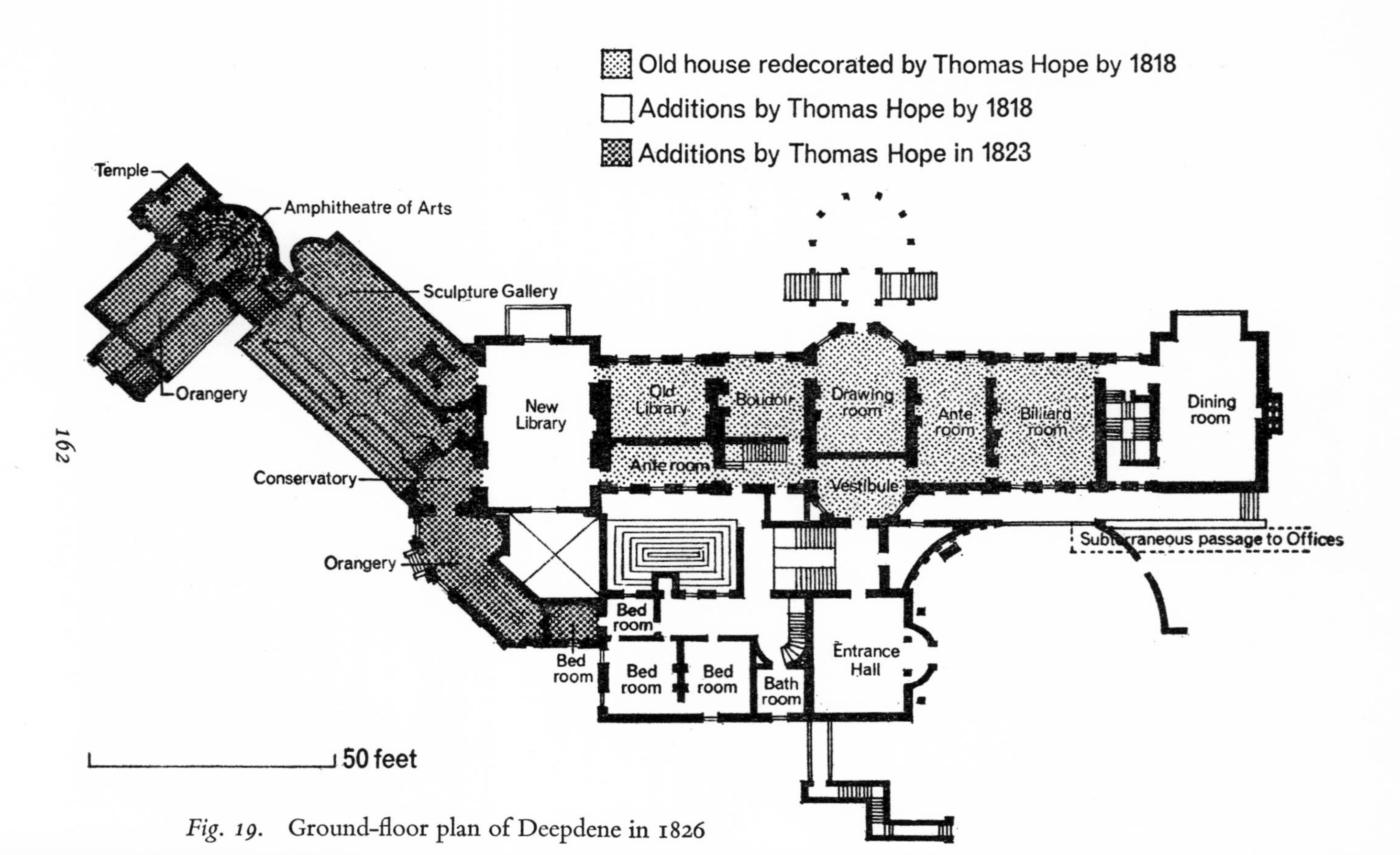

Fig. 19. Ground-floor plan of Deepdene in 1826

the Honourable Charles Howard which Sir William's wife composed in 1792 and caused to be inscribed on a 'votive tablet'[11] within his laboratory-cave. This tablet is preserved in the entrance-vestibule of the house.

With the house that he found, Hope seems to have been content for a number of years. Thus in June 1809 when his friend Miss Berry stayed at the house, she admired the 'irregularity of the ground' but observed that 'it wants much doing to it'.[12] But the estate was being improved in other ways. Hope's brother Henry Philip generously purchased for him from Sir Charles Talbot, Bart., the estate of Chart Park which adjoined the Deepdene on the south. To commemorate this, Hope erected on the top of the amphitheatrical hill at the Deepdene a vaguely Etruscan temple (Plate 56)—now demolished—bearing the inscription, '*Fratri Optimo*. H.P.H.' and a further inscription in Arabic inside. The estate ultimately grew to a size of over four hundred acres.

The first building operation of whose date we have a precise record is the Mausoleum, which was consecrated as a burial place in the autumn of 1818 by Dr. John Beresford, Bishop of Raphoe.[13] Standing just outside the southernmost extremity of the Chart Park estate, it is a simple building with an attractive iron-work door and railings.

For establishing the dates and chronology of Hope's additions to the house itself, we have the following facts to guide us. It is unlikely that anything of any consequence had been added by 1813 since there is no description of the house in the Surrey volume of John Britton's *Beauties of England and Wales* which appeared in that year. Thomas Hope was out of the country from 1815 to the summer of 1817. In the autumn of the following year we hear of the consecration of the Mausoleum. At the same moment, an engraving of the remodelled Deepdene, clearly showing the new side wings and the principal tower, appeared as a small calendar illustration for September 1818. Of equal interest is an account of the house written in April 1819 by the novelist Maria Edgeworth.[14] In that month she spent ten days with the Hopes at the Deepdene and makes it clear, in a letter, that much had been done to the house. She refers to 'The stables at the bottom of the hill . . . like a vast square brick manufactory . . . [and the] house . . .

grotesque and confused among trees in no one particular taste.' She describes the interiors as 'magnificently furnished', mentioning the French furniture, the decoration of the staircase-hall and passages, the Egyptian room and the Raphael room. It is clear, also, that the building operations were not yet quite complete, since she observes that 'he intends next year to stucco his house'.[14] In June 1823 it was reported in the *Repository of Arts* that Hope was in the process of adding to the house a sculpture gallery and conservatory; and a view of the house shows the entrance-front complete. It is evident, then, that in 1818–19 Hope redecorated according to his own ideals the rooms of the eighteenth-century house; added on to it two side wings, one capped by a tall tower; formed a new entrance-front and staircase-hall; and constructed the detached and irregular groups of offices and stables. The next main building phase came in 1823 when he threw out to the south-west, at an angle of forty-five degrees to the body of the house, an orangery, conservatory, sculpture-gallery, and amphitheatre forming one bizarre unit. The *Repository* article of 1823 also helps to establish a *terminus ad quem* for Hope's numerous additions to the park. Observing that the house 'is at present undergoing considerable improvements', the author goes on to point out that 'Not a seat but bears the mark of a master hand ... bridges, entrance gates, lodges, greenhouses, orangeries, pineries, all have some elegant peculiarity.'[15]

What we lack in the way of detailed circumstantial evidence for the dating of the house is more than made up to us by the remarkably complete record of its appearance given in two MS. volumes prepared in the 1820s under the direction of John Britton. It was the discovery of these on different occasions and in different places which, as much as anything, made the present study possible. Their existence was first referred to in an Appendix to volume II of Britton's *Autobiography*, published in 1848. In this Appendix we read that:

> A history and description of Deepdene, the seat of Thomas Hope Esq. with notices of eminent persons connected with the place, was also begun by him [i.e. John Britton]. This was not intended for publication, but as a manuscript volume, to accompany a series of highly-finished drawings of that seat, which had been made for Mr. Hope under Mr. Britton's direction by Bartlett, Penry Williams, etc. A great portion of the work,

including some interesting biographical matter, was written, but the volume has never been completed.

A volume, begun in 1821 and containing the uncompleted biographical and descriptive text, a plan of the house and thirty-six illustrations, came to light recently in the possession of Mrs. H. W. Law of Cambridge.[16] The second far more elaborate volume, dated 1826, survives at the Minet Library, Brixton, and contains an introduction, a plan of the estate, and twenty-nine illustrations. It is clear that the final arrangement would have been considerably different. The volume of text would have contained the plan of the estate now in the Minet Library volume, but no other illustrations at all. Those that it contains now are preparatory drafts for those in the Minet Volume and were evidently pasted in when it became clear that the text was not going to be completed. Moreover, a number of architectural drawings probably by Hope and Atkinson have found their way into the Minet volume almost certainly after Hope's death. Most of the illustrations from this volume are here reproduced, all of them for the first time; and the rather complicated composition of the two volumes is clarified in a complete catalogue of their illustrations given in Appendix C.

Britton's *History of the Deepdene* is of especial interest in that it can be seen as a parallel or companion volume to his book of 1827 on Sir John Soane's Museum entitled *The Union of Architecture, Sculpture and Painting*. The sub-title of the Deepdene history is *The Union of the Picturesque in Scenery and Architecture with Domestic Beauties*, which appears displayed within an elaborate Gothic quatrefoil on the title-page of the Minet Library volume. If the Soane Museum volume showed how the Picturesque could be achieved in a town-house, the Deepdene volumes showed how it could be achieved in the ampler setting of a country house and estate. The dedication of the first volume 'To the Honourable Mrs. Hope' observes how her husband's gift of 'drawing with facility and accuracy enables him to design numerous architectural improvements in the house and outbuildings; and also to embellish the house scenery', so that instead of the small red-brick house which he found, there is now 'a spacious mansion of pleasing colour, diversified and varied in its features'. The titles were then given of the six chapters of which the book was to be composed: *Descriptive Account of the County from Clapham, The Deepdene and Park Scenery, Historical Particulars of the Manor of the Deepdene and Successive Possessors, Biographical Anecdotes of the most eminent possessors, Description of the Mansion and its Contents*, and *Description of the Vicinity and other Seats*. Various sections of the first four chapters were completed but the last two were not even begun. That the *Description of the Mansion and its Contents* was not attempted is a loss, but in fact we have a lengthy version of this in the account which he wrote, after Henry Hope's alterations, for the five-volumed *Topographical History of Surrey*, which he published with Brayley during the 1840s. The best and longest contemporary account is that of 1826 in Neale's *Views of Seats*. Neale thought so highly of this, or perhaps it was Hope who did, that he also published it separately in the same year, bound up as a book on its own.

Hope employed the successful country-house architect William Atkinson (*c.* 1773–1839),[17] to execute his own plans for the alterations at the Deepdene. A pupil of Wyatt, he entered the Royal Academy Schools in 1796 and at the end of that year competed for the Medal for the Best Drawing in Architecture of the South View of Somerset House. The other competitors were Robert Smirke and John Dixon, an assistant of Wyatt. Atkinson and Dixon received but one vote apiece, Smirke nineteen.[18] Draughtsmanship seems never to have been Atkinson's strongest point. However, in December 1797, he won the Gold Medal with a design for Courts of Justice in Ireland.[19] In 1805 he made himself known to a wider audience by publishing a book of rather unalluring *Picturesque Views of Cottages*. But it was not in the design of cottages that his future lay. His first important work, Scone Castle, Perthshire, for the Earl of Mansfield, set the pattern for his commissions and patrons during the next quarter of a century. There are two Gothic schemes preserved at Scone, dated January 1802 and January 1803. 1804 saw the beginning of his work for the Earl of Mulgrave at Mulgrave Castle, Yorkshire. His patronage by Lord Mulgrave was to have the most fruitful consequences for him. Mulgrave, a close friend of Sir George Beaumont and Lord Ashburnham, was *persona grata* in the influential world of connoisseurship in London. He and Beaumont were the earliest patrons and supporters of Wilkie and Haydon;[20] Ashburnham and Beaumont both employed George Dance in these years to design country-houses for them in his novel Gothic manner; while Lord Mulgrave chose the then little-known William Atkinson. Perhaps it was on Mulgrave's recommendation that Hope came to employ the same architect. It was certainly Lord Mulgrave who, in 1813, gave him the post of Surveyor of the Ordnance. Atkinson thus scored a point over his old Silver Medallist rival Smirke, for whom Lawrence had been attempting to obtain the appointment. Lord Mulgrave argued that Atkinson deserved the appointment because he had a large family to support, and that he had known him for twenty years. Smirke saw the matter in a different light and explained to Farington that Atkinson had a wharf at Westminster to which he shipped materials for his special Roman cement—materials which he bought from Lord Mulgrave who dispatched them to London from his Yorkshire estates.[21]

Following Loudon's use, in his *Country Residences* (1806), of the term 'mixed Gothic' to describe the irregular castellated style, Rowan observes that in the earliest nineteenth century only Smirke and Atkinson achieved a personal statement in the mixed Gothic; and that Atkinson, unlike Smirke or even Wyatt, employed irregular ground plans. 'Atkinson', he writes, 'had perhaps more feeling for the true qualities of an asymmetrical design than many of his fellow practitioners.'[22] This may be so, but the impression left on many people by an Atkinson façade in the Gothic or Baronial taste is one of flatness and baldness and a feeling that the obscurity in which the architect has been left may not be wholly unjustified. Happier are his classical interiors of 1809–11 at Broughton Hall, Yorkshire, and his remodelling of Hylands, Essex, for the banker and collector P. C. Labouchère, who was a partner in Hope & Co. from 1802–11. His classical additions to Gorhambury, Hertfordshire (1816–17), and to Himley Hall, Staffordshire (1824–7), are virtually featureless. At Tullyallan in Fifeshire he designed in 1817–20 for the 1st Viscount Keith a castellated mansion of which Burke observed that 'It boasts of no particular style.' However, in the park was a small mortuary chapel into the doorway of which Atkinson had worked two columns of polished granite brought back by Lord Keith from Egypt. Atkinson's gardens were 'disposed in all styles ... amongst the most admired . . . is the French garden . . . in tiny beds, with gravel walks between'.[23] This picturesque assembly of gardens of different styles, periods, and countries—more than hinted at by Repton—is a parallel to the architectural eclecticism of the Deepdene.

We are now ready to make our own tour of the Deepdene. A plan of the house is shown in Fig. 19. Of the principal entrances, the surviving East Lodge can probably be attributed to Hope but the main or North Lodge (Plate 57), on the Dorking to Reigate road, was rebuilt by Hope's son. Thomas' original version was in a Tuscan vernacular style with broadly projecting eaves and a strange almost Ledoux-like barrel-vaulted porch. From here one had already 'a fine view of the luxuriantly wooded knoll, on the sides of which are seen the upper parts of the house, with its ornamental parapets, and lofty turrets, rising amidst the foliage' (Plate 43).[11]

After Neale's description of the house as though it were some pinnacled Gothic fantasy one would not have been surprised when, having driven southwards along the straight drive for a quarter of a mile, one turned suddenly to the right under a heavily castellated Gothic archway. In fact this was constructed by Hope merely to carry a public road, which crossed his estate, over his private drive, but by giving it corner-towers he made it seem like the dramatic entranceway to some castle. On the east front, despite its segmental arch, it was Gothic in feeling, but on the west there was a quite accurate little Norman arcade. The visitor was further to be impressed by the arms of Hope and Beresford boldly carved on each front of the archway. From here the drive passed behind the stables and then making a great loop out to the foot of the amphitheatrical valley returned to halt before the east or entrance front of the house (Plate 58). This was an archaeological assembly of classical motifs with a weirdly detailed semicircular porch flanked by a pair of obelisks supporting lamps and surmounted on the first floor by a tripartite composition with a window in the centre and divided by four square piers with cushion capitals, a Hopeian version of canephorae. This entrance was on the short eastern end of a long rectangular wing which Hope erected just to the south of the old house and linked to it by a hemi-cycle of pilasters supporting a balustrade punctuated by prominent antifixae in the form of antique masks. In front of this screen wall stood a bronze cast of

'The Wrestlers'. From the south front of the entrance wing projected an archway supporting an open-work loggia on to which opened Mrs. Hope's first-floor apartments. This Italianate loggia was protected by simple criss-cross railings and surmounted by a flat roof with far-projecting eaves and large antifixae. A stairway descending from the loggia in three broken flights, adorned with antique vases, *cippi* and fragments of architecture, led away picturesquely into a pine-grove.

At the other side of the entrance front from this, the ground sloped eastwards steeply away from the house. On this abrupt descent, embowered by trees, Hope chose to place a 'T'-shaped group comprising kitchen and dairy (Plate 59). This notion of grouping the offices so that they form with the house itself an irregular and Picturesque composition is doubtless inspired by Uvedale Price's observation that: '... in general nothing contributes so much to give both variety and consequence to the principal building, as the accompaniment, and, as it were, the attendance of the inferior parts in their different graduations'.[24] The flat roof of the dairy was topped by a tall strange loggia, large but, one imagines, quite useless. A close parallel to this, though on a far grander scale, is the great tower or belvedere which Wyatville added at the end of his new wing at Chatsworth (*c.* 1820).[25] This opening up of architecture to nature so that the winds can blow through it is, of course, a Picturesque idea and seems, again, to be in part inspired by Uvedale Price. He particularly recommended flat roofs, because '... the edge of the sloping roof... is incapable of receiving decorations' and points out how Vanbrugh at Blenheim, 'having been probably struck with the variety of outline against the sky in many Gothic and other ancient buildings ... has raised on the top of that part, where the slanting roof begins in many houses of the Italian style, a number of decorations of various characters'.[26] This whole group of dairy, kitchens, and offices was crowned by a little spire. The architectural inspiration for this, I think, is not English but Italian. Such little spirelets often appeared in the romantic groups of hill-top buildings which Gilbert Laing Meason was to record in 1827 in his book *Landscape Architecture of the Great Painters of Italy*. A little way to the East were the stables which, though picuresquely sited, were less picturesque in architectural detail than the group of dairy and kitchens and with their austere row of blind arcading were dismissed by Maria Edgeworth as recalling '. . . a vast square brick manufactory'.[14]

It was the long south wing which revealed Hope at his most original and enchanting (Plate 60). From the north-west corner of the house he threw out in 1823 at an angle of about 45 degrees a south-facing chain of bizarre and exotic conservatories, sculpture galleries, and orangeries, the whole forming a perfect epitome of Regency taste. To begin with, the house had itself at the south-west corner gone through another change of style from which it had emerged decked out in Atkinson's never very accurate Gothic taste with a corner turret, battlements and single-light pointed windows as well as Tudor windows and oriels (Plate 61). At the foot of this Gothic corner was the Orangery, eccentric in plan and with bays divided externally by piers supporting urns and linked by an almost Gothic parapet. Between the tubs of orange trees were probably displayed copies of antique sculpture. The Orangery opened into a small nearly circular room (Plate 62), which formed part of the Conservatory but which also opened into the library. In the niche stood a statue of Psyche by Thorvaldsen, centrally placed on the axis of the long Conservatory. This charming statue shows the young girl returning from Hell with the box, which she is uncertain whether to open, containing the perfume of beauty. This little room also contained a fine table supported on animal monopodia, which was originally made for the Duchess Street mansion and appears in plate 15 in *Household Furniture*. It is now owned by the Victoria and Albert Museum. A circular vaulted ceiling was adorned with feigned rope-work decoration and a short flight of steps led down into the Conservatory. In the centre of this was a small fountain and aligned with this in the garden outside was an impressive American aloe plant (Plate 63). This exotically spiked plant stood between two marble pedestals supporting bronze vases ornamented with masks of fauns. The large light Conservatory had little external adornment save for a roof-line of miniature pediments flanked by acroteria. It opened into the Amphitheatre which was on a lower level and approached by a flight of steps (Plate 64). This was a curious conceit, for along its terraced seats were displayed busts and *cippi* behind which were five rectangular recesses containing antique statues. The roof was reminiscent of the coverings thrown over

59. THOMAS HOPE and WILLIAM ATKINSON, Kitchen and Dairy, Deepdene, 1818–23

THOMAS HOPE and WILLIAM ATKINSON, Deepdene, 1823
60. South Wing 61. South West Corner

ancient theatres to protect the audience from the sun, and the floor was made up of a mosaic from Hadrian's Villa at Rome. The façade (Plate 66) was in a highly inventive style, impossible to pin down to any period, the principal feature of which was the triangular-headed openings of doors and windows. This stylistic detail had made an earlier appearance on a little arcade in the dairy and kitchen wing. Attached to the north-west corner of the Amphitheatre was a small Temple, the function and appearance of which remain a mystery. From the Amphitheatre it was possible to pass almost directly into the Sculpture Gallery (Plate 65) which, rather curiously, was placed immediately adjacent and parallel to the Conservatory. This was a long, austere, top-lit room with a raised clerestory of continuous round-headed lights. In the frieze below, lion masks alternated with wreaths. At the east end a flight of steps led up to a columned recess which opened into the Library; at the opposite end there was a semi-circular exedra. Down the centre of the room, from west to east, were placed a superb marble *tazza* on a pedestal adorned with four winged horses, a richly carved *cippus* and a large marble tripod. Facing each other on the side walls were colossal busts of, on the left, Roma and, on the right, Jupiter Ammon. Next to the Jupiter was a sumptuous candelabrum which had formerly adorned the sculpture gallery at Duchess Street (Fig. 7). Facing this was a statue of Venus and, diagonally opposite this, Pisani's copy of the Medici Venus. Facing each other about half way down the room were square piers or pedestals supporting small statues of, on the left, a Bacchanalian figure and, on the right, Silenus. These pedestals each contained three open recesses in which were placed fragments of ornaments, Greek sculpture, and casts. Elsewhere there were statues of Augustus, Apollo, Cupid, and Psyche, a head of Medusa and a marble bust of Mrs. Hope by Behnes.

We have now completed a tour of this particular chain of apartments and can step outside into the garden to admire how, in Neale's words, 'The foreground is very irregular, and descents are made by small flights of steps, with vases on the pedestals' (Plate 67).[27] In looking at this whole complex and terraced system we remember Hope's words in his essay on Picturesque gardening of 1808 that we must seek '. . . for variety, for contrast and for brokenness of levels . . . only in arcades and in terraces, in steps, balustrades, regular slopes and parapets'. There can be no doubt that in this imaginative sequence of house and garden we see Hope's clearest statement of his views of 1808, a statement which compellingly evokes his observation that: 'The cluster of highly adorned and sheltered apartments that form the mansion ... shoot out as it were into ... ramifications of arcades porticos, terraces, parterres, treillages and avenues.'

The house itself now partakes of the same sudden contrasts of height, level, shape, and style as the garden, and moves with astonishing versatility from Gothic to Classic, from Greek to Italian, from a style combining elements of both to another style of such originality that it can be pinned down to neither. The function of this whole setting is likewise the result of a new and varied synthesis. The rooms are filled with plants, and the gardens with sculpture and pots. The fountain has been moved indoors or, at any rate, into the conservatory, and the conservatory is a continuation of the library. In a room like the Psyche alcove, it is impossible to tell whether we are indoors or out. In looking at the plan of this complex network it is insufficient to say that the spirit of the garden has invaded the house, or vice-versa. Both have combined to create something wholly new: a Picturesque vision of the civilized man of taste, dedicated to culture in both art and nature so that the old barriers between the two are broken down, a man whose mind, supposedly liberated from formal conventions and tradition, can draw inspiration from and merge into a new unity the cultural expressions of past societies. As Christopher Hussey wrote: 'Picturesque architecture, then, is not, except in rare instances, a style, but a method of using and combining styles.'[28] John Britton sounded exactly the right note when he described the Deepdene as creating a new 'Union of the Picturesque in Scenery and Architecture with Domestic Beauties'. Hope's arrival in England in the 1790s, when the new theories of the Picturesque were being hotly disputed, was especially propitious as there emerged from these discussions a guiding discipline which gave direction and purpose to his employment of the mass of artistic knowledge which he had acquired during his lengthy tours of the Continent and the Eastern Mediterranean.

We have seen one way in which Hope achieved the broken variety which was always an essential feature of the Picturesque. For an architect designing in the Gothic manner with its towers and battlements this was, of course, a relatively simple matter; but in the classical manner it was rather more difficult. Uvedale Price, as so often, pointed to a solution when he spoke of the '. . . analogy between the general effect of rocks and of buildings', observing that the house, 'if divided into certain large portions, (as, for instance, into round or square towers), will not only be more varied, but appear of greater magnitude'.[29] The tower was an obvious solution, as Vanbrugh had realized at Vanbrugh Castle, Walpole at Strawberry Hill, Payne Knight at Downton Castle, Wyatt at Fonthill, and Nash at Cronkhill. Hope, however, was the first to elaborate on the rustic loggia-topped towers of North Italian domestic architecture in order to lend to his skyline the necessary touch of piquant drama. Thus, what Neale described as 'a curious open tower, constructed in the Tuscan or Lombard style',[30] and probably unique in English architecture, rose aloft over the staircase-bay which Hope added at the eastern end of the house to link his new dining-room wing with the old house (Plate 68). This surprising tower with its heavy balcony and broadly projecting flat eaves stands as an isolated pointer in the medley of Regency taste to the bulkier campaniles that were so soon to adorn the early Victorian villa. Towers were a feature of the Deepdene. If one stood with one's back to the north-west front of the house and the great tower, another tower loomed into sight on the steep slopes before the house (Plate 69). Bartlett's water-colour shows it rising dramatically at the end of a pathway shaded by the fronds of the cactus and the pine. Its canted sides rose to a balcony supported on heavy brackets giving the appearance of machicolation. The whole was surmounted by a tall domed *tholos* or cupola. Looking back from this point one could make out the north-west front of the old house which Hope had extended at each end. What appeared to be a third tower rose over the new dining-room wing (Plate 70). In fact this was an unusually elaborate chimney-stack on the design of which, in accordance with Price's recommendations, Hope had lavished especial care. The body of the chimney-stack was adorned with blind arches above which was a frieze of paterae and a projecting cornice with a heavily serrated top. The six chimney-pots were disguised as oil-jars, a device later popularised in Loudon's *Encyclopaedia*. The dining-room and library wings which

Hope added on to this north-west front, though adorned with the prominent neo-Greek acroteria so popular in furniture and architectural design at this moment, break out into the un-Greek bay-windows without which, it seems, the English house is rarely complete. This curious half-Tudor, half-Greek form reappears in 1834 at Swithland Hall in Leicestershire, a fine late-classical house designed by James Pennethorne (1801–1871) for the 4th Earl of Lanesborough.[31]

A series of designs has survived for the conversion of a tower in the kitchen gardens into a substantial gardener's cottage. These are almost certainly in the hand of Atkinson with pencilled alterations probably by Hope (Plate 71). The cottage is designed in that Picturesque combination of the Italianate and the castellated styles which is, ultimately, a part of the revived enthusiasm for the irregular effects of Vanbrugh.

Before we move indoors, a word should be said on the quality of the watercolours by W. H. Bartlett and Penry Williams[32] which have enabled us to make this external tour. They are in their own right a work of the Picturesque (see Plates 72, 73, and 74). Deliberately but subtly they heighten the effect of all that they choose to depict. The steep Surrey hills are made that much steeper and more dramatic; the plants and flowers more luxuriant; the gaps between the various portions of the house and the offices are enlarged and the trees which fill those gaps denser and more profuse. To turn through these richly detailed and sometimes quite ravishing water-colours is to be transported into a fantasy world almost Firbankian in its festive impermanence. In place of the cold archaeology that somehow one can never rid oneself of expecting from Hope, there is a hot-coloured exoticism both indoors and out. That scarlet and gold glory of Beckford at Fonthill and the Prince Regent at Brighton is never very far from Hope's picture. Costly peacocks and china urns add brilliance to the opulent terraces with their fountains, masses of bright flowers, sudden secluded corners enclosed by prickly and mysterious plants, and occasional unexpected Italianate vistas of the steep wooded Surrey hills beyond.

J. C. Loudon coined an adjective to describe Hope's Picturesque effects at the Deepdene. In his lengthy discussions in his *Encyclopaedia* (1833) of the problems of designing Picturesque country-houses, he observed that: 'As graphic illustration of the principles which we have endeavoured to lay down we shall refer to the villa of the late Thomas Hope, Esq. at Deepdene, Surrey ... the finest example in England of an Italian villa, united with the grounds by architectural appendages.'[33] Loudon had already elaborated this theme in an article in the *Gardener's Magazine* in 1829. There, he had described how in the house and offices Hope had:

> ... combined in them all the finest parts of what may be called the landscape architecture and sculpture of Italy, has formed a whole, the greatest praise that we can bestow on which is to say, that it will delight such men as Sir Uvedale Price and Gilbert Laing Meason ... [It] forms a group so rich in classic forms and combinations, that no one can duly appreciate its beauties, whose mind is not thoroughly imbued with Italy and the fine arts. It is, in short, an example of what the Germans call the ecstatic in architecture. There is not one English architect who would of his own accord have designed such a house; nor, if he had designed it, could he have found more country gentlemen by whom it would have been understood or carried into execution, than the Gard. Mag. would find readers if it were published in Greek.[34]

So Hope is to be responsible for the creation of a new category of the Picturesque: the Ecstatic! The Ecstatic takes us beyond the Beautiful and the Sublime to that combination of intellect and imagination in which each is heightened to an extreme degree. It is not surprising then, that as Loudon laments, there were few prepared to emulate the Deepdene. Thus it was to rectify this state of affairs that Loudon deliberately popularized Hope's work in the *Gardener's Magazine* and in his *Encyclopaedia.*

A case could be made for the Ecstatic being the missing term in the critical vocabulary of late neo-classical romanticism. In painting it is evocative of the atmosphere of Blake, Fuseli, Gandy, and John Martin.[35] In architecture, also, it seems right for those buildings which can hardly be contained within the agreeable confines of the Picturesque: Fonthill and the Brighton Pavilion, the external effects of the Deepdene, and the strange interiors of Soane. The Ecstatic was a guiding aesthetic in the Romantic 1800s. It was an age of fantastically heightened responses to the visual and literary arts. To appreciate this one has only to read some of the hundreds of accounts of Regency houses and gardens written in this period, all in amazingly heightened and exaggerated language, conjuring up a sort of Aladdin's Lamp atmosphere of magic and drama, of dazzling colours, of infinite vistas, and so on. And of course the reality, when one visits it—the little rock-gardens and conservatories, the mirrors placed to reflect views, the baby Stonehenges and the trivial cascades—rarely comes up to the descriptions. One of the reasons for this fever of enthusiasm was precisely that it was literary and theoretical through force of circumstances, the circumstance being the Napoleonic Wars which made large scale private building-projects almost impossible and thus encouraged this Ecstatic theorizing.

Such a pitch, of course, could hardly be maintained for long. The over-complex Italianate Picturesqueness of the Deepdene faded off gradually into the merely Italianate. That process will be shown later, but first let us inspect the interiors of Thomas Hope's house as they were when he left them. The tour would begin with the Entrance Hall. This was entered from a segmental projection on the east side which was flanked inside by a pair of fluted Greek Doric columns. These columns immediately struck a clear neo-classical note in marked contrast to the richer Picturesque orchestration of the exteriors of the house. This note was taken up elsewhere in the Hall. Thus in the centre of the wall opposite the entrance to the staircase-hall stood a copy of the Canova Venus which adorned Hope's sculpture-gallery in Duchess Street. The statue was placed between a pair of marble sarcophagi on pedestals, and slabs of rare marbles were let into the walls to serve as backgrounds for a large number of statues, busts, and vases. In the four corners of the room stood Corinthian columns of antique marble and in the centre was a circular table inlaid with variegated marble. An unexecuted design for this room, probably in Atkinson's hand (Plate 83), shows its reticent almost Palladian calm.

In the adjacent staircase-hall the first floor landing was supported by a Greek canephora, the unsuitability of which to its function, so Maria Edgeworth thought, caused her to describe it scornfully as '... a resigned female Caryatide of white stucco whose head in eternal pillory supports a heavy staircase, while her feet stand on a globe so small that it never could support her and it always seems to be slipping from under her ...'.[14] The bronze banisters in the form of elegant palmettes, have, unlike the stucco caryatid, survived all the vicissitudes of the last century and a half.

The drawing-room occupies the centre of the house and opened out through a porch on to a semi-circular platform adorned with urns, from which flights of steps led down into the gardens (Plate 74). All these were additions by Thomas Hope. The walls of the drawing-room were decorated with blue satin panels and there was an organ at the south end. The chimney-piece, which still survives, is bold and plain, save for gilt-bronze mounts, and has the great semi-circular opening so dear to Victorian designers. Over it is a tall mirror in which the glass elegantly returns round the corners of the chimney-breast on either side. The mirrors are divided by the tall, slender colonettes with lotus capitals at top and bottom, so much favoured in French Empire interiors. In this room were hung some of Hope's more distinguished modern paintings including a 'Narcissus' and an 'Italian scene' by Benjamin West, Westall's 'Damocles', an 'Andromache' by George Dawe and a portrait by Reynolds of Mrs. Hope's mother, Lady Decies.

Adjacent to the drawing-room is the boudoir or small dining-room (Plate 75) which of all the Deepdene interiors is the one of which we know most. There are two reasons for this. Firstly, it seems to have been a favourite of Hope's and a detailed water-colour was made of it for Britton's *History of the Deepdene*; and secondly, its chimney-piece and table (Plate 36) still survive intact. The chimney-piece is of green Mona marble flanked by pairs of coupled columns with ormolu capitals of lotus form. Above was a mirror framed by broad strips of unmoulded red marble adorned with a pair of sconces and gilt-bronze mounts. Hope's gilt cornice to the room, and the coving beneath it decorated with small red flowers, still survives though the frieze of swags below that is lost. Opposite the windows was a pedimented structure hung with tasselled draperies and containing a long day-bed or sofa, the whole linked to the side walls of the room by crimson curtains hung in quadrant form from a crested pelmet probably of brass. These 'tent-beds' with their martial Roman associations were, of course, especially popular in France though rarer in England. Whole tent-rooms, however, were actually introduced in the 1830s by Gandy-Deering at Shrubland Park, Suffolk, and J. B.

Papworth at Cranbury Park, Hampshire. Hope's smaller structure was surmounted by two large figures of swans; and within its curtained recess were hung five frames containing wax impressions from classical gems. In the centre of the room stood a circular table probably the superb mahogany one, with ornamental details in ebony and silver, made for Duchess Street which is illustrated in plate 39 of *Household Furniture*, and is now in the Victoria and Albert Museum. The fine Regency oil-lamp pendant from the centre of the ceiling might be compared stylistically with those, of ten years later by Barry, surviving at the Travellers' Club. The doors of this room, now dating from the 1890s, were originally inlaid with woods from the Deepdene estate and decorated with brass mouldings. Two Venetian views by Canaletto were hung here, both visible in the water-colour, together with copies of some of the Vatican frescoes.

Next to the Boudoir was the Old Library (Plate 76), the round-headed windows of which contained examples of Flemish stained glass possibly introduced by the Norfolks. Here also, was a narrative historical painting by Hilton showing Queen Philippa interceding for the citizens of Calais; a composite picture of bas-reliefs and architectural fragments from Ephesus; a bronze statue of Napoleon and another of Blucher made, appropriately, from cast-iron. In the centre of the ceiling is a large plaster rose. This is Adamish in decorative detailing yet the bold clarity of its composition and execution is suggestive of a later neo-classicism. So this could either be dated to the period *c.* 1780 when the house was built or to *c.* 1818 when Hope altered it. The frieze, curiously painted in green, was fully modelled in bas-relief and is closely paralleled by those of the 1790s at Cairness, Aberdeenshire, by the elder Playfair. The chimney-piece was a French affair with sprawling winged figures in white marble bearing torches, set in a tall round-headed recess filled with mirror. Penry Williams' water-colour of this chimney-piece shows us how the sparkling Hopeian-Empire manner of Duchess Street had mellowed over the years into a style that anticipated the comfortable domesticities of the Early Victorian home. Here are the warm darkish colours, the cosy floral wallpaper, the great semi-circular arches of mirror and chimney-piece opening, the scrolly fender, even the glass-domed clock, which all make up an atmosphere that we associate with a date later than

62. Thomas Hope and William Atkinson, Circular Conservatory
Deepdene, 1823

63. THOMAS HOPE and WILLIAM ATKINSON, Entrance to the Long Conservatory, Deepdene, 1823

Thomas Hope and William Atkinson, Deepdene, 1823

64. Interior of the Amphitheatre

65. Sculpture Gallery

66. THOMAS HOPE and WILLIAM ATKINSON, Exterior of the Amphitheatre, Deepdene, 1823

Hope's and that is still distinctly present in, say, Tenniel's *Alice* illustrations of the 1860s. The tall panelled doors in this room are decorated with classical patterns stencilled in gilt (Plate 77). This device reappears in the new anteroom (see below), which Hope probably created between 1826 and 1831. The Old Library doors may have been given their present form at that time, though it is not beyond the bounds of possibility that all this stencilled work was added by Henry Hope in the late 1830s.

The New Library was adjacent to the Old. The broad frame of a mirror on the south wall, just visible through the open door in the water-colour of the Conservatory (Plate 62), was ornamented with twelve medallions containing bas-relief portraits of members of Napoleon's family. Above this was a glazed partition letting in light from an internal yard. At the other end of the room was a classical oriel window which contained busts of the Duke of Wellington and of Field-Marshal the Viscount Beresford, a cousin of Mrs. Hope's, who was to become her second husband. Also in the room were displayed a statue by Behnes of Hope's youngest son playing with a rabbit, and a bust by Bartolini of his eldest son.

On the first and second floors there were thirty-three bedrooms and two drawing-rooms. The Lilac Room was so-called from the colour of its hangings and from the decorative details on its chimney-piece. These were thin strips of mauve marble inlaid to form lozenge-shaped intersecting outlines, an unusual and pleasing device. The doors were of mahogany inlaid with buhl and between the windows was hung a bronze gilt medallion by Thorvaldsen representing Night. On the pier-table before this stood a silver-gilt *tazza* probably executed by Paul Storr. There can be no doubt that this was a particularly sumptuous and femininely elegant room. It was further adorned with ancient Limoges enamels, a number of miniatures, two '*Fêtes Champêtres*' by Watteau, and a marble bas-relief by Flaxman depicting the birth of Bacchus. This room was directly over the Boudoir on the ground-floor. Elsewhere on the first floor was the Egyptian Room. China and pictures of lesser quality were displayed here, and the principal feature was, to quote Maria Edgeworth's unenthusiastic description, '. . . a bed made exactly after the model of Denon's Egyptian bed, a sofa bed wide enough for two aldermen, embosssed gold hieroglyphic *frights* all pointing with their hands distorted backwards at an Osiris or a long-armed monster of some sort who sits after their fashion on her hams and heels and hath the likeness of a globe of gold on her lappeted, scaly lappeted head'.[14] Despite Miss Edgeworth's scepticism, it must have made a bold display and one hard to parallel in England at that date.

Adjacent to the Egyptian Room was a Bathroom containing four representations of Raphael's 'grotesque' decorations in the Vatican loggie. In this sumptuous little High Renaissance room the bath was placed in a recess of looking-glass. The room existed at the time of Maria Edgeworth's visit in April 1819, but she cared no more for the decorative style of Raphael than for that of the Egyptians.

Mention must now be made of two more rooms on the ground floor (Fig. 20) which both seem to be the work of Thomas Hope but are not accounted for either in the plan of the house in Britton's *History of the Deepdene* nor in Neale's detailed tour of the house of 1826. The more important of these rooms must have been created between 1826 and 1831 on the site of an internal yard which had previously been occupied by the roof of the servants' hall in the basement. The new room was lit by a window facing west into another small internal yard at the south end of the new Library. Although the glazing bars have been altered, this room retains its original appearance at the time of writing more completely than any other in the house. Chimney-piece, doors, mirror, shutters, and painted cornice all survive, if in a battered state. The semi-circular opening of the chimney-piece is flanked by pairs of Bearded Bacchus terms, marble versions of the similar wooden terms dividing the cupboards in the 1st Vase Room at Duchess Street. These terms are themselves flanked by panels of scrolled anthemion detail. There is an acanthus frieze round the room, above which is a Greek key pattern combined with fleurs-de-lis. The walls and door-cases are bordered with laurel decoration, pairs of leaves alternating with pairs of berries, painted in gold on a dark red ground. Precisely this decoration adorned the borders of the segmental ceiling in the Indian Room at Duchess Street. Also reminiscent of Duchess Street is the unusual detailing of some of the doors (Plate 78). On the panels of these are inlaid in brass, figures and wreaths taken

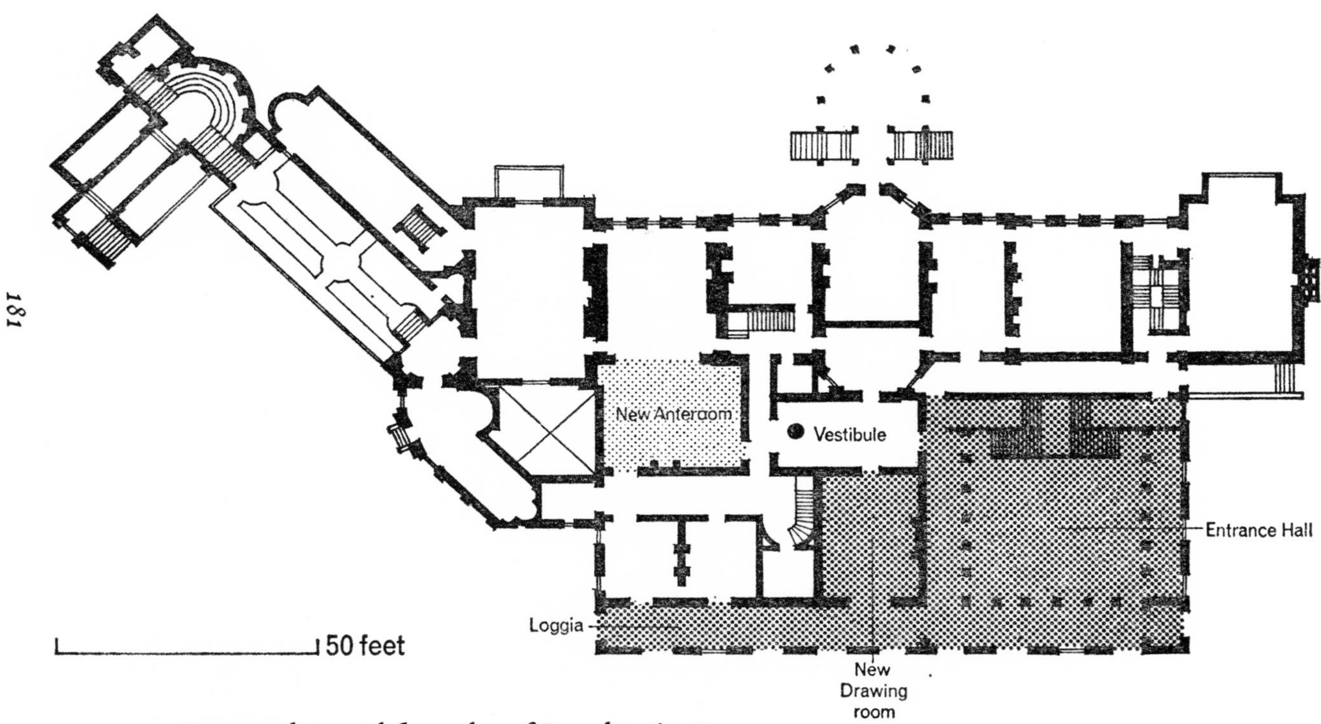

Fig. 20. Suggested ground-floor plan of Deepdene in 1840

from vase paintings. This device had been employed by Hope on the doors in the new Gallery at Duchess Street in 1819. The other room which poses a problem of dating is the long windowless vestibule which opens out of the existing entrance-hall. Stylistically it seems to be the work of Thomas Hope with its astylar door-cases, yet it partly occupies the site of his staircase-hall. We must assume, therefore, that either Hope himself in the last five years of his life re-sited his main staircase thus involving himself in considerable structural alterations or, more likely, that his son in adding the new entrance-hall and staircase simply lifted his father's staircase out of the old staircase-hall and, making good the details, turned that into the vestibule which still survives. Exactly this progress is envisaged in the design, probably by Atkinson, shown in Plate 83. Here, however, the new staircase occupies the site of what was to be Henry Hope's new South Drawing-room.

In the 1830s Henry Hope began the process of transforming the house into a sumptuous High Renaissance *palazzo* which was completed in 1840 (Plates 79, 80, and 81; and Fig. 20). The date is not exactly certain, but Loudon observed in 1836 that 'Extensive improvements are making . . . at the Deepdene by H. T. Hope, Esq.';[36] in October 1840 Disraeli and his wife stayed at the house and, in a letter to his sister, Disraeli wrote: 'In the midst of romantic grounds and picturesque park Hope has built, or rather is still building, a perfect Italian palace, full of balconies adorned with busts. On the front a terraced garden, and within a hall of tesselated pavement of mosaics, which is to hold his choicest marbles';[37] and in 1845 the remodelling was described as having taken place 'a few years ago'.[38] Hussey and Nairn, who alone in modern times have discussed the Deepdene, have both fallen into the error of describing the existing façades of the house as though they were Thomas Hope's work. Thus Hussey observed in 1927 that the house was 'as a whole . . . an Italian villa, with its campaniles, terraces, and loggias; the parent of Dorchester House and innumerable suburban villas';[39] and in 1958 that 'Hope's Deepdene synthesis perceptibly influenced Gandy-Deering's remodelling of Shrubland, and, through Barry's *palazzos*, begot the race of Victorian villas of which Osborne was to be the type.'[40] In the *Buildings of England* volume on Surrey, Nairn reproduced a photograph[41] of the

Italinate work of Hope's son over a caption attributing it to Thomas Hope and Atkinson.

Yet, having said this, one is still able to confirm in part Hussey's observations about the house. The reason is that bound up with the Minet Library volume of Britton's History are eight architectural drawings or sketches for the hall and exteriors of the house, none of which correspond exactly with what was ultimately executed (Plates 82–86). I suggest that the first six represent improvements to the house envisaged by Thomas Hope between 1826, when the major remodelling was complete, and 1831, the year of his death. Nos. 7 and 8 are clearly later in architectural style as in spirit and it is more than likely that they are the work of Hope's son, Henry.

What the first six drawings reveal is that Hope himself, towards the end of his life, was toying with the idea of creating a grand new staircase-hall and south front by extending to the east the south wing which he had added a few years earlier. The new entrance front would be eleven bays by three with, behind it on the ground floor from east to west, a staircase-hall, a drawing-room, and a sequence of three smaller rooms. The wing which Hope's son had added by 1840 was to be exactly of this size and disposition. What the drawings further reveal is that Thomas Hope had shifted stylistically away from his original additions to the Deepdene, which were Italianate in the Picturesque Claude-like sense, to the more precise Italianism of the 1830s which was based fairly closely on fifteenth and sixteenth-century models. It is easy to regard this new style merely as an example of 'the growing historicism' of the nineteenth century, but there is no reason why it should not be seen as the natural heir to English Palladianism, which is not normally described as an 'historicist' style.

Hope's design no. 1 (Plate 82) for the staircase end of the proposed new hall is an elegant exercise in the round-arched Italianism which was still rare in the 1820s. In fact, Henry Hope's work of the late 1830s follows this design closely although, unlike his father, he retained, surprisingly, his father's metal staircase railings. A quite different scheme for the hall is presented in design no. 2 (Plate 83). Here, the aedicular treatment of the doors is a close parallel to that of the windows on the Pall Mall front of Barry's Travellers' Club (1829–31). In any discussion of the nineteenth-century Italianate revival Barry must inevitably play a large part. His villa at Brighton for Thomas Attree, his church of St. Andrew's, Hove, and the Travellers' Club are the first English examples of this style and in their restraint are very close to the contemporary Deepdene designs. Indeed, the Italianate details of the Pall Mall façade of the Travellers' are so subtle as probably to pass unobserved. The garden front is more obviously Italianate but inside nothing is except the plan. It is not always realized how sophisticatedly eclectic the interiors are. Thus the Library is entirely Palladian in character, save for the Bassae frieze which would, properly speaking, be as out of place in an English Palladian as in an Italian Renaissance apartment. The Staircase has a distinctly late seventeenth-century English touch, and what is now the Dining-room is a restrained version of the Graeco-Roman manner of Henry Holland.[42]

Hope's design no. 3 has an open ground-floor loggia or colonnade, an idea which Henry Hope was eventually to adopt. The perspective sketch in design no. 6 (Plate 85) is of interest in that it shows what Hope imagined the effect would be when the façade in no. 5 (Plate 84) had been added on to the existing house. He intended to leave intact the old kitchen and dairy wing and the great loggia-topped tower, but he had now developed further the use of terraces and balustrades which had added Picturesque irregularity to the foreground of the conservatory wing. Thus the new entrance wing is linked to the grounds by means of long balustraded walls adorned with urns, the larger wall being punctuated with tall semi-circular headed niches containing statues. The whole conception is still merged irregularly with trees and represents a half-way stage in the development of the Italianate 'architectural garden'.

Designs nos. 7 and 8 (Plate 86), perhaps by Henry Hope, display as was implied earlier, the difference between the earliest Renaissance revival of the late 1820s and the heavier and more confident Italianism of a decade later. Here, now, the ground floor of the entrance-front is rusticated, there is a raised central belvedere of round-arched openings —a close parallel to that projected at the Travellers' Club—and the roof is pantiled. At the same moment Barry introduced these tiles into England[43] at Walton House, Surrey (1835–9), now demolished. Design no. 8 (Plate 86), for the remodelled garden-front, shows the central canted bay capped by a French domelet and beneath the first-floor windows those chunky balconies which Barry first used on the garden front of the Travellers'.

Henry Hope's eventual remodelling differed in a number of particulars from these two sketches. The main differences were on the entrance front (Plate 79) which was given a greater depth and richness. The central five bays of the second floor were considerably recessed exactly as at Vulliamy's Dorchester House (1848–63), and the space thus provided was used as a loggia. Behind and above this rose a fourth storey, of five bays, on which the window surrounds and the tapered pilasters were familiar from Italian Mannerist architecture. The end bays of this raised storey were surmounted by small square belvederes or loggias, with three round-arched openings on each face. Such details were based on Genoese and Roman villas like the towered Villa Medici. On the north-west or garden-front (Plate 80) the chief innovation was the addition of a third storey to the wings of the original house which contained the Billiard Room and the Old Library. These wings were further heightened by balustrades with tall square chimneys at the four corners, a device later used by Barry to articulate the Green Park front of Bridgewater House (1847–57). The French dome, however, was not executed, with the result that the central bay is considerably lower than the side wings—a most unhappy effect. Although the whole front was refaced in a heavier style, the actual shape of the window-openings was not altered. Nor were Thomas Hope's internal decorations and his long projecting south-west wing tampered with. The only new reception-rooms of any consequence provided by the remodelling were the huge entrance-hall and the adjacent south drawing-room, occupying the site of Thomas Hope's entrance-hall. The new entrance-hall (Plate 81) follows fairly closely suggestions made by Thomas Hope and Atkinson, with colonnades on the ground- and first-floors and a flat coffered ceiling with a central lantern. This monumental galleried and colonnaded hall was executed, it seems, exactly at the moment of that at Barry's Reform Club. Characteristic of the new age are the mosaic floor whose thin scrolly decoration is recognizably Early Victorian and, in the drawing-room, an ostentatious caryatid-flanked 'Barocco' chimney-piece with the letter 'H' triumphant in the centre.

With the architectural shift from Poussinesque Italianate to Renaissance Italianate went the corresponding shift in garden design from the Picturesque to the Gardenesque, presaged in Thomas Hope's design no. 6. In the *Gardener's Magazine* for 1836,[36] Loudon refers to the improvements being effected in the gardens at the Deepdene, and discusses generally the new taste for the Gardenesque of whose cause, from this moment, he became one of the principal champions. So far as the architecture itself is concerned, the Deepdene is either antecedent to or contemporary with the major examples of Victorian Italianization on the grand scale. Trentham was begun in the 30s, but it seems that even there the most characteristic parts were the product of a decade later.[44] Thomas Hope's projects of the late 20s are obviously in part responsible for the Deepdene's early arrival at the masked ball of Italianized Georgian country houses.

The Italianate manner has this in common with the Picturesque: it is an 'organic', freely growing style, ideal for use in adaptions and alterations of existing buildings. Thus Osborne manages, perversely, to look exactly like a remodelled Georgian house.

For the student of the Picturesque, as the student of the Deepdene must be, the Italianate revival is a phenomenon of especial interest. There is a sense, indeed, in which the Italianate revival can be regarded merely as another stage in the development of the Picturesque. Thus Summerson, writing of the garden-front of the Travellers' Club, observed:

> The whole effect was vigorous and picturesque, in contrast to the extreme restraint imposed by the Athenian school. The building was the answer to the *malaise* discernible in all the work of the later Greek Revival, the feeling that the capture of Periclean refinement was not an absolute goal after all: that there was still beauty in roughness and in deep, complex shadows.[45]

Roughness and shadows were obviously a feature of the new entrance-front of the Deepdene, as they had also been of the aesthetic theory formulated by Price and Knight. The following quotation from Mrs. Jameson's diary of the 1820s tells us much about the moment of transition: 'Had I never visited Italy I think I should never have understood the word *picturesque* . . . A snug English villa with its shaven

67. THOMAS HOPE and WILLIAM ATKINSON, Steps to the South Wing, Deepdene, 1823

THOMAS HOPE and WILLIAM ATKINSON, Deepdene, 1818–23

THOMAS HOPE and WILLIAM ATKINSON, Deepdene

70. North West Front, 1818 71. Design for Gardener's Cottage

72. William Bartlett, The Dene from the Terrace at Deepdene, 1825

William Bartlett
73. Holm Wood from the Terrace at Deepdene, 1825
74. The Terrace at Deepdene, 1825

75. Thomas Hope and William Atkinson, Boudoir, Deepdene, 1818

THOMAS HOPE and WILLIAM ATKINSON

76. Chimney-piece in the Old Library, Deepdene, 1818

77. Detail of Door in the Old Library, Deepdene, 1818

78. Door in the Ante-Room, Deepdene, 1826–31

HENRY THOMAS HOPE, Deepdene, 1836–40

79. Entrance Front 80. North West Front

lawn, its neat shrubbery, and its park, is a delightful thing—an Italian villa is probably far less *comfortable*, but with its vineyards, its gardens, its fountains, and statues, is far more picturesque.'[46] It might, moreover, be hard to attack the historian who regarded the whole of nineteenth-century architecture as a developing essay in the Picturesque, from Pugin's screened interiors through the bold massing of Scott's Foreign Office to Shaw's towering chimneys and sweeping roofs. And as a postscript there would be the valiant attempts made by the *Architectural Review*, immediately after the second world war, to introduce Picturesque principles into contemporary town-planning.

It should be pointed out that it was at the Deepdene in the 1840s that the political movement called Young England was born. The reason for doing so is that if ever there was a political movement deserving the title of Picturesque, then it was Young England. It was a last colourful fling, before the more solemn movements of the mid-Victorian decades, by those who were aristocrats by background or aspiration like Lord John Manners, Disraeli, and Henry Hope. They stood for a highly romantic and picturesque society and government that was aristocratic and agrarian, half-feudal and half-*ancien régime*. This, of course, was the moment for the revival of lost titles by the old Catholic families and for their creation of romantic and evocative settings for themselves. This is what Goodhart-Rendel called, in a caption to a plate of Pugin's Scarisbrick Hall, 'The Catholic Seigneury'.[47] What Walter Scott did for the Gothic Revival, Benjamin Disraeli did for the Italian. *Coningsby*, published in 1844 as the first of Disraeli's great trio of political novels, is actually dedicated to Henry Hope. The dedication explains, moreover, that the novel was 'conceived and partly executed amid the glades and galleries of Deepdene.' The sequence of Disraeli's novels offers fascinating insights into the Picturesque and the Italianate, as well as showing how the former faded off imperceptibly into the latter. The late 'Regency' years brought to a fine art the costly Picturesque magnificence of neo-classicism as well as its heightened ideals of connoisseurship in art and life. There is probably no better evocation of this, the atmosphere of Duchess Street and the Deepdene, than Disraeli's novel, *Henrietta Temple* (1834). I propose, therefore, to quote from descriptions in the novel of an English neo-classical country house, a *palazzo* in Rome and a London town-house. At Ducie Bower:

> A façade of four Ionic columns fronted an octagon hall, adorned with statues, which led into a saloon of considerable size and fine proportion. Ferdinand thought that he had never in his life entered so brilliant a chamber. The lofty walls were covered with an Indian paper of vivid fancy ... [There were] ... most inviting couches, cabinets of choice inlay, and grotesque tables covered with articles of vertu ... A large lamp of Dresden china was suspended from the painted and gilded ceiling. The three tall windows opened on the gardens, and admitted a perfume so rich and various ... [In the dining-room,] ... the ceiling was painted in grey tinted frescoes of a classical and festive character, and the side table, which stood in a recess supported by four magnificent columns, was adorned with choice Etruscan vases. The air of repose and stillness which distinguished this apartment was heightened by the vast conservatory into which it led, blazing with light and beauty, groups of exotic trees, plants of radiant tint, the sound of a fountain, and gorgeous forms of tropic birds.

Moving from Ducie Bower to the palace in Rome of an English connoisseur, we are taken into a room evocative of Hope's Flaxman Room at Duchess Street:

> At the end of the principal gallery, Henrietta perceived an open door which admitted them into a small Octagon chamber, of Ionic architecture. The walls were not hung with pictures, and one work of art alone solicited their attention. Elevated on a pedestal of porphyry surrounded by a rail of bronze arrows of the lightest workmanship, was that statue of Diana which they had so much admired at Pisa. The cheek, by an ancient process, the secret of which was recently been regained at Rome, was tinted with a delicate glow.

Finally, Lady Bellair's town mansion is consciously Hopeian in detail:

> Bellair House was the prettiest mansion in Mayfair. It was a long building, in the Italian style ... All the reception rooms were on the ground floor, and were all connected. [In the centre was] ... an octagon library, lined with well-laden dwarf cases of brilliant volumes, crowned with no lack of marble busts, bronzes, and Etruscan vases. On each side opened a magnificent saloon, furnished in that classic style which the late accomplished and ingenious Mr. Hope first rendered popular in this country. The wings,

projecting far into the gardens, comprised respectively a dining-room and a conservatory of considerable dimensions.[48]

Now *Henrietta Temple* was written exactly three years after the death of Thomas Hope, exactly three years before the accession of Queen Victoria—that is at the last moment at which this half-Regency glitter was still fashionable. The Regency ideal of connoisseurship, epitomized by Thomas Hope, gradually found its natural setting to be the sumptuous High Renaissance *palazzo*, epitomized by his son's remodelling of the Deepdene. Partly as a result of his friendship[49] with Henry Hope, Disraeli's settings keep pace with the growing Italianism of the day so that a late novel, like *Lothair*, actually has Barry's Trentham for a background. Perhaps it is too fanciful to point out that Henry Hope's daughter shared her Christian name with Henrietta Temple. At all events, Henrietta Hope more than fulfilled all the expectations of her father (and grandfather, had he been alive) by marrying in 1861 the son and heir of the 5th Duke of Newcastle. This was the Duke whose commissioning of Barry in 1857 to remodel Clumber resulted in the project which, according to Hitchcock, 'represented Barry's ultimate ideal for the country palace of an English peer' and was considered to be too Picturesque, 'much too boldly plastic',[50] to be included within the Early Victorian category. It is a strange irony that the same opulent Italianism should have been the ideal of both the reforming party, at the Reform Club, and the conserving party, at the Deepdene. Strange, also, that there should survive an undated design for an Italianate house labelled: 'Erwood, Cheshire, as not completed' (Fig. 21),[51] signed by Alexander Beresford Hope, Thomas' otherwise resolutely High Church, High Gothic offspring. However, there is a Picturesquely sited Gothic chapel nearby, and the whole is close to his remodelling of his house Bedgebury in Kent.[52]

Since we have dwelt on the significance of Henry Hope's work at the Deepdene and its connections with his father, some reference should be made to the town house which he built in Piccadilly to replace his father's in Duchess Street, demolished in 1851. The new house was erected between 1849 and 1851 to designs by the French architect P.-C. Dusillion with the assistance of T. L. Donaldson.[53] There is no need to recount here Hitchcock's description of it,[54] though I would add to it the fact that its lavish decorative detailing, all by French craftsmen, cost as much as £18,000[53] and that its façades anticipated the street architecture of 1900 as much as that of the English Second Empire style. One of the main reasons for mentioning this house at all is that it helps to show how ingrained in the Hope family were the

Fig. 21. Alexander Beresford Hope, *et al.*, 'Erwood, Cheshire, as not completed'

ideals of opulent, up-to-the-minute connoisseurship which we have noticed in the character of Thomas Hope.

There can be little doubt that the career of his eldest son would have afforded Thomas Hope the very highest satisfaction. The mid-nineteenth century took more enthusiastically to its bosom the opulent offspring of commercial transactions than had the stricter matron of Regency society. Thus, though both were Vice-Presidents of the Society of Arts, Henry Hope was also a founder in 1836 of the Art Union of London and of the Royal Botanical Society; he also had a hand in the arrangement of the Great Exhibition of 1851 and, to crown all, became Chairman of the Eastern Steam Navigation Company, founded to launch Brunel's ship *Leviathan*. He was made the subject of an adulatory article in *The Illustrated London News* in 1858,[55] was father-in-law to a prospective Duke and played superbly the combined rôles of squire, connoisseur, and host when, for example, the Surrey Archaeological Society, of which he was President, met at the Deepdene.[56]

Between Henry Hope's death in 1862 and the year 1917, the Deepdene survived as a comfortably inhabited country house in very much the same architectural and decorative form that he and his father had given it. His daughter Henrietta saw her eldest son, as 7th Duke of Newcastle, inherit Clumber in 1879; to her second son, Lord Henry Francis Hope Pelham-Clinton-Hope, she bequeathed the Deepdene. A few years after her second husband's death in 1892 she let the house to Colonel Lord William Beresford, who had taken as his wife in 1895 the already twice-married Lilian, Duchess of Marlborough. They introduced a number of small decorative details into the old entertaining rooms such as wooden over-doors with intertwined L's surmounted by coronets. Perhaps it was also at this moment that Thomas Hope's projecting conservatory and sculpture-gallery wing was replaced by two short parallel wings running westwards and terminating in a large circular conservatory. The appearance of house and grounds in these palmy days was marvellously recorded in a series of photographs taken by *Country Life* in 1899,[57] showing the immaculately-kept grounds punctuated by gas-lamp and monkey-puzzle tree.[58]

Four years after inheriting the Deepdene from his mother in 1913, Lord Francis Hope—as he was known for short—was tragically obliged to sell the contents of the house and much of the property.[59] Curiously enough, the result of this mammoth sale, conducted by Christie's in the summer of 1917, was ultimately to enhance not dissipate the reputation of Thomas Hope since much of his furniture was bought by Edward Knoblock, who may be said to have initiated the Regency Revival. (For a brief account of this Revival, see Appendix E.) With Maxwell Ayrton as architect, Knoblock created, immediately after the first world war, a superbly convincing yet imaginative setting for his Hope and other neo-classical pieces at Beach House,

Worthing, originally built in 1820 for a Mr. Helmes by J. B. Rebecca.[60]

But if furniture 'in the Thomas Hope manner' now reflects in the dealers' advertisements all the glitter of the costly and the fashionable, no such hopeful rays have illumined the subsequent history of the Deepdene. After a period between the wars as an hotel, owned for a time by the notorious Maundy Gregory, who sold peerages for Lloyd George,[61] the house was used as British Railway Offices until 1966. During its occupancy by the railway authorities the house was reduced to an uniquely detestable state, disgusting beyond all powers of description. At the time of writing, this deeply depressing carcase is hopefully being offered for sale. The Picturesque, one may conclude, is a plant too frail to survive the blasts of modern life.

VII

The Hope Style: Sources, Parallels, and Influences

This chapter must begin with a reassertion of the individuality of the Hope style. The search for contemporary sources—beyond the decorative details collected in the modern books to which Hope refers in the bibliography to *Household Furniture*—does not reveal anything immediately obvious or convincing. The one possible exception is the furniture style, which is a parallel to, though not necessarily a derivative of, the work of Percier and Fontaine. At Duchess Street and at the Deepdene, Hope was governed by different sets of aesthetic considerations which were more or less unique to himself. These have already been more than hinted at in the chapters devoted to these houses.

At Duchess Street there was firstly the desire to present coherently the whole, cumulative, antique vision as it had affected successive civilizations in Greece, Italy, Turkey, Syria, and Egypt. This romantic eclectic synthesis, the direct result of Hope's extensive travels between 1787 and 1795, was further heightened by an insistent desire to create a symbolic language so that every object in the house could tell its own story: a story that would echo and indicate the function of the object and its function in the iconography of the room as a whole. This conception is probably French in origin and may be seen as a direct parallel to the *architecture parlante* of the 'Revolutionary' architects. That a highly symbolical art had been extensively employed to popularize the Revolution, and later appeared in different form in interior decoration and furniture is obvious, but that it ever played in French interiors so dominant and ubiquitous a rôle as at Duchess Street must remain doubtful until a detailed study of the use of allegory in Empire furniture is undertaken. It was certainly present at a theoretical level. A characteristic instance occurs in 1801 in the first volume of the influential *Annales du Musée*. We know from *Household Furniture* that Hope used this series as a source; and from volume II Charles Kelsall borrowed a design for the Observatory at his Ideal University (Fig. 5). The design in volume I is for a bookase, the lower half of which is flanked by animal monopodia and decorated with anthemia, the upper half being flanked by seated Egyptian priests and surmounted by the names in Latin of Homer and Virgil. It is a clumsy piece, but the

Fig. 22. Thomas Hope, Chimney-piece at Duchess Street, *c.* 1800

accompanying text justifies its combination of styles in exactly the same way that Hope justified his decorative synthesis at Duchess Street:

> la composition est un assemblage du style grec pour la partie basse, égyptien pour les figures, et romain ou toscan pour l'architecture. Ce mélange de style est autorisé par l'usage auquel ce meuble est destiné. Une bibliothèque est une dépôt de science; et, sous ce rapport, quelles nations ont plus de droits à notre reconnaissance que celles que l'artiste a eu l'intention de rappeler d'une manière symbolique par la choix de ses accessoires?[1]

81. Henry Thomas Hope, Hall, Deepdene, 1836–40

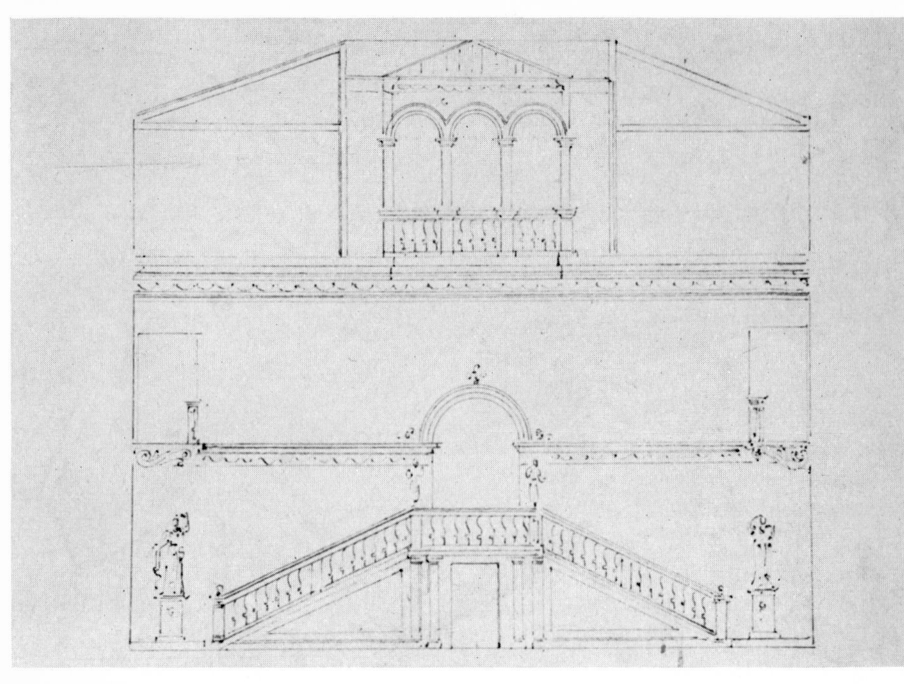

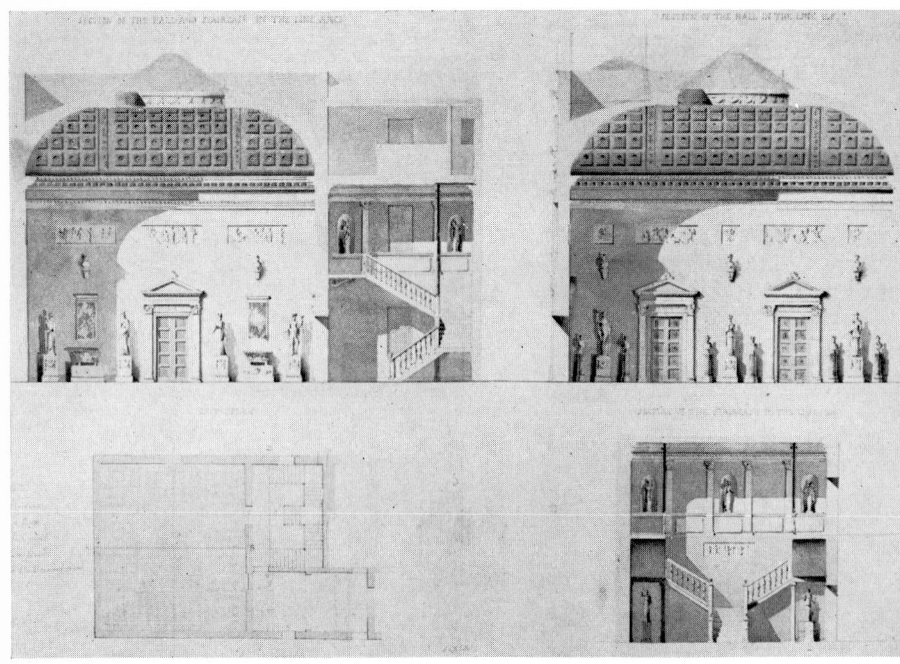

THOMAS HOPE and WILLIAM ATKINSON, Deepdene, 1826–31

82. Design for the Hall 83. Design for the Hall, Sections and Plan

THOMAS HOPE and WILLIAM ATKINSON, Design for the Entrance Front, Deepdene, 1826–31

84. Elevation 85. Perspective View

86. Henry Thomas Hope?, Design for North West Front, Deepdene, 1836–40

87. Roman Throne Legs

88. Column from the Temple c
Viss Vissha, Benares

A typical example of this technique at Duchess Street was a white marble chimney-piece (Fig. 22) adorned with bronze ornaments elaborating the theme of fire: wreaths containing the heads of Vulcan and Vesta, and a candelabrum placed between pairs of Mithraic figures. Elsewhere, was a sumptuous bed of mahogany and bronze (Fig. 23), on the ends of which were two elegant figures of Night

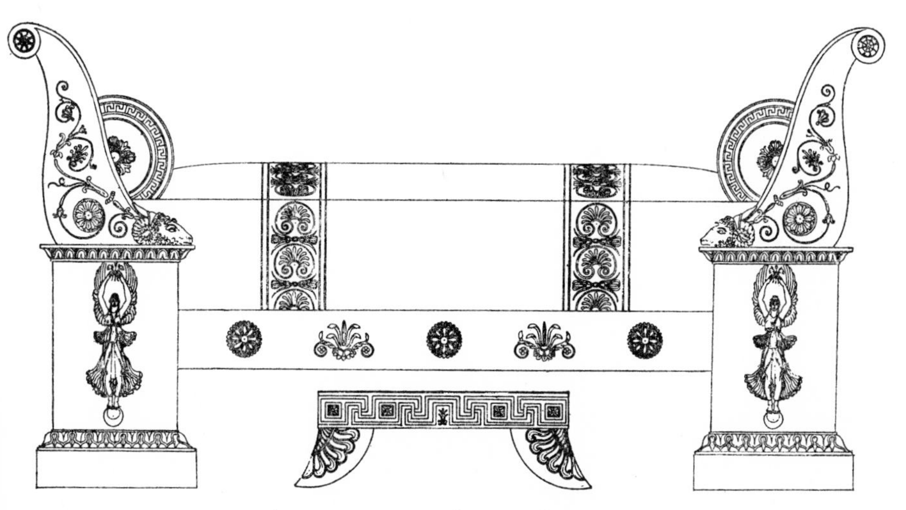

Fig. 23. Thomas Hope, Bed at Duchess Street, *c.* 1800

riding on a crescent-moon and scattering her poppies—a frequent decorative device on Empire furniture. Similarly, on an elaborate gilt-bronze chandelier (Fig. 24), a thick wreath of Deadly Nightshade was surmounted by a diadem of stars—a visual pun suggesting the victory of light over dark. The rather overpowering Hope cradle (Fig. 25), anticipating that made by Jacob-Desmalter and Thomire in 1811 for the King of Rome,[2] was elaborately but elegantly adorned with classical emblems of night, sleep, dreams, and Hope—and to emphasize the point was prominently inscribed *Spes*.

Thus the Hope style created a new iconology which would give complete meaning to every detail of the house's arrangements, such as had been experienced before only in the sequence of religious art within a great church. As Flaxman was perceptively to observe: 'Mr. Hope's principle affords us an excellent hint for adapting the

Fig. 24. Thomas Hope, Chandelier at Duchess Street, *c.* 1800

furniture, decoration, and symbols to the Edifice and its purposes, whether it be the Church or the Fortress, the Palace, Museum, private dwelling or cottage.'[3] In accordance with this aim, therefore, Hope's iconology was literary or narrative. It requires no very special gifts of foresight to see how this points forward to the immense emphasis upon narrative art of all kinds which was to be so characteristic of the nineteenth century, as exemplified particularly by the sentimental

Fig. 25. Thomas Hope, Cradle at Duchess Street, *c.* 1800

literariness of the furniture at the Great Exhibition. From the aesthetic behind the Hope cradle it is but a step to that behind a chair described in the catalogue of 1851 as 'The Day Dreamer'. Indeed, its maker's description could almost be taken from *Household Furniture*:

The chair is decorated at the top with two winged thoughts—the one

> with bird-like pinions, and crowned with roses, representing happy and joyous dreams, the other with leather bat-like wings—unpleasant and troubled ones. Behind is displayed Hope, under the figure of the rising sun. The twisted supports of the back are ornamented with poppy, heartsease, convolvulus and snowdrop, all emblematic of the subject.[4]

Just as the meaning of the decorative details of the Hope style was emphasized by the addition of words like *Φιλιππος* and *Spes*, so was there to be Victorian furniture of which the meaning could be appreciated fully only with mottoes. And the interiors and exteriors of Victorian public and domestic buildings came more and more to be adorned with mottoes, texts, and quotations, either explanatory or moral, or both. One can suggest that Hope was at the forefront of a movement almost Puritan in its way, which believed that all ornament must be justified by having a purpose other than the merely aesthetic; the nineteenth century came very close to saying that all ornament must have a moral; and it has been left to the twentieth century to declare that all ornament is immoral anyway.

In Hope's letter of 1805 to Matthew Boulton—perhaps the most interesting of his few surviving letters, and already quoted in Chapter II—he offers a clear statement of his approach to ornament, design, and the antique. Rehearsing to Boulton the advice he had given to his protégé Phillp, Hope insisted

> that if there was any novelty in my house, it was only in the application of very *old* forms. That if the forms of my furniture were more agreeable than the generality of those one meets with, it was only owing to my having, not servilely imitated, but endeavoured to make myself master of *the spirit* of the Antique. That consequently imitating me was only imitating the imitator; and that he would do better still by applying at once to the fountain-head, to those sources of beauty which lay open to every body: I mean the most approved books on ancient Art: Sir Wm. Hamilton's Vases, Winckelman, Piranesi, Stuart's Athens, Ionian Antiquities &c. &c. &c. Beauty consists not in ornament, it consists in outline—where this is elegant and well understood the simplest object will be pleasing: without a good outline, the richest and most decorated will only appear tawdry. Ornament can only be of use after we have sufficiently surveyed and dwelt upon the perfection of the whole, to make us find new pleasure in examining the details. But for that reason

> it should aways appear to be subordinate, particularly in objects of utility.[5]

Hope seems to be saying here about the applied arts what Pugin was soon to say about architecture in such oft-quoted tags as: 'there should be no features about a building which are not necessary for convenience, construction, or propriety' and 'all ornament should consist of enrichment of the essential construction of the building'.[6] And certainly there is a striking contrast between Hope's dictum that 'Beauty consists not in ornament, it consists in outline', and the published plates of Percier and Fontaine. The King of Spain's study at Aranjuez,[7] for example, seems to be entirely enmeshed by an ubiquitous calligraphic ornament that is almost Beardleyesque in its disregard for the varied objects it covers.

The precise sources for the Hope style in the applied arts and especially in furniture are numerous and complex. The daring recreation of the domestic interiors of the ancient world, initiated in the later eighteenth century, is one of the most remarkable achievements of neo-classicism. Greek furniture was known through vase-paintings and reliefs; Roman through frescoes at Pompeii, sarcophagi, tombstones, and a few surviving pieces. The types of Greek furniture were as limited as their forms were simple. Beyond the throne, chair, couch, stool, chest, and table the Greek designer hardly looked. His most sophisticated and characteristic product was probably the *klismos* chair, and of the animal parts, which were to be so prominent a feature of the Empire style, he made but the most infrequent use. These were a Roman elaboration. Thus in Thomas Hope's, as in French Empire furniture, the primary source must be regarded as Roman not Greek. But whereas the Percier and Fontaine style, as we have hinted above, is marked by an attraction towards the greater sumptuousness of Roman decoration, so is the Hope style towards the greater elegance of Greek. Variants of the *klismos* chair are therefore frequent in Hope's designs, rare in those of Percier and Fontaine.

By the time that Hope was ready to make his own contribution in *c.* 1799 there were at least six principal sources on which the designer could draw. These and the relationship of Hope's furniture to them will now be successively examined. (A list of surviving objects designed by Hope will be found in Appendix E.)

I. MARBLE FRAGMENTS AND RELIEFS IN MUSEUMS AND PRIVATE COLLECTIONS

Hope himself possessed a set of four elaborately decorated Roman throne legs (Plate 87),[8] now in the Fitzwilliam Museum, of a type familiar from Greek vase-paintings. These are close to the supports of a sumptuous State Chair made for Napoleon and clearly depicted in the Ingres portrait of him in 1803 as First Consul.[9] They were exactly copied by Jacob-Desmalter in 1809 on a gilt wooden armchair in the Empress' State Drawing-room at Compiègne.[10] The ends of a tea-table (Fig. 26), designed by Hope for Duchess Street, were clearly based on the so-called Tomb of Agrippa in the Pantheon. This tomb had had a long history of delineation, appearing in the works of Desgodetz, Piranesi, and Tatham.[11] The sides of the lower half of a red marble throne in the Vatican[12] were also used extensively for furniture designs in our period. Similar in form to the ends of the Agrippa tomb they were more elegantly decorated with anthemia. Gauffier had used them as early as 1790 for the design of a table in his painting 'La Charité des Dames Romaines' (in the Musée des Beaux Arts, Poitiers), as also had Hope (Plate 98) and, before 1801, Percier and Fontaine.[13] Tatham had reproduced a similar design in 1799 from a marble seat in 'a chapel near Rome'.[14] A sumptuous marble seat like that in the Louvre[15] furnished Hope with the idea for his four thrones in the Picture Gallery at Duchess Street (Fig. 8), their sides formed by winged sphinxes. In the Indian Room (Fig. 12), the large winged lions forming the sides of the two armchairs (Fig. 27) were based on sarcophagi decorated with chimaerae in the collection of Prince Braschi at Rome.[16] The frieze, depicting a row of twelve gods, on the sofa (Fig. 27) in the Lararium was copied from one round an antique well-head in the Capitoline Museum; Hope especially praised 'the old stiff style of workmanship', and Reade rightly emphasizes how characteristic this 'stiffness' is of the work of both Flaxman and Hope.[16] The terminations of a heavy sofa elsewhere in the house (Fig. 28) were based on some marble chimaerae that Hope had seen in the studio in Rome of Bartolommeo Cavaceppi.[17] These were doubtless antique fragments which Cavaceppi, the unscrupulous restorer of the Weddell Venus, was going to work up into some new recreation.

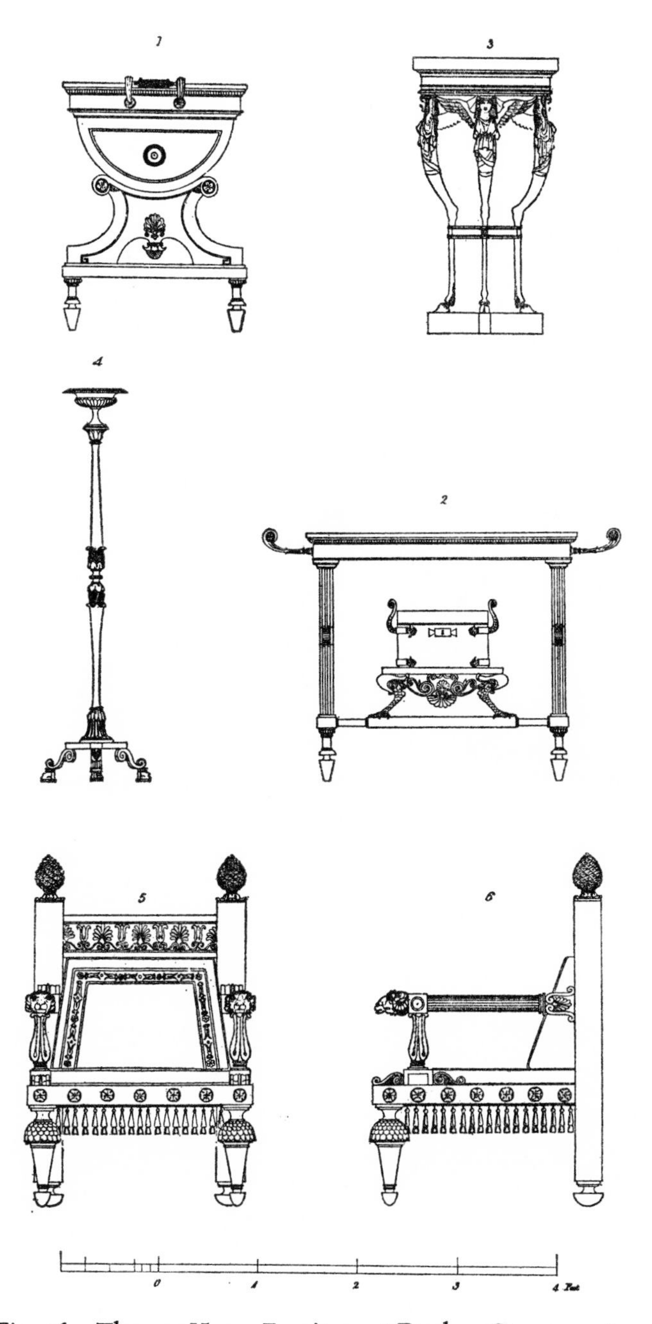

Fig. 26. Thomas Hope, Furniture at Duchess Street, *c.* 1800

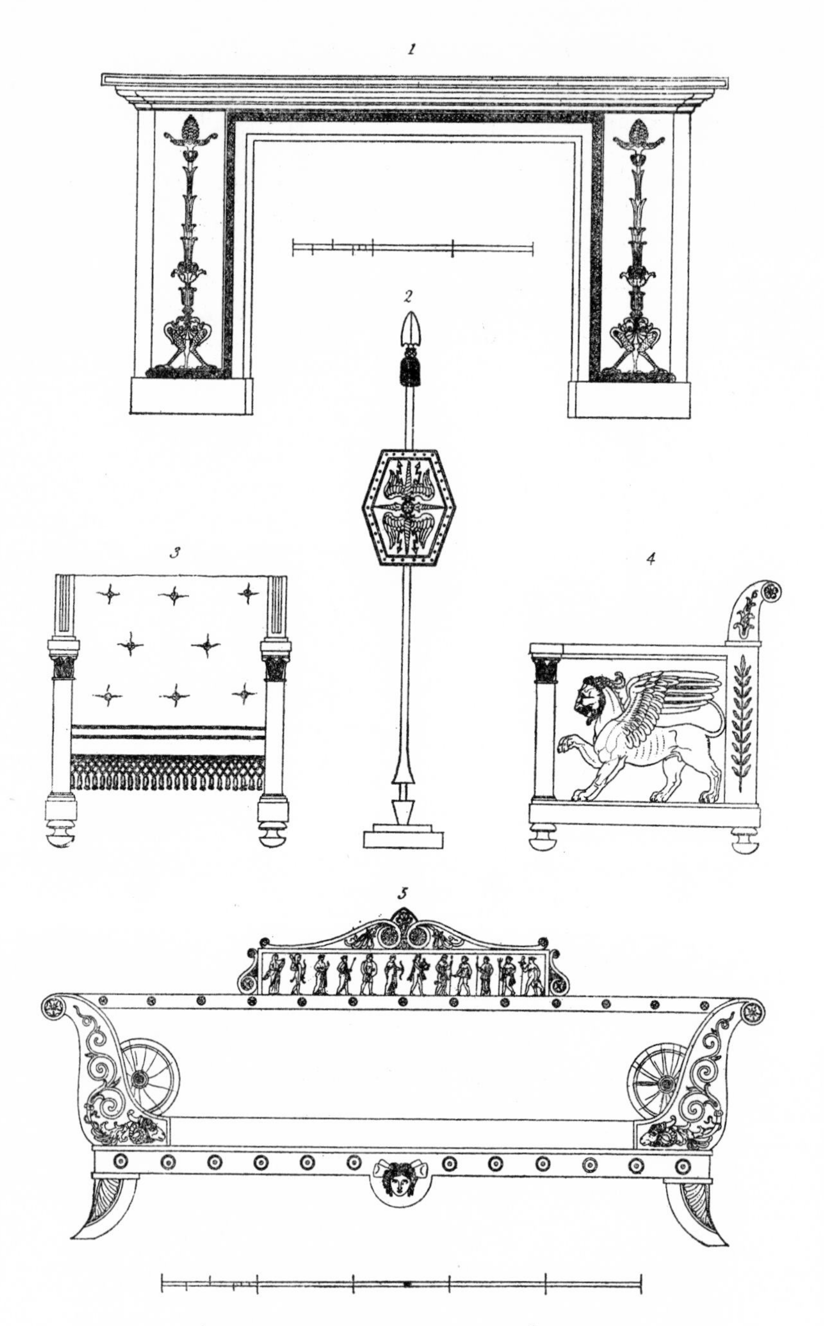

Fig. 27. Thomas Hope, Furniture at Duchess Street, *c.* 1800

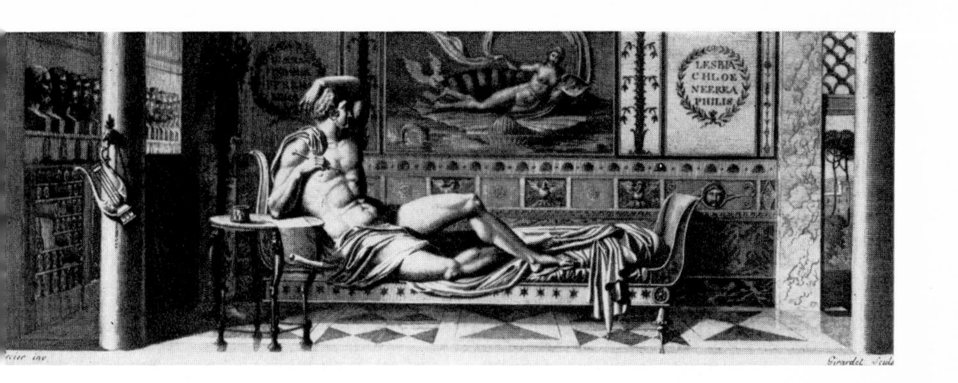

89. Charles Percier, Illustration to Didot's edition of Horace, 1799
90. James Playfair the Elder, Egyptian Room, Cairness House, 1792–7

91. C. H. TATHAM, Detail of Ball Room Chimney-piece, Wilton Park, 1803–5
92. Winged stool, *c.* 1810

Fig. 28. Thomas Hope, Furniture at Duchess Street, *c.* 1800

The impressive obelisk-like pedestals of a sideboard (Fig. 29) were inspired by an Etruscan altar preserved at the Villa Borghese.[18] A pair of Greek female terms on a simple table in a Dressing-room were based

Fig. 29. Thomas Hope, Pedestal from Sideboard at Duchess Street, *c.* 1800

on antique terms in the Museum at Bologna.[19] Elsewhere there were vases and *cippi* from originals in the Albani and Barberini Collections;[20] and the general outline and handles of a magnificent bronze and gold vase were copied from a Greek vase in white marble in the museum at Portici, the elegant group on it of a Genius and Apollo with a lyre being taken from a bas-relief in the British Museum.[21]

2. FURNITURE DISCOVERED AT POMPEII AND HERCULANEUM

By 1800 this was well known and had already played a part in the development of the Adam style in furnishings. Nevertheless, Hope based more than one piece on these bronze tripods and tables. The legs of one such table, shown in his plate 25, no. 2, comprised of long winged sphinxes standing on animal legs adorned with masks, were directly copied from a table then in the Museum at Portici.[22]

3. VASE-PAINTINGS

These were most widely known through the engravings by D'Hancarville and Tischbein of those on the vases in Sir William Hamilton's collections. But before being transcribed to any great extent into modern furniture, these formed the basis of an important intermediary stage. This is represented by Flaxman's illustrations to Homer and Aeschylus, and, to a lesser degree, by Percier's to an edition of Horace published by Didot in 1799 (Plate 89). The Horace vignettes, which showed that Percier had not yet adopted the outline technique, were described by Hope as 'exquisite representations of the mode in which the ancient Romans used to decorate their town and country houses'.[23] However, the Flaxman drawings, which he acquired, were for him 'the finest modern imitations I know of the elegance and beauty of the ancient Greek attire and furniture, armour and utensils'.[23] Flaxman returned the compliment by pointing out, in an unpublished passage from a review of *Household Furniture*, that: ' it is but justice to Mr. Hope to acknowledge he is the first in this country who has produced a system of furniture, collected from the beautiful examples of antiquity, whose parts are consistent with each other, and the whole suited to domestic ease and comfort.'[24] But it was only in the *Odyssey* illustrations that Flaxman had illustrated furniture to any great extent. There is little in the *Iliad*, less in the *Aeschylus*. The chairs shown are mostly of the *klismos* type and the other furniture is confined almost entirely to tripods and stands, beds, or couches.

4. NEO-CLASSICAL FURNITURE IN THE EIGHTEENTH CENTURY

England

James Stuart (1713–88) is well known for his revival of Greek themes in architecture at Hagley and Shugborough and in interior decorations at the Greenwich chapel. His Painted Room of *c.* 1759 at Spencer House is regarded as the earliest complete example of the revived 'Etruscan' taste, but it is important to remember that to complete the antique picture for Lord Spencer he added a set of six arm-chairs and four sofas, now at Kenwood House.[25] These made prominent use of antique griffons to a degree hardly paralleled before 1800. Whole end pieces are made up of these creatures, their wings becoming unhappily involved in the upholstery and their realistic feet and paws serving as chair-legs. The griffons are echoed by others supporting medallions in the coved ceiling of the Great Room. Severely neo-classical is an austere and solid mahogany cupboard, now at Althorp, incised with a bold Greek key pattern.[26] The theme of the Spencer House arm-chairs was taken up in the set of four such chairs or thrones designed by Hope for the Picture Gallery at Duchess Street. By now, however, the composition is far more architectural and monumental and the huge winged sphinxes are detached from the upholstery. It was probably a combination of these with the round-backed throne in the church of San Gregorio Magno, Rome,[27] which inspired the pair of gilt council-chairs made for Carlton House.[28] In his exquisite bas-relief of the 'Death of Germanicus' (1774),[29] Thomas Banks had introduced an elegantly curved *klismos* chair, anticipating by several years the furniture depicted in David's paintings.

The work of Adam must also find a place here, as so often the Empire style was to be merely a harsher more masculine reshuffling of decorative details which in Adam's hands had been purely a pretty surface decoration. However, in the colder austerity of rooms like entrance-halls Adam sometimes came close to the late neo-classical manner. Some long table-like stools[30] designed in 1768 for the hall at Lansdowne House were copied from the Tomb of Agrippa which we have already mentioned. Hall chairs designed for the Hill Street house of Sir Abraham Hume, Bart. in 1778[31] are, in their witty economy, close to a number of designs in *Household Furniture* like 12, no. 3, and 19, no. 4 (see also Fig. 28).

Wyatt reiterated Adam's neo-classical hints, and especial mention should be made of a pair of pedestal-lamps, which he designed in *c.* 1795 for the Etruscan Room at Heveningham Hall.[32] These elegant and imaginative recreations, painted by Rebecca with figures from vases, are decorated with animal parts and support imitation Greek vases.

The work of Henry Holland (1745–1806) marks an important transitional phase. Into interiors at Southill, which he had panelled and adorned in the Louis XVI manner, he inserted from 1796 numerous pieces of furniture which, through information provided him from Rome by Tatham, anticipated the Hope style in many details. Thus, as Watson points out,[33] a pair of single-ended couches in the drawing-room shares certain characteristics with one in plate 28, no. 2, of *Household Furniture*; and the lion monopodia on the five side-tables in the dining-room were soon to be popularized in the same book.

France

With the execution in 1787 by Georges Jacob of the 'Etruscan' furniture for Marie-Antoinette's dairy at Rambouillet,[34] the Empire style can be said to have been born. It is unlikely that Hope would have seen these strange antique mahogany pieces designed by Hubert Robert, but he would doubtless have known through David's paintings the similar pieces of furniture which had been executed at about the same time by Jacob from designs by David himself.[35] One such piece, indeed, may have inspired the Southill and Hope couches mentioned above. In the 1790s the painter Louis Gauffier (1762–1801), extensively patronized by Hope, owned pieces of Directoire-type furniture which he introduced into such paintings of his as 'The Ambassador Miot and his Family' and a scene of a mother giving jewels to her daughter.[36]

The significance should be emphasized of the fact that the new style first manifested itself in the properties of a kind of glorified stage setting, be it the make-believe dairy of the Queen or the heroic dream-world conjured up by the studio of David. The theme was taken up in the illustrations of Flaxman and Percier. And was not the Empire of Napoleon as romantic an antique vision as the interiors at Duchess Street?

The work of the architect L.-M. Berthault (*c.* 1771–1823) in 1798 at the *hôtel* Récamier should be mentioned for its early date, its high quality, and—through the medium of Krafft's *Plans, Coupes, Elévations* ... (1801–2)[37]—its influence. The house seems to have been opened, like Hope's, to the public, and in 1802 Hope's intimate friend Mary Berry wrote a detailed description of Mme Récamier's bedroom, admiring especially the great swan-ended bed.[38] The pier-table in this room probably inspired that in Hope's Flaxman Room (Fig. 13) supported by the four Horae, and a similar table made for Malmaison by Georges Jacob. In 1801 Berthault designed for the *hôtel* of the Duchess of Kurland a tented Turkish boudoir adorned with crescent moons and stars picked out in black and gold.[39] With its hangings of rose-pink silk draped in front of a large mirror, the total effect of this room must have been close to a number of interiors at Duchess Street, especially the Flaxman or Star Room. It was illustrated by Krafft in *c.* 1802, and the Hopes are known to have visited the house after further alterations in 1814.

Italy

Thomas Hope had early come into contact with the influential work of Piranesi. An important fact, not remarked upon in modern times, is that before Hope's birth his father had acquired from Piranesi and brought to their house in Amsterdam a magnificent chimney-piece.[40] This was a characteristic Piranesian composition of some interest since, as its creator observed of it: 'Le cariatidi, l'architrave e gli altri pezzi di marmo sono avanzi di opere antiche da Cavaliere Piranesi uniti insieme.'[40] This cumulative and imitative technique Hope was to make especially his own, though his classical quotations were assembled with a greater concern for relevance and meaning than were Piranesi's. Hope also owned a large and elaborate candelabrum (Fig. 7 and Plate 65), which had been imaginatively worked up from antique fragments in the manner of Piranesi. Such sumptuous pieces were also to have considerable influence on the designs of Percier and Fontaine.

5. EIGHTEENTH-CENTURY ENGRAVINGS OF ANTIQUE ART

These were used as a source for ornamental details. Particularly useful were the Comte de Caylus' *Receuil d'Antiquités Egyptiennes, Etrusques et Romaines* (1752–67), and, from the 1780s onwards, publications like Guattani's *Monumenti inediti di Roma* and Visconti's ponderous series on the contents of the Roman museums. As sources for furniture decoration these were largely superseded in this country by Tatham's popular *Etchings . . . of Ancient Ornamental Architecture; drawn from the Originals in Rome and other Parts of Italy, during the years 1794, 1795, and 1796* (1799). Coming at the end of the century this was, in a sense, a retrospective work of synthesis more than a work of original scholarship. Thomas Hope did not refer to it in the bibliography to *Household Furniture*. He probably regarded it as too popular a handbook and considered that he had acquired his own anthology of 'ancient ornamental architecture'. He may have met Tatham in Rome, for he was a subscriber to the first edition of his book. He also possessed copies of the editions of 1803 and of a further two books by Tatham,[41] both published in 1806, entitled *Etchings representing Fragments of Grecian and Roman Architectural Ornaments* and *Designs for Ornamental Plate*. A chimney-piece and mirror, designed by Tatham in 1803–5 for Wilton Park, Buckinghamshire, is shown in plate 91. This rare example of Tatham's executed work shows the full English late neo-classical style. Though bolder and stronger than the Henry Holland manner, it incorporates details like the winged lions with torches, of which Holland had employed variants—based on drawings by Tatham—to adorn the pier-mirrors in the library at Southill.[42]

6. PERCIER AND FONTAINE

The relationship of the Hope style to that of Napoleon's designers is problematical. The chronology suggests parallels rather than influences. The remodelling and furnishing of Duchess Street were begun in 1799 and were complete by 1803–4. This exactly coincides with the Consulate, during which period Percier and Fontaine began the lengthy task of refurnishing the old royal palaces. Although they began to issue their *Receuil de décorations intérieures* as early as 1801—and it cannot be doubted that this stimulated the production of Hope's own book—very little of their work had been executed at that time, and the plates of this rare edition of 1801 formed little more than half the number of those in the much better-known 1812 edition. Thus, the popular view, expressed by Grandjean in the most recent study of Empire furniture, that 'it was not long before some of these designs were adopted abroad by decorators of renown—Thomas Hope in England, Pietro Ruga in Italy . . . '[43] is probably an over-simplification. For example, Percier's illustrations to Horace are probably inspired by Flaxman's to Homer. In the vignette heading the second book of *Satires* the outline of a table and its method of delineation are similar to 'Ulysses at the Table of Circe' from the *Odyssey*. If Flaxman was in close contact with Hope in these formative years in Rome in the 1790s, he was equally in touch with Percier. He corresponded with Percier, his junior by nine years, as early as 1791, and in 1802 addressed him as 'carissimo amico'.[44] Percier's illustrations show a range of antique furniture that includes animal-monopodia tables, lamps, *klismos*, and winged lion chairs and elegant curved couches. A bold star-studded frame enclosing the illustration to the second book of *Carmina* may well have inspired Hope's very similar frames to the picures in the Egyptian Room at Duchess Street (Fig. 14). But setting aside the problem of chronology—which might be clarified in the detailed study that is still lacking of Percier and Fontaine, despite M.-L. Biver's interesting book, *Fontaine* (Paris, 1964)—the total aesthetic of the Hope style at Duchess Street is, as has been indicated elsewhere, rather different from that of the French designers.[45]

* * *

For his essays in the Egyptian taste Hope used the standard neo-classical sources: Norden's *Travels in Egypt and Nubia* (1757), Piranesi's *Diverse Maniere d'Adornare i Cammini* (1769), and Denon's *Voyages dans la Basse et la Haute Egypte* (1802). But Hope, probably uniquely among English designers at that moment, had actually visited Egypt itself. Volume III of the Hope drawings contains Egyptian costumes, craft on the Nile, and the catacombs at Alexandria. Volume IV, labelled on the spine *Egyptian Drawings* though containing much Greek and Turkish material, includes 'sketches of Egyptian landscapes, mosques, palaces, interiors, friezes, reliefs, architectural details, etc. with the Sphinx and the Pyramids, remains of ancient temples, peasant groups, camels, etc.'[46] Hope had considerable difficulty in implementing this first-hand information in the execution of interior furnishings, and since he could find no carvers of high quality he was obliged to acquire from Italy numerous models and casts in order to bypass one whole stage in the process of production. Fortunately, there had been discovered and deposited in 1748 at the Capitoline Museum a number of Egyptian antiquities: the fruits of Hadrian's Egyptian campaign which he had housed in his villa at Tivoli.[47] Thus, while the general idea of the chimney-piece in the Egyptian Room at Duchess Street (Fig. 14) came from a rock temple in Southern Turkey, the shelf and fender ornaments were based on statues and bas-reliefs either exhibited in the Capitoline and Vatican Museums, or depicted in the publications of the Accademia Ercolanese and Denon.[48] Similarly, the decorative details of the four impressive arm-chairs (Plate 40) in the same room were based on Egyptian originals preserved in Italian museums: the seated priests supporting the arms were copied from 'an Egyptian idol in the Vatican', the winged Isis on the rail from a mummy-case in the museum at Bologna, and the little canopic vases on top from the Capitoline Museum.[48] The few remaining decorations, however, were actually taken from buildings at Thebes and Tentyris.

A little-known contemporary parallel to Hope's Egyptian Room is at Cairness House, Aberdeenshire (1792–7; Plate 90).[49] Designed by James Playfair the elder (?–1794) for Charles Gordon, it closely anticipates Hope's work at Duchess Street with its segmental vault, double-doors, hieroglyphic friezes, and monumental little chimney-piece. After Hope came an elaborate Egyptian recreation of *c.* 1810 by J. B. Papworth or S. P. Cockerell for the Duke of Marlborough at Whiteknights, Berkshire. Here was a tri-partite library adorned with Egyptian hieroglyphics, wall-paintings, and statuary.[50]

A few more random eclectic sources may be cited: a pair of massive nail-studded doors were copied from some in the Uffizi in Florence,[45] and a large box (Fig. 28) from a sarcophagus of verd-antique serving, when Hope saw it, as an ablutionary fountain in the Kilise Djami at Constantinople;[17] and a long couch with feet in the form of Egyptian lotus leaves and the frame decorated with Greek anthemia, boasted at its lower end a figure of a sleeping greyhound likened by Hope to those 'on Gothic sarcophagi' (Fig. 30).[51]

What of the total effect of this amazingly scholarly and eclectic synthesis that we must call the Hope style? There can be little doubt that it must have been massive, strong, and colourful; romantic, exotic, and poetic; and, ultimately, overpowering in the ruthless almost fanatical persistence with which the mind of a single man had solidly patterned every object with a relentless iconography. That the colour was strong, varied and imaginative has been shown in Chapter IV. Indeed, some of the surviving furniture—especially the Egyptian,

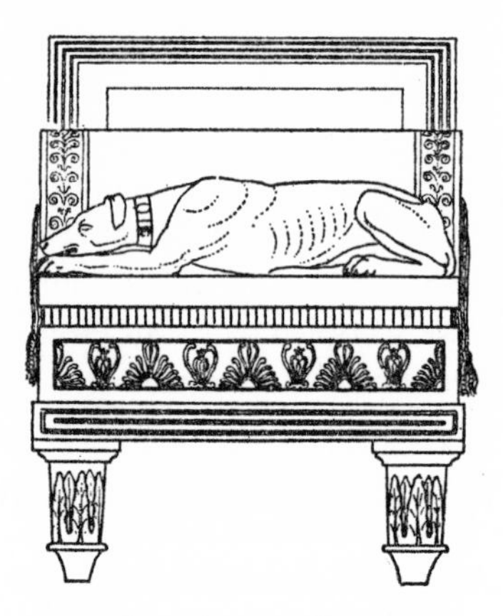

Fig. 30. Couch end at Duchess Street, *c.* 1800

in its strident gold and black—is almost fair-groundish in its lively exuberance. And yet the modern verdict—inspired by the outline engravings in *Household Furniture*—has been, in Colvin's words, that the furniture 'was too cold and esoteric to inspire much imitation',[52] or, in Musgrave's, that it was remarkable only for its 'frigid accuracy' and that its creator's 'vein of pedantic archaeological accuracy was contrary to the spirit of his time, which was marked by vitality, informality, and exuberance, and above all by a sense of romantic poetry'.[53] These last qualities the Hope style, as in the Flaxman room, for example, surely possessed in abundance—save for 'informality', which is perhaps not especially characteristic of the Regency: licence and freedom in some cases, but not the casual modern slackness suggested by 'informality'.

By a happy chance it was in the company of Farington that George Dance made his first visit to Duchess Street one afternoon in March 1804, so that, inevitably, his every reflection was recorded for posterity. The rather odd reaction of this great architect tells us much about the rather odd style of the house: 'Dance told me', Farington dutifully recorded, 'He thought it better than He expected, & that by the singularity of it good might be done as it might contribute to emancipate the public taste from that rigid adherence to a certain style of architecture & of finishing & unshackle the Artists.'[54] Strange that Hope's elaborate system of decoration, linked together like chain-mail by a thousand classical or pre-classical allusions, should be thought likely to 'unshackle the Artists'—but no better authority than Dance could be desired for a statement of the neo-classical aesthetic. Interesting, too, that Dance did not regard the house as an experiment in 'bringing the French Empire style to England', as modern writers tend to, but concentrated precisely on its 'singularity', its highly personal individuality. And whereas Musgrave discussed it in a chapter entitled 'Thomas Hope and Classical Purity', when Julius Angerstein visited it in 1808 he was perturbed to find it conceived in 'imitation of a *barbarous taste*, not of that which is deemed classical'.[55] Again, it is the uniqueness of the Hope style that is stressed by his son Alexander when writing in 1861 of the impact it had on him:

> The position which my father occupied in the artistic movement of our age has never been appreciated or even understood . . . As this house [the Duchess Street mansion] is now unhappily numbered with the things that no longer exist, I may be allowed to leave on record that impression of early but vivid recollections of the taste, the fancy, the eye for colour and for form, which characterized the whole conception. The style was not suited for practical use, and so the experiment broke down; but it was the experiment of a man of genius, and not to be confounded with the contemporary and parallel, but far more insipid, 'Empire' epoch of French art. The great fact for which Thomas Hope deserves the gratitude of posterity . . . was that he, first of Englishmen, conceived and taught the idea of art-manufacture, of allying the beauty of form to the wants and productions of common life.[56]

Hope's emphasis was thus on the need for ever higher standards of personal craftsmanship—a tradition continued from Ruskin to the Art Nouveau and not reversed until the ultimate acceptance of the Modern Movement—and was quite categorically against the machine. Despite this, Musgrave argues that Hope's importance lay in designing objects which 'lent themselves admirably to execution by the new industrial methods that were then being developed' and in forming, amazingly, 'part of the movement that lead [*sic*] to a purification of style, and to the functionalism of the modern age'.[57]

It was, as much as anything, Hope's self-conscious search for a new style that anticipated the dominant trends of the nineteenth century. The following passage from his *Historical Essay on Architecture* could be taken from almost any nineteenth-century theoretician, from Rickman, Ruskin, or Scott:

> No one seems yet to have conceived the smallest wish or idea of only borrowing of every former style of architecture, whatever it might present of useful or ornamental, of scientific or tasteful; of adding thereto whatever other new dispositions or forms might afford conveniences or elegancies not yet possessed; of making the new discoveries, the new conquests, of natural productions unknown to former ages, the models of new imitations more beautiful and more varied; and thus of composing an architecture which, born in our own country, grown on our soil, and in harmony with our climate, institutions, and habits, at once elegant appropriate, and original, should truly deserve the appellation of 'Our Own'.[58]

This must be the earliest statement of what was to become the characteristic Victorian dilemma. It is interesting to observe how its Picturesque eclecticism contrasts strikingly with Pugin, whose lack of stylistic catholicism was as un-Victorian as his Roman Catholicism. The ultimate future lay with Hope rather than with Pugin; or, at least, with Hope's attitudes but not his styles, and Pugin's style but not his attitudes.

By publishing the designs for the contents of the Duchess Street mansion Hope invited yet more publicity and appreciation for his achievement. A book so lavish in its form, so uncompromising and eccentric in its contents as *Household Furniture*, was an ideal subject for the reviewer's pen in the numerous artistic and literary periodicals of the day. The *Edinburgh Review* was first in the field in July 1807 with a long and philistine account of Hope's book by Sydney Smith. It is significant that not only were Hope's methods and aims attacked but the very existence of the book at all: 'we confess we are not a little proud of this Roman spirit, which leaves the studies of those effeminate elegancies to slaves and foreigners, and holds it beneath the dignity of a free man to be eminently skilled in the decoration of couches and the mounting of chandeliers'. If it was considered ungentlemanly and frivolous to take an interest in the design of furniture at all, then Hope's battle was lost before it had begun. The persistence of this attitude in the nineteenth century heightened the professionalism or commercialism of the designer—which they all, including the architects, were anxious to promote—thus creating a gap between him and his patron which had its own effect on the character of Victorian furnishings and decoration. The very seriousness of Hope's manner is made the subject of irony:

> If the salvation of Europe depended upon Mr. Hope's eloquence, he could not have exerted it with more earnestness and animation; and we are convinced, that neither the restorers of learning nor the reformers of religion, ever spoke of their subject in terms half so magnificent, nor of their abilities with such studied and graceful modesty, as this ingenious person has here done, in recommending to his countrymen a better form for their lamps, sideboards, and cradles.

Smith's observation, however, is undoubtedly true. And it has been a part of our concern in this study to indicate Hope's almost religious emphasis upon the need for culture and cultural education. Smith goes on to condemn the actual furniture for its immense weight and bulk and its emblematic or symbolic character, which combined to make it more suitable for 'the vestibule of an academical museum'[59] than for a private dwelling.

A short-lived journal called *The Satirist or Monthly Meteor* soon rose to Hope's defence. In October 1807 the following 'communication' was printed preceded by the observation that it would 'be attended to, if possible, in our next Number': 'We, the little sylvan boys and fauns, who sport and revel among the gallery and round the vases of Mr. Thomas Hope, having been scared by certain rude and ugly satyrs of the north, calling themselves *Edinburgh Reviewers*, do humbly crave your favourable notice ... We throw ourselves on your protection, trusting that you are able to protect us.' The November edition of *The Satirist* begins with an article entitled *Meublomanie, or Rage for Furniture*. This, far from being the protection desired by the sylvan boys, ends with a very intelligent parody of *Household Furniture*, of which the following lines well convey the flavour:

> No. 1. represents a piece of furniture for a library, supported by a negro. His *arms* form two of the legs, and thus constitute a regular quadruped; in addition to the drawers which surround the circle of this table, the body of the figure may be so constructed as to form a receptable for pamphlets and memoranda; opening *a posteriori*, with a handle descriptive of the *tail* so ingeniously ascribed to our primitive parents by the late Lord Monboddo;

or again: 'No. 7. is a work-table, the top of which is sustained by the ghost of an owl in a winding-sheet, intended to adorn a lady's boudoir, emblematically signifying that wisdom in such a place is but a shadow.' The reasoned defence of Hope, which the October edition of *The Satirist* had led its readers to expect, appears later in the November edition. 'For the first time', its author began, 'we see them [the Edinburgh reviewers] anxious to distinguish themselves in the fine arts.' He finds it surprising and unfortunate that this welcome attempt is marred by the attribution to Hope of lack of patriotism for being concerned with interior decoration at a time when the country should be geared for war. He sees that Hope is concerned with something more than the fanciful decoration of fald-stools—which was as far as Sydney Smith was prepared to look—but that 'the *principles of ornament*, on which couches, &c., must depend in common with more important matters, is the real subject, though under an humbler title'. He sees the importance and quotes Hope's own statement of his aim to give to 'each object a peculiar countenance and character, a pleasing outline and an appropriate meaning'. The review is continued in the December issue. The fire-screen in the form of a Roman shield placed on a javelin (Fig. 27), so derided in the *Edinburgh Review*, is here justified since the words screen and shield are interchangeable and since who 'will be offended at the idea ... that a warrior has suspended his shield on a spear, and placed it to defend female beauty?' The reviewer comes close to defining the significance of *Household Furniture* when he observes: 'Unfortunately for society, art and literature in this country seldom grow on the same stock. This we have long lamented as a radical defect in the constitution of our universities. We hope the patron of Downing College will reflect on it, and that the arts, which in general are only known to the literati by rote, will be cultivated with letters.'[60] It was precisely this concern that created Kelsall's *Phantasm of an University*.

In the same month as the *Satirist* review, another account that was both favourable and perceptive appeared in the *British Critic*. Its author believed it impossible for a nation to produce distinguished architects, sculptors, and painters, 'while the body of the people is uninstructed in the arts of design, unconscious of the superiority of genius, and wholly destitute of the emotions which should be excited by the contemplation of works of taste'. This situation, however, he believed was being remedied, 'and we believe there can be no doubt, that to Mr. Hope as much of this kind of improvement is to be attributed as it is possible for an individual to have accomplished'. He confirms Hope's own observations about the extent to which his designs had been imitated:

> On turning over the engravings in the book which lies before us, Mr. Hope seems to present us with nothing which we have not formerly seen under some modification. We were not at first aware, that it is to this gentleman we are indebted for them; that he gave the model after which the artisan has wrought; and that the drawings which he has now published, are the originals from which so many copies have been taken.

He found the concept of the narrative in interior decoration sufficiently appealing to observe that: 'It is in the principle of association that the charm lies'. However, he thought that association had been somewhat overdone in the Flaxman Room and that in seeking to recreate the effects of dawn, Hope 'has attempted to do that which is quite beyond the power of his materials'. In his concluding lines the reviewer, in warning designers against falling into what he clearly considered to be Hope's excesses, comes close to the aesthetic of the Modern Movement by insisting on simplicity and truth to materials:

> [Those] who have to imitate this style of decoration must take care they do not attempt too much; they must keep in view the nature of their materials, and be cautious not to proceed on obscure allegories; they must take simplicity of form as the highest point of excellence; and not advance at once to that profuse assemblage of ornament, which marks in the inventor the decay of taste rather than the richness of fancy.[61]

Household Furniture was discussed in articles in two more journals, both published in 1809: the *Monthly Review; or Literary Journal, Enlarged* and *The Annual Review, and History of Literature.* The critic in the *Monthly Review* closely followed Sydney Smith's lead, though without his pompous Whig vituperation. He believed that the modern 'furniture-mania' was merely the outlet for the superfluous wealth of the *nouveaux riches.* He cared little for the modern museum-spirit and, coupling Hope and Soane together, observed that: 'as little good taste is manifested in overloading our walls with the symbolical images of antiquity, as in making our national Bank resemble a Mausoleum.' Similarly, of Hope's vases, he remarked that they 'are well adapted for the furniture of a Museum; but in their present mode of arrangement, they excite rather the idea of an apothecary's shop on a very grand scale'.[62]

In Flaxman's anonymous account in the *Annual Review,* which has already been quoted, he regretted that 'the richness of effect in the colours, and light and shadow, are entirely lost in a publication of mere outlines', and wished that 'vignettes had been introduced of shadowed engravings of the same kind with those beautiful designs by Percier in Didot's *Horace*'.[63]

The Hope style in its most Grecian aspects was perhaps best epitomized in the volume of plates engraved for Thomas Hope in 1812 by Henry Moses, under the title of *Designs of Modern Costume.* These were doubtless closer than the plates in *Household Furniture* to what Flaxman had in mind as a more realistic and appealing presentation of the Duchess Street interiors. Though there are references to this book in most of Hope's obituaries and in *A Biographical Dictionary of Living Authors* as early as 1816, there appears to be no copy of it in any of the major European or American libraries.[64] Recent enquiry, however, fortunately resulted in the discovery of what must almost certainly be this work. It consists of twenty plates signed by

93. Chair with winged arm supports, *c.* 1807

94. Chair with x-shaped legs, *c.* 1807

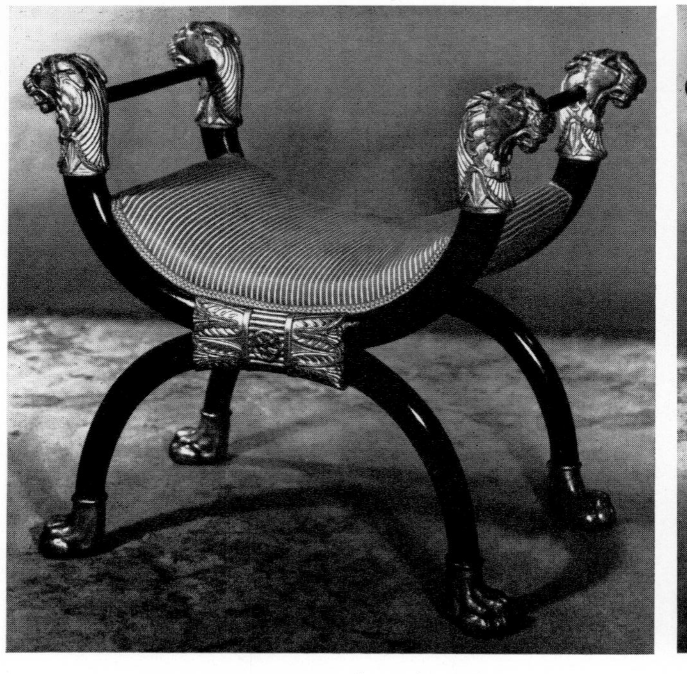

95. Thomas Hope, x-shaped stool, *c.* 1800

96. x-shaped stool, *c.* 1807

Henry Moses, stitched together in a paper cover. There is no publication date but external evidence suggests that it was bought in *c.* 1812 by Edward Henry Nevinson (1779–1850).[65] Mention must now be made of the book published in 1823 as *A series of twenty-nine designs of Modern Costume drawn and engraved by Henry Moses, Esq.* This seems to have been put together as a rather more pretentious commemorative volume of the 1812 edition. The 1823 volume contains all of the twenty plates of the 1812 edition, though in a different order, together with nine additional plates. Further reasons for believing that these twenty plates must be the missing work by Hope are that in 1814 in the preface to his *Collection of Vases* . . . , Moses expressed his gratitude to Hope 'for various acts of kindness'; secondly, they are related to the costume of 1800–10, rather than to that of 1823; thirdly, the plates depict actual pieces of furniture from the Duchess Street mansion and, in one case, a whole room; and, finally, the level of artistic imagination and creativity is so high as to suggest a master-mind other than Moses' behind the scene, for superb draughtsman though Moses was, there is no evidence of his having published anything apart from these engravings that was not straightforward copying from life or art.

A comparative list of the plates in the two volumes is given in Appendix D and, for the moment, it will suffice to point out that the only plate to remain in the same position in the 1823 edition as in the 1812 is the first, entitled *Le Beau Monde* (Fig. 31). It depicts a number of elegant ladies and gentlemen of fashion disporting themselves in a room based on the Greek Doric picture-gallery at Duchess Street. The persons shown throughout the book—in what are, effectively, a series of conversation pieces—are dressed in modernized versions of the ancient Greek costumes which Hope had recreated from antique sculpture and vase-paintings and had first presented to the public, for the especial use of history painters, in his *Costume of the Ancients* (1809). He doubtless knew Caylus' *Tableaux tirés de l'Iliade et de l'Odyssée d'Homère et de l'Enéide de Virgile*; *avec des observations générales sur le costume* (1757), a work of considerable importance, although lacking the illustrations its title suggests. As the neo-classical style in furniture was influenced by the background 'properties' in the paintings of David, so neo-classical dress was similarly to be based on costumes employed by painters to evoke the antique past. The neo-classical was ever a theatrical or a dream world. With men's costumes, however, Hope's vision broke down. They are all standard Regency, elegant to modern eyes but antique to none. The women's costumes are an enchanting compromise between the fashions of the fifth century B.C. and of 1810; and as such they appear to be unique in the history of Regency costume. What Hope has done is to take the

LE BEAU MONDE.

Fig. 31. 'Le Beau Monde' from *29 Designs of Modern Costume drawn and engraved by Henry Moses,* 1823

woman's dress of 1810, lengthen it, add to it decorative borders like the anthemion palmettes which ran round the frieze of every Regency drawing-room, and adorn its wearer's head with the pretty little pointed caps, of which there were numerous plates in his *Costume of the Ancients.* What he made no attempt to do was to abandon the high 'Empire' waist-line for the loosely flowing top-draperies which were a universal characteristic of Greek costume. If anything, his waist-lines reach a height rarely achieved in England at that time.[66]

Like the Art Nouveau designer Henri van de Velde (1863–1957), Hope designed costumes for his wife to match her architectural settings. This must almost certainly be true of her clothes in the Dawe portrait of 1812 (Plate 11). Moreover, as was suggested earlier, Hope may actually have demanded that the artist base this portrait on a Greek vase painting (Plate 12).

The Dawe portrait belongs to the year of publication of *Designs of Modern Costume* and such clothes were widely imitated, being at once sufficiently close to moden types to be economically functional and sufficiently different to create an agreeable surprise though not a vulgar shock. Of one such lady in the earliest nineteenth century it was said that:

> Her gown was white satin trimmed with white velvet, cut in a formal pattern, then quite a rage, a copy from some of the Grecian borders in Mr. Hope's book; she had feathers in her hair and a row of pearls round her neck, from which depended a large diamond locket; the gown was short-waisted and narrow-skirted, but we thought it beautiful.[67]

Had *Designs of Modern Costume* been printed in any quantity in 1812 instead of in 1823, Hope's influence on Regency dress would have been even more marked. He probably had as few sets of plates printed from Moses' drawings in 1812 as he had from Flaxman's Dante drawings in 1792. Perhaps he considered them to be too slender a collection to present to the world. His other published books were all large, expensive, and highly finished from every point of view.

For an appreciation of the Hope style Moses' plates are of especial value since they depict his monumental furnishings actually in use, which would not otherwise always be easy to visualize (Fig. 32). Particularly delightful is a scene in the nursery which exactly reproduces the elaborate Hope cradle together with a variant on the chairs in the second Vase Room. A full list of furniture dependent on pieces at Duchess Street is given in Appendix D. Altogether, half of the twenty plates of 1812 contain furniture derived from this source; and three of the nine plates added in 1823.

Influence from designs in *Household Furniture* can also be traced in some of the works of the greatest of English neo-classical goldsmiths, Paul Storr (1771–1844), who had once been employed by Hope. A pair of silver candelabra and a two-handled silver bowl,[68] made between 1807 and 1809, have handles formed by pairs of intertwined serpents holding an egg in their mouths—a detail taken directly from a pattern in *Household Furniture* (Fig. 3). A silver basket (Fig. 2), furnished Storr with the idea for the fruit-baskets on a magnificent pair of silver-gilt tripods[69] which he made in 1810–11 for the Duke of Wellington. Storr's superb creations, both of everyday domestic utensils

Fig. 32. 'At the Writing Table', from *29 Designs of Modern Costume drawn and engraved by Henry Moses,* 1823

and of monumental compositions for patrons like the Prince Regent, not only form one of the high points of the neo-classical achievement but are of interest because of the method of their production. That is to say, designs were commissioned or taken from men of high repute like Hope and Tatham, Flaxman, Stothard, and the elder Theed. To complete this successful picture, moreover, Storr was himself a director from 1807 of the leading firm of Regency goldsmiths, Messrs. Rundell, Bridge, and Rundell. It was, of course, precisely such a fruitful combination of antique art, modern designers, craftsmen, and trade that Hope was anxious to promote, and he must have been gratified that his own designs had been found of some use. Indeed he particularly mentioned Philip Rundell (1743–1837) by name in an article of 1807 on *The Utility of Remains of Antiquity*. It must never be forgotten that for all these men antique art came first, and in this article Hope described how 'the first Musaea or repositories of the Muses (as they were appropriately denominated) ... [were the] nurseries of... modern art',[70] producing first a Raphael and a Michelangelo, and today, bearing fruit once more, a Flaxman and a Westmacott, a Wedgwood, and a Rundell. In the attempt to improve the artistic standard of industrial design Matthew Boulton had been a pioneer, and it has been shown in an earlier chapter how he made use of Hope's own designs at Duchess Street.

In 1937 the present Duke of Wellington observed enthusiastically in one of the earliest articles to discuss the work of Hope, that 'as the poetry of Shakespeare is to the rest of Elizabethan poetry, so is the furniture of Thomas Hope to the rest of Regency furniture'.[71] The influence of Hope's furniture is therefore not hard to trace. This has been well demonstrated in two publications of 1961, John Harris' *Regency Furniture Designs* and Clifford Musgrave's *Regency Furniture*, and can also be easily appreciated from an inspection of the fine collection of photographs assembled by H. Blairman & Sons.[72] Typical of countless inferior versions of Hopeian furniture is the painted chair (Plate 93), with its winged supports like those in Hope's plate 20, no. 6. A more elegant and imaginative chair (Plate 94) has a linear sweep reminiscent of that in Hope's plate 20, no. 3. A genuine Hope stool from Duchess Street (Plate 95) is immediately distinguishable from a copy (Plate 96) marred by coarse carving. On the other hand, a pair of gilt wood tripods (Plate 97) is an outstandingly accurate and excellent copy of the bronze tripods at Duchess Street (Fig. 26). Hope himself observed of his furniture in 1807 that: 'even these few earliest attempts ... had already met with sufficient approbation from the public at large, to induce several professional men, up-holders, cabinet-makers, and others, to abandon ... the old beaten track ... [for] a direct imitation of the individual objects, of which I had planned the designs for my own exclusive use'. He goes on to say that he has therefore decided to publish: 'geometrical and other views, sufficiently faithful and detailed to prevent ... extravagant caricatures, such as of late have begun to start up in every corner of this capital . . . most wretchedly distorted, most injudiciously applied'.[73]

That Hope's furniture was extensively copied before publication is confirmed in the article from the *British Critic* of November 1808 which we have already quoted. Moreover, John Britton observed in 1827 that:

> To Mr. Hope we are indebted, in an eminent degree, for the classical and appropriate style, which now generally characterizes our furniture and ornamental utensils. Like most other innovations, his was decried as whimsical and puerile by some persons . . . whilst others caricatured the system by cramming their apartments with mythological figures and conceits, jumbled together without propriety or meaning . . .
>
> *Household Furniture and Interior Decoration* has not only improved the taste of cabinet-makers and upholsterers, but also that of their employers.[74]

Rudolph Ackermann's *Repository of Arts* (1809–28) was one of the most influential media for the transmission of the new style, since in it were published month by month works by the leading Regency furniture-manufacturers: George Bullock, Morgan and Sanders, Allen of Pall Mall, and others. Ackermann also published in 1817 and again in 1819 three volumes entitled *A Selection of Ornaments*, comprising one hundred and twenty plates which must have been partly responsible for carrying through the English Empire manner into the third decade of the century. Even before the publication of *Household Furniture*, advertisements, some of which led one to expect the worst, were appearing in great numbers, like the following from *The Times*: 'Daniel Curling, furniture printer, 18, Cheapside: Collection of printed furnitures, with Borders and chair-seats in suite, in the Grecian, Etruscan, Egyptian, and Indian styles'. On the same day, 17 April 1806, *The Times* also carried an advertisement from George Smith (1783–1869), who, describing himself as 'upholder Extraordinary to H.R.H. the Prince of Wales', claimed that he had 'completed the second part of his work *Designs for Household Furniture* . . .' and was now in a position to manufacture furniture from his designs. Smith's important book is now commonly supposed to have appeared for the first time in 1808[75] and this reference to it doubtless supplies the answer to the question: to what exactly was Hope referring when he described how his example had encouraged

> several professional . . . up-holders . . . to abandon . . . the old beaten track . . . and to attempt exhibiting, either in reality or in engravings, not only a general approximation to the style for which I wished to introduce a taste, but frequently a direct imitation of the individual objects, of which I had planned the designs for my own exclusive use.[73]

We know that Hope's library contained two copies of Smith's book of 1808 and that in his *Cabinet-maker's and Upholsterer's Guide* (1828), Smith mentioned having received 'many flattering testimonies from Mr. Thomas Hope'.

Whereas Smith's first publication popularized where it did not vulgarize the Hope style, the Italian Gaetano Landi, who described himself as an 'architectural painter', published in February 1810 a collection of designs which formed a far more original if rather grotesque parallel to Hope's work. Although hopefully entitled, *Architectural Decorations: a Periodical Work of Original Designs invented from the Egyptian, the Greek, the Roman, the Etruscan, the Attic, the Gothic, etc., for Exterior and Interior Decoration and whatever relates to furniture* . . . , this was in fact to be the first and only number. It presumably exhausted Landi's financial as well as imaginative resources. Its exotic highly-coloured plates introduce a hot Latin note that is immediately striking, even amidst the verve and colour of English Regency. There is a wondrously over-elaborated Empire chimney-piece, a 'Grand Egyptian Hall' (Plate 99)—grand, indeed, with much Egyptian detail of Piranesian grossness and intensity—and a breath-taking Chinese Room complete with a Soaneic saucer-dome, segmental lunettes, and an elaborate system of colonettes. However, five of the plates of designs for furniture, somehow spared the addition of the lurid colours, were considered sufficiently close to the Hope style to be bound in at the end of a copy of the 1812 edition of Hope's *Costume of the Ancients* by that same E. H. Nevinson to whom we owe the copy of Hope's *Designs of Modern Costume*.

The obsession, which Landi's designs reveal as much as Hope's, with furniture based on the limbs of real or imaginary animals is hard to understand or to sympathize with. One of the more ludicrous products of this short-lived fashion is shown in Plate 92. Hope's principal effort in this vein (Plate 37, extreme right) is close to the chairs in Landi's 'Grand Egyptian Hall' and to a remarkable Roman chair illustrated by Piranesi in 1778.[76] That a winged or pawed chair might occasionally be introduced as a novelty, in imitation of some Roman prototype, seems reasonable; that such furniture should lurk, half alive, in every corner, ready now to flap aloft to the ceiling, now to shamble out of the room altogether, is surely an exaggerated if not an absurd conceit. Probably Thomas Hope was not remarkable for his sense of humour. Certainly his smooth curvaceous chairs based on Greek originals—that is the various versions of the popularly-named 'Trafalgar' chair, analysed and described by Musgrave—if less imitated by Smith are more appealing to modern taste. Landi's designs were too exotic and elaborate to invite much imitation, and after Smith's publication of 1808 the next popular book of designs to appear was Richard Brown's *The Rudiments of Drawing Cabinet and Upholstery Furniture . . . after the manner of the antique* (1820). Brown specifically acknowledges his debt to 'Mr. Hope's mythological work on Household Furniture',[77] to George Smith and to Percier and Fontaine, in that order. Brown carried Hope's principle of symbolical and narrative ornament 'almost to the point of mysticism',[78] as it was sometimes complained. He also looked to the Victorian future in recommending the introduction of decorative forms based on plants from the English countryside.

In this survey of the Hope style, the Deepdene will not be mentioned because its influence was so much a part of the Picturesque and Italianate movements which we have discussed in detail elsewhere. Moreover, only a few friends were invited to the Deepdene, whereas everyone came to Duchess Street. The favourable reaction to Hope's London house of George Dance has already been indicated. Benjamin West, while regarding Dance as 'the first architect in the country in respect of true taste and judgement', claimed a yet greater status for Hope, since after a visit to Duchess Street he described it as 'the finest specimen of true taste . . . either in England or in France'.[79] West's friend Dr. Burney declared, yet more enthusiastically, 'that if the best parts were taken out of the ten best houses in England they would not together make up so much of good taste as in that single instance'.

97. Pair of tripods, *c.* 1807

98. Thomas Hope, Table, *c.* 1800

99. Gaetano Landi, Design for Grand Egyptian Hall, 1810

100. John Nash, Drawing Room, Caledon, 1812

Country Life

101. THOMAS DANIELL, Indian Temple, Melchet Park, 1800

Farington tells us that 'Woodforde, Rossi, &c., also approved it much'.[79]

At the time of visiting Duchess Street, Dance was remodelling Stratton Park, Hampshire, and the heavily Pompeiian panels in the library, for which his drawings survive,[80] are Hopeian in character. They have the dark backgrounds which always indicate vase-paintings as a source. Dance could certainly claim to have 'unshackled' himself from conventional taste to produce an 'emancipated' style, to use the words with which he described the effect he hoped Duchess Street would have. His curious stripped Gothic would fit well into this stylistic category and we know that Hope had seen Dance's designs in this vein. His plans for Coleorton, Leicestershire, were exhibited at the Royal Academy in the spring of 1804, and on 16 April Lady Beaumont brought a number of friends, including Thomas Hope, to admire the designs for her remarkable new home.[81] Enthusiastic though Dance was about the possible effects of the Hope style, he felt obliged to observe of the Duchess Street mansion that, 'however much of amusement or interest there might be in seeing it, it certainly did not excite much idea of comfort as a dwelling'.[54] But Dance was the last architect who could afford to throw stones where a cheerful cosiness was concerned. In domestic interiors of his, such as the bleak hall at Laxton (Plate 54), comfort does not seem to have been uppermost in the architect's mind. The point about Duchess Street was that, like Soane's house in Lincoln's Inn Fields, it was a high-minded neo-classical compromise between a dwelling and a museum. Nor did this pass unobserved at the time. At a dinner-party given by Sir George Beaumont in April 1804, the Duchess Street mansion served as a talking-point, Sir George declaring that 'it was more a *Museum* than anything else'.[82] Precisely the same comment was made of the house by Lord Lonsdale in 1812.[83] Remarks such as these prompt us to a closer analysis of the relationships between Duchess Street and Sir John Soane's Museum.

The first point to be made is that Hope's remodelling at Duchess Street between 1799 and 1803 ante-dates the principal work at the Soane Museum by something approaching ten years. The Soane Museum, as we know it today, is largely the result of remodellings in 1812 and 1824. Soane visited Duchess Street on more than one occasion. On 29 March 1804 he wrote to Hope thanking him for 'the high gratification in viewing again some days since your collections', which he described as 'a lasting monument of your civic spirit and classical taste'. He went on to say: '[I would be] happy on further occasions to avail myself of your kindness and taste'.[84]

Hope's example may well have stimulated Soane's desire to create an eclectic museum-like setting for intellectual life in London. There are small technical similarities which may not be coincidental. In 1812 Soane formed to contain his vases what were known as 'the Catacombs'. In reality this was a small room which, in Summerson's words, was 'originally lined with three tiers of box-like recesses containing cinerary urns. It was then top-lit, but altered when the ground-floor ante-room was formed in 1889–90.'[85] The undoubted similarity of this room to Hope's catacomb-like vase-room with its funerary recesses need hardly be pointed out. It has been observed elsewhere that Hope's Mummy, occupying the place of honour in the Egyptian Room, was acquired twenty years before Soane's sarcophagus of Seti I. Another case where Hope seems to have made a novel suggestion which Soane developed further is the use of hinged panels for the display of pictures. This was a feature of the Picture Gallery which Hope added to Duchess Street in 1819. Five years later the same feature turned up in Soane's new Picture Room at 14, Lincoln's Inn Fields, where Summerson describes it as a 'device, which appears to be unique'.[86] Here it was made the most striking feature of the room, for three entire walls could be made to fold back displaying successive layers of pictures. Hope and Soane had each allowed his special collection—vases with Hope, architectural sculpture and casts with Soane—to create, as it were, its own characteristic setting. The weird Museum, rising through three storeys at the back of Soane's house, is the hub, the *raison d'être* of the whole; Hope's string of tomb-like vase-rooms carried to an extreme degree his principle of creating iconographically appropriate and narrative settings for works of art. Soane's answer was the more spatially imaginative, but the problem in each case was the same: that of creating a personal yet semi-public museum. Soane's house was probably closer in spirit to Hope's than to any other.

If no house was so eclectic as Duchess Street, we know of one where Hope's precedent was, in certain matters, very closely followed. This was 22, St. James's Place which the poet Samuel Rogers (1763–1855) remodelled for himself in 1803–4 with Wyatt as architect.[87] Through the large numbers who congregated there, it must have been as well known and influential as Duchess Street itself. Hope and Rogers, both offsprings of wealthy banking families, though personally devoted to the cause of literature and the arts, were attempting in the same years to make an impression on intellectual society in London by the *avant-garde* style of their houses. Clayden observed of Rogers that by January 1803: 'He had made notes of household arrangements he had seen in houses in which he had visited; had given much study to questions of decoration and ornament; and had designed the furniture himself, with the assistance of Hope's work on the subject.'[88] While it would have been impossible for him to have made use of *Household Furniture*, since that was not published until four years later, it is more than likely that Hope showed his friend the original designs for the Duchess Street furniture and allowed him to make notes from them. Rogers further followed Hope's example by commissioning Flaxman to design chimney-pieces and decorations for him. In February 1803 Flaxman charged him £23. 11s. 6d. for altering three existing chimney-pieces and five guineas for 'drawing and modelling on a frieze' in the drawing-room. A new chimney-piece by Flaxman with side figures of Mnemosyne and a Muse with a lyre, inserted into the drawing-room in March 1804, cost £105.[89] Rogers even employed the same wood-carver as Hope, the Flemish Bogaert, and as a result young Chantrey, then employed by the carver, worked on both their houses.[90] Clayden gives a few more details about Rogers' interiors:

> Stothard designed a cabinet for antiquities, ornamenting it with paintings by his own hand... Much of the work was done under Rogers' personal supervision ... The furniture and decorations followed the Greek models, and one of the striking features of the house was its large and beautiful collection of Greek vases. 'Round the staircase', says his nephew, 'was added a frieze, taken from the Panathenaic procession among the Elgin marbles.'[88]

Like Hope's, much of Rogers' inspiration was French, and he had spent the autumn and early winter of 1802 in Paris studying at the Louvre and elsewhere.

Typical of Regency decorative schemes that suggest a dependence on *Household Furniture* are the interiors designed by William Atkinson in the second decade of the century for Stephen Tempest at Broughton Hall, Yorkshire. Especially characteristic are the segmental vaults, the areas of plate glass, and the tight careful decoration. The chimney-piece in the red drawing-room, supplied in 1810, has Egyptian sphinx terms and a steel grate of 1814 that manages to combine Greek, Gothic, and Baroque details. In the austerely decorated dining-room of 1814, the iconography of the masks at the intersections of the reeded bands surrounding the doors and the segmental sideboard-recess was dictated by a Hopeian concern for accuracy and relevance. Atkinson wrote of them in a letter to his patron: 'I think Ceres the goddess of plenty will be as proper a Deity to preside with the god of libations as his father Silenus, although either would be proper and classical.'[91]

John Nash produced fine English Empire interiors with sophisticated mural decorations and consciously Hopeian furniture in the library (1806–10) at Barnsley Park, Gloucestershire, and in the oval drawing-room (1812; Plate 100) at Caledon, County Tyrone, with its curious gilt paper reliefs. The long gallery of Nash's house at 14–16, Regent Street (1822–4), later transported to East Cowes Castle, Isle of Wight, was close in form and conception to Hope's New Gallery of 1819 at Duchess Street.[92]

A town house in an amazingly bulky and self-confident Empire style must be mentioned here. This is 3, Seamore Place, at the west end of Curzon Street, completely remodelled for the 2nd Earl of Ducie by J. B. Papworth as late as 1835.[93] Five and a half storeys high yet only three bays wide, encased by elaborate ironwork of eccentric design and dominated by four very large caryatids, this was a *tour de force* as unique in London as was Hope's own house.

One way of appreciating the atmosphere and impact of the Duchess Street mansion is to read a popular three-volumed novel by T. S. Surr, published in 1806 under the title, *A Winter in London; or, Sketches of Fashion*. The novel begins with an account of a wealthy banker suddenly elevated to the peerage at the end of the eighteenth century, but soon shifts to the youthful hero's experiences in London society. It is at this point, in volume II, that a description is given of a town-mansion which is almost certainly based on Thomas Hope's in Duchess Street. Every effect is, inevitably, heightened to an exotic degree, but the similarities are too close to be coincidental. Even the timing is exactly right: the year 1804. The occasion of the description is 'a grand masked gala', given at Roseville House by way of 'opening the fashionable campaign of 1804–5':

> 'No longer let the descriptions of entertainments recorded in the *Arabian Nights*', Surr begins romantically, 'be regarded as fabulous, when the nobility, and even the merchants of London, can charm away the hours of winter with such fetes as these.
>
> 'The mansion of Lord Roseville stood upon a large space of ground, and formed a noble quadrangle, in the centre of which were spacious gardens.' The first apartment which the guests entered, 'represented "the rich alhambra of the Moorish kings".
>
> 'The Earl of Roseville and his countess [were] habited in exact costume as a Moorish prince and princess . . . [and] musicians, who welcomed the company with notes of Moorish melody, were all dressed in corresponding habits . . .
>
> 'Passing through this apartment, the visitor next entered a long gallery, which was formed into an Egyptian temple . . . [it] formed one side of the quadrangle.' The quadrangle itself was 'converted into the gardens and pavilions of a Turkish seraglio . . .
>
> '. . . Beautiful young ladies, in the dress of Grecian slaves, were . . . playing on musical instruments, while others danced, and others again were bearing refreshments or perfumes . . . a pavilion erected in this garden . . . was built in rotondo form . . . Here it was intended that supper should be served to the Prince of Wales . . .'
>
> The dress of Lady Emily Roseville 'was precisely that of the beautiful Fatima, described by Lady Mary Wortley Montagu . . .
>
> 'The fourth scene was intended as a contrast to the Turkish one . . . the spectator, upon quitting the brilliantly illuminated pavilion, again entered the house, the north quadrangle of which was in general used as a picture gallery; for which purpose three stories had been thrown into one, and the light was admitted from the top.
>
> 'The paintings . . . were sent into temporary banishment; and the apartment, under the skilful management of Carbonel, Loutherbourg, and that promising young artist Kerr Porter . . . now became the exact representation of a tract of the dreary desert of Arabia, at the hour of midnight . . . ladies actually shrieked at the well counterfeited howlings

> of beasts of prey . . . At the extremity of the scene was a well executed design of the ruins of a species of ancient temple . . . Behind the remains of an uncouth arch . . . appeared a light issuing through the mouth of a cavern, from the fires of a troup of wandering Arabs, whose camels were seen crouching among the ruins.
>
> 'The interior of the cave was excellently designed; and the parts of the robbers were well supported by several young noblemen . . .
>
> 'Other groups of these wild Arabs were discernible by the light of the fires, round which they sat . . . and consisted of professional singers, who from tent to tent answered one another in a wild hunting or warlike chorus.'[94]

The reader who has patiently followed these extracts through will surely agree that they throw much light on the 'Ecstatic' fantasy-world which the Regency so loved to create round itself. If life was to be lived in a museum of past styles, that museum was at least as picturesque and exotic as a stage setting. Life, art, and drama became indistinguishable. Loutherbourg has already been mentioned in an earlier chapter for the South Pacific landscape scenery which he designed for a play about the Tahitian native Omai; Carbonel was a well-known stage designer; and Sir Robert Ker Porter (1777–1842) won early success by his panorama-paintings, those Regency theatres-in miniature which surrounded the spectator on all sides. In 1799 Porter had exhibited a panorama of the Taking of Seringapatam; and Boase has described him as 'a restless figure, whose Russian journeys and marriage and Eastern travels were as romantic as the adventures in his sister's novels'.[95]

It need hardly be pointed out that at the Hope mansion as at Roseville House there was a top-lit Picture-gallery on the north side of the quadrangle, as well as Egyptian and Turkish or Indian rooms. Visitors were greeted by a full-length portrait in the staircase hall of Thomas Hope in Turkish dress with a hookah, painted in 1798, and in the *Fratri Optimo* temple at the Deepdene there was an Arabic inscription. *Anastasius*, moreover, was Roseville House converted back into novel-form. A parallel may also be found in the excited excursions *à la Turque* which occasionally enliven the Romantic Classical music of Mozart, hinting at a more fiery world beyond the gentle ecstasies of controlled melancholy. And at the end of the nineteenth century a romantic like Wilfred Scawen Blunt sought to liberate himself from the conventions of his time by assuming Arab dress and the Moslem faith, while keeping up a country house in Sussex designed by himself in the Queen Anne taste.

Some sources and parallels related to Hope's Egyptian Room have been mentioned earlier and the same must now be done for his Indian Room. We shall spend a little more time on the Indian Revival, however, since it was both more important and more serious than the Egyptian as well as being essential to an understanding of the full neo-classical outlook.

After the playful Eastern freaks of Sir William Chambers' garden-buildings at Kew in the 1760s,[96] the first serious landmark in the Indian Revival is Reynolds' recommendation to architects in his thirteenth Discourse (1786) to imitate 'The Barbarick splendour of those Asiatick buildings'[97] being published by William Hodges in his *Select Views in India.* Hodges' discovery on Hindu temples at Benares, and particularly on a column of the 'temple of Viss Vissha' (Plate 88), of plausibly Greek decoration encouraged him to speculate on the relative position of the Indian to the other great cultures. His daring suggestions were given to the world in his *Travels in India* of 1793. A passage from this book has already been quoted as the possible inspiration for Hope's juxtaposition at Duchess Street of a stalactite from the grotto at Antiparos with a fragment from the Parthenon frieze; and it should not be forgotten that Hope owned a considerable collection of Indian and Graeco-Indian carvings in carboniferous rock-stone dating from the third century B.C. to the thirteenth century A.D. Moving on from his consideration of the column-like effect of stalactites, Hodges discusses how caves, encrusted with these architectural growths, must have been used as habitations by early man. Thus, when these caverns eventually became insufficient for a growing population,

> their improvements and enlargements . . . must naturally bring on imitations of their forms by artificial excavations of rocks, or artificial grottos, caverns, and catacombs . . . the several species of stone buildings, which have been brought more or less to perfection (I mean the Egyptian, Hindoo, Moorish, and Gothic architecture), instead of being copies of each other, are actually and essentially the same . . . The pyramid, the

> obelisk, the spire steeple and minaret, are evidently bold, stupendous imitations of the romantic forms of spiry, towering rocks.[98]

In just such a way does Hope describe the development from 'congelations and stalactites' to 'the flicker, of light and shade'[99] of the Turkish border with which he framed the title-page of *Household Furniture*. Repton, champion of the Indian Revival, developed the theme that Indian architecture was derived from rock-formations; and this whole Romantic movement, beginning, perhaps, with the discovery of Fingal's Cave in 1772,[100] was given a late and masterly expression in Gandy's strange painting of 1836 entitled 'Architecture: its Natural Model'.[101]

William Hodges serves as a stepping stone to the first building which displayed serious hints of Indian influence, Warren Hastings' house at Daylesford (1788–96) in Worcestershire (now part of Gloucestershire).[102] Hastings owned a series of eight paintings of Indian landscapes and buildings which he had commissioned from William Hodges, engravings of which illustrated Hodges' *Travels in India* (1793). His architect was S. P. Cockerell, whose brother, Sir Charles Cockerell, formed a friendship with him while serving in the East India Company from 1776 to 1800. Hastings was an horticulturalist and a trained botanist with an accompanying interest in architecture. In the 1770s he built himself a country house at Alipore in India, and on his return to England, 'erected on the banks of the Thames a house on the model of his home at Alipore'.[103] At Daylesford he 'laid out the grounds after the fashion of his Indian country seat',[103] and even brought plants to it from India.[104] Cockerell provided the house with a double-curved dome adorned with leaf-forms and an elongated pinnacle. Inside there were rich decorations in gold and crimson with 'oriental alcoves', an Eastern gaming-room in the basement[105] and on the first-floor two fine chimney-pieces carved by Thomas Banks in 1792 and *in situ* by 1794.[106] That in the west drawing-room boasts a pair of caryatids in the form of Indian women returning from the Ganges, with a central panel above depicting life in a Harem. A panel in the chimney-piece in the centre drawing-room shows the god Brahma between two elephants. In 1827 George Cumberland mentioned that it was he who had suggested that Banks might imitate ancient Persian paintings in his designs for the Daylesford chimney-pieces, and observed perceptively that the sculptor ended up 'by Grecianizing . . . these Persian *Peruginos*'.[107] The refined allusive spirit of Banks' Eastern work would certainly have appealed to Hope. Moreover, Cumberland was to preface a book on Bonasoni, published in 1793, with *A Plan for the Improvement of the Arts in England* in the course of which he noted that: 'he has observed of late, some painters and sculptors open their eyes to the latent beauties of Hindoo compositions; many of which contain actions that Phidias might have, and, perhaps had studied: for . . . it would not be difficult to advance strong proofs of the Greeks having received art from India, as well as mythology'.[108]

The remarkable aesthetician Cumberland was also artistic adviser to Thomas Johnes,[109] creator of Hafod, Caernarvonshire, where the Indian note was next struck. Here in 1794,[110] John Nash[111] gave the octagonal library a little dome in the form of a 'flattened Moghul cap'.[112] If this looks back to Capability Brown's remarkable Tong Castle, Shropshire (1765), it equally looks forward to the Brighton Pavilion (1815–21).[113]

In 1797 Flaxman who was to approve of Hope's mingling of classical and oriental sources at Duchess Street, agreed to subscribe to a life of William Hodges[114] and executed a monument for University College Chapel, Oxford, to the oriental scholar Sir William Jones, which shows him compiling his digest of Hindu and Mohammedan laws.

Hope's Oriental Room comes next chronologically, since the first of the Daniell pictures for it was commissioned in August 1799. The room was probably similar in spirit to the pretty romanticism of the *boudoir turc* formed in the *hôtel* Beauharnais during the sumptuous remodelling of 1803 by Bataille.[115] Hope's attempt to evoke an Eastern atmosphere without much recourse to strict Oriental detail echoed the Turkish Room at '*Fonthill Splendens*'. This room, probably dating from William Beckford's remodelling of his father's house in the last quarter of the eighteenth century, was decorated with a bold colour-scheme pointing forward to Duchess Street. We know of this unusual room that its walls were hung with orange silk curtains alternating with large mirrors, and that there were also orange silk blinds before the windows, and a 'reddish etruscan brown'[116] carpet. The chimney-piece was designed in the form of an antique marble altar and disposed about the room were numerous candelabra and piles of cushions. It is worth noting that the house which Beckford designed for himself in Lisbon in 1795 also contained a 'Turkish Saloon'.[117]

The first complete Indian building to be erected came in the year following the conception of Hope's Oriental Room. It was a garden-temple—like the first revived Greek Doric buildings of nearly fifty years before—erected at Melchet Park, Wiltshire (Plate 101) (now in Hampshire), by Major Sir John Osborne in honour of his friend Warren Hastings.[118] It was designed by Thomas Daniell in the chastest Hindu taste, executed in artificial stone by Rossi and contained a bust of Hastings on a plinth decorated with Indian lotus forms and classical acroteria—just the combination that had been justified by Hodges' discoveries at the temple of Viss Vissha and which was being worked out in Hope's furniture. One could suggest as a source for this little building, with its porch and pyramidal roof, the Hindu temples at Agori on the river Son, which the Daniells had visited and drawn just ten years before, in January 1790.[119]

An engraving by William Daniell of the Melchet temple was accorded a place of honour in the Oriental Library at the new East India House, Leadenhall Street, completed in 1800 from designs by Henry Holland. The significance in the Indian Revival of the premises of the East India Company has not before been pointed out. Here in the centre of London was a rich collection of original sources of Eastern life and art. The library contained 1600 Sanskrit manuscripts presented by R. H. Colebrook as well as Chinese, Siamese, and Malay manuscripts. There were several volumes of drawings of Indian plants and of the arts, customs, and dress of the orientals. There were botanical collections and a large museum containing such objects as models of Chinese scenery and temples and the gold footstool, in the form of a tiger's head, from the throne of Tipoo Sahib. English artists, too, had combined to weld these alien fragments into a suggestive neo-classical whole. The main pediment of the building contained a large sculptural group by Bacon in which appeared figures symbolic of the Ganges and of Asia, seated on a camel. The General Court Room boasted a white marble chimney-piece with terminal figures in the form of Brahmins and, above, a sculptured plaque with female figures representing India, Asia, Africa, and so on. Throughout the principal rooms there were allegorical paintings, portraits, and busts, including two paintings by Buttersworth of the Battles of Algiers and of the Nile.[120]

It will now be appreciated how the Indian Revival was, in a sense, a microcosm of the whole late neo-classical period since it both combined and was the result of two quite different realms of thought and activity. Firstly, there was the Picturesque tradition of the landscape movement. Into that picture fit the Daniells and their approach to Indian architecture, which was to paint it in a landscape as they imagined Poussin would have done. Secondly, there was the serious study of the Sanskrit language and literature then being conducted under the aegis of Warren Hastings. Two little-known Indian garden temples of the end of the eighteenth century well exemplify this double level. At Stanmore Hall, Middlesex, an octagonal temple was erected for James Forbes to contain sculpture given him by the Brahmins of Hindustan in gratitude for his assiduous care of them whilst occupying a post in the East India Company. He had at the same time filled 150 volumes with notes on Indian life, re ligion, flora and fauna.[121] And at the Picturesque end of the scale, there is the folly at Werrington Park in Devon, erected for the Duke of Northumberland, with three Indian sugar-loaf excrescences on top doubtless derived from some Picturesque landscape scene by the Daniells.[122]

This double-eyed or ambivalent outlook is of the very essence of our period. Take, for example, A. L. Millin (1759–1818), the influential French scholar and author whose works on antique art and whose friendship with Hope have been referred to elsewhere. At the same time as fulfilling the functions of Conservateur des Medailles, des pierres gravées et des Antiques de la Bibliothèque du Roi, Professeur d'Archéologie and, later, Conservateur du Musée des Antiques à la Bibliothèque Nationale, he was also, in Robin Middleton's words, one of 'the three great protagonists of Gothic study and enthusiasm in these years', together with Lenoir and Châteaubriand. He also lectured on Egypt art and antiques and from 1795 edited the *Magasin*

Encyclopédique, a journal of his own invention, which Middleton describes thus: 'It contains detailed discussion of the works of Kant, highly coloured tales, supposedly derived from Indian, Chinese and Persian sources ... There are articles on Erse poetry, oriental languages and Ourang Outangs ... Frenzied reviews of Mrs. Radcliffe's novels are tossed at readers.'[123]

The age of Romantic Classicism occasionally amazed even those who lived in it by its constant ambivalence. Thus there were many[124] who at first found it impossible to believe that the Thomas Hope they thought they knew was the author of *Anastasius*. J. W. Croker succintly expressed in a letter to John Murray what most people felt about *Anastasius*: 'Tom Hope's late body is now the tabernacle of Byron's soul.'[125]

A critical account of *Anastasius* has been regarded as outside the scope of this study. But apart from this, the investigation of the Hope style undertaken in this and in previous chapters has involved us in the architecture and all the visual arts, fine and applied, of the Regency period. This tells us much not only about Thomas Hope's activities but about the universality of the neo-classical manner. Thus, a figure from a Greek vase would be found in a modern history-painting; the chair on which it sat in a modern drawing-room, itself possibly inspired by a Greek temple; the decorative border of its garment not only adorning modern costume but echoed in plasterwork and silverware. Perhaps only in the stricter moments of the Gothic Revival with Pugin's Gothic puddings and even babies did any past style leave so universal and ubiquitous an imprint on contemporary life.

But the style was universal in another way. It brought designers and scholars from different countries into intimate contact with each other to an almost unparalleled degree, at least so far as the English were concerned. If Piranesi, Clérisseau, and Adam were involved together in the early years of neo-classicism, it can be shown that at the height of the movement Canova, Millin, Percier, Flaxman, and Hope, to look no further, were all known to each other. Letters survive written in Italian between Percier and Flaxman from 1791 to 1815;[126] Hope referred to Percier as 'an artist of my acquaintance[127] and corresponded in French with Canova;[128] and Millin knew Flaxman, describing his

Aeschylus drawings in a letter to him as a 'belle composition ou se retrouvent [*sic*] tout le génie des anciens'.[129]

The spirit of cosmopolitan connoisseurship is evoked perfectly by an occasion in the autumn of 1819. Canova was in London, perhaps to view the Elgin Marbles,[130] and he and Flaxman had been asked to a breakfast-party by Thomas Hope, after which they were both invited to make a little tour of Hope's more modest collections.[131]

What we have called in this study, for the purposes of convenience, 'the Hope style', was formed through contacts made in London, Paris, and Rome; and it would be pointless were it not impossible to say which of these cities made the greatest contribution. What we can say is that it seemed to many people at the time that it was Thomas Hope who caused the new style to become fashionable and popular in England, or that, at any rate, 'to Mr. Hope as much of this kind of improvement is to be attributed as it is possible for an individual to have accomplished'.[132]

Conclusion

As it has been my aim throughout this study to relate the achievement of Thomas Hope to the neo-classical age as a whole, it seems fitting that at least a valedictory page or two should be devoted to relating that age to those which have succeeded it. At the risk of appearing tendentious and prophetical I would do that by indicating those nineteenth- and twentieth-century developments to which, I think, the dominant trends of neo-classical and picturesque thought have led.

This study has suggested that the nineteenth century inherited from late neo-classicism all those preoccupations which have often been regarded as its own unique contribution. I refer to a combined conception of art and its moral value; art-education, the museum, and the public building generally; a contemporary style at once narrative and picturesque; and an historical preoccupation with past styles coupled with a passionate search for a new style. That in every nineteenth-century city these interests and theories were put into practice to an amazing degree will doubtless be revealed more and more frequently as a result of the present growth in Victorian studies. In the twentieth century the museum-spirit has become more pervasive if sometimes in a less tangible form, and it has already been suggested that the *Musée Imaginaire* devised by André Malraux is a parallel to Thomas Hope's achievement in his Duchess Streeth ouse and particularly in his Lararium, his museum of religions. And there is another invention of Malraux's which has much in common with the picturesque museum, and that is '*Son et Lumière*.' Sir John Soane's house in Lincoln's Inn Fields is a '*Son et Lumière*' house in reverse, for while it must have seemed in his lifetime far more like a museum than most other houses, today it seems far more like a house than most other museums. Thomas Hope's house was even closer to the '*Son et Lumière*' house which is accessible by ticket on special occasions, floodlit and set out to suggest that it is lived in. To see, say, the great gallery at Chenonceaux across the river lit up at night for a make-believe ball, tape-recorded laughter and music wafting across the water, floodlights switched on within the chapel so that the stained-glass windows glow in the dark to the sound of records of choirboys coming from within—is to my mind an utterly macabre and, indeed, 'ecstatically' Picturesque experience which Gandy, in his wilder flights of fancy, might just have dreamed of.

But for the most complete realization of the vision of Romantic Classicism[1]—the combination of nature, art, morality in a landscaped setting, the cult of the moment to abstract virtue in the artificially natural park, the preoccupation with the tomb, death and decay, so characteristic of the artistic sensibilities of Ledoux and Gilly, Dance and Gandy—it is, I suggest, to North America that we must turn, to the Cemetery of Forest Lawn. A few quotations from the *Property Owner's Guide and Pictorial Map of the Forest Lawn Memorial Park, Glendale, California*, will suffice to convey the atmosphere:

> 'If your time permits be sure to visit the Great Mausoleum—eleven floors of art masterpieces, rare imported marbles and more than three hundred stained-glass windows. Here too are masterpieces of statuary; the magnificent St. George by Donatello and Michelangelo's greatest sculpture. Forest Lawn is the only place in the world where these may be seen together. If your time is limited, leave the Great Mausoleum in time to see the next hourly showing of the Crucifixion Painting, America's largest religious painting.' You can also visit the Freedom Mausoleum which 'reflects our great American heritage in softly glowing rare marble, magnificent stained glass and statuary . . . the Forest Lawn Museum which contains every coin mentioned in the Bible and other mementoes of historical and cultural interest . . . [including] a radiant stained-glass recreation of Leonardo's Last Supper . . . '[There is] the Church called the Wee Kirk o' the Heather in which the matchless love story of Annie Laurie is told in the stained-glass windows' and you can wander through the landscaped park which contains 'The Mystery of Life Garden, the Freedom Mausoleum, the Masonic Monument, the Temple of Santa Sabina, the Court of Freedom, the Shrine of Love, and Apollo and Daphne' and you can visit 'Vesperland, Harmony, Graceland and Memory Slope'.

It seems to me that a case can be made, although I can understand if there be those who find the idea unsympathetic or unconvincing, that Forest Lawn achieves at a popular level what we have seen tentatively expressed at a sophisticated and private level in the neo-classical period. Thus at Forest Lawn the different religions of the world are finally united together in terms of their artistic, romantic, and sentimental appeal so that art, nature, and morality merge in the midst of a picturesque landscaped setting in which the urgency and permanence of the message is brought home by the ubiquitous presence of death, by the touched-up face within the tomb.

APPENDIX A

Charles Kelsall: A Bibliography

(The place of publication is London unless otherwise stated)

1812 *A Letter from Athens addressed to a Friend in England.* 95pp

1812 *A Translation of the Two Last Pleadings of Marcus Tullius Cicero against Caius Verres: to which is added a Post Script containing Remarks on the State of Modern Sicily.* 365pp

1814 *Phantasm of an University: with Prolegomena.* 174pp

1818 *Constance and Eugenie, or an Evening on Mount Vernon, the Seat of General Washington: a Political Dialogue discussing the Constitution of the United States.* By Junius Secundus. (Brussels)

1818 *A Translation from Italian into English of the Funeral Oration by Navagero on the Death of the Doge Loredano at Venice.* (The *Pamphleteer*, vol. XII, 1818, pp. 187–229)

1820 *Classical Excursion from Rome to Arpino.* (Geneva.) 254pp. (Reprinted in *New Voyages and Travels*, vol. IV, 1821)

1822 *Remarks touching on Geography, especially that of the British Isles.* By Mela Britannicus. 79pp

1823 *First Sitting of the Committee on the Proposed Monument to Shakespeare.* By Zachary Craft. (*The Pamphleteer*, vol. XXII, 1823, pp. 169–97)

1827 *A Letter to the Society of Dilettanti on the Works in Progress at Windsor.* By Mela Britannicus. 81pp

1828 *Carluccio and Signore Violina.* (The Morden College copy is inscribed by Kelsall: 'a musical jeu d'esprit by Charles Kelsall after he had fruitlessly attempted to make some progress on the violin')

1828 *Poematia Tria Latina.* By Laurea Arpinata

1830 *Esquisse de mes travaux, de mes voyages et de mes opinions.* By Mela Britannicus. (Frankfurt.) 234pp

1831 *The Apparatition of the Castle.* By Junius Minimus. 36pp

1836 *Horae Viaticae.* By Mela Britannicus. 412pp. (A 2nd edition was printed at Bristol in 1839)

1836 *A Letter on Bells: with a novel mode of ringing them.* 43pp. (Written for a mechanics institute)

—— *Song of the Three Witches from 'Macbeth'*, Act 1, with violin accompaniment. (Single printed sheet of music, with no date)

Appendix

KELSALL MSS. AT MORDEN COLLEGE LIBRARY

Las Maravillas de España, a pocket-guide written *c.* 1800.
Sketchbook used in the Auvergne in 1814.
Sketchbook used in Devon and Arpino in 1819.
Three architectural drawings for a Monument to Milton.
Four architectural drawings for the proposed new library at Morden College, Blackheath, in the Elizabethan style.

APPENDIX B

Chronologies of the Introduction into England, France and Germany of Greek Doric Orders up to 1810

Only executed projects (except in the case of Germany), of reasonably certain date, are included.
Unless otherwise stated, it is to be assumed that
1. in the English examples the Greek Doric order is employed on external porticos or colonnades; and that
2. the French examples are to be found in Paris.
Abbreviations: 'ext.': exterior;
'int.' : interior.
The numbers after the names refer to pages where the buildings are discussed. Numbers in brackets are fig. or plate references.

GREEK DORIC

1758	Hagley, Worcs. (temple). 2nd Earl of Lyttelton. Stuart.
1758 ('65?)	Shugborough, Staffs. (temple). Thomas Anson. Stuart.
c. 1766	Standlynch, Wilts. Henry Dawkins. Revett. (Delian order.) 87
1772–78	Downton Castle, Herefs. (chimney-piece). Payne Knight for himself. 89
1778	Ayot St. Lawrence church, Herts. Revett. (Delian order.) 87, 88–9
1780	Aston Hall, Salop. (gateway). — Moultrie. Mylne.
1789	Great Packington church, Warwicks. (int.). Bonomi.
c. 1790	Gresford Lodge, Cheshire. (gateway). J. Parry. Wyatt. 86
c. 1790	All Saints, Newcastle. Stephenson.
c. 1791?	Castle Goring, Sussex. (ext. & int.). Bysshe Shelley. Rebecca. 280
1793	Hammerwood, Sussex. — Sperling. Latrobe. (stopped flutes.) 89
1793–1820	Chester Castle. Harrison. 61, 71, 86
1795	Tyringham, Bucks. (int.). W. M. Praed. Soane. (stopped flutes.) 89
1795–7	Cleveland House, St. James's. 3rd Duke of Bridgewater. J. Lewis.
c. 1795	Ottershaw Park, Surrey. (lodges). — Wyatt. 86

c. 1797	Hanworth Park, Middlesex. Wyatt.
1798	Bentley Priory, Middlesex. (int.). 1st Marquess of Abercorn. Soane. (stopped flutes). 89
1799	Woolley Park, Berks. Revd. P. Wroughton. Jeffry Wyatt. 89
1800	Duchess Street mansion. (int.). Hope for himself. 103 (Fig. 8)
c. 1800	The Mote, Kent. (temple). 3rd Baron Romney. S. Nelson. (31)
c. 1800	Stoke Park, Bucks. John Penn. Wyatt. 86, 89
Between 1802 & '08	Sacombe Park, Herts. George Caswell. —.
1803	Hyde Hall, Herts. (int.). 2nd Earl of Roden. Wyatville.
1803	Weedon Barracks, Northants. —.
c. 1803	Phoenix Fire Office, Charing Cross. Gandy.
1804	Bank of England vestibule (int.). Soane. 89
1805	Dodington church, Gloucs. (int.); and Dairy (ext.) between 1798 & 1808. Christopher Codrington. Wyatt.
1805	Paultons, Hants. Hans Sloane-Stanley. John Kent.
1806	Osberton, Notts. F. F. Foljambe. Wilkins. 64 (18)
1806	Lower Assembly Rooms, Bath. Wilkins. 71
1806–9	Manchester Exhange. Harrison.
1807	Desenfans Mausoleum, Charlotte-st. (int.). Sir Francis Bourgeois. Soane.
By 1807?	Newlands Park, Bucks. T. Allen. —.
1807–17	Belsay, Northumberland. Sir Charles Monck, Bart., for himself. 67, 69 (20 & 21)
1808	Chester News Room. Harrison.
1808–9	Letheringsett Hall, Norfolk. Wm. Hardy for himself. (½ stopped). 89, 91 (29)
1808–10	North Gate, Chester. Harrison.
1808 & '11	Storrs Hall, Westmoreland. J. Bolton. Gandy. (stopped flutes). 89, 280 (28)
1809	Grange Park, Hants. Henry Drummond. Wilkins. 69–70, 91 (22 & 51)
1809	Moggerhanger, Beds. Godfrey Thornton. Soane. (partly stopped flutes). 89
1809	Covent Garden Theatre. Smirke. 71
1809–12	Bayfordbury, Herts. William Baker. —.
1810	Newcastle Moot Hall. Stokoe.
1810	Wakefield Court House. —.

1810	Buckland Filleigh, Devon. (int.). J. I. Fortescue. Green. 89, 280

UNFLUTED GREEK DORIC OR 'PRIMITIVIST'

Between 1774 & '89	Villa at Mill Hill, Middlesex. Peter Hammond. Paine, Jr.
1779–82	Warwick Gaol. Johnson. (intended to be fluted). 87
1783	Hammells Park, Herts. (bark dairy). Hon. Philip Yorke. Soane. 87
1786	Langley Park, Norfolk. (lodges). Sir Thomas Proctor Beauchamp, Bart. Soane.
1786–90	Stansted House, Sussex. Richard Barwell. Wyatt & Bonomi. (with astragals).
1789	Sydney Lodge, Hants. Hon. Mrs. Yorke. Soane.
1792	Tyringham, Bucks. (lodges). W. M. Praed. Soane. 89
1793–1820	Chester Castle. Harrison. 61, 71, 86
1795	Hereford Gaol. Nash.
1798	Malvern Hall, Warwicks. (brick barn). H. G. Lewis. Soane.
1799	Betchworth Castle, Surrey. (bark dairy). Henry Peters. Soane. 87
c. 1800	Goodwood House, Sussex. 3rd Duke of Richmond. Wyatt.
1802	Macartney House, Greenwich. (int.). Hon. G. F. Lyttelton. Soane.
1803	Stratton Park, Hants. Sir Francis Baring. Dance. 70, 89 (23)
1805	Paultons, Hants. (int.). Hans Sloane-Stanley. John Kent.
c. 1810	Doric House, Bath. Thomas Barker. Gandy. 88 (27)
1810	Buckland Filleigh, Devon. J. I. Fortescue. Green. 89, 280

Ireland, Scotland, and Wales have been regarded as rather outside the orbit. However, Francis Johnston's *Townley Hall, Co. Louth*, of 1794 ought to be mentioned for its use of both the fluted Greek Doric, and the 'Primitivist' orders. Ireland also has *Castle Coole*, but that is by an English architect. In 1810 another English architect, Richard Elsam, designed in the Nash/Dance gaol-style the *County Prison at Cavan*, an ambitious project that cost £12,000. Home-grown products, though trained by Nash, were the brothers George and James Pain, (1793–1838) and, (1779–1879), respectively, who jointly produced the fine *Male Prison at Cork* in the rare Delian Doric order. Scotland had the seeds of a local talent that were to flower into the eventual transformation of Edinburgh into the Athens of the North. The elder Playfair (?–1794) used unfluted Greek Doric columns at *Cairness* in the 1790s. Peter Nicholson (1765–1844) had built *Carlton Place at Partick* by 1806 in the Greek Doric taste for Fulton Alexander; and crossed the border to design in 1812–17 the fine Greek Doric *Corby Castle, Cumberland,* for Henry Howard.

SHORT COMPARATIVE LISTS FOR FRANCE AND GERMANY

GREEK DORIC

1772	Hôtel Montmorency. Ledoux. 85
1775	Theatre, Besançon. Ledoux. 57
1777	Grotto at the Folie de Ste. James, Neuilly. Belanger. 85
1778–81	Hôpital de la Charité. J.-D. Antoine. 85
1782	Capt. Cook Monument, Parc de Méréville, nr. Etampes. A. Pajou. 85, 154–5 (26)
1784	Barrière de Monceau. Ledoux. 85
1784	St. Médard. Petit-Radel.
1790	Maison Chenot, rue de Provence. Bruneau. 85
1802	Lecture Theatre, Jardin des Plantes. Legrand & Molinos.

UNFLUTED GREEK DORIC OR 'PRIMITIVIST'

1772	Hôtel Montmorency. Ledoux. 85
1775	Saltworks entrance, Arc et Senans. Ledoux.
1775	Pagoda, Chanteloup. Le Camus de Mézières.
1778	Maison de la Thuille, rue Poissonière. Durand.
1778	No. 1, rue Pepinière. De Wailly.
1778–81	Hôpital de la Charité. J.-D. Antoine. 85
1778–81	Hôtel Thelusson, rue de Provence. Ledoux.
1780	Pyramid Monument, Parc de Maupertuis. Brongniart. (Ledoux?).
c. 1780	Cottage, Parc de Maupertuis. Brongniart. 87
1781	Capuchin Convent. Brongniart. 87
1784–89	Barrières by Ledoux: Bonshommes, Chopinette, Courcelles, Réservoir, Reuilly and Villette.
1785	Maison de Champs, Pantin. Belanger.
1785–87	Church at Romainville. Brongniart.
1787	Maison Belanger, rue Neuve des Capucines. Belanger.
1790	Maison Vassal, rue Pigal. Henry.
1792	Maisons Hosten, nos. 1, 2, 3, & 6. Ledoux.

1793	Maison Damesme, rue Richer. Damesme.
1795	Greenhouse, Jardin des Plantes. Molinos.
1797	Château Bienaimé, Courbevoie. Bienaimé.
1798	Rue des Colonnes. Poyet.
1801	Maison le Beau, rue St. Lazare. Moitte.
1801	The Bourse, St. Petersburg. Thomas de Thomon. 72, 76
1803	Hôtel-Dieu, Parvis de Notre Dame. Clavareau.

GREEK DORIC

1798–1800	Old Mint, Berlin. Gentz.
1800–5	Vieweg House, Brunswick, D. Gilly.
1802–4	Staircase in the Schloss at Weimar. Gentz.
1804–5	Banqueting Hall, Shooting-lodge, Weimar. Gentz.
1810	Mausoleum in the Park at Charlottenburg. Gentz.

UNFLUTED GREEK DORIC OR 'PRIMITIVIST'

1792	Riding School, Berlin.
1798	Municipal Theatre, Danzig. Held.
c. 1799	Municipal Theatre, Glogau.
1801–4	Vieweg House, Brunswick. D. Gilly.
1804	Schloss Steglitz. D. Gilly.
1808	Fürstenhaus, Liebenstein.
1809–10	Women's Prison, Würzburg. Speeth.

UNEXECUTED DESIGNS

GREEK DORIC

1787	National Monument to Frederick the Great. H. C. Genelli.
1790s	Sketches for exts. & ints. F. Gilly.
1793–4	Town cemetery. Weinbrenner.
1796–7	National Monument to Frederick the Great. F. Gilly.
1797	Market Place, Karlsruhe. Weinbrenner.
1798	National Theatre. F. Gilly.
1808	Monument to Kant. H. C. Genelli.
1809 & '10	Walhalla. K. von Fischer.

UNFLUTED GREEK DORIC OR 'PRIMITIVIST'

1790s	Sketches for exts. & ints. F. Gilly; Weinbrenner.

APPENDIX C

Catalogue of the Illustrations in John Britton's *Illustrations of the Deepdene. Seat of T. Hope Esqre., 1825-6.* Now in the Minet Library, Brixton

This sumptuous volume, 19″ × 13⅛″ in size, now badly damaged, is bound in red leather with gilt tooling to match that on the Deepdene Album. The illustrations are mounted on pages of stiff grey-brown card or paper and separated from each other by two pages of white paper (watermark, J. Whatman 1825). They are by W. H. Bartlett, save for nos. 23–8 and the peacock in no. 16, which are the work of Penry Williams. Two are lost: 'Stables and House from Entrance Road' and 'South East Entrance'. The numbers in this catalogue give the order of the illustrations as they appear in the volume.

PLAN

1. The Estate. Water-colour, 10″ × 7½″.*

EXTERIORS

10. House from the Drying Grounds. Water-colour, 13″ × 9½″.
11. Entrance Front. Water-colour, 10″ × 6½″.
13. Entrance Court, looking towards Tower. Water-colour, 7⅝″ × 7⅛″.
14. Gothic Wing and Loggia to Mrs. Hope's Apartments. Sepia and wash, 10″ × 8¼″.
15. View from Amphitheatre. Water-colour, 10¾″ × 7½″.
16. Steps to the Amphitheatre. Water-colour, 11″ × 8⅛″.
17. Amphitheatre, Conservatories and Gothic Wing. Water-colour, 13⅞″ × 8⅛″.
18. Terrace before the Drawing-room. Water-colour, 11⅜″ × 7¾″.
19. Dining-room Wing and Tower. Water-colour, 6¾″ × 4⅝″.

INTERIORS

23. View from the Long Conservatory. Water-colour, 9⅝″ × 6⅞″.
24. Circular Conservatory. Water-colour, 9¼″ × 7″.
25. Amphitheatre. Water-colour, 8¼″ × 7″.
26. Statue Gallery. Water-colour, 9⅛″ × 7″.

*The plan is kept separately at the Library since it is not bound into the Volume.

27. Library Chimney-piece. Water-colour, $10\frac{7}{8}'' \times 7\frac{1}{2}''$.
28. Boudoir. Water-colour, $9'' \times 7''$.

BUILDINGS IN THE GROUNDS

4. Entrance Lodge. Sepia and wash, $7\frac{1}{8}'' \times 4\frac{3}{4}''$.
6. Castellated Archway of Approach, East Side. Sepia and wash, $6\frac{3}{4}'' \times 4\frac{3}{4}''$.
7. Ditto, West Side. Sepia and wash, $9\frac{1}{4}'' \times 6\frac{7}{8}''$.
8. Stables. Sepia and wash, $7\frac{1}{8}'' \times 4\frac{7}{8}''$.
9. Kitchen and Dairy. Sepia and wash, $7\frac{1}{8}'' \times 5\frac{5}{8}''$.
12. Temple. Pencil, $7\frac{3}{4}'' \times 4\frac{7}{8}''$. A later insertion over the original caption, 'The South East Entrance'.
29. Tower in Kitchen Gardens. Sepia and wash, $8\frac{3}{4}'' \times 5\frac{1}{2}''$.
30. Tower before the North-West Front. Water-colour, $8'' \times 6\frac{1}{4}''$. A later insertion.

VIEWS IN THE GROUNDS AND ADJACENT COUNTRY

2. Box Hill from Dorking Mill. Water-colour, $7\frac{7}{8}'' \times 5\frac{3}{8}''$.
3. View of Dorking, Deepdene, and Woods from the Denbies. Water-colour, $11\frac{1}{8}'' \times 8\frac{7}{8}''$.
5. The Denbies and Dorking Lime Quarries from Deepdene. Water-colour, $7'' \times 5''$.
20. The Dene and Flower Gardens from the Terrace. Water-colour, $7\frac{5}{8}'' \times 6\frac{5}{8}''$.
21. Holm Wood and Distant Country from the Terrace. Water-colour, $13\frac{1}{2}'' \times 9\frac{3}{8}''$.
22. Sandy Lane with Gnarled Trees. Sepia, $8\frac{5}{8}'' \times 6\frac{1}{2}''$.

ARCHITECTURAL DRAWINGS LATER INSERTED AT RANDOM

ENTRANCE- AND STAIRCASE-HALLS

1 Plan, 1 Elevation and 2 Sections. Sepia and water-colour on a single sheet, $20\frac{1}{2}'' \times 13\frac{3}{4}''$.

Sketch for Staircase-end of Hall. Indian ink, $7\frac{1}{4}'' \times 4\frac{1}{2}''$.

EAST FRONT

3 Elevations with part plans:

(*a*) sepia and water-colour, $21'' \times 13\frac{3}{4}''$.

(*b*) pencil and water-colour, $19\frac{1}{4}'' \times 11\frac{7}{8}''$.
(*c*) sepia and water-colour, $21'' \times 13\frac{3}{4}''$.

Perspective View. Sepia, $15'' \times 10''$.
Sketch. Indian ink, $7'' \times 4\frac{3}{8}''$.

WEST FRONT

Sketch. Indian ink, $7\frac{1}{4}'' \times 4\frac{1}{2}''$.

PROPOSED CONVERSION OF TOWER IN KITCHEN GARDENS INTO GARDENER'S COTTAGE

4 Elevations:
(*a*) sepia and water-colour, $16'' \times 9\frac{3}{4}''$.
(*b*) sepia and water-colour, $16'' \times 10\frac{1}{4}''$.
(*c*) sepia and water-colour, on the same sheet
as (*d*) sepia and water-colour, $15'' \times 10''$.

3 Sections. Sepia and water-colour on a single sheet, $16\frac{1}{4}'' \times 9\frac{3}{4}''$

Catalogue of the Illustrations in John Britton's *History etc. of the Deepdene. Seat of Thos. Hope Esqr. 1821-6.* Now in the Drawings Collection, R.I.B.A. Library.

Bound in blue leather and $13'' \times 8''$ in size, this volume was intended to contan historical accounts of the estate and its owners, and plans of the estate and the house. It was the companion volume to the more splendid volume of illustrations now at the Minet Library. However, the MS. accounts were not completed and in their place were loosely pasted on to the lined paper over 30 preliminary sketches and water-colours. Some of these are inscribed by the artist with pencilled notes which have not been repeated here. The numbers in this catalogue give the order of the illustrations as they appear in the volume. 'WB' indicates that the illustration is signed by W. H. Bartlett.

PLANS

1. The Estate. Water-colour, $11\frac{1}{4}'' \times 7\frac{1}{2}''$. Water-mark, H. Smith & Son 1825.
2. Ground Floor of house. Indian ink on brown paper, $16\frac{3}{4}'' \times 12''$.

EXTERIORS

4. Approach to House. Water-colour, $10\frac{1}{8}'' \times 6''$. WB, Sept. 1825.
3. Entrance Front. Water-colour, $9\frac{5}{8}'' \times 6\frac{1}{2}''$. WB.

15. Entrance Court, looking towards Tower. Water-colour, $9\frac{1}{4}'' \times 7''$. WB, Sept. 1825.
28. Preparatory sketch for tower. Pencil, $8\frac{3}{4}'' \times 5\frac{1}{2}''$. *Verso*, figures on horseback. Sepia.
8. House from Drying Grounds with Dairy and Kitchen. Unfinished water-colour, $12\frac{1}{2}'' \times 7\frac{7}{8}''$.
16. Ditto. Water-colour, $8\frac{7}{8}'' \times 6\frac{1}{8}''$.
11. House and Dairy. Pencil, $9'' \times 6\frac{3}{4}''$.
10. Dairy and Kitchen. Pencil, $10\frac{1}{4}'' \times 7''$.
5. Kitchen Roof. Water-colour, $9\frac{3}{4}'' \times 6\frac{1}{2}''$.
13. Amphitheatre. Water-colour, $9'' \times 6''$.
14. Amphitheatre, Conservatory and Gothic Wing. Water-colour, $9\frac{7}{8}'' \times 6''$.
17. Amphitheatre looking towards Valley. Water-colour, $10\frac{3}{4}'' \times 7\frac{1}{2}''$.
32. Ditto. Unfinished water-colour, $10\frac{1}{4}'' \times 7\frac{1}{2}''$.
38. North-West Front and Tower. Pencil, $10'' \times 5\frac{5}{8}''$. WB.
25. View of House from Stables. Unfinished water-colour and sepia, $11'' \times 7\frac{1}{4}''$.
19. Distant View of House. Unfinished water-colour, $6\frac{3}{4}'' \times 4\frac{1}{2}''$.
33. Distant View of House through Valley. Pencil, $12\frac{1}{2}'' \times 6\frac{7}{8}''$. Watermark, Joseph Coles 1822.

BUILDINGS IN THE GROUNDS

7. Castellated Archway of Approach. Sepia, $9'' \times 6\frac{5}{8}''$. WB, Sept. 1825.
9. Ditto. Pencil and wash, $7'' \times 5''$.
22. Open Wooden Bridge over Ravine. Unfinished pencil, $7\frac{3}{4}'' \times 7''$. *Verso*, castellated archway of approach, unfinished pencil.
12. Tower before North West Front of House. Pencil, $9'' \times 6\frac{1}{2}''$. WB, Sept. 1825.
6. View in Kitchen Garden with Tower. Unfinished water-colour, $8\frac{3}{4}'' \times 5\frac{1}{2}''$.

VIEWS IN THE GROUNDS AND ADJACENT COUNTRY

20. Betchworth Park from Box Hill. Pencil and wash, $10'' \times 6\frac{1}{2}''$. WB.
30. Box Hill from Deepdene. Water-colour, $6\frac{1}{2}'' \times 4\frac{5}{8}''$.
37. Box Hill with Deepdene in distance. Pencil, $9'' \times 6\frac{1}{4}''$. WB.
31. Valley near Deepdene. Pencil, $7'' \times 6''$.
36. Valley in Norbury Park. Pencil, $7'' \times 5''$. WB.
23. Scene with Water-mill. Pencil, $9\frac{7}{8}'' \times 7''$.

18. Tree on Sandy Slope. Water-colour, $7\frac{5}{8}'' \times 4\frac{3}{4}''$.
34. Tree. Pencil, $9\frac{3}{4}'' \times 6\frac{5}{8}''$. Water-mark, Britannia in crowned medallion.
21. Trees. Pencil, $4'' \times 2\frac{5}{8}''$.

MISCELLANEOUS

29. Random sketches and notes. Unfinished pencil, $10\frac{5}{8}'' \times 6\frac{5}{8}''$. *Verso*, distant view of Dorking, pencil.
35. Ruined Gothic towers among trees. Pencil, $7'' \times 4\frac{1}{4}''$. *Verso*, Sept. 1825, and part of letter (by Bartlett?).

APPENDIX D

Sources for *Designs of Modern Costume* (1812) in *Household Furniture* (1807).

First numbers are of plates from *Designs of Modern Costume*; others are from *Household Furniture.*

1. Picture-gallery in 2.
3. Table from 15 i; sofa from 18 v.
4. Table from 39; chair from 2.
6. Table from 19 v.
9. Chair from 59 i.
11. Chair leg from 59 i.
12. Table from 39; chair from 25 iv.
19. Cradle in 44; chair from 26 vi; tripod from 50 iii.
20. Chair from 2.

A Series of twenty-nine designs of Modern Costume drawn and engraved by Henry Moses. Esq. (1823) adds nine plates, some of unrelated subjects like 'Hebe and the Angel', 'Pericles', 'Two Flying Angels with Harps', and 'Echo and Narcissus'. Of the nine additional plates, the following contain furniture derived from *Household Furniture.*

17. Table from 19 v; chair from 25 iv.
22. Plaque in 27 ii; table in 54 i.
29. Chair from 2.

APPENDIX E

Surviving objects designed by Thomas Hope with a Note on the Regency Revival

The principal source for our knowledge of these is the Christie's Sale Catalogues of 1917. Thirty-nine objects, which had been illustrated in *Household Furniture* and were almost certainly designed by Hope, were sold in 20 lots. In the following list, numbers in square brackets refer to sale and lot numbers; in round brackets to plates in *Household Furniture*; and all others to plates or figs. in the present book. An * indicates that the attribution to Hope is uncertain. Most of the furniture without catalogue numbers was disposed of in September 1917 by Messrs. Humber and Flint.

Circular table [99, 297]; (32); 36. (Victoria and Albert Museum.)
Tripod table [99, 298]; (39). (Victoria and Albert Museum.)
2 tables. (12); 98. (Ashmolean Museum, Oxford.)
Pier-table (7 & 13); Fig. 13.
Pier-table (7 & 15). (Ex Knoblock Collection.)
Writing-desk. (Ex Knoblock Collection.)
Sofa (18); 37, Fig. 27. (Ex Knoblock Collection.)
2 Egyptian couches and 4 chairs [99, 306]; (8, 17, 46); 39, 40, Fig. 14. (1 couch & two chairs at Buscot Park, Berkshire.)
2 elbow chairs [99, 293]; (22); Fig. 26. (Royal Pavilion, Brighton: there is also a pair at the Victoria and Albert Museum.)
2 Egyptian chairs 37 extreme right. (James Watson-Gandy-Brandreth.)
4 chairs. (Ashmolean Museum, Oxford.)
2 X-shaped chairs [99, 302]; (20). (Edward James.)*
2 X-shaped stools [99, 304]; (12); 95.
Bookcase. (James Watson-Gandy-Brandreth.)
Clock (7 & 13); 38. (Royal Pavilion, Brighton; there is a variant at Buscot Park.)
2 fire-screens (6); 36 and Figs. 12 & 27. (Ex Knoblock Collection.)
2 fire-screens [99, 300]; (28).
2 wall-lights (6). (Royal Pavilion, Brighton.)*
2 wall-lights (8); Fig. 14. (Duke of Wellington.)
2 bronze *torchères* [99, 291]; (22); Fig. 26.
2 *torchères* (28). (Royal Pavilion, Brighton.)
2 wine-coolers [99, 301]; (24).
2 *tazze* [99, 29].

2 candlesticks [99, 273]; (15 & 49).
2 circular vegetable-dishes [98, 42]; (47); Fig. 3.
Oviform tea-urn [98, 54]; (49 & 52); Fig. 2.
2 vases with ormolu mounts [99, 252A]; (13).*
2 Chinese vases with ormolu mounts [99, 121]; (31).*
Vase [99, 239]; (48).
2 greyhounds [99, 224]; (10); Fig. 17.*
2 greyhounds [99, 237]; (28); Fig. 30.*
2 leopards [99, 282]; (46).*
Nymph [99, 232]; (48).*

The Regency or Empire Revival began far earlier than is commonly supposed (e.g. Musgrave, *op. cit.*, pp. 27–8). It did not spring suddenly into being in the 1920s, but had been prepared for in the gaily Gallic days of Edward VII. Few large Edwardian hotels or liners were complete without 'Empire suites', sometimes of considerable finesse. But the most remarkable of all such experiments was, surprisingly enough, in the heart of the city, near Temple Bar; the sumptuous headquarters of the United Kingdom Provident Association, erected in *c.* 1907 from designs by the prolific and competent architect, Henry T. Hare (1860–1921). The domed General Office and the 1st floor Hall, with lavish decorative details in ormolu and bronze by Lynn Jenkins, are Percier and Fontaine seen, as it were, through a rich haze of brandy fumes and cigar smoke.

The important part played by Edward Knoblock immediately after the first world war has already been stressed. His London house at 11, Montague Terrace (Plates 36 and 37), was a straightforward and convincing recreation of Hopeian ideals. But it was soon found that the smartly intellectual, sometimes almost flashy, character of Regency furnishings had much in common with the artistic tastes of the 1920s and 30s, and could be expensively and sophisticatedly combined with the 'gloss and glass' of the period. This phase of the Regency Revival, described by Osbert Lancaster as 'Vogue Regency' (*Homes Sweet Homes*, 1939, p. 74), is typified by the remodelling of the following London houses: 8, Devonshire Place, by Guy Elwes for himself; 17, Park Square East, by Lord Gerald Wellesley for H. J. Venning; 5, Belgrave Square, with decorations by Lord Gerald Wellesley and Michael Gibbons, for Henry Channon, M.P.; 11, Titchfield Terrace, by Lord Gerald Wellesley for himself; 13, Crawford Street, by H. S. Goodhart-Rendel for himself; and the incredible Mulberry House, Smith Square, a Lutyens house transformed for Lady Melchett by Darcy Braddell, with decorations by Glyn Philpot and C. S. Jagger including jazz-modern neo-Greek murals in silver-foil and a bronze relief depicting

'Scandal', combined with Greek Doric columns and a genuine Greek head—the perfect setting for scenes in any one of Evelyn Waugh's early novels. At a more scholarly level, the culmination of this enthusiasm was the re-publication in 1937, by John Tiranti, Ltd., of the plates from Hope's *Household Furniture.*

Today, the initiative seems finally to have passed from the private collector to the public museum. But under the guiding hands of Clifford Musgrave, the Brighton Pavilion has gradually been restored to a condition as dazzling as, if not more dazzling than, its original appearance under George IV. Clearly the public today—as Pevsner, perhaps, just hinted at (*The Buildings of England. Sussex*, 1965, pp. 441–2)—is finding increasing delight and relief in forgetting, for a colourful moment, the shoddiness and the brutality of much modern architecture.

Bibliography

The first 4 sections of the Bibliography list the major instances of sustained reference to Thomas Hope which have been used in writing this book. Most of the references are to published works; all MS. sources are cited individually in the Notes. The place of publication is London unless otherwise stated.

1. Biographies of Hope
2. The Hope Collection
3. The Duchess Street Mansion & The Deepdene
4. Furniture Design by Hope
5. Hope's Writings: (a) Books & Pamphlets; (b) Articles

1. BIOGRAPHIES OF HOPE

Annual Biography and Obituary, vol. XVI, 1832.

Baumgarten, S. *Le Crépuscule Néo-Classique. Thomas Hope*, Paris, 1958.

Colvin, H. M. *A Biographical Dictionary of English Architects. 1660–1840*, 1954.

Biographie Universelle, vol. 19, Paris, 1857.

Dictionary of National Biography, vol. XXVII, 1891.

Elias J. E. *De Vroedschap van Amsterdam. 1578–1795*, 2 vols., Haarlem, 1903–5 (Amsterdam, 1963), vol. II.

Gentleman's Magazine, vol. CI, part i, 1831.

Law, H. W. & I. *The Book of the Beresford Hopes*, 1925.

Sass, E. K. *Thorvaldsens Portraetbuster*, 3 vols., Copenhagen, 1963–5.

Thieme, U. & Becker, F. *Allgemeines Lexikon der bildenden Künstler*, 37 vols., Leipzig, 1907–50, vol. 17.

2. THE HOPE COLLECTION

Annals of the Fine Arts, vol. IV, 1820, no. 12.

Christie, Manson and Woods, Ltd. *Sale Catalogues*, vol. VI, 1917, July–August.

98. Old English and Foreign Silver and Silver-Gilt, Jewels, Miniatures, and Enamel Portraits . . . from the Deepdene.
99. Objects of Art, Porcelain, Old English, and Other Furniture . . . from the Deepdene.
100. Important Pictures by Old Masters and Family Portraits . . . from the Deepdene.

101. Celebrated Collection of Greek, Roman, and Egyptian Sculpture and Ancient Greek Vases . . . from the Deepdene.

102. Valuable Library of Books on Architecture, Costume, Sculpture, and Antiquities, etc., formed by Thomas Hope . . . from the Deepdene.

Fosbrooke, G. D. *The Outlines of Statues in the Possession of Mr. Hope (never published); for which illustrations were furnished by G. D. Fosbrooke,* 1813.

Michaelis, A. *Ancient Marbles in Great Britain*, Cambridge, 1882.

Tillyard, E. M. W. *The Hope Vases*, Cambridge, 1923.

Victoria & Albert Museum Library (51.H.36). *Hope Marbles*, (*c.* 1820) a collection of 34 plates including some of vases and paintings.

Waagen, G. F. *Treasures of Art in Great Britain*, 4 vols., 1854–7, vol. II.

Wertheimer, A. *The Hope Collection of Pictures of the Dutch and Flemish Schools*, 1898.

3. THE DUCHESS STREET MANSION AND THE DEEPDENE

Ackermann, R. ed. *Repository of Arts*, 1823, vol. I, no. VI.

Brayley, E. W., Britton, J., etc. *A Topographical History of Surrey*, 5 vols., 1841–8, vol. V.

Britton, J. *History, etc., of the Deepdene. Seat of Thos. Hope Esqr.*, 1821–6. (Drawings Collection, R.I.B.A.)

Britton, J. *Illustrations of the Deepdene. Seat of T. Hope Esqre.*, 1826. (Minet Library, Brixton.)

Britton, J. & Pugin, A. C. *Illustrations of the Public Buildings of London*, 2 vols., 1825, vol. I.

Country Life, vol. V, 1899, *The Deepdene.*

Gardener's Magazine, vol. IV, 1828; & vol. V, 1829.

Loudon, J. C. *Encyclopaedia of Cottage, Farm and Villa Architecture*, 1833.

Magazine of the Fine Arts, vol. I, 1821.

Nairn, I. & Pevsner, N. *The Buildings of England. Surrey*, 1962.

Neale, J. P. *Views of Seats of Noblemen and Gentlemen in England, Wales, Scotland, and Ireland*, 11 vols., 1818–29, 2nd series, vol. III, *The Deep-Dene, Surrey.*

Westmacott, C. M. *British Galleries of Painting and Sculpture*, 1824.

4. FURNITURE DESIGN BY HOPE

Harris, J. *Regency Furniture Designs*, 1961.

Musgrave, C. *Regency Furniture*, 1961.

Symonds, R. W. 'Thomas Hope and the Greek Revival', *Connoisseur*, vol. CXL, 1957.
Wellesley, Lord Gerald. 'Regency Furniture', *Burlington Magazine*, vol. LXX, 1937.

5. HOPE'S WRITINGS

(a) BOOKS AND PAMPHLETS

1. 'Observations on the Plans and Elevations designed by James Wyatt, Architect, for Downing College, Cambridge, in a letter to Francis Annesley, esq., M.P. by Thomas Hope', 1804.
2. 'Household Furniture and Interior Decoration executed from Designs by Thomas Hope', 1807.
New Editions: 1937 and 1946 (both lacking the text).
3. 'Costume of the Ancients', 2 vols., 1809.
New Editions: 1812, 1826 (Brussels), 1841, 1842 (in C. Martin, *The Civil Costume of England*), 1875, 1956 (U.S.A.) and 1962 (U.S.A.).
4. 'Designs of Modern Costume', 1812.
For an enlarged version, see H. Moses, *A Series of Twenty-nine Designs of Modern Costume*, 1823.
5. 'Anastasius or the Memoirs of a Modern Greek, written at the Close of the 18th Century', 3 vols., 1819.
New Editions: 1820 (2 eds.), 1827, 1831, 1836, and 1849 (U.S.A.: 1831 and 1832).
French Translation: 1820, 1831, 1844, and 1847.
German Translation: 1821 (2 eds.) and 1825 (2 eds.).
Flemish Translation: 1821–2.
6. 'An Essay on the Origin and Prospects of Man', 3 vols., 1831.
7. 'An Historical Essay on Architecture . . . illustrated by Drawings made . . . in Italy and Germany', 2 vols., 1835.
See also E. Cresy, *An Analytical Index to an Historical Essay on Architecture by Thomas Hope*, 1836.
New Editions: 1835, 1840, and 1843.
French Translation: 1839 and 1852.
Italian Translation: 1840.

(b) ARTICLES

1. Review of Royal Academy Exhibition. *Morning Post*, 5 May 1804.

2. 'On the Structure of Our Theatres', *The Director*, 1807, vol. I, pp. 171–6, 240–7; vol. II, pp. 329–36.
For other versions see *Review of Publications of Art*, 1808, vol. IV, pp. 306–14; and *Belle Assemblée*, 1809, vol. II, pp. 272a–b; and vol. III, pp. 111b–112b.
3. Letter on the Design of English Theatres, *Belle Assemblée*, 1809, vol. III, p. 96.
4. Letter on the Ballet, *The Director*, 1807, vol. II, pp. 65–8.
5. 'The Utility of Remains of Antiquity', *The Director*, 1807, vol. II, pp. 198–205.
6. A Letter on Instruction in Design, *The Artist*, vol. I, no. VIII, 2 May 1807, pp. 1–7.
7. B. R. Haydon's 'Rest on the Flight into Egypt', *Review of Publications of Art*, 1808, no. II, pp. 110–12.
8. 'On the Art of Gardening', *Review of Publications of Art*, 1808, no. II, pp. 133–44.
Reprinted in Mrs. B. Hofland, *A Descriptive Account of . . . White-Knights*, 1819, pp. 3–13.
9. 'On Grecian and Gothic Architecture', *Review of Publications of Art*, 1808, no. IV, pp. 297–303.

List of Abbreviations used in the Notes

Baumgarten	S. Baumgarten, *Le Crépuscule Néo-Classique: Thomas Hope*, Paris, 1958.
Brayley	E. W. Brayley, J. Britton, etc., *A Topographical History of Surrey*, 5 vols., 1841–8, vol. V.
Colvin	H. M. Colvin, *A Biographical Dictionary of English Architects. 1660–1840*, 1954.
Croft-Murray/Flaxman	*An Account Book of John Flaxman, R.A.* (British Museum Add. MSS. 39784 B.B.) Ed. by E. Croft-Murray, *Walpole Society*, vol. 28, 1939–40, Oxford, 1940.
Farington typescript	J. Farington, *Diary. 1793–1821*, 28 vols. (Print Room, British Museum.)
Household Furniture	*Household Furniture and Interior Decoration executed from Designs by Thomas Hope*, 1807.
Law	H. W. and I. Law, *The Book of the Beresford Hopes*, 1925.
Neale	J. P. Neale, *Views of the Seats of Noblemen and Gentlemen in England, Wales, Scotland and Ireland*, 11 vols., 1818–29, 2nd series, vol. III, 1826, *The Deep-Dene, Surrey*.
Observations	*Observations on the Plans and Elevations designed by James Wyatt, Architect, for Downing College, Cambridge; in a Letter to Francis Annesley, Esq., M.P., by Thomas Hope*, 1804.

Notes

PREFACE

1. Our knowledge of Hope was enormously enlarged by Sandor Baumgarten in his *Le Crépuscule Néo-Classique: Thomas Hope*, Paris, 1958. Although it is useful for suggesting sources it is extremely irritating to use through the presence of over one hundred and fifty minor errors, inaccurate or mis-spelt footnotes, and so on. Baumgarten's interest in Hope was as a literary and social figure and, above all, as the author of *Anastasius*. To these aspects of his career Baumgarten devotes two-thirds of his text. For a pertinent review of the book, see D. Irwin, *Burlington Magazine*, vol. CI, December 1959, p. 461.
2. For a recent elaboration of this theme, see H. Hawley and R. G. Saisselin, *Neo-Classicism: Style and Motif*, Cleveland Museum of Art, U.S.A., 1964.
3. See the important articles by S. Eriksen: 'Lalive de Jully's Furniture *à la grecque*', *Burlington Magazine*, vol. CIII, August 1961, pp. 340–7; 'Marigny and *Le Goût Grec*', *ibid.*, vol. CIV, March 1962, pp. 96–101; and 'Early Neo-Classicism in French Furniture', *Apollo*, vol. LXXVIII, August 1963, pp. 344–51.

I. BACKGROUND AND LIFE

1. A. Chuquet, ed., *Recollections of Baron de Frénilly*, 1909, pp. 30–1.
2. In 1811 Westall told Farington that at Lord Stafford's and Thomas Hope's houses the servants received money from visitors (Farington typescript, p. 5835). See also the perceptive comment of Miss Mitford: 'He knew to a fraction the expense of every day: nothing ever approached the exactness of his establishment—a strange union with such magnificence and such taste—perhaps the Dutch blood might have some influence' (Revd. A. G. L'Estrange, ed., *The Friendships of Mary Russell Mitford*, 1882, vol. II, p. 164). She later observed of Hope's eldest son that, 'like his father, he keeps his own accounts and won't be cheated. It's a mind like Napoleon's' (*ibid.*, p. 305).
3. L. W. Labarc and W. J. Bell, Jr., eds., *The Papers of Benjamin Franklin*, Yale, 1959—in progress, vol. 9, 1966, p. 367, letter of 10 October 1761; and Sir J. Reynolds, *The Literary Works*, 1835, vol. II, pp. 207–8.
4. See D. J. Watkin, 'The Hope Family by Benjamin West', *Burlington Magazine*, vol. CVI, December 1964, pp. 571–2. The first person to doubt that the principal sitter was Adrian Hope was C. H. Collester in *Notes and Queries*, 1922, p. 311, but he had insufficient facts at his disposal to offer an alternative.
5. Farington typescript, p. 2019.

6. Revd. D. Lysons, *Environs of London*, 2nd ed., 1811, vol. II, pt. ii, p. 550.
7. Farington typescript, pp. 988–9. Quotations from the typescript in the British Museum of the Farington Diary in the Royal Archives, Windsor, are published by gracious permission of Her Majesty the Queen.
8. P. W. Clayden, *The Early Life of Samuel Rogers*, 1887, p. 348.
9. See J. Rosenberg, S. Slive, and E. H. ter Kuile, *Dutch Art and Architecture, 1600–1800*, 1966, pp. 250–1 and pl. 203 (B). The index wrongly gives Williams Hope the credit for commissioning this house.
10. See D. J. Watkin, 'Charles Kelsall. The Quintessence of Neo-Classicism,' *Architectural Review*, vol. CXL, August 1966, pp. 109–12.
11. J. E. Elias, *De Vroedschap van Amsterdam. 1578–1795*, Haarlem, 1903–5, vol. II, p. 934.
12. L. Lewis, *Connoisseurs and Secret Agents in 18th Century Rome*, 1961, pp. 198–199; F.M.A. de Voltaire, *Oeuvres Complètes*, L. Moland, ed., 52 vols., Paris, (1877)–85, vol. 41, p. 5, letter to Capacelli of 3 October 1760; and J. J. Winckelmann, *Briefe*, H. Diepolder and W. Rehm, ed., 4 vols., Berlin, 1952–7, vol. 3, p. 52, letter to Stosch of 12 August 1764. Voltaire writes of 'un cavaliere chiamato M. Hope, mezzo Inglese, mezzo Ollandese, e richissimo, dunque tre volte libero. Egli va a videre tutta l'Italia et la Grecia ancora.' We cannot be entirely certain that Albani, Voltaire, and Winckelmann all refer to the same member of the Hope family.
13. *Blackwood's Edinburgh Magazine*, vol. X, October 1821, p. 312. Letter from Hope of 9 October 1821. See also *Observations*, pp. 7–9.
14. See E. Gibbon, *The History of the Decline and Fall of the Roman Empire*, with notes by Dean Milman and M. Guizet, ed. with addnl. notes by W. Smith, 8 vols., 1854–5, vol. I, p. 70, n. 1.
15. *Conversations of Lord Byron with the Countess of Blessington*, ed. 1893, p. 64.
16. *Anastasius*, 2nd ed., 1820, vol. I, p. 68.
17. *Monthly Magazine*, vol. I, 1831, p. 515.
18. Amsterdam Municipal Archives, *Notarieele Archieven*, Baumgarten, p. 25.
19. Historical Manuscripts Commission, Fifteenth Report, 1898, Appendix to Part VII, p. 257.
20. British Museum, Add. MSS. 39781, ff. 16–18. Hope to Flaxman, 6 December 1794.
21. A. de Montaiglon, ed., *Correspondance des Directeurs de l'Académie de France à Rome*, Paris, vol. XVI, 1907, pp. 412–13.
22. See Kew, Library of the Royal Botanic Gardens, Banks Correspondence, vol. 2, no. 184, Frederick Hornemann to Bryan Edwards, Cairo, 18 October 1797.
23. Farington typescript, p. 290.

24. Croft Murray/Flaxman, p. 56.
25. J. Evans, *A History of the Society of Antiquaries*, Oxford, 1956, p. 93, and n. 7.
26. L. Melville, ed., *The Berry Papers. 1763–1852*, 1914, p. 127.
27. P. W. Clayden, *op. cit.*, p. 346.
28. F. Bickley, ed., *The Diaries of Sylvester Douglas*, 1928, vol. I, pp. 239–40.
29. St. Marylebone Ratebooks, 1799. I am grateful to Mr. A. J. D. Stonebridge, former Librarian at the St. Marylebone Central Public Library, for his kind assistance over the Ratebooks.
30. Revd. R. Tweddell, *Remains of the Late John Tweddell*, 1815, pp. 346 and 402.
31. Clayden, *op. cit.*, p. 438.
32. Museo Civico Bassano, Manoscritti Canoviani, quoted in Baumgarten, p. 239.
33. Duchess of Cleveland, *The Life and Letters of Lady Hester Stanhope*, 1914, p. 41.
34. See J. M. Thiele, *Thorvaldsen's Leben*, Leipzig, 1852–6, vol. I.
35. Bibliothèque Nationale, Nouv. Acq., 3231, f. 115. Hope to Millin, 29 September 1815.
36 Sir L. Cust and S. Colvin, *History of the Society of Dilettanti*, new ed., 1914, p. 146.
37. Farington typescript, p. 1950.
38. The quotations in the story of Hope's difficulties with the Royal Academy are taken from the Farington typescript, pp. 2519–2664.
39. The text of *Hope's Garland* quoted here is taken from a contemporary MS. version in the possession of Mr. and Mrs. Paul Mellon. This MS. contains an unpublished poem on the same subject, longer and less interesting but presumably also by Tresham. Copies of *Hope's Garland* are bound in at the end of the copies of Hope's *Observations* at Sir John Soane's Museum and at the Victoria and Albert Museum Library.
40. Farington typescript, p. 2867.
41. L'Estrange, *loc. cit.*, p. 164.
42. Farington typescript, p. 3040.
43. *Ibid.*, p. 3272.
44. G. H. Powell, ed., *Reminiscences and Table-talk of Samuel Rogers*, 1903, p. 175.
45. A. Hare, ed., *Life and Letters of Maria Edgeworth*, 1894, vol. I, p. 209.
46. Cust and Colvin, *op. cit.*, pp. 127 and 226–8.
47. He was again in Tunbridge Wells in December 1806, when he wrote to the popular miniaturist Ozias Humphrey, R.A. (1742–1810), that he was unable to accept his 'offer of the pictures painted by Mr. Barry' (Bodleian Library, MSS. Montagu, d. 7, f. 512, Hope to Humphrey, 3 December 1806).

48. P. W. Clayden, *Rogers and his Contemporaries*, 1889, vol. I, p. 25.
49. Right Honourable Lord John Russell, M.P., ed., *Memoirs, Journal and Correspondence of Thomas Moore*, 8 vols., 1853–8, vol. VII, p. 241.
50. L. Melville, *The Life and Letters of William Beckford of Fonthill*, 1910, p. 238.
51. B. Alexander, *England's Wealthiest Son*, 1962, p. 33.
52. Beresford, born in 1788, was the natural son of Louisa's uncle, the 1st Marquess of Waterford. There is a good account of his remarkable career in Law, ch. III-V.
53. F. P. Cobbe, *Beresford of Beresford: Eight Centuries of a Gentle Family*, Preliminary Sketch, Part III, Leek, 1893 (no page numbers).
54. A. M. Stirling, *The Letter-Bag of Lady Elizabeth Spencer-Stanhope. Compiled from the Cannon Hall Papers*, 1913, vol. I, p. 51.
55. See the Deepdene Sale Catalogue, 1807. (Copy preserved in the R.I.B.A. Library.)
56. See *The Deepdene Album* in the possession of Mrs. H. W. Law; and Law, pp. 51–8.
57. Lady Theresa Lewis, ed., *Journals and Correspondence of Miss Berry*, 1865, vol. II, pp. 382–3.
58. *Ibid.*, pp. 379–80.
59. Russell, *op. cit.*, vol. VIII, p. 70.
60. E. Inglis-Jones, *The Great Maria. A Portrait of Maria Edgeworth*, 1959, p. 159,
61. Lewis, *loc. cit.*, p. 113.
62. Bickley, *loc. cit.*, p. 239.
63. Lewis, *loc. cit.*, p. 379.
64. A. F. Stewart, ed., *The Diary of a Lady in Waiting by Lady Charlotte Bury*, 1908, vol. I, p. 183.
65. Bickley, *op. cit.*, vol. II, pp. 100–1.
66. Royal Library, Windsor Castle, Georgian MSS. 18736–7. I am indebted to Dr. J. Mordaunt Crook for drawing my attention to the existence of this MS.
67. Russell, *loc. cit.*, p. 174.
68. R. Edgcumbe, ed., *The Diary of Frances, Lady Shelley*, 1912, vol. I, p. 56.
69. Russell, *loc. cit.*, p. 191.
70. Baronne de Wimpffen, ed., *Lettres de Mme. Reinhard à sa Mère. 1798–1815*, Paris, 1900, p. 420.
71. J. C. L. Sismondi, *Epistolario*, C. Pellegrini, ed., Florence, 1933–55, vol. II, pp. 75, 90–1, 95, and 115.
72. Farington typescript, p. 6650.
73. Law, pp. 46–9.

74. Marquess of Anglesey, ed., *The Capel Letters*, 1955, p. 177.
75. L.-G. Pellissier, *Le Portefeuille de la Comtesse d'Albany*, Paris, 1902, p. 305.
76. W. M. Rossetti, ed., *The Diary of Dr. John William Polidori*, 1911, p. 209.
77. V. Foster, *The Two Duchesses*, 1898, pp. 425–6.
78. Lewis, *loc. cit.*, p. 445.
79. Museo Civico Bassano, Manoscritti Canoviani, quoted in Baumgarten, pp. 240–1.
80. Archivio dello Stato, etc., quoted in Baumgarten, p. 163.
81. Honourable F. Leveson Gower, ed., *Letters of Harriet, Countess Granville*, 1894, vol. I, pp. 115–16.
82. Bishop of Guildford's Registry, Muniment Book, 1818.
83. Writing in 1820, A. J. B. Defauconpret well conveys the impact of *Anastasius:* '. . . la seconde édition, attendue pendant un mois, a offert le phénomène d'être epuisée en vingt-quatre heures, et on attend encore la troisième! . . . la traduction de cet ouvrage est sur le point de paraître, et comme il join l'intérêt du romain à la fidelité de l'histoire, je serais surpris s'il n'avait pas, à Paris, le même succès qu'il a obtenu à Londres' (*Londres en mil huit cent vingt*, Paris, 1821, p. 121).
84. S. Smiles, *Memoir and Correspondence of John Murray*, 1891, vol. II, p. 75.
85. Bickley, *loc. cit.*, p. 336.
86. *Annals of the Fine Arts*, 1820, vol. IV, no. 14, p. 490.
87. E. Beresford Chancellor, ed., *The Diary of Philipp von Neumann*, 1928, vol. I, pp. 22 & 70.
88. Earl of Ilchester, ed., *Lady Holland to her Son. 1821–1845*, 1946, p. 18.
89. Russell, *op. cit.*, vol. IV, pp. 172–3.
90. Earl of Ilchester, ed., *Journal of the Honourable Henry Edward Fox*, 1923, pp. 186–7 & 189.
91. Leveson Gower, *loc. cit.*, p. 238.
92. Russell, *loc. cit,*. p. 236.
93. Law, pp. 58–9.
94. *Ibid.*, p. 61.
95. Beresford Chancellor, *loc. cit.*, pp. 136, 186, & 195.
96. *Ibid.*, vol. II, p. 203.
97. *Lady Holland to her Son*, p. 7.
98. Russell, *op. cit.*, vol. V, p. 152.
99. Law, p. 38.
100. Edgcumbe, *op. cit.*, vol. V, p. 152.
101. Duke of Wellington & F. Bamford, ed., *The Journal of Mrs. Arbuthnot*, 1950, vol. II, p. 80.
102. *Ibid.*, vol. I, p. 222.

103. Law, p. 63.
104. *Lady Holland to Her Son*, p. 110.
105. Hare, *op. cit.*, vol. II, p. 177.
106. Law, p. 66.
107. L'Estrange, *loc. cit.*, p. 163.
108. Hare, *loc. cit.*, p. 178.
109. *The Times*, 4 February 1831; and the *Examiner*, 6 February 1831.
110. Register of Deaths, p. 155, no. 1234. Baumgarten, p. 229.
111. Somerset House, Will of Thomas Hope, vol. Tebbs, 1831, Vol. I, no. 153, f. 5.
112. Of the mausoleum's 33 tomb-recesses only 9 were filled, the last interment being that of the 8th Duke of Newcastle in 1941. I am grateful to Mr. C. G. Stableforth, Agent to the Newcastle Estates, for kindly sending me a plan and a photograph of the mausoleum.
113. Farington typescript, p. 2643. In 1813 Farington observed that 'Thomas Hope's father left £900,000 divided equally between three sons, but Thomas had the advantage through being some time a partner' (*ibid.*, p. 6392).
114. As Miss Mitford observed: 'Above all there was about him a little tinge of shyness, a modesty, a real and genuine diffidence' (L'Estrange, *loc. cit.*, p. 163).
115. *Observations*, p. 7.
116. He was a 'sleeping partner' in Hope & Co. from 1790–1814 (Elias, *loc. cit.*).
117. *An Historical Essay on Architecture*, 3rd ed., 1840, vol. I, p. xii.

II. COLLECTOR AND PATRON

1. C. M. Westmacott, *British Galleries of Painting and Sculpture*, 1824, p. (211).
2. British Museum, Add. MSS. 39780, f. 57. Flaxman to parents, 3 March 1792.
3. Croft-Murray/Flaxman, p. 56.
4. M. Whinney & R. Gunnis, *The Collection of Models by John Flaxman R.A. at University College London*, 1967, pp. 52–3.
5. Bodleian Library, MSS. Autog. d. 11, f. 319. Flaxman to Hamilton, 13 March 1792.
6. British Museum, Add. MSS. 39781, f. 16. Hope to Flaxman, 6 December 1794. See also Westmacott, *op. cit.*, p. 213.
7. R. Gunnis, *Dictionary of British Sculptors. 1660–1851*, 1953, p. 149; and M. Whinney, *Sculpture in Britain, 1530–1830*, 1964, p. 188 & pl. 144 (A).
8. Fitzwilliam Museum, Flaxman Letter-box, no. 3. Mrs. Flaxman to Hayley, 22 July 1793, ff. 1–2.
9. See G. E. Bentley, Jr., & R. J. Wolfe, *The Early Engravings of Flaxman's*

Classical Designs, New York, 1964, pp. 48 & 50; and *Annual Biography and Obituary*, 1828, vol. XII, p. 23.

10. Comte de Caylus, *Tableaux tirés de l'Iliade et de l'Odysée d'Homère et de l'Enéide de Virgile . . .*, Paris, 1757, pp. vii–viii.
11. T. Sadler, ed., *Diary, Reminiscences, and Correspondence of Henry Crabb Robinson*, 3 vols., 1869, vol. I, p. 319.
12. J. W. von Goethe, *Werke*, ed. S. von Sachsen, Weimar, 133 vols., 1887–1918, vol. 47, 1896, pp. 245–6 (first published in *Propyläen*, 1799); and A. W. von Schlegel, *Sämmtliche Werke*, Leipzig, 1846, vol. IX, pp. 102–57.
13. M. Bishop, ed., *Recollections of the Table-Talk of Samuel Rogers*, 1952, p. 112.
14. Christie's Catalogue of the Library from the Deepdene, July 1917.
15. Fitzwilliam Museum, Flaxman Letter-box, no. 4. Flaxman to Hayley, 26 October 1793, ff. 1–2.
16. *Annals of the Fine Arts*, vol. IV, 1820, p. 97.
17. Croft-Murray/Flaxman, pp. 68 & 80.
18. British Museum, Add. MSS. 39791, f. 50. Moreover, a volume bound in red morocco containing eight letters in Hope's hand from Hope to Flaxman appeared as Lot 730 in the sale at Sotheby's of a *Portion of the Library of the Rt. Hon. A. J. B. Beresford-Hope*, 27–30 July 1892. Its present whereabouts is not known.
19. A. de Montaiglon, ed., *Correspondance des Directeurs de l'Académie de France à Rome*, 18 vols., Paris, 1887–1912, vol. XVI, 1907, pp. 412–13.
20. G. A. Guattani, *Memorie Enciclopediche Romane sulle belle arti, antichità &c.*, 5 vols., Rome, 1806–7, vol. III, p. 91.
21. J. Dallaway, *Of Statuary and Sculpture Among the Ancients*, 1816, pp. 355–6.
22. A convenient account is G. F. Waagen, *Treasures of Art in Great Britain*, 4 vols., 1854–7, vol. II, pp. 20–1.
23. For details of purchasers and prices see *ibid.*, pp. 485–503; and W. Buchanan, *Memoirs of Painting, with a chronological list of the importation of pictures by the great masters into England since the French Revolution*, 2 vols., 1824, vol. I, pp. 1–216. Thomas Hope's purchases were described as: 'St. Lawrence' by Francesco Albano; 'Venus and Cupid' by Alessandro Allori; a Domenichino 'St. Jerome'; a 'Temptation of Christ' attributed to Titian; two Veroneses, 'Wisdom Accompanying Hercules' and 'Paul Veronese between Virtue and Vice'; and a 'Caesar Borgia' attributed to Correggio. The titles of Henry Hope's purchases—some of which found a home at Duchess Street—were: 'Christ Bearing His Cross' by Andrea Sacchi; 'Rinaldo and Armida' by Alessandro Padovanino; 'The Celebrated Poets of Italy' attributed to Vasari; a Velasquez of 'Lot and his Daughters'; two paintings by Guido Reni, 'The Magdalen' and 'The Force of Love'; and a 'Holy Family' attributed to Michel-

angelo. Each later acquired a painting not disposed of at the original sale: to Thomas came a small 'Virgin and Child' attributed to Raphael, and to Henry a 'Danaë' by Correggio. For a list of Thomas Hope's paintings as they had been augmented by 1824, see Westmacott, *op. cit.*, pp. 224–8.

24. It was certainly in his possession by May 1813—see A. M. Jaffé, 'The Death of Adonis: by Rubens', *Duits Quarterly*, no. II, 1967. The painting is owned by Mr. Clifford Duits to whom I am grateful for permission to see and to reproduce it.
25. Sir J. Reynolds, *The Literary Works*, 1835, vol. II, pp. 199–202.
26. G. Glück, *Van Dyck*, Stuttgart, 1931, p. 543 & pl. 225.
27. Farington typescript, p. 3972.
28. See A. Wertheimer, *The Hope Collection of Pictures of the Dutch and Flemish Schools*, 1898.
29. E.g. D. Irwin, *English Neo-Classical Art*, 1966, p. 61 & pls. 66–7.
30. E. Edwards, *Lives of the Founders of the British Museum*, 2 parts, 1870, pt. I, p. 357.
31. A. L. Millin, *Monuments Antiques, Inédites ou nouvellement expliqués*, 2 vols., Paris, 1802–6, vol. II, p. 88, n. 7.
32. *Ibid.*, p. 15.
33. *Archaeologische Zeitung*, Berlin, 1875, p. 16.
34. Christie's Catalogue of the Collection of Greek, Roman, and Egyptian Sculpture and Ancient Greek Vases from the Deepdene, July 1917.
35. *Archaeologischer Anzeiger*, Berlin, October 1849, p. 97.
36. O. Manning & W. Bray, *History and Antiquities of the County of Surrey*, new ed., 1814, vol. III, p. 390; & Westmacott, *op. cit.*, p. 214.
37. Now at the Kunsthaus, Zürich.
38. For accounts of this, see J. M. Thiele, *Thorvaldsen's Leben*, Leipzig, 1852–6, vol. I; and R. Zeitler, 'Klassizismus and Utopia', *Figura*, 5, Uppsala, 1954, pp. 146–51.
39. F. Novotny, *Painting and Sculpture in Europe, 1780–1880*, 1960, p. 213. Indeed Jason's head and sensitively modelled face are closely based on Canova's Perseus of 1800. This sensitive grace is entirely absent from Henry Moses' severely neo-classical engraving of the Perseus. That Moses' engravings have long been the principal medium in this country of knowledge of Canova's work has probably encouraged the conception of Canova as being less of a 'Romantic Classical' artist than Thorvaldsen.
40. Thorvaldsens Museum, Copenhagen, Archives. Letter from Patricio Moir to Thorvaldsen, 8 April 1806, partly published in Baumgarten, Appendix VI.
41. Baumgarten, p. 76.
42. Thiele, *loc. cit.*, pp. 349–50.

43. Thorvaldsens Museum, Copenhagen, Archives. Letter from Thorvaldsen to Torlonia & Co., 21 August 1821, partly published in Baumgarten, p. 77, n. 79.
44. See letters between Thorvaldsen and Hope, quoted in Thiele, *op. cit.*, vol. II, pp. 192–3.
45. Thorvaldsens Museum, no. 518a.
46. *Ibid.*, no. 414.
47. E. K. Sass, *Thorvaldsens Portraetbuster*, 3 vols., Copenhagen, 1963–5, vol. I, pp. 281–301.
48. Neale, p. 11.
49. Sass, *op. cit*, vol. II., pp. 195–200; and vol. III, pp. 95–6 and 159, n. 307.
50. Thiele, *op. cit.*, vol. I, p. 153.
51. C. E. Bell, ed., *Annals of Thomas Banks*, Cambridge, 1938, pp. 62–3. Letter from Hope to Revd. E. Forster of 22 April 1805.
52. See E. Bassi, *Canova*, Bergamo, 1945, p. 30; and Museo Civico Bassano, Manoscritti Canoviani, 6 letters from Hope to Canova concerning the Venus. Published in Baumgarten, Appendix VII.
53. A. C. Quatremère de Quincy, *Canova et ses ouvrages*, Paris, 1834, pp. 136–40.
54. Brayley, p. 85.
55. See the fine outline engravings of them by Henry Moses in his *The Works of Antonio Canova*, 3 vols., 1822–4, vol. I.
56. For a detailed account of Dubost's experiences, see his pamphlet, *Hunt and Hope* (1810).
57. A fuller version is given in W. T. Whitley, *Art in England, 1800–1820*, Cambridge, 1928, pp. 172–6.
58. *The Times*, 13 May 1807.
59. This quotation from the Whitley Papers, vol. IV, p. 465, is published by courtesy of the Trustees of the British Museum.
60. Farington typescript, p. 4573.
61. *Examiner*, 8 July 1810, p. 427; see also 16 December 1810, pp. 794–5, and 30 December 1810, pp. 828–9.
62. E. H. Coleridge, ed., *The Poetical Works of Lord Byron*, 1905, 'Hints from Horace', p. 111.
63. *Political Register*, 12 December 1810.
64. Farington typescript, p. 4587.
65. *London Chronicle*, 7 December 1810, pp. 550–1. In 1812 Dubost attempted to export the painting clandestinely, but it was seized by the Customs Officials. (See *The Times*, 4 May, 1812.)
66. Whitley, *op. cit.*, p. 15.
67. A. de Montaiglon, *loc. cit.*, p. 405.

68. Formerly in the possession of Mrs. Astley Smith. Reproduced in Law, pl. facing p. 31.
69. Exhibited at the Royal Academy in 1799. See W. Roberts, *Sir William Beechey, R.A.*, 1907, p. 67. The portrait was dispatched to Christie's in 1967 by the Trustees of the Duke of Newcastle and was acquired by the National Portrait Gallery. The Turkish jacket and waistcoat worn by Hope in this picture still survive in the possession of Mrs. H. W. Law.
70. K. Garlick, *Sir Thomas Lawrence*, 1954, p. 74.
71. Christie's Catalogue of . . . Old Masters and Family Portraits . . . from the Deepdene, July 1917.
72. D. E. Williams, *The Life and Correspondence of Sir Thomas Lawrence*, 2 vols., 1831, vol. II, p. 430. For engravings of this portrait by Edward Scriven (1775–1841) see British Museum, Dept. of Prints & Drawings, Engravings of Portraits by Thomas Lawrence, vol. V. See also *La Belle Assemblée*, 1831, vol. XI, p. 185.
73. For further information see Farington typescript, p. 4031; and M. A. Shee, *The Life of Sir Martin Archer Shee*, 2 vols., 1860, vol. I, pp. 319–20.
74. Law, pl. facing p. 55.
75. *Monthly Retrospect of the Fine Arts*, July 1811.
76. The property of the Duke of Newcastle, Shockerwick House, Bath.
77. *Annals of the Fine Arts, loc. cit.*, p. 95.
78. F. N. Jackson, *Ancestors in Silhouette*, 1921, p. 142.
79. Brayley, p. 86, & Gunnis, *op. cit.*, p. 46.
80. Gunnis, *op. cit.*, p. 41.
81. *Annals of the Fine Arts, loc. cit.*, p. 93. In 1806, incidentally, Hope was to refuse to acquire some paintings by the pioneer of history painting, James Barry (1741–1806) (Bodleian Library, MSS. Montagu, d. 7, f. 512, Hope to Humphrey, 3 December 1806).
82. Farington typescript, pp. 2639 & 2867.
83. A. L. Millin, *op. cit.*, vol. I, p. 287 & pls. XXIX–XXX.
84. Farington typescript, p. 2949.
85. *Ibid.*, p. 5825. See also *Works of Art from Midland Houses*, City of Birmingham Museum and Art Gallery, 1953, no. 75.
86. Farington typescript, p. 4036.
87. Exhibited at the R.A. in 1810. See also 'George Dawe. A Biography', *Library of the Fine Arts*, vol. I, 1831, pp. 9–17.
88. Farington typescript, p. 2593.
89. T. A. Buckley, ed., *The Iliad of Homer translated by Alexander Pope*, 2 vols., 1853, vol. II, book XIX, p. (165), lines 5–7.
90. Irwin, *op. cit.*, p. 51. Moses' engraving, referred to in *The Examiner*, 12 May

1811, p. 300, appears as Plate I in his *The Gallery of Pictures painted by Benjamin West*, 1811.

91. A. P. D. Penrose, ed., *The Autobiography and Memoirs of Benjamin Robert Haydon*, 1927, p. 37.
92. *Ibid.*, p. 41.
93. *Ibid.*, p. 45.
94. *Ibid.*, p. 620.
95. See *Annals of the Fine Arts, loc. cit*, pp. 95–6.
96. W. T. Whitley, *Thomas Heaphy*, 1933, pp. 15–17.
97. Brayley, p. 87.
98. *Annals of the Fine Arts, loc. cit.*, pp. 121–3.
99. T. Balston, *John Martin*, 1947, pp. 48–50. At the Hope Sale in 1917 it fetched only 65 guineas and at a further sale in 1937 as little as 2 guineas. The painting is now believed to be in Iceland.
100. For the purchase details of these Daniell pictures see Farington typescript, pp. 1616, 1808, & 2573.
101. W. G. Constable, *Canaletto*, Oxford, 1962, vol. II, p. 325.
102. Farington typescript, p. 3986.
103. W. T. Whitley, *Art in England: 1800–1820*, Cambridge, 1928, pp. 117–8.
104. *Annals of the Fine Arts, loc. cit.*, p. 123.
105. See also *The Outlines of Statues in the Possession of Mr. Hope (never published) for which illustrations were furnished by G. D. Fosbrooke*, 1813. (Library of the Victoria and Albert Museum, 37.b.90.)
106. See A. Joubin, 'L'Athéna Hope', *Académie des Inscriptions, Monuments et Mémoires*, vol. III, 1896; and A. Preyss: 'Athena Hope und Pallas Albani', *Kaiserlich Deutsches Archäologischen Institut Jahrbuch*, vol. XXVII, 1912, pp. 88–128, and 'Athena Hope und Winckelmanns Pallas', *ibid.*, vol. XXVIII, 1912–13, pp. 244–65.
107. See W. Fuchs, 'Zum Antinoos Hope und zum 'Cacciatore' im Kapilotinischen Museum', *Archäologischer Anzeiger*, Berlin, 1966, vol. I, pp. 76–86.
108. Westmacott, *op. cit.*, p. 215. For reference to Egyptian influence under Hadrian, see S. Lang & N. Pevsner, 'The Egyptian Revival', *Architectural Review*, vol. CXIX, May 1956, pp. 243–54.
109. Westmacott, *op. cit.*, p. 218.
110. A. Michaelis, *Ancient Marbles in Great Britain*, Cambridge, 1882, p. 285.
111. The account is reprinted in P. Noble, *Anne Seymour Damer. A Woman of Art and Fashion: 1748–1828*, 1908, pp. 160–1; see also pp. 156–8 & pl. facing p. 150.
112. Farington typescript, p. 3986.
113. Gunnis, *op. cit.*, p. 128.

114. Westmacott, *op. cit.*, pp. 213–14.
115. Sir L. Cust & S. Colvin, *History of the Society of Dilettanti*, new ed., 1914, pp. 127 & 226–8.
116. British Museum (Natural History), Dept. of Botany, Copies of Banks Correspondence, 1805–6, vol. XVI, Payne Knight to Townley-Standish, 17 May 1805. For the complicated history of the terms of Charles Townley's bequest, see Edwards, *loc. cit.*, p. 379.
117 J. Evans, *A History of the Society of Antiquaries*, Oxford, 1956, p. 201 & n. 20.
118. *The Charter and Bye-Laws of the Royal Institution of Great Britain*, 1803, p. 59; and H. B. Jones, *The Royal Institution*, 1871.
119. Evans, *op. cit.*, p. 93 & n. 7.
120. Royal Society, Archives, Volume of Certificates: 1801–19. Quoted in Baumgarten, p. 56, n. 7.
121. Royal Society of Arts, Archives, 23 May 1804. I have to thank Mr. D. G. C. Allan, Curator-Librarian, for kindly ascertaining the exact date for me.
122. Whitley, *op. cit.*, p. 106.
123. Public Record Office, T. 27/53, f. 400.
124. Farington typescript, p. 3617.
125. Windsor Castle, Royal Library, Georgian MSS., 18736–8. Her Majesty the Queen has graciously given permission for this passage to be quoted.
126. Farington typescript, p. 1996.
127. *Ibid.*, p. 2639.
128. *Ibid.*, p. 4516.
129. *Ibid.*, p. 3010.
130. *The Artist*, vol. I, no. VIII, 2 May 1807, pp. 1–7.
131. British Museum, Add. MSS. 29320, f. 25.
132. Victoria & Albert Museum, Haydon MSS. 86.J.16.
133. See Q. Bell, *The Schools of Design*, 1963.
134. *Household Furniture*, p. 13.
135. S. Sitwell, *Conversation Pieces*, 1936, p. 7.
136. *Household Furniture*, p. 10.
137. *Ibid.*, and A. Dubost, *Hunt and Hope* (1810), p. 40.
138. G. Jones, *Sir Francis Chantrey, R.A. Recollections of his Life, Practice and Opinions*, 1849, p. 4.
139. *Literary Gazette*, 12 February 1831, p. 107.
140. J. Pye, *Patronage of British Art*, 1845, p. 306, note D.
141. *Household Furniture*, pp. 2–5.
142. A. J. B. Beresford Hope, *The English Cathedral of the 19th Century*, 1861, note to pp. 63–4.
143. Assay Office, Birmingham, Boulton Papers, Hope to Boulton, 14 September

1805, ff. 2 & 4. I am indebted to Mr. John Cornforth for drawing my attention to the existence of this letter. See also H. W. Dickinson, *Matthew Boulton*, Cambridge, 1937.

144. For details of work by Storr and by Rundell, Bridge and Rundell, see Christie's *Catalogue of the Old English and Foreign Silver and Silver-Gilt, Jewels, Miniatures and Enamel Portraits . . . from the Deepdene, July 1917.*
145. Farington typescript, p. 4154.
146. See B. D. Wyatt, *Observations on the Principles of the Design for the Theatre now building in Drury Lane*, 1811 (rev. ed. 1813), where he claims, incidentally, to have been the first in this country to employ the horseshoe-shaped auditorium (p. 34).
147. *The Pamphleteer*, 1814, vol. III, pp. 329–43.
148. *Annals of the Fine Arts, loc. cit.*, pp. 348–51.
149. See B. Kaye, *The Development of the Architectural Profession in Britain*, 1960.
150. T. Hope, *Costume of the Ancients*, enlarged ed., 2 vols., 1841, pp. xi–xii.
151. T. Hope, 'The Utility of Remains of Antiquity', *The Director*, 1807, vol. II, pp. 198–205.
152. The books are: J. M. Gandy, *Designs for Cottages* . . . 1805; E. Aikin, *Designs for Villas* . . . , 1808; J. Britton, *Architectural Antiquities of Great Britain*, 1805–27, vol. II, 1809; and H. Moses, *A Collection of Vases, Altars, Paterae, Tripods* . . . , 1814.
153. H. Walpole, *Anecdotes of Painters in England*, J. Dallaway & R. N. Wornum, ed., 3 vols., 1849, vol. III, p. 776.

III. HOPE AND THE GREEK REVIVAL

1. *Satirist*, vol. I, 1808, p. 254.
2. R. Willis and J. W. Clark, *Architectural History of the University of Cambridge*, 4 vols., 1886–7, vol. II, pp. 756–7.
3. G. Walkley, 'A Recently Found James Wyatt Design', *R.I.B.A. Journal*, vol. 45, 1938, pp. 970–4 and 1014–15.
4. The Revd. H. W. Pettit Stevens, *Downing College*, 1899, pp. 79 ff. The college archives shed no light on Hope's relationship with Annesley. I am indebted to Mr. Peter Bicknell, F.R.I.B.A., Fellow of Downing College, for showing me the archives.
5. On a small scale James Lewis (*c.* 1751–1820) was a sophisticated neo-Greek architect. See the fluted Greek Doric portico on his north front of Cleveland House, St. James's, 1795–7 (*Survey of London*, vol. XXX, 1960, p. 494 and pl. 233 (b)) and his unfluted Doric colonnade at Woolmers, Hertfordshire, 1802. He had published designs for a Greek villa as early as 1779 in his *Original Designs in Architecture*, vol. I, pl. 1.

6. The quotations from Hope's *Observations* are taken from pp. 16–29.
7. *Ibid.*, p. 14.
8. The three perspective elevations by Wyatt, now at the R.I.B.A. Library, show a huge quadrangle with an entrance archway in the middle of the north range. The south range, with the chapel in the centre, is continued to the east and west in long wings projecting out beyond the quadrangle itself. But it is clear that there were two separate designs, one of which was three-sided and open to the south (*Observations*, pp. 30–1). Hope recommended that this open character be heightened but made more subtle. The most revolutionary feature—the provision within the college of houses for married professors—was not due to Wyatt, Hope, or Wilkins but to those who drafted the statutes of the new college.
9. The Revd. R. Tweddell, *Remains of the Late John Tweddell*, 1815, p. 337.
10. *Ibid.*, p. 348.
11. These volumes of drawings appeared in Christie's Deepdene Library Catalogue, 1917, Lots 295–7, but, it seems, had been withdrawn before the sale took place. They next turned up in an undated Sale Catalogue (*c.* 1930) of *100 Old, Rare or Unique Illustrated Books, Collections of Original Drawings, Designs, Engravings, etc., offered for Sale by B. T. Batsford, Ltd.* B. H. Blackwell Ltd., to whom Batsford's Antiquarian Department has passed, inform me that they believe the volumes were sold to 'the Chicago Art Museum'. Enquiry and advertisement in Chicago and elsewhere in America has not so far resulted in the discovery of these drawings. Fortunately, a detailed catalogue and description of them is given in the Batsford Catalogue of *c.* 1930, Section IX, *Oriental Art*, Item 93, pp. 62–3. Typical of many of these drawings must be a view in Hope's hand of Constantinople (see pl. 19) pasted into *The Deepdene Album.*
12. *Observations*, pp. 13–14.
13. Tweddell, *op. cit.*, 'Correspondence', pp. (27)–340; & 'Appendix', pp. (341)-479.
14. The Revd. R. Tweddell, *An Account of the Examination of the Elgin-box at the Foreign-Office in Downing Street, Nov. 7, 1816. In a letter to James Losh, Esq.*, Manchester, 1817.
15. The Revd. R. Tweddell, *Remains of the Late John Tweddell*, 1815, p. 483.
16. *Ibid.*, pp. 268, 282.
17. See *Country Life*, vol. LXXXVIII, 1941, pp. 300 ff. and 324 ff.
18. See *Dictionary of National Biography* articles on Sir William Gell (1777–1836); and Edward Dodwell (1767–1832).
19. See *The Life and Remains of the Revd. E. D. Clarke, LL.D.*, ed. by The Revd, W. Otter, 1824; and E. D. Clarke, *Greek Marbles brought back from the Shores*

of the Euxine, Archipelago, and the Mediterranean, and deposited in the Vestibule of the Public Library of the University of Cambridge, Cambridge, 1809.

20. See the *Orthodox Journal*, August 1819, p. 303; and the *Quarterly Review*, no. 19, p. 223: 'His religious sentiments and political principles are equally liberal.'
21. The exterior of Belsay, however, is extremely close to Dufourny's Il Ginnasio at Palermo of 1789–92 (C. L. V. Meeks, *Italian Architecture: 1750–1914*, Yale University Press, 1966, fig. 28). Had Monck seen this?
22. Although Downing had not been Picturesque, Haileybury was planned with an Arcadian landscape—a transition well shown by J. M. Crook in *Haileybury and the Greek Revival*, 1964.
23. Kelsall does not appear in the *Dictionary of National Biography*. The principal source for the details of his life offered here is his *Esquisse de mes travaux, de mes voyages et de mes opinions*, published in Frankfurt in 1830 under the pseudonym, *Mela Britannicus*. I am indebted to the late Mr. Reginald Saw of Morden College, Blackheath, for drawing my attention to the existence of this work (not mentioned in the *Dictionary of Anonymous and Pseudanonymous Literature*) and for making available to me the Kelsall Archives and Library at Morden College.
24. *A Letter from Athens addressed to a Friend in England*, 1812, p. 37. Hope's *Anastasius*, moreover, may actually have influenced the later Cantos of *Don Juan*. See E. F. Boyd, *Byron's Don Juan. A Critical Study*, U.S.A., 1958, pp. 132–5.
25. *Phantasm of an University*, 1814, p. 135.
26. *A Letter from Athens addressed to a Friend in England*, 1812, p. 41.
27. *Phantasm of an University*, 1814, p. (127).
28. *Ibid.*, pp. 34–5.
29. See W. B. O'Neal, *Jefferson's Buildings at the University of Virginia*, Charlottesville, 1960.
30. *Phantasm of an University*, 1814, p. 174.
31. A.-P. Prieur and P.-L. van Cléemputte, *Collection des Prix*, Paris, 1787–*c.* 1796.
32. C. P. Landon, *Annales du Musée*, Paris, 1805, vol. II, pl. 64 & p. 127.
33. *Phantasm of an University*, 1814, pp. 152–3.
34. *On the Costume of the Ancients*, new ed. 1841, vol. I, p. 48.
35. *Phantasm of an University*, 1814, pp. 129 & 131.
36. G. H. Hamilton, *The Art and Architecture of Russia*, 1954, p. 209.
37. *Phantasm of an University*, 1814, p. 129 n. See N. Pozza, ed., *Disegni di Giacomo Quarenghi*, Bergamo & Venice, 1967.
38. Dem. 1954. See A. J. Rowan, *The Castle Style*, unpublished Cambridge Ph.D. thesis, 1965, p. 301.

39. *Phantasm of an University*, 1814, p. 165.
40. *Ibid.*, p. 174.
41. *Magasin Encyclopédique*, 1814, vol. V, no. 113, pp. 355–6.
42. *Classical Excursion from Rome to Arpino*, Geneva, 1820, p. 33.
43. Quoted in Baumgarten, p. 244.
44. *Classical Excursion from Rome to Arpino*, Geneva, 1820, p. 224.
45. *Ibid.*, p. 215.
46. See A. Neumayer, 'Monuments to "Genius" in German Classicism', *Journal of the Warburg Institute*, vol. II, 1938–9, pp. 159–63.
47. *Horae Viaticae*, 1836, p. 310.
48. *Ibid.*, pp. 285–6.
49. *Ibid.*, p. 312.
50. *Ibid.*, p. 389. (The italics are mine.)
51. *Remarks touching on Geography, especially that of the British Isles*, 1822, pp. 78–9.
52. *The Diary of Benjamin Robert Haydon*, ed. by W. B. Pope, Massachusetts. 1960, vol. III, p. 267.
53. *Observations*, p. 9.
54. *Ibid.*, p. 25.
55. Sir J. N. Summerson, *Architecture in Britain: 1530–1830*, 4th ed. 1963, p. 302.
56. 'On Grecian and Gothic Architecture', *Review of Publications of Art*, no. IV, 1808, pp. 297 & 299.
57. New ed., 1843, p. 48. See also p. 41.
58. See P. Mebes, *Um 1800*, Munich, 1908, vol. I, p. 76.
59. J.-Ch. Krafft, *Recueil d'Architecture Civile*, Paris, 1812, pl. 109.
60. A. de Laborde, *Nouveaux Jardins de France*, Paris, 1808, pl. 55 and pp. 109–110.
61. J.-Ch. Krafft and N. Ransonnette, *Plans, Coupes, Elévations des plus belles Maisons et des Hôtels construits à Paris . . .*, Paris, 2 vols., 1801–2, vol. II, pl. 114.
62. *Ibid.*, pl. 50.
63. For further evidence, see D. Lewis, *Greece and the Greek Revival*, unpublished Cambridge B.A. thesis, 1962 (in the Library of the Fine Arts Faculty).
64. I am indebted to Dr. Hugh Plommer, Curator of the Museum of Classical Archaeology, Cambridge, for some valuable suggestions concerning this tricky problem.
65. L. V. Thiéry, *Guide des amateurs et des étrangers voyageurs à Paris*, Paris, 1787, vol. II, p. 135.
66. J. S. de Sacy, *A.-T. Brongniart*, Paris, 1940, pp. 55–6.
67. W. Ison, *The Georgian Buildings of Bath*, 1948, p. 182.

68. M. Whiffen, *Stuart and Georgian Churches outside London*, 1947–8, p. 59.
69. In fact the central columns of the Propylon on the Athenian Acropolis were placed not two but three metopes apart, but this was to allow sufficient passage for the Sacred Way.
70. I attribute this house to Green on the evidence provided in the account of the house in *Repository of Arts*, 1827, vol. X, no. 59. See also Neale, 2nd series, *Views of the Seats* . . . vol. I, 1824 and Thomas (Fortescue) Lord Clermont, *A History of the Family of Fortescue in all its branches*, privately printed, 2nd ed. 1880. For Green's career, see *Minutes of the Proceedings of the Institute of Civil Engineers*, vol. IX, 1849–50, pp. 98–102; and C. Hadfield: 'James Green as Canal Engineer', *Journal of Transport History*, vol. I, 1953–4, pp. 45–56; *The Canals of Southern England*, 1955; and *The Canals of South Wales and the Border*, 1960, *passim*. I am grateful to Dr. Fortescue-Foulkes and Mr. M. R. G. Williams for their assistance and hospitality at Buckland Filleigh.
71. Gandy exhibited designs for Storrs Hall at the Royal Academy in 1808 and 1811. The house was complete at least as early as 1814 since in that year it was drawn by J. C. Buckler (see pl. 28). For a previous owner of Storrs Hall, Sir John Legard, Bart., Gandy had designed *c.* 1804 a boathouse and a Temple of the Heroes, both erected on the shores of Lake Windermere. For the Temple, see *Country Life*, vol. CXXXII, 1962, p. 1338.
72. In fact this was the Temple of Isis. The flutes in the lower half of the columns are carved to about half the depth of those in the upper part.
73. For a more detailed account of the house, see my article in *Country Life*, vol. CXLI, 1967, pp. 18–21.
74. G. Richardson, *New Vitruvius Britannicus*, vol. II, 1808, pls. 36–8.
75. Castle Goring, however, 'was built in 1791, by the late Sir Bysshe Shelley, after a singular idea of his own . . . which he did not live to complete' (Sir B. Burke, *A Visitation* . . . 1st series, vol. I, 1852, p. 15). Shelley died in 1815 and we cannot be sure whether the Greek Doric parts of the house were complete by then. The Greek Doric colonnade on the garden-front does not fit stylistically with the Henry Holland-like Graeco-Palladianism of the façade itself. Rebecca, the architect of the house, died in 1808. See J. Evans, *Picture of Worthing*, 1805, p. 96; A. J. Rowan, *op. cit.*,; and I. Nairn and N. Pevsner, *The Buildings of England: Sussex*, 1965, pp. 125–7 and pls. 46–7.
76. See N. Pevsner and S. Lang, 'Apollo or Baboon', *Architectural Review*, vol. CIV, December 1948, pp. 271–9.
77. The title of the MS. journal by the architect Edmund Bartell is: *Notes . . . of Picturesque Effects . . . made in a Tour through Derbyshire, Cheshire, part of Flintshire and Denbighshire and the Northern Counties of England* . . . .
78. See *Country Life*, vol. CXXX, 1961, p. 455.

IV. THE DUCHESS STREET MANSION

1. See D. Lysons, *Environs of London*, 2nd ed., 1811, vol. II, pt. ii, p. 550; *Gentleman's Magazine*, vol. LXXXI, pt. i, 1811, pp. 292–3; and Farington typescript, *passim*.
2. Farington typescript, pp. 290 & 598.
3. A. T. Bolton, *Robert and James Adam*, 1922, vol. II, pp. 99–101.
4. St. Marylebone Ratebooks, 1771–99.
5. Christie's Catalogue of the Library from the Deepdene, July 1917.
6. Sir John Soane's Museum, Adam Drawings: Vol. XIV, 57–8: ceilings; vol. XXIII, 160 & 230: chimney-pieces; vol. XXIV, 280–4: shutter-panels; vol. XLIV, 1–9: 2 elevations, 4 sections & 3 plans.
7. I owe this suggestion to Sir John Summerson.
8. Bolton, *loc. cit.*, p. 100.
9. J. Britton & A. C. Pugin, *Illustrations of the Public Buildings of London*, 1825, vol. I, p. (310).
10. Bolton, *loc. cit.*, p. 99.
11. *Magasin Encyclopédique*, Paris, 1800, no. 34, vol. IV, p. 114.
12. F. Bickley, ed., *The Diaries of Sylvester Douglas*, 1928, vol. I, pp. 239–40.
13. A belated reference to the completion of the alterations appears in the *Daily Advertiser*, 15 November 1804, where the sculpture collection is described as being worth more than £60,000. In 1807 Hope referred to the reconstruction as having taken place 'a few years ago'.
14. *Tour of Germany, Holland and England, in the years 1826, 1827 and 1828 . . . in a series of letters by a German Prince*, 1832, vol. III, p. 380.
15. Croft-Murray/Flaxman, pp, 68, 74, & 89.
16. A Fremantle, ed., *The Wynne Diaries*, 1940, vol. III, p. 114.
17. *Literary Gazette*, 12 February 1831, p. 107.
18. M. A. Shee, *Elements of Art*, 1809, p. 25.
19. C. M. Westmacott, *British Galleries of Painting and Sculpture*, 1824, p. 212.
20. St. Marylebone Ratebooks, 1851.
21. *Household Furniture*, p. 15.
22. Westmacott, *op. cit.*, p. 215.
23. *Household Furniture*, pp. 19–20.
24. *Ibid.*, p. 21.
25. *Ibid.*, p. 22.
26. 'The Utility of Remains of Antiquity', *The Director*, 1807, vol. II, pp. 202–3.
27. *An Historical Essay on Architecture*, 3rd ed., 1840, vol. I, p. 491; and 'On Grecian and Gothic Architecture', *Review of Publications of Art*, no. IV, 1808, p. 299.

28. Westmacott, *op. cit.*, pp. 229–30.
29. *Household Furniture*, p. 23.
30. *Ibid.*, pp. 24–5.
31. Westmacott, *op. cit.*, p. 217.
32. *Anastasius*, 2nd ed., 1820, vol. I, p. 70.
33. See J. Britton, *The Union of Architecture, Sculpture and Painting*, 1827.
34. See Lord Gerald Wellesley, 'Regency Furniture', *Burlington Magazine*, vol. LXX, May 1937, pl. II B.
35. See *The Royal Pavilion. Souvenir Catalogue of the Regency Exhibition*, Brighton, 1966, p. 27, no. 90.
36. *Household Furniture*, p. 25.
37. I am grateful to Mr. John Cornforth for drawing my attention to this clock, and to Mr. Lennox Money for showing it to me and kindly providing the photograph of it.
38. Reproduced in C. Musgrave, *Regency Furniture*, 1961, pl. 84.
39. Westmacott, *op. cit.*, p. 218.
40. W. Hodges, *Travels in India. 1780–1783*, 1793, p. 74.
41. Westmacott, *op. cit.*, p. 214.
42. I am indebted to the Duke of Wellington for providing information about his and Edward Knoblock's purchases of objects designed by Hope.
43. On this furniture see R. W. Symonds, 'Thomas Hope and the Greek Revival', *Connoisseur*, vol. CXL, December 1967, pp. 226–30.
44. For references to the Egyptian Room and its furnishings see *Household Furniture*, pp. 27 & 43–4.
45. Sir J. Soane, *Lectures on Architecture*, A. T. Bolton, ed., 1929, p. 21.
46. Christie's Catalogue of the Paintings from the Deepdene, July 1917.
47. Sir J. N. Summerson, *A New Description of Sir John Soane's Museum*, 1955, p. 36.
48. *Household Furniture*, pp. 46–7.
49. *Ibid.*, p. 28.
50. C. Percier & C. F. L. Fontaine, *Recueil de décorations intérieures*, Paris, 1812 ed., pl. 31.
51. Westmacott, *op. cit.*, p. 219.
52. See A. Malraux, *Le Musée Imaginaire de la Sculpture Mondiale*, Paris, 1952.
53. Westmacott, *op. cit.*, p. 230; and Britton & Pugin, *loc. cit.*, p. 312.
54. *Household Furniture*, p. 29.
55. *Ibid.*, p. 16.
56. *Ibid.*, p. 35.
57. R. Brown, *The Rudiments of Drawing Cabinet and Upholstery Furniture*, 2nd ed., 1822, pp. xiii–xiv.

V. HOPE AND THE PICTURESQUE

1. The engraving of Blenheim reproduced in pl. 42 originally appeared as a decoration for the month of September in a small calendar for the year 1825.
2. *The Complete Works of Sir John Vanbrugh*, ed. by B. Dobrée and G. Webb, vol. IV, 1928, pp. 29–30.
3. D. Green, *Blenheim Palace*, 1951, p. 85.
4. H. A. Tipping and C. Hussey, *English Homes*, Period IV, vol. II, 1928, pp. 2, 9, & 22.
5. L. Whistler, *The Imagination of Vanbrugh and his Fellow Artists*, 1954, pl. 90.
6. For the Bordeaux temple and the Paris Observatory, see C. Perrault, *Vitruvius*, Paris, new ed., 1684, pp. 13–15 & 217–19.
7. For a survey of this subject, see N. Pevsner, 'Good King James's Gothic', *Architectural Review*, vol. CVII, February 1950, pp. 117–22. Apart from this article, the Jacobean Revival of the eighteenth century has not received the attention it deserves.
8. *The Letters of Horace Walpole, 4th Earl of Orford*, ed. by P. Cunningham, 1891, vol. V, p. 403. Letter dated 12 August 1772.
9. *The Works in Architecture of Robert and James Adam*, vol. I, 1773, pp. (3)–4.
10. Sir J. Reynolds, *Discourses on Art*, ed. R. R. Wark, San Marino, 1959, pp. 242–44. See also R. C. Boys, 'Sir Joshua Reynolds and the Architect Vanbrugh', *Michigan Academy of Science, Arts and Letters*, vol. XXXIII, 1947.
11. *Price on the Picturesque*, ed. by Sir T. D. Lauder, Bart., 1842, pp. 344–7.
12. R. P. Knight, *An Analytical Inquiry into the Principles of Taste*, 1805, p. 221.
13. *Lectures on Architecture*, ed. by A. T. Bolton, 1929, Lecture 2, p. 175.
14. *Country Life*, vol. LVIII, 1925, p. 396 ff.
15. J. Fleming, *Robert Adam and his Circle*, 1962, pl. 47 (from the Sir John Clerk collection).
16. N. Pevsner, *An Outline of European Architecture*, 7th ed. 1963, p. 32.
17. *Observations*, p. 33. Hope, of course, knew Hagia Sophia at first hand; others knew it from engravings in Fischer von Erlach's *Entwurff Einer Historischen Architektur*, Leipzig, 1725, vol. III, pl. 6.
18. Cunningham, *op. cit.*, vol. V, pp. 294 & 386.
19. A. T. Bolton, 'The Classical and Romantic Compositions of Robert Adam', *Architectural Review*, vol. LVII, January to May 1925; and P. Oppé, 'Robert Adam's Picturesque Compositions', *Burlington Magazine*, vol. LXXX, March 1942, pp. 56–9.
20. *The Works in Architecture of Robert and James Adam*, Vol. II, 1779, no. III, pl. VII, and no. IV, pl. VII.
21. Bolton, *op. cit.*, Lecture 5, p. 90.
22. *Poems of Alexander Pope*, vol. III, ii, 1951, ed. by F. W. Bateson, p. 138. The

second couplet is quoted in J. Britton, *The Union of Architecture, Sculpture and Painting*, 1827, p. (24); the text is largely by W. H. Leeds (see p. (ix)).

23. *Review of Publications of Art*, no. II, 1808, pp. 133–144.
24. Mrs. Hofland, *A Descriptive Account of the Mansion and Gardens of White-knights, Seat of the Duke of Marlborough*, 1819, pp. 3 & 8.
25. N. Pevsner, 'The Genesis of the Picturesque', *Architectural Review*, vol. XCVI, November 1944, pp. 139–46.
26. Hofland, *op. cit.*, pp. 9 & 11–13.
27. *Poems of Alexander Pope*, vol. VI, 1954, ed. by N. Ault and J. Butt, p. 317.
28. See H. F. Clark, 'Lord Burlington's Bijou, or Sharawaggi at Chiswick', *Architectural Review*, vol. XCV, May 1944, pp. 125–9.
29. Lauder, *op. cit.*, p. 308.
30. Knight, *op. cit.*, p. 215.
31. I am indebted to Mrs. H. W. Law for kindly allowing me to have these photographed. The designs, one on each side of a single sheet of paper (water-mark: fleur-de-lis in a shield over P.D.V. & Co.) have been inserted into *The Deepdene Album*. The page following is inscribed: 'N.B. the design for a Villa mounted on the opposite page is by, and in the autograph of Mr. Thomas Hope.' The fact that on the same page as the elevation is a drawing for a dish-handle identical to one made for Hope in 1801 by Storr (Fig. 3) may date the villa designs to as early as 1801.
32. Knight, *op. cit.*, pp. 216–19.
33. Lauder, *op. cit.*, p. 376.
34. *Observations*, p. 15.
35. Farington typescript, p. 2595.
36. *Life at Fonthill*, tr. and ed. by B. Alexander, 1957, pp. 48 and 339.
37. See E. F. English, ed., *Views of Lansdowne Tower . . . From drawings by W. Maddox*, 1844; and W. Ison, *The Georgian Buildings of Bath*, 1948, p. (186).
38. H. A. N. Brockman, *The Caliph of Fonthill*, 1956, p. 191.
39. Quoted from a letter written by Beckford in 1837. See Brockman, *op. cit.* p. 189.
40. Lauder, *op. cit.*, pp. 347–8.
41. Information about the house (known since 1920 as Bathwick Grange) from title deeds; from a letter in the *Bath Weekly Chronicle*, 21 February 1942; and from R. E. M. Peach, *Street-Lore of Bath*, 1893, p. 96. I am indebted for their help and kindness to the Honourable Mary Loder, owner of the house, and to Mr. P. Pagan, Director of the Bath Municipal Library.
42. Peach, *op. cit.*, p. 100.
43. Quoted in B. Little, *The Building of Bath*, 1947, p. 25.
44. The Revd. G. N. Wright, *The Historic Guide to Bath*, Bath, 1964, p. 366.

45. This point was confirmed in another way in the *R.I.B.A. Journal*, vol. XL, 1932, pp. 135–6, where Professor Geoffrey Webb referred to a volume of early nineteenth-century drawings of the Grange in the possession of Mrs. C. L. Wingfield at Tiverton Castle. These Picturesque views, he wrote, 'combined the elegance of the Greek with all the charms of Claude and seventeenth-century Baroque landscape'. I have to thank Mrs. V. de Smidt, a daughter of Mrs. Wingfield, and Professor Webb for their help in my so far fruitless attempt to discover the present whereabouts of these drawings.
46. T. Hope, 'On Grecian and Gothic Architecture', *Review of Publications of Art*, no. IV, 1808, p. 299.
47. *Gardener's Magazine*, vol. I, 1826, pp. 106–7.
48. *An Historical Essay on Architecture*, 1835, vol. I, p. 491.
49. G. F. Prosser, *Select Illustrations of Hampshire*, 1833.
50. *Gardener's Magazine*, *op. cit.*, pp. 107–8.
51. *Ibid.*, vol. II, 1827, pp. 170–1.
52. See the *Gentleman's Magazine*, 1805, p. 599 and 1806, p. 34.
53. M. Fouché, *Percier et Fontaine*, Paris (1905), pls. facing pp. 84 and 88.
54. *Ibid.*, pl. facing p. 96.
55. *The Works of Ruskin*, Library Edition, 39 vols., 1903–12, vol. VIII, p. 63; vol. X, p. 22 and n; and vol. XII, pp. 186–7. A. J. B. Beresford Hope, in his *The English Cathedral of the 19th Century*, 1861, p. 133, observed that: 'The words in which my father described the phenomenon' (i.e. of the Early Christian use of the basilica) 'in days when there were few people in England who would so much as care to understand the question, are still so clear and apposite that I make no excuse for availing myself of them in several long extracts, rather than having recourse to my own inferior phraseology.'
56. Quoted in H. Sedlmayr, *Art in Crisis*, tr. by B. Battershaw, 1957, p. 28.
57. *Magazine of the Fine Arts*, vol. I, 1821, p. 7.
58. *The Works of the Late Aaron Hill, Esq.*, 1753, vol. I, pp. 190–3 & 199–120. The interests of both Hill and Lady Walpole were serious and technical: e.g., Hill writes, 'my servants . . . informed me, that your ladyship seem'd desirous to know, what *compositions* I use, in cementing the *pebbles*, and *shell-work*, and where and at what rates, the blue stones are to be procured . . .'
59. N. Pevsner, *The Buildings of England: Buckinghamshire*, 1960, p. 251.
60. Farington typescript, p. 1361; see also pp. 1400–1.
61. E. F. Henderson, *Symbol and Satire in the French Revolution*, New York, 1912, p.v. See also J. A. Leith, *The Idea of Art as Propaganda in France 1750–1799*, University of Toronto Press, 1965.
62. Henderson, *op. cit.*, pp. 356–70; and D. L. Dowd, *Pageant-Master of the Re-*

public: Jacques-Louis David and the French Revolution, University of Nebraska, 1948, pp. 110–19.

63. For a well-illustrated account of these see D. J. Watkin, 'Some Dufour Wallpapers', *Apollo*, vol. LXXXV, June 1967, pp. 432–5.
64. See N. McClelland, *Historic Wall Papers*, Philadelphia, 1924, ch. XII.
65. Reynolds, *Discourses, ed. cit.*, p. 242.
66. See L. Whistler, *A Guide to the Gardens at Stowe*, 1956.
67. Pevsner, *op. cit.*, p. 82.
68. A. de Laborde, *Nouveaux Jardins de France*, Paris, 1808, pl. 55 and pp. 109–10. For a general account of the landscaping at Méréville by Hubert Robert and Belanger, see J. Stern, *François-Joseph Belanger*, Paris, 1930.
69. Cunningham, *op. cit.*, vol. VI, p. 496. Letter to the Countess of Ossory, dated 9 August 1784. For an account of Kingsgate, see *Country Life*, vol. CXIV, 1953, pp. 1968–9.
70. N. Pevsner and J. Harris, *The Buildings of England: Lincolnshire*, 1964, p. 311. Harris gives Roberts' Christian name as James, but perhaps he is to be identified with the Henry Roberts who is known to have travelled on Cook's second voyage. There appear to be no further sources of information about Roberts in the Lincolnshire County Archives or at the Lincoln City Library. A design for a Tahitian hut was published in 1799 in J. G. Grohmann, *Ideenmagazine für Liebhaber von Gärten*, Leipzig, 1779–1805, vol. XXV, pl. 9.
71. See B. W. Smith, *European Vision and the South Pacific: 1768–1850*, Oxford, 1960, pp. 58–9. This excellent study indicates the impact of the South Pacific on many of the arts, but not on monuments in landscaped parks or on wallpaper design.
72. *Ibid.*, pp. 80–1.
73. W. T. Whitley, *Artists and their Friends in England, 1700–1799*, Cambridge, 1928, vol. II, p. 354.
74. Smith, *op. cit.*, p. 82.
75. See C. Mitchell, 'Zoffany's "Death of Captain Cook"', *Burlington Magazine*, vol. LXXXIV, March 1944, pp. 56–62.
76. L. A. de Bougainville, *Voyage Round the World*, trans. by J. R. Forster, 1772, pp. 219, 244–5, & 249.
77. MS. in the Commonwealth National Library, Canberra. Quoted in Smith, *op. cit.*, p. 26.
78. See H. C. Hatfield, *Winckelmann and his German Critics*, New York, 1943, p. 140.
79. McClelland, *op. cit.*, pp. 175–80.
80. *Repository of Arts*, 1823, vol. II, no. 11.
81. See *Country Life*, vol. CXXIX, 1961, pp. 455–6; and *Voyages and Travels of*

Her Majesty Caroline, Queen of Great Britain . . . by one of Her Majesty's suite, 1822.

82. D. Irwin, *English Neo-Classical Art*, 1966, p. 146 and n. 4.
83. McClelland, *op. cit.*, p. 403. I quote from this translation, since there is no known copy of the pamphlet in England.
84. A suggestion made in Smith, *op. cit.*, p. 26.
85. Knight, *op. cit.*, pp. 208–9.
86. For a valuable discussion of the relationship between the Picturesque and the Exotic, see Smith, *op. cit.*, p. 150.

VI. THE DEEPDENE AND THE DEVELOPMENT OF THE PICTURESQUE

1. I. Nairn & N. Pevsner, *The Buildings of England. Surrey*, 1962, p. 12.
2. For Wotton and Albury the main source is E. S. de Beer, ed., *The Diary of John Evelyn*, 6 vols., Oxford, 1955. The exact date of these gardens is hard to ascertain because of Evelyn's baffling system of 'forward references', i.e. unacknowledged additions made to the diary at a later date when the entries were transferred from one book to another. De Beer, significantly, refers to Evelyn's 'feeling for the visual beauty of landscape, regardless of its utility or associations . . . still rare in the 17th. century'. Moreover, on his Italian tour of 1644–5, Evelyn gave detailed and enthusiastic descriptions of the major High Renaissance villas and gardens. (De Beer, vol. II, *passim.*)
3. There is a photograph of this temple in the *Architectural Review*, vol. CIII, March 1948, p. 124.
4. De Beer, *op. cit.*, vol. III, p. 154.
5. W. Camden, *Britannia*, new ed. by E. Gibson, 1722, vol. I, p. 186.
6. J. Aubrey, *The Natural History and Antiquities of the County of Surrey*, 1718, vol. IV, pp. 164–6.
7. De Beer, *op. cit.*, pp. 561–2.
8. See N. Pevsner, 'Humphrey Repton. A Florilegium', *Architectural Review*, vol. CIII, February 1948, pp. 53–9.
9. Information from Neale, p. 3; and from Brayley, pp. 79–80.
10. This figure comes from the Sale Deeds, preserved in the Burrell Archives at Knepp Castle, quoted in A. J. Rowan, *The Castle Style*, unpublished Cambridge Ph.D. Thesis, 1965, p. 259, n. 3.
11. Neale, p. 4.
12. Lady Theresa Lewis, ed., *Journals and Correspondence of Miss Berry*, 1865, vol. II, p. 382.
13. Bishop of Guildford's Registry, Muniment Book, 1818.
14. Quoted by Baumgarten, p. 244, and, in a slightly different form, by E. Inglis-Jones, *The Great Maria. A Portrait of Maria Edgeworth*, 1959, p. 158.

15. *Repository of Arts*, 1823, vol. I, no vi, pp. 312–3.
16. The 1st vol. had been at Bedgebury Park in the library of her grandfather, A. J. B. Beresford Hope. She has since graciously donated it to the R.I.B.A. Library. The 2nd vol. was sold at Sotheby's on 26 May 1960 to the London bookseller Mr. Stanley Crowe, who later sold it to the Minet Library for their Surrey Collection.
17. Information from Neale, Brayley, and the entry on Atkinson in the Architectural Publication Society's *Dictionary of Architecture*, vol. I, 1852, p. 119. Neale and Brayley give no precise dates, the A.P.S.D. gives 1819–26. For reasons set out in the text I believe that there were two main building-phases of 1818–19 and 1823. There has been much speculation as to the dates of Hope's work, ranging from the tentative queries in J. Harris (*Regency Furniture Designs*, 1961, p. 16, n. 27) to Hussey's more fanciful observation that: 'there are reasons for thinking he began not long after purchasing the property in 1802, though the date usually given is twenty-seven years later' (C. Hussey, *English Country Houses. Late Georgian 1800–1840*, 1958, p. 21).
18. Farington typescript, pp. 854–5.
19. *Ibid.*, p. 1166.
20. It was while Beaumont, Wilkie, and John Jackson, R.A. (1778–1831) were staying at Mulgrave Castle in September 1806 that Lord Mulgrave suggested the subject for one of Haydon's best known pictures, the 'Assassination of Dentatus', painted between 1807 and 1809 (A. P. D. Penrose, ed., *The Autobiography and Memoirs of Benjamin Robert Haydon*, 1927, pp. 35–6). On Beaumont, see M. Greaves, *Regency Patron: Sir George Beaumont*, 1966.
21. Farington typescript, p. 6396.
22. Rowan, *op. cit.*, p. 232.
23. Sir B. Burke, *A Visitation of the Seats and Arms of the Noblemen and Gentlemen of Great Britain and Ireland*, 2nd series, vol. II, 1858, p. 51.
24. Sir T. D. Lauder, ed., *Sir Uvedale Price on the Picturesque*, 1842, p. 331.
25. It is interesting that as recently as 1949 the tower could be described as 'hideous'—see F. Thompson, *A History of Chatsworth*, 1949, p. 200.
26. Lauder, *op. cit.*, p. 344.
27. Neale, p. 7.
28. C. Hussey, *The Picturesque*, 1927, p. 217.
29. Lauder, *op. cit.*, p. 343.
30. Neale, p. 10.
31. The house survives but the only view of it seems to be that in Revd. F. O. Morris, *County Seats*, *c.* 1877, vol. II. See also J. Gwilt, *Encyclopaedia of Architecture*, new ed. by W. Papworth, 1891, p. 1150.
32. The Deepdene views were the first commissions of these two highly suc-

cessful water-colourists. W. H. Bartlett (1809–54) showed a precocious talent and was articled to John Britton at the age of 14. Penry Williams (*c.* 1800–85) studied under Fuseli at the Royal Academy Schools and in 1827 settled in Rome where his romantic landscapes were much in demand.

33. J. C. Loudon, *An Encyclopaedia of Cottage, Farm and Villa Architecture and Furniture*, 1833, pp. 783–4.
34. *Gardener's Magazine*, vol. V, 1829, pp. 589–90. Professor Pevsner kindly tells me that neither he nor Dr. Robson-Scott knows of the word 'ecstatic' being so used.
35. G. Grigson's argument in 'Painters of the Abyss', *Architectural Review*, vol. CVIII, October 1950, pp. 215–20, would lend support to this suggestion.
36. *Gardener's Magazine*, vol. XII, 1836, p. 621.
37. *Lord Beaconsfield's Correspondence with his Sister. 1832–52*, 1886, p. 164.
38. Brayley, p. 84. In some editions the engraving of the new front is dated 1845, although the volume did not appear until 1848.
39. Hussey, *op. cit.*, p. 223.
40. C. Hussey, *English Country Houses. Late Georgian 1800–1840*, 1958, p. 21.
41. Nairn & Pevsner, *op. cit.*, pl. 46 (b).
42. Similarly Barry designed fine Louis Seize style chimney-pieces at Walton House, Surrey (1835–9).
43. A. Barry, *Memoir of the Life and Works of the late Sir Charles Barry*, 2nd ed., 1870, p. 108.
44. H.-R. Hitchcock, *Early Victorian Architecture in Britain*, 2 vols. 1954, vol. I, pp. 164–6.
45. Sir J. N. Summerson, *Georgian London*, 1945, p. 233.
46. Mrs. A. B. Jameson (anon.), *Diary of an Ennuyée*, 1826, pp. 357–8.
47. H. S. Goodhart-Rendel, *English Architecture since the Regency*, 1953, p. 85.
48. B. Disraeli, 1st Earl of Beaconsfield, *Novels and Tales*, Bradenham Edition, 1927, vol. VIII, pp. 93–4, 284, & 213.
49. For further evidence of the close relationship between the two men, see W. F. Monypenny, *The Life of Benjamin Disraeli, Earl of Beaconsfield*, vol. II, 1912, p. 197 and *passim*.
50. Hitchcock, *loc. cit.*, p. 205.
51. The drawing was pasted into *The Deepdene Album* when it was kept at Bedgebury Park. It is doubtless a design for what Beresford Hope called 'religious watering-places' (see Law, ch. VII, *passim*).
52. This seventeenth-century house was remodelled by Viscount Beresford in the 1830s and by his stepson, Alexander Beresford Hope, in the 1850s. The architect on the second occasion was R. C. Carpenter (see Law, pp. 113 & 179–81).

A model of the house before the nineteenth-century alterations is in the possession of Mrs. H. W. Law.

53. See the *Builder*, vol. VII, 1849, pp. 393–4, 498–9, & 534; and J. Timbs, *Curiosities of London*, new ed., 1867, p. 551.
54. Hitchcock, *loc. cit.*, pp. 209–10.
55. *The Illustrated London News*, 3 April 1856, p. 352.
56. *Ibid.*, 4 July 1857, p. 22.
57. *Country Life*, vol. V, 1899, pp. 624–8.
58. At this time the sculpture was discreetly shut away out of sight in the grottoes and caves in the garden, but Sir Shane Leslie, Bart., who stayed in the house during the occupancy of Lilian, Duchess of Marlborough, tells me that he remembers the interior decoration as being both lavish and highly coloured.
59. Lord Francis Hope's elder brother, the 7th Duke of Newcastle, acquired a number of objects at this sale which he took to Clumber. Lord Francis succeeded as 8th Duke in 1928 but with the Clumber Sale of 1937 all stability of private ownership of Hope objects was brought to an end. I am indebted to the present Duke of Newcastle for his kind assistance in clarifying certain details of the history of his family and its heirlooms.
60. Knoblock's autobiography *Round the Room* (1939) is marked by no stylistic or imaginative felicity, but this must not be allowed to detract from our appreciation of his achievement, with Ayrton, as a popularizer and recreator of Regency design. On Beach House see *Country Life*, vol. XLIX, 1921, pp. 126–33; and J. Guthrie and A. Dale, *Beach House*, Worthing, 1947. Pls. 9–10 in E. Beresford Chancellor's *Life in Regency and Early Victorian Times* (1926) and *Country Life*, vol. LXIX, 1931, pp. 450–6, show Knoblock's rooms in London. As early as 1918 Arnold Bennett, a close friend of Knoblock, presented a detailed picture of his Regency Revival rooms at Albany in his novel *The Pretty Lady*. This must be the first popularization of the Hope style in the present century, and it is no coincidence that Knoblock appears in the novel under the name of 'Hoape'—see also M. Praz, *Gusto Neoclassico*, 2nd ed., Naples, 1959, p. 360.
61. G. Macmillan, *Honours for Sale*, 1954, p. 121.

VII. THE HOPE STYLE: SOURCES, PARALLELS AND INFLUENCES

1. C. P. Landon, ed., *Annales du Musée*, vol. I, 1801, p. 27 & pl. 12.
2. The cradle is now in the Louvre. The more elaborate original version is in the Kunsthistorisches Museum, Vienna.
3. Gennadius Library, American School of Classical Studies, Athens, MS. review by Flaxman of *Household Furniture*, f. 7.
4. Quoted in N. Pevsner, *High Victorian Design*, 1951, p. 112; see fig. 18.

5. Assay Office, Birmingham, Boulton Papers, Hope to Boulton, 14 September 1805, ff. 2–4.
6. A. W. N. Pugin, *The True Principles of Pointed or Christian Architecture*, 1841, p. (1).
7. C. Percier & P. F. L. Fontaine, *Recueil de décorations intérieures*, Paris, 1812, ed., pl. 61. See also the even more Beardsleyesque bed shown in pl. 19.
8. L. Budde & R. Nicholls, *A Catalogue of the Greek and Roman Sculpture in the Fitzwilliam Museum*, Cambridge, 1964, pp. 111–12 & pl. 61.
9. In the Liége Museum.
10. S. Grandjean, *Empire Furniture*, 1966, p. 67 & pl. 49A.
11. A. B. Desgodetz, *Edifices Antiques de Rome*, Paris, 1682, pl. V; G. B. Piranesi, *Opere Varie*, Rome, 1750, pl. 112; and C. H. Tatham, *Etchings . . . of Ancient Ornamental Architecture*, 1799, pls. 96–7. The plate-numbers in Tatham's book are erratic and unreliable, probably because many plates were added in 1800.
12. G. M. A. Richter, *The Furniture of the Greeks, Etruscans and Romans*, 1966, fig. 504.
13. Percier & Fontaine, *op. cit.*, pls. 13 & 16.
14. Tatham, *op. cit.*, pl. 78.
15. G. M. A. Richter, *Ancient Furniture: a History of Greek, Etruscan and Roman Furniture*, Oxford, 1926, fig. 281. See also Tatham, *op. cit.*, pls. 82 & 85.
16. *Household Furniture*, p. 33. See also B. Reade, *Regency Antiques* 1953, pp. 56–7.
17. *Household Furniture*, p. 36.
18. *Ibid.*, p. 35.
19. *Ibid.*, p. 40.
20. *Ibid.*, p. 45.
21. *Ibid.*, p. 39.
22. G. M. A. Richter, *The Furniture of the Greeks, Etruscans and Romans*, 1966, fig. 567. It had been popularized by Piranesi in *Vasi, Candelabri*, 1778, vol. 2, pl. 44.
23. *Household Furniture*, p. 53.
24. Flaxman, *op. cit.*, f. 4.
25. See *Country Life*, vol. LX, 1926, pp. 757–9.
26. *Ibid.*, vol. LXXVIII, 1935, pp. 204–5.
27. Richter, *op. cit.*, figs. 162–5.
28. See C. Musgrave, *Regency Furniture*, 1961, pls. 28A & B.
29. Property of the Earl of Leicester, Holkham Hall.
30. Sir John Soane's Museum, Adam Drawings, vol. 17, no. 76. Reproduced in E. Harris, *The Furniture of Robert Adam*, 1963, pl. 111.

31. Sir John Soane's Museum, *loc. cit.*, no. 98. Reproduced in Harris, *op. cit.*, pl. 119.
32. Property of the Trustees of the Heveningham Hall Estate. See *English Taste in the 18th Century*, R.A. Catalogue, 1955–6, pl. 58; and Harris, *op. cit.*, pl. 154.
33. F. J. B. Watson, 'The Furniture and Decoration', *Southill, A Regency House*, 1951, p. 29.
34. See Ch. Mauriche-Beaupré, 'Un mobilier de G. Jacob dessiné par Hubert Robert', *Bulletin des Musées de France*, April 1934, pp. 76–80.
35. See M. E. J. Delécluze, *Louis David, son école et son temps*, Paris, 1855, pp. 20–1.
36. See P. Marmottan, 'Le peintre Louis Gauffier', *Gazette des Beaux-Arts*, 5th period, vol. 13, Paris, 1923, pp. 281–300; and M. R. Crozet, 'Le peintre Louis Gauffier', *Bulletin de la Société de l'Art français*', Paris, 1941–44, pp. 100–113. John Harris notes that Reynolds and Gavin Hamilton introduced neo-classical furniture into their paintings as early as the 1760's (J. Harris, 'Early Neo-Classical Furniture', *Furniture History*, vol. II, 1966, pp. 1–6.)
37. J.-Ch. Krafft & N. Ransonnette, *Plans, Coupes, Elévations des plus belles Maisons et des Hôtels construits à Paris et dans les environs*, 2 vols., Paris, 1801–2, vol. II, pls. 90–2. Up to 1812 this important book, published with texts in German and English, was more widely known and more influential than Percier and Fontaine's published plates.
38. Lady T. Lewis, ed., *Journals and Correspondence of Miss Berry*, vol. II, 1865, p. 191.
39. Krafft & Ransonnette, *loc. cit.*, pl. 89.
40. G. B. Piranesi, *Diverse Maniere d'Adornare i Cammini*, Rome, 1769, pl. 2. The relationship between Piranesi, the Empire Style and Hope is discussed in a review, and in the many letters it provoked, in the *Times Literary Supplement*, February–July 1953, pp. 100, 413, 445, 461, 477, & 493.
41. Christie's Catalogue of the Library from the Deepdene, July 1917.
42. Watson, *loc. cit.*, pp. 32–3 & pls. 12a & b.
43. Grandjean, *op. cit.*, p. 24.
44. Fitzwilliam Museum, Cambridge, Flaxman Letter-book, inserted between ff. 71–2, Flaxman to Percier, 13 October 1791; and f. 49, Flaxman to Percier, 2 November 1802.
45. Censuring the term 'English Empire', John Gloag has recently argued for the independence from French types of Hope's work and the Regency style. *A Social History of Furniture Design*, 1966, pp. 172–5.
46. *One Hundred Old, Rare or Unique Illustrated Books . . . offered for Sale by B. T. Batsford Ltd.*, Section IX, no. 93, p. 63.
47. Sir William Chambers refers to the Egyptian Revival under Hadrian in the

preface to his *Designs of Chinese Buildings*, 1757. He justifies it with the observation that: 'variety is always delightful, and novelty . . . sometimes takes the place of beauty'.

48. *Household Furniture*, pp. 43–4. The fanciful notion that Hope's Egyptian pieces 'are almost identical with some of the furniture found in the tomb of Tut-ankh-amen' (E. Knoblock, *Round the Room* (1939), p. 64), is entirely without foundation.
49. Drawings for this house, though not for the Egyptian Room, are preserved in the Playfair Portfolio, Sir John Soane's Museum.
50. Papworth is known to have designed the elaborate garden-buildings (see W. Papworth, *J. B. Papworth*, 1879, p. 38). S. P. Cockerell and Francis Bernasconi worked at Whiteknights in 1810–11 (information from account-books, Blenheim Palace, Muniment Room, Tray 4, F. 157). See also Mrs. B. Hofland, *A Descriptive Account . . . of White-Knights* 1819, pp. 42–4.
51. *Household Furniture*, p. 37.
52. Colvin, p. 298.
53. Musgrave, *op. cit.*, pp. 35 & 52.
54. Farington typescript, p. 2599.
55. *Ibid.*, p. 4102.
56. A. J. B. Beresford Hope, *The English Cathedral of the 19th Century*, 1861, pp. 63–4.
57. Musgrave, *op. cit.*, p. (53).
58. *An Historical Essay on Architecture*, 3rd ed., 1840, vol. I, p. 492.
59. *Edinburgh Review*, vol. X, 1807, pp. 478–9 & 484.
60. *Satirist*, vol. I, 1808, pp. 47, 117–18, 143, 148, 252, & 254.
61. *British Critic*, vol. XXXII, 1809, pp. 441, 445, 447, and 452.
62. *Monthly Review*, vol. LVIII, 1809, pp. 176 & 180.
63. *Annual Review*, vol. VII, 1809, p. 632.
64. See Baumgarten, p. 139.
65. The book is inscribed by E. H. Nevinson, as also is a copy of the 1812 edition of Hope's *Costume of the Ancients*. Nevinson's library seems to have been formed in his Cambridge years or, at any rate, before his marriage in 1813. I am indebted for this information and for help with the history of Regency dress to Mr. J. L. Nevinson, F.S.A.
66. France, of course, had led the way, as can be appreciated from the clothes worn by Napoleon's mother in her portrait of 1803 by François Gérard (1770–1837), now in the Versailles Museum.
67. E. Grant of Rothiemurchus, *Memoirs of a Highland Lady*, ed. 1950, p. 39.
68. See N. M. Penzer, *Paul Storr. The Last of the Goldsmiths*, 1954, pp. 126 & 132, pls. XXIV & XXVII.

69. *Ibid.*, p. 144 and pl. XXXIII.
70. 'The Utility of Remains of Antiquity', *The Director*, 1807, vol. II, pp. 202–3.
71. Lord Gerald Wellesley, 'Regency Furniture', *Burlington Magazine*, vol. LXX, May 1937, p. 239.
72. I am grateful to Mr. G. J. Levy of H. Blairman & Sons for making this collection available to me.
73. *Household Furniture*, pp. 11–12.
74. J. Britton, *The Union of Architecture, Sculpture and Painting*, 1827, pp. 22–3 & n.
75. But Musgrave, *op. cit.*, p. 54, notes that the plates are dated 1804–7.
76. G. B. Piranesi, *Vasi, Candelabri*, Rome, 1778, vol. 2, pls. 81–4.
77. R. Brown, *The Rudiments of Drawing Cabinet and Upholstery Furniture*, 2nd ed., 1822, p. x.
78. Musgrave, *op. cit.*, p. 79.
79. Farington typescript, p. 2597.
80. Sir John Soane's Museum, Dance Shrine, Slider 1, Set 3. Summerson writes: 'The rooms have delightful and surprising details very freely adapted from Pompeiian, Egyptian, or *cinquecento* decoration' (*Architecture in Britain: 1530–1830*, 4th ed., 1963, p. 275). But the photographic survey by the N.M.R. shows only Pompeiian panels in the library. With the exception of the portico, the house has since been demolished.
81. Farington typescript, p. 2617.
82. *Ibid.*, p. 2637.
83. J. Greig, ed., *The Farington Diary*, 1922–8, vol. VII, p. 122. This section of the diary is not included in the British Museum typescript.
84. Drafts of Soane's correspondence, preserved at Sir John Soane's Museum.
85. Sir J. N. Summerson, *A New Description of Sir John Soane's Museum*, 1955, p. 34.
86. *Ibid.*, p. 20.
87. See Survey of London, vol. XXX, 1960, *Parish of St. James, Westminster*, Pt. I, *South of Piccadilly*, pp. 536–8; and Christie's *Catalogue of the . . . Collection . . . of the late Samuel Rogers*, 1856.
88. See P. W. Clayden, *The Early Life of Samuel Rogers*, 1887, pp. 448–9.
89. See Croft-Murray/Flaxman, p. 77; and G. F. Waagen, *Works of Art and Artists in England*, 1838, vol. II, p. 133.
90. M. Bishop, ed., *Reminiscences and Table-Talk of Samuel Rogers*, 1952, pp. 112–13.
91. *Country Life*, vol. CXI, 1950, p. 958.
92. For these houses by Nash see T. Davis: *John Nash*, 1966, pp. 37–8 & 53; and *The Architecture of John Nash*, 1960, p. 24 & pl. 40.

93. See A. E. Richardson, 'The Empire Style in England', *Architectural Review*, vol. XXX, December 1911, p. 324.
94. T. S. Surr, *A Winter in London*, 1806, vol. II, pp. 215–23.
95. T. S. R. Boase, *English Art: 1800–1870*, Oxford, 1959, p. 56.
96. See J. Harris, 'Exoticism at Kew', *Apollo*, vol. LXXVIII, August 1963, pp. 103–8.
97. Sir J. Reynolds, *Discourses on Art*, ed. R. R. Wark, San Marino, 1959, p. 242.
98. W. Hodges, *Travels in India, 1780–3*, 1793, pp. 62–3 & 75–6.
99. *Household Furniture*, p. 19.
100. G. Grigson, 'Fingal's Cave', *Architectural Review*, vol. CIV, August 1948, pp. 51–4.
101. Now at Sir John Soane's Museum. Gandy states the argument for this 'elemental' approach to architecture in 'The Philosophy of Architecture', *Magazine of the Fine Arts*, vol. I, 1821, pp. 289–93 & 370–9.
102. British Museum: Warren Hastings Diary, Add. MSS. 39881, 25 July 1788, first instructions from Hastings to Cockerell on design of house; Warren Hastings Papers, Add. MSS. 29231, ff. 2–4, paintwork completed in 1793; final payments made 1796.
103. Lord Curzon of Kedlestone, *British Government in India*, 1925, vol. I, p. 141.
104. British Museum, Warren Hastings Papers, Add. MSS. 29232, ff. 392–410.
105. P. F. Norton, 'Daylesford: S. P. Cockerell's Residence for Warren Hastings', *Journal of the Society of Architectural Historians*, U.S.A., vol. XXII, October 1963, p. 131.
106. See C. F. Bell, ed., *Annals of Thomas Banks*, Cambridge, 1938, pp. 88–90 & 102, pls. XXI–XXIII.
107. G. Cumberland, *An Essay on the Utility of Collecting the best works of the Ancient Engravers of the Italian School, accompanied by a Critical Catalogue*, 1827, p. 19.
108. G. Cumberland, *Some Anecdotes of the Life of Julio Bonasoni*, 1793, pp. 4–5.
109. British Museum, Cumberland Papers, vols. I–XXVI, Correspondence, Add MSS. 36491–36516. These include 80 letters from Johnes to Cumberland, many on artistic matters, from *c.* 1790–1810.
110. *Ibid.*, Add. MSS. 36497, f. 337.
111. The attribution to Nash is now made certain by a reference in an unpublished journal of 1806 by C. R. Cockerell: ' . . . the library is a good room but affected as Nash's things generally are'. The journal is the property of Mrs. Anne Crichton and is on loan to Mr. D. Pepys Whiteley who kindly showed it to me. Professor Sir Albert Richardson had access to it in writing a brief article on Cockerell in *Architecture*, vol. IV, May 1925, pp. 30–33.
112. J. Piper, *Buildings and Prospects*, 1948, p. 36.

113. For recent accounts of Johnes and Hafod see G. Grigson, 'Kubla Kahn in Wales', *Cornhill Magazine*, 1947, vol. 162, pp. 275–83; and E. Inglis-Jones, *Peacocks in Paradise*, 1950.
114. Irwin, *op. cit.*, p. 141, n. 3, gives as source, Yale University Library, MSS. Flaxman to Hayley, 1797.
115. See G. Pillement, *Les Hôtels du Faubourg Saint-Germain*, Paris, 1950, pp. 30–1; and L. Hautecoeur, *Histoire de l'Architecture Classique en France*, vol. V, Paris, 1953, fig. 296.
116. J. Britton, *The Beauties of Wiltshire*, 3 vols., 1801–25, vol. I, p. 213.
117. B. Alexander, *England's Wealthiest Son*, 1962, pl. facing p. 118.
118. *European Magazine*, vol. 42, December 1802, pp. 448–9.
119. Reproduced in *Architectural Drawings from the Collection of the R.I.B.A.*, 1961, pl. 22.
120. J. Britton and A. C. Pugin, *Illustrations of the Public Buildings of London*, 1825, vol. II, pp. 77–89.
121. James Forbes (1749–1819) was the author of *Oriental Memoirs*, 4 vols., 1813–15. See also W. W. Druett, *The Stanmores and Harrow Weald*, Uxbridge, 1938, pp. 192–3.
122. N. Pevsner, *The Buildings of England. North Devon.* 1952, p. 163.
123. R. D. Middleton, *Viollet-le-Duc and the Rational Gothic Tradition*, unpublished Cambridge Ph.D.Thesis, 1958, vol. I, pp. 66–9. The long opening chapter of this remarkable study is the best account in English of French neo-classical architecture.
124. For example, the novelists Mary Russell Mitford and Cornelia Knight.
125. S. Smiles, *Memoir and Correspondence of John Murray*, 1891, vol. II, p. 76. And in *Anastasius* itself, the hero observes of himself: 'I always seemed to be composed of two distinct persons: the one argumentative, sophistical; the other entirely under the influence of my imagination . . . which . . . never . . . amalgamated' (2nd ed., 1820, vol. III, p. 349).
126. Fitzwilliam Museum, Cambridge, Flaxman Letter-book, ff. 49 & 72–4.
127. *Household Furniture*, p. 14.
128. Museo Civico Bassano, Manoscritti Canoviani, Hope to Canova, 24 December 1802.
129. Fitzwilliam Museum, Cambridge, Flaxman Letter-book, f. 76, Millin to Flaxman, 26 April 1803, f. 1.
130. W. T. Whitley in *Art in England. 1800–1820*, Cambridge, 1928, p. 251, notes that Canova had visited London for this purpose in 1815.
131. T. Sadler, ed., *Diary, Reminiscences, and Correspondence of Henry Crabb Robinson*, 1869, vol. II, p. 133.
132. *British Critic, loc. cit.*, p. 441.

CONCLUSION

1. It is not always appreciated that the first to describe the eighteenth century as an age of 'romantic classicism' was Geoffrey Scott in *The Architecture of Humanism*, 1914, p. 48. Siegfried Giedion followed with *Spätbarocker und romantischer Klassizismus*, Munich, 1922, and Pevsner popularized the notion though not the name in *An Outline of European Architecture*, 1st ed., 1943. The name was returned to by Fiske Kimball in 'Romantic Classicism in Architecture', *Gazette des Beaux-Arts*, vol. 25, 1944, pp. 95–112, and was used at last with complete confidence by H.-R. Hitchcock in *Architecture: 19th and 20th centuries*, 1st ed., 1958. The most recent contribution to this discussion has been the fascinating if inconclusive study by R. Rosenblum, *Transformations in Late Eighteenth Century Art*, Princeton, 1967.

Index

Modern authorities and present locations of works of art are not indexed

Index

Index

Index

Index

Index

Index

Index

Index

Index